MUSIC AND JEWISH CULTURE
IN EARLY MODERN ITALY

MUSIC AND THE EARLY MODERN IMAGINATION
MASSIMO OSSI, *editor*

MUSIC AND JEWISH CULTURE IN EARLY MODERN ITALY

NEW PERSPECTIVES

Edited by LYNETTE BOWRING,
REBECCA CYPESS, *and* LIZA MALAMUT

INDIANA UNIVERSITY PRESS

This book is a publication of

Indiana University Press
Office of Scholarly Publishing
Herman B Wells Library 350
1320 East 10th Street
Bloomington, Indiana 47405 USA

iupress.org

© 2022 by Indiana University Press

All rights reserved
No part of this book may be reproduced or utilized in any form or by any means, electronic or mechanical, including photocopying and recording, or by any information storage and retrieval system, without permission in writing from the publisher. The paper used in this publication meets the minimum requirements of the American National Standard for Information Sciences—Permanence of Paper for Printed Library Materials, ANSI Z39.48-1992.

Manufactured in the United States of America

First printing 2022

Library of Congress Cataloging-in-Publication Data

Names: Bowring, Lynette, editor. | Cypess, Rebecca, editor, writer of introduction. | Malamut, Liza, editor.
Title: Music and Jewish culture in early modern Italy : new perspectives / edited by Lynette Bowring, Rebecca Cypess, and Liza Malamut.
Other titles: Music and the early modern imagination.
Description: Bloomington, Indiana : Indiana University Press, 2022. | Series: Music and the early modern imagination | Includes bibliographical references and index.
Identifiers: LCCN 2021032568 (print) | LCCN 2021032569 (ebook) | ISBN 9780253060105 (hardback) | ISBN 9780253060099 (paperback) | ISBN 9780253060082 (ebook)
Subjects: LCSH: Jews—Italy—Music—16th century—History and criticism. | Jews—Italy—Music—17th century—History and criticism. | Music—Italy—16th century—History and criticism. | Music—Italy—17th century—History and criticism.
Classification: LCC ML3776 .M82 2022 ML290.2 (print) | LCC ML3776 ML290.2 (ebook) | DDC 780.89/924045—dc23
LC record available at https://lccn.loc.gov/2021032568
LC ebook record available at https://lccn.loc.gov/2021032569

Publication of this book has been aided by a grant from the Donna Cardamone Jackson Fund of the American Musicological Society, supported in part by the National Endowment for the Humanities and the Andrew W. Mellon Foundation.

For my parents, Graham and Barbara Bowring,
whose support never wavered.
—L. B.

For my parents, Drs. Roberta and David Schaefer,
who taught me to love learning.
—R. C.

In memory of Professor Joel Sheveloff, who listened.
—L. M.

CONTENTS

List of Figures   ix
List of Musical Examples   xi
List of Tables   xiii
Editorial Principles   xv
Acknowledgments   xvii

Introduction: Rebecca Cypess   1

1. Written in Italian, Heard as Jewish: Reconsidering the Notated Sources of Italian Jewish Music / *Francesco Spagnolo*   23

2. Miriam's Timbrel: The *Decameron* as Exodus / *Aaron Beck*   37

3. Traces of Jewish Music and Culture at the Urbino Court of Federico da Montefeltro / *J. Drew Stephen*   63

4. The Peripatetic Career of a Converted Jew: The Music Theorist Pietro Aaron / *Bonnie J. Blackburn*   92

5. A Fire, a Fight, and a Knight: Elye Bokher in Verse and Song / *Avery Gosfield*   111

6. The Bassanos at the Court of Henry VIII: A Story of Cooperation and Protection / *Dongmyung Ahn*   144

7. Jewish and Converted Musicians and Musical Instrument Makers in Southern Italy in the Fifteenth through Early Seventeenth Centuries / *Luigi Sisto*   165

8. Salamone Rossi's *Songs of Solomon*: The Pleasures and Pains of Marginality / *Stefano Patuzzi*   185

9. Orality and Literacy in the Worlds of Salamone Rossi / *Rebecca Cypess and Lynette Bowring*   197

10. L'Accademia degli Impediti: A Reevaluation / *Liza Malamut*   233

Bibliography   259

Index   285

LIST OF FIGURES

Figure 1.1. Casale Monferrato, MS 479, Montefiore Library, London. The whereabouts of this manuscript are unknown at present, but a microfilm has been digitized at the National Library of Israel at https://web.nli.org.il/sites/NLI/Hebrew/digitallibrary/pages/viewer.aspx?presentorid=MANUSCRIPTS&docid=PNX_MANUSCRIPTS990001131470205171-1#|FL29607698 (accessed January 8, 2021), image no. 150.

Figure 1.2. Salamone Rossi, "'Ein kelohenu," Canto part of Choir II, from *Ha-shirim 'asher li-Shlomo* (Venice: Bragadini, 1622–1623). Image courtesy of the Bibliothèque nationale de France.

Figure 2.1. Miriam at the Sea (detail), full-page illumination in color and gold, Haggadah for Passover (the "Golden Haggadah"), 1320–1330, Add MS 27210, fol. 15r, British Library, London.

Figure 2.2. Miriam and her timbrel (detail), Sarajevo Haggadah, ca. 1350–1360. Courtesy of the National Museum of Bosnia and Herzegovina, Sarajevo.

Figure 3.1. Paolo Uccello, *Miracle of the Profaned Host*, predella of the Corpus Domini Altarpiece, 1468. With permission of Ministerio dei bene e delle attività culturali e del turismo—Galleria Nazionale delle Marche, Urbino.

Figure 3.2. Joos van Ghent, *Communion of the Apostles*, main panel of the Corpus Domini Altarpiece, 1474. With permission of the Ministerio dei bene e delle attività culturali e del turismo—Galleria Nazionale delle Marche, Urbino.

Figure 3.3. Joos van Ghent, *Music*, oil on poplar, ca. 1470s. © The National Gallery, London, reproduced with permission.

Figure 4.1. Pietro Aaron as teacher in the *Toscanello in musica* (Venice: Bernardino & Matheo de Vitali, 1529). Photo: author.

Figure 5.1. "Śėrėfę lid." Oxford, Bodleian Library, MS Canonici Or. 12, fol. 258r. Reproduced with permission from the Bodleian Libraries, the University of Oxford.

Figure 5.2. "HaMavdil lid." Oxford, Bodleian Library, MS Canonici Or. 12, fol. 203r. Reproduced with permission from the Bodleian Libraries, the University of Oxford.

Figure 5.3. "Tzur mi-shelo" (text). Munich, Universitätsbibliothek der Ludwig-Maximilians-Universität München, 4° Cod. MS 757, fol. 96r, upper page.

Figure 5.4. "Tzur mi-shelo" (music). Munich, Universitätsbibliothek der Ludwig-Maximilians-Universität München, 4° Cod. MS 757, fol. 95v, lower page.

Figure 5.5. Salmo decimosettimo a tre "Diligram te Domine": "Intonazione degli Ebrei Tedeschi sopra המבדיל וגו׳." Benedetto Marcello, *Estro poetico-armonico* (Venice: Domenico Lovisa, 1724–1726), vol. 3, unpaginated.

Figure 7.1. Cristoforo Scacco, *L'incoronazione della vergine coi Ss Marco e Giuliano* (ca. 1500), Museum of Capodimonte, Naples (tempera and gold on wood). With permission of the Ministry for Cultural Heritage and Activities and for Tourism—Museo e Real Bosco di Capodimonte.

Figure 7.2. Sebastian Virdung, *Musica getutscht* (Basel: M. Furter, 1511), fol. Bij. Image courtesy of the Bibliothèque nationale de France.

Figure 7.3. Giovanni Battista (Sansone) known as "Il Siciliano / Ciciliano" (Lat. *Siculus*) from Nikolaus Reusner, *Icones sive imagines vivae* (Basel: Conr. Valdkirch, 1589). Image courtesy of the Bibliothèque nationale de France.

Figure 8.1. Salamone Rossi, title page of sesto partbook, from *Ha-shirim 'asher li-Shlomo* (Venice: Bragadini, 1622–1623). Image courtesy of the Bibliothèque nationale de France.

LIST OF MUSICAL EXAMPLES

Example 5.1. Transcription of "Tzur mi-shelo 'okhalnu." Munich, Universitätsbibliothek der Ludwig-Maximilians-Universität München, Cod. MS 757 (40), fol. 95v–96r. Transliterations to the Roman alphabet follow Ashkenazic pronunciation.

Example 5.2. Text: Elye Bokher, "Dås lid ouf di śėrėfẹ v̄un Wėnėdig," written ca. 1512. Oxford, Bodleian Library, MS Canonici Or. 12, fols. 258r–261v (based on a transcription by Simon Neuberg). Music: "Tzur Mi-shelo 'okhalnu." Munich, Universitätsbibliothek der Ludwig-Maximilians-Universität München, Cod. MS 757 (40), fol. 95v.

Example 5.3. Salmo decimosettimo a tre "Diligram te Domine": "Intonazione degli Ebrei Tedeschi sopra המבדיל וגו׳." Benedetto Marcello, *Estro poetico-armonico* (Venice: Domenico Lovisa, 1724–1726), 3:94. Transliterations to the Roman alphabet follow Ashkenazic pronunciation.

Example 5.4. Text: Elye Bokher, "HaMav̄dil lid." Oxford, Bodleian Library, MS Canonici Or. 12, fols. 203r–207r (based on a transcription by Simon Neuberg). Music: "Intonazione degli Ebrei Tedeschi sopra המבדיל וגו׳." Benedetto Marcello, *Estro poetico-armonico* (Venice: Domenico Lovisa, 1724–1726), 3:94.

Example 9.1. Salamone Rossi, "Canzon [prima] per sonar," from *Il secondo libro delle sinfonie è gagliarde à tre voci* (Venice: Amadino, 1608), mm. 1–6 and mm. 22–26.

Example 9.2. Salamone Rossi, "Sonata sopra l'aria della Romanesca," from *Il terzo libro de varie sonate, sinfonie, gagliarde, brandi, e corrente* (Venice: Vincenti, [1613?]), incipits.

Example 9.3a. Salamone Rossi, "'Ein kelohenu," from *Ha-shirim 'asher li-Shlomo* (Venice: Bragadini, 1622–1623), mm. 46–53, Chorus I (Chorus II omitted).

Example 9.3b. Salamone Rossi, "'Ein kelohenu," from *Ha-shirim 'asher li-Shlomo* (Venice: Bragadini, 1622–1623), mm. 59–100.

LIST OF TABLES

Table 2.1. Inset songs in Boccaccio's *Decameron*.

Table 5.1. Selected examples of linguistic crossover by Jewish poets in sixteenth-century Italy.

Table 5.2. Selected examples of evidence for the sung performance of poems written by Jewish authors in sixteenth-century Italy.

Table 7.1. Instruments and musicians in Naples before and in 1601, as described in Scipione Cerreto, *Della prattica musica vocale, et strumentale* (Naples: G. G. Carlino, 1601), 3:154–160.

EDITORIAL PRINCIPLES

The spellings of names and titles in the early modern period, no matter the original language, vary widely. We have brought these into standardized style for this volume, but in cases where we quote the work of authors who have used different spellings, we have retained the style of the quotations. Thus the name of the Jewish Mantuan composer Salamone Rossi also appears in quoted sources as *Salomone*, which is consistent with his own usage in some instances. Musical examples have likewise been brought into conformity with modern conventions, including through the use of standardized measure lines and accidentals. English-language titles follow headline-style capitalization; German-language titles have common nouns capitalized; and capitalization in all other titles has been minimized.

The romanization of Hebrew is not an exact science. However, we have adopted the following general principles:

- א and ע are differentiated by means of apostrophes facing in different directions (' and ' respectively).
- Hard כ is rendered as *k* and ק as *q*.
- Soft כ is rendered as *kh* and ח as *ḥ*.
- Prefixes are separated from main words via a hyphen (e.g., *ha-shirim* = *the songs*).
- ת is consistently rendered as *t*.
- The vowel שְׁוָא נָע (schwa mobile) is rendered as an *e*, while the שְׁוָא נָח (resting schwa) is not indicated at all.

ACKNOWLEDGMENTS

This volume is the result of years of work and patience on the part of its authors, who have displayed unfailing graciousness and good humor throughout the process. We thank them for allowing us to include their work in this book. Massimo Ossi, editor of the series Music and the Early Modern Imagination, provided invaluable feedback on the first version of the manuscript, and we are grateful for his careful reading and conceptual vision. The feedback from our anonymous reviewers helped to improve the volume dramatically, and we thank them for their insightful questions, wise suggestions, and judicious corrections. Remaining faults are, of course, our responsibility.

We thank Allison Chaplin, acquisitions editor at Indiana University Press, for shepherding this volume through the editing and publication process so adeptly, and Sophia Hebert, assistant acquisitions editor, for her support and assistance. We also express our thanks to the many libraries and archives, cited in the footnotes and bibliography, that made their materials available to us and our contributors for use during this project. The librarians and library systems at Rutgers University and Yale University were especially helpful as we prepared the final manuscript during the COVID-19 pandemic in 2020–2021. Work on this volume would have ground to a halt without their assistance.

Finally, we express our thanks to our families and friends for their unwavering support of our work.

Lynette Bowring, *New Haven, Connecticut*
Rebecca Cypess, *Highland Park, New Jersey*
Liza Malamut, *Medford, Massachusetts*
February 2021

MUSIC AND JEWISH CULTURE
IN EARLY MODERN ITALY

Introduction

REBECCA CYPESS

The English traveler Thomas Coryat (1577–1617) was comically out of place nearly everywhere he went. His travel diary, published in 1611 as *Coryat's Crudities*, is full of tales of his misadventures. Among the many locations in which he felt confused and alienated was a synagogue in Venice, and one of the causes of his confusion was the singing that he heard there. Surprised by the participatory and disorganized nature of this liturgical music, led by a single cantor but joined ad libitum by members of the congregation—whether they were trained or untrained in singing—Coryat described what he heard as "an exceeding loud yaling, undecent roaring, and as it were a beastly bellowing of it forth. And that after such a confused and hudling manner, that I thinke the hearers can very hardly understand him [i.e., the cantor]: sometimes he cries out alone, and sometimes againe some others serving as it were his Clerkes hard without his seate, and within, do roare with him, but so that his voyce (which he straineth so high as if he sung for a wager) drowneth all the rest."[1]

Coryat's description, with its comparison of Jews to animals, betrays an obvious anti-Jewish bias—a manifestation of the millennia-old phenomenon that Ruth HaCohen has called "the music libel against the Jews."[2] As HaCohen has shown, Christian listeners and critics contrasted their own music, which they deemed harmonious and orderly, with the music of the Jews, perceived as noisy and undisciplined—an aural manifestation, these critics claimed, of the Jews' religious degeneracy. Indeed, Coryat passed negative judgment not only on Jewish musical practices but, in keeping with the mores of his Christian world, on their religious views as well. Accosting a Jewish passerby in the ghetto, he entered into an argument about the Jews' errant beliefs and attempted to convert his interlocutor. He thus marginalized the Jews, rendering them opposite to or other than himself, but still engaged them in debate and even sought to save them. He likewise took the time to visit their place of worship, granting them both his visual and aural attention only to determine (as if it were ever in doubt) that their musical practices were inferior to those he knew already.

Despite Coryat's biased self-positioning, one might well understand his confusion upon hearing the participatory liturgical singing in the synagogue. In contrast to the tightly regulated polyphony that he was used to hearing in church, which he described as "a sober, distinct, and orderly reading," synagogue prayer must have seemed disorienting, its multiplicity of voices threatening the stability of the soundscape to which he was accustomed. In fact, some of the same tensions are evident in the writings of Leon Modena (1571–1648), one of the most musically inclined rabbis, authors, and communal leaders in Jewish history. It is perhaps to be expected that Modena provides a description of synagogue music that is more objective than Coryat's; he confirms that a cantor is one who "sings prayers louder than others" while those "others" participate in music making according to the needs of the liturgy.[3] In line with Coryat's observations, the cantor might have been the leader, but musical worship in the Italian Synagogue (Scuola italiana) in Venice, where Modena served as cantor from 1610 until his death in 1648, was a participatory and polyphonic experience. Still, Modena also sought to bring what he perceived as more tightly regulated, orderly music into the synagogue. Having received, like many educated Jews of his age, training in singing and instruments as a youth,[4] Modena advocated for the creation of a body of art music for the synagogue during an age when there was virtually none. His support for—and collaboration with—the Mantuan Jewish composer and instrumentalist Salamone Rossi in the publication of Rossi's collection of polyphonic Hebrew motets, *Ha-shirim 'asher li-Shlomo* (*The Songs of Solomon*, 1622–1623),[5] is well known, but Modena participated in numerous other musical ventures as well.[6] As early as 1604, he had attempted to introduce learned polyphonic music into the synagogue practice at Ferrara; although most listeners were pleased with the result, one communal leader in attendance, Rabbi Moses Coimbram, objected, citing a Talmudic passage prohibiting *zemer* (song) from synagogue practice entirely. The passage from the Babylonian Talmud to which this listener was doubtless referring is Tractate *Gittin* (7a), which claims that, as a sign of mourning following the destruction of the Temple, all song—indeed, all music—was prohibited from Jewish life. While this Talmudic position was apparently not broadly applied as *halakha* (Jewish law) in Renaissance Italy, it was accepted enough to have prompted objection from Modena's Ferrarese listener.[7] Some years later, Modena presided over a Jewish musical academy in Venice, the Accademia degli Impediti, again seeking to inscribe polyphonic art music in Jewish communal life, but his academy was apparently decimated by the plague that struck in 1629–1630.[8] Nevertheless, these and other cases, some of which are discussed in the chapters of this volume, point to an awareness within Jewish communities on the Italian peninsula of differences and tensions between Jews' and non-Jews' musical practices.

Within the context of the religious upheavals of sixteenth-century Italy, the place of Jews and Jewish communities was paradoxical. On the one hand, church officials, members of the Christian nobility, and political leaders perceived Judaism as a threat to existing institutions, and they sought to contain Jewish communities and mitigate their effects on the predominantly Christian society in which they lived, most obviously, in the sixteenth and early seventeenth centuries, through the creation of ghettos. At the same time, and perhaps partly as a result of this communal containment, aspects of Jewish culture—including musical culture—flourished. Among other activities in which they engaged, Jewish musicians notated and sometimes published their work; authored treatises on music theory and history; expanded on forms of musical theater; performed as instrumentalists, singers, and dancers; taught these subjects to both Jews and Christians; performed in private homes of adherents to both religions; and participated in the rich environment of instrument design and creation. Some of these innovations manifested themselves primarily within Jewish communities, but in many cases, influence, collaboration, and discursive counterpoint among Jewish musicians and theorists and their non-Jewish contemporaries are readily discerned. Such cases of influence and counterpoint range from the presence of humanist theories of music in Hebrew writings to stylized imitations of Hebrew song in the musical compositions and practices of non-Jewish composers.⁹ Such cross-cultural exchange persisted despite increasing restrictions on Jewish musicians in the late sixteenth and early seventeenth centuries.¹⁰

Scholarly work on the intersection of music and Jewish culture in early modern Italy began with the nineteenth-century movement known as Wissenschaft des Judentums, and until the mid-twentieth century, treatments of this topic have largely adhered to the project of that movement. Authors of monumental studies, such as Cecil Roth, Israel Adler, and Abraham Idelsohn, placed Jewish musical culture in early modern Italy within far-reaching historical narratives, seeking out unifying historical tendencies that sometimes obscured the multiple divergent experiences of Jews and their interactions with their non-Jewish contemporaries.¹¹ These studies sought, moreover, to establish Jews as "contributors" to European musical traditions and aesthetic categories without questioning the primacy of those categories. (Jews who converted to Christianity, whether by choice or by force, were rarely incorporated into these historical narratives, notwithstanding considerable evidence that Jewish self-identification could, in some cases, be fluid and flexible.¹²)

The case of Salamone Rossi helps to elucidate historiographical tendencies in the treatment of music within Jewish culture in early modern Italy. Rossi's polyphonic settings of Hebrew liturgical and paraliturgical texts and Psalms have long been cited, both within specialized histories of Jewish music and in general histories of Western music, and frequently compared to sacred Christian compositions of their day.¹³ In such treatments, Rossi himself seems to emerge as a latter-day prophet who anticipated the polyphonic art music that emerged in nineteenth-century Germany as part of the Reform movement. At the same time, Rossi's Hebrew vocal works, *Ha-shirim 'asher li-Shlomo*, appear as curiosities. If this is true with respect to their typography, which contains both conventional staff notation and texts printed in Hebrew characters, their novelty is underscored still further by their status as the first polyphonic Hebrew compositions ever printed. Nevertheless, consideration of the rich musical life of the Jewish community that occupied the ghetto of Mantua, where Rossi lived, casts them in an entirely different light. Far from mere curiosities, Rossi's *Shirim* emerge as manifestations of an active culture of liturgical practice, instrumental music, improvised singing, musical theater, treatments of music in the Jewish legal tradition, discussions of music in the tradition of Qabbalah, and humanist musical theory. Rossi's works were experimental, to be sure, but they were the results of decades or centuries during which Jews cultivated music and musical thought. Likewise, the significance of Leon Modena as an advocate for Rossi's work, and for the cultivation of art music in the style of his Christian neighbors, cannot be overstated. At the same time, the resistance that Modena encountered attests to the strength of competing cultures and conceptions of music among other Jews in his community. The status of Rossi and Modena as exceptional individuals should not eclipse these other standpoints.

And yet, until the mid-twentieth century, histories of "exceptional" figures formed the basis of both general histories of Jews in early modern Italy and histories of Jewish music, whether in Italy or elsewhere. Since the mid-nineteenth century, historians encountering the overwhelming number of sources related to Jews as practitioners and theorists of music have attempted to interpret and synthesize those sources, demonstrating, too, their relationship to the fickle tides of broader cultural and political events during this era. Cecil Roth, for example, saw the history of Jews in Renaissance Italy as a component of the "great historic role of the Jewish people during the past two thousand years." He understood these Jews as "great internationalists—if only because at this time the world was filled with Jewish refugees, forced to remove from one country to another—bringing with them new currents, ideas and conceptions."[14] Yet Roth also sought to uncover the stories of exceptional "individual Jews—volatile, impressionable, perhaps ambitious, or forced to seek a livelihood by any means that offered itself—living in the purlieus of the Renaissance courts and acting there in the most unexpected capacities." Roth devotes a chapter of this study to Jewish involvement in "music and the dance," surveying the figures who stand out from the historical record for their achievements in publication, performance, or teaching. He concludes that Jewish involvement in these arts, especially in the secular sphere, forms one link in a long chain of history that extended into his own day: "The remarkable participation of Jews in the musical life of modern Europe and America is basically not a recent development, but has a memorable ancestry extending back to, and antedating, the Renaissance."[15]

In his critique of Jewish historiography, Moshe Rosman questions the tendency of historians since the Wissenschaft des Judentums movement of the nineteenth century to conceive of Jewish history in terms of such grand narratives. Roth's dubious attempt to connect Jewish participation in mid-twentieth-century musical culture with similar participation by Jews of the Italian Renaissance is an obvious example. Moreover, Rosman cites Roth as one prominent historian who argued for the legitimacy of the field of Jewish history through what Rosman calls the "contribution discourse," which claims such legitimacy as a function of Jews' "contributions" to Western civilization.[16] Such an approach, warns Rosman, "can readily be interpreted as implicit acceptance of racial theory. It virtually grants the validity of antisemites' [to whom Roth was responding] fundamental assertion that the Jews were a race, differing only by insisting that the Jewish race was in possession of positive traits."[17] Instead, Rosman advocates meeting Jewish history on its own terms: "Jewish studies ... should be engaged in, first of all, on the basis of the belief that Jewish culture in all of its manifestations has an intrinsic value that requires no justification other than its existence as a constituent part of human culture."[18]

Steps in that direction were undertaken by the late Don Harrán, whose vast output of writings and editions formed a significant contribution to modern-day understandings of Jewish musical culture in late-Renaissance Italy, including studies of repertoire, musical practices, and humanist musical theory. In addition to Harrán's complete-works edition and biography of Salamone Rossi,[19] he published studies of Rossi and the question of his Jewish identity.[20] Harrán's writings on Rossi's sister, Madama Europa, as well as the poet and intellectual Sarra Copia Sulam, demonstrate the participation of these remarkable women in both their Jewish and non-Jewish musical environments.[21] Likewise, Harrán's translations and explanations of Hebrew-language music-theoretical works that participate in both Jewish and humanist discourses are invaluable resources for expanding discussions of Jewish musical culture in this rich and diverse musical-cultural environment.[22]

Despite these advances, however, Harrán's work tacitly accepts many of the underlying assumptions that inform the work of Roth and his mid-twentieth-century contemporaries. For example, as Edwin Seroussi has pointed out, in placing such exceptional figures as Rossi at the foreground, Harrán reinforced the quest to legitimize Jewish musical practice through reference to the mythology of "great composers."[23] In addition, as Seroussi notes, Harrán circumvented some of the complex historiographic questions surrounding Jewish life during this period; for example, to what extent were Jews as a whole involved in the intellectual world of the Renaissance? Did Jews experience a Renaissance alongside their Christian contemporaries? To what extent were the experiences of figures such as Rossi, Leon Modena, Guglielmo Ebreo, and Sarra Copia Sulam, often perceived as exceptional, representative of Jews' wider engagement with musical thought and practice? Seroussi himself has pointed the way forward by reading surviving musical sources from early modern Italy to discern evidence of their unwritten practices and their lived encounters at the margins of Jewish and Christian experiences.[24] Moreover, as Daniel Jütte demonstrates, engagement with music in a range of forms was widespread among the Jews of early modern Italy, and music constituted one of the most significant sites of interaction between Jews and their non-Jewish neighbors.[25]

Work of Seroussi, Jütte, and others has established a number of important modes of musical expression and institutions of musical culture among Italian Jews of this period. Exploring more specific cases within the history of musical practice and theory, scholars, including some contributors to this volume, have begun to move beyond the goal of creating a unifying narrative, allowing the specific circumstances to call forth their own interpretations. Still, sources remain unpublished and personalities and case studies little known; the vibrant exchanges of ideas and practices among Jews and non-Jews, even within a sometimes hostile environment, have yet to be fully explicated. Recent reevaluations of the social, cultural, political, economic, and religious circumstances that shaped the lives of early modern Jews in Italy demand new accounts of music in those lives. It is the hope of the editors of this volume that the essays contained in it will help to open the discussion of music and Jewish culture in early modern Italy to new ideas and directions.

It is worthwhile at this point to pause over the title of this volume—*Music and Jewish Culture in Early Modern Italy: New Perspectives*—and to acknowledge some of the key methodological questions that it raises, if only to frame the discussions in the chapters that follow. Why "music and Jewish culture" rather than, for example, "Jewish music"? What is meant by "early modern," a term that is often used as a vague catchall? And, given the fractious political situation on the Italian peninsula in the era before its political unification in the nineteenth century, is it appropriate to write about "Italy"?

While the phrase "Jewish music" continues to be used in some scholarly situations today, it traces its roots to the nineteenth century, when, as Seroussi notes, "conceptions about the essence of Jewish nationhood, often formulated in racial terms, germinated among Jews on European soil."[26] Inherent in the notion of Jewish music was a search for a set of traits that simultaneously unified Jews across time and place and set them apart from the local societies in which they lived. Leaving aside its political associations, the phrase "Jewish music" thus raises a set of expectations around, on the one hand, internal Jewish communal cohesion and, on the other, separation from non-Jews that cut against the grain of some aspects of Jews and their experiences with music in the early modern era. Especially on the Italian peninsula, Jewish experience with music was highly varied, and as several of the chapters in this volume demonstrate, it sometimes involved immersion in and close contact with musical practices in which both Jews and non-Jews participated. Moreover, our volume also considers the ways in which the experiences of recent converts to Christianity continued to be shaped by their Jewish past. In some cases, this aided them in careers in music; for example, Luigi Sisto shows that converts drew on their extensive international connections to facilitate their participation in the trade of musical instruments. In other cases, the musical careers of converts were hindered by their Jewish origins, as Bonnie J. Blackburn demonstrates in her study of Pietro Aaron. The phrase "music and Jewish culture" allows this book to consider these stories alongside those of Jews who remained within the Jewish community and navigated its various attitudes toward music in diverse ways.

Use of the phrase "early modern" in the title of this book likewise requires explanation. David B. Ruderman's important metastudy *Early Modern Jewry* identifies five key factors that characterized Jewish communities across central and eastern Europe, the Netherlands, Italy, and the Ottoman Empire in the early modern period. In Ruderman's view, these five characteristics help to define "a connected early modern Jewish culture," representing aspects that were "distinctive and unprecedented about this era."[27] The first of Ruderman's five elements of early modern Jewry is "accelerated mobility"—the movement of increased numbers of people across lands—which in turn may have helped to spread ideas and cultural practices and bring peoples into contact with one another in new ways. In his study of Jewish life in Renaissance Italy, Robert Bonfil, too, sees a new "dynamism" in this period. Bonfil identifies the Italian peninsula as a "land of immigration"—a situation aided by its geographical situation—starting with the advent of French Jews after the majority were expelled in 1394 and German Jews after the plague of 1348.[28] Ruderman's second element of early modern Jewry is "communal cohesiveness" represented by a heightened self-awareness of the community in relation to the "other." In some Italian cities, this cohesion took on a new aspect, as I will discuss in what follows, with the introduction of ghettos starting in the sixteenth century.

A third element that Ruderman identifies as central to this period is a "knowledge explosion" among Jews, accelerated by the printing press but also manifested in an extensive manuscript culture and exemplified in an "expanded curriculum of Jewish learning," as well as in an interest in Jewish and Hebrew books on the part of Christian readers. This "knowledge explosion" was perhaps especially pronounced on the Italian peninsula, where rates of literacy among Jews were quite high and where the production of printed Hebrew books started and was fueled by collaborations with non-Jewish printers.[29] The new engagement with literacy played out in musical terms in the emergence of theoretical, historical, and polemical writings on music—for example, in the works of Leon Modena, Judah Moscato, and Abraham Portaleone; it also affected aspects of musical practice, including, most famously, the experiments with notated polyphonic music undertaken by Salamone Rossi in collaboration with Modena, as will be discussed in the present volume in the chapter by Stefano Patuzzi as well as that by Rebecca Cypess and Lynette Bowring.

Ruderman's fourth aspect of early modern Jewry is a "crisis of rabbinic authority," which led, in its most extreme forms, to radical messianism, a topic that we do not address in this volume. However, this crisis is connected to the fifth element that Ruderman sees as central to early modern Jewry—namely, the "blurring of religious identities." This can be seen in the increased collaboration between Jews and non-Jews in the production of synagogue music, as discussed in the chapter by Francesco Spagnolo. It is also manifested in the cases of individuals who converted (some of whom later returned to their Jewish faiths); as already noted, Blackburn shows that the trajectory of a convert such as Pietro Aaron was shaped in significant ways by his Jewish origin. And it can be seen in the increased interest among

Christians in Hebraic language and writing. The engagement with Qabbalah in the mid-seventeenth-century writings of the Jesuit polymath Athanasius Kircher is a noteworthy example of this trend.

In Ruderman's view, these five key aspects of early modern Jewry transcended local and national boundaries. Without denying the importance of the details of individual experiences, Ruderman argues that such a meta-understanding of Jewry is helpful for framing such individual histories. As he notes, these factors "reveal in their entirety the pressures this period exemplifies on the notion of religious and social boundaries between Jews and other Jews and between Jews and members of other faiths and ethnic groups." Moreover, they "complicate the borders imposed by Jewish law and Christian society on its Jewish minority," and they "suggest a blurring of what constitutes Jewish identity with a variety of new options for Jewish self-definition and for representing Jewish civilization in the non-Jewish world."[30] As we shall see throughout the chapters in this study, these ideas can be readily discerned in the study of musical thought and practice in early modern Italy.

Having thus justified our use of the phrases "music and Jewish culture" and "early modern" in the title of this volume, I turn to the last word, perhaps equally problematic: "Italy." The Italian peninsula was a place of great diversity, with each locale differing in political leadership, systems of government, and approaches to its Jewish community. Nevertheless, Jews were united, in some respects, by their position within Italian societies. Robert Bonfil's treatment of the peninsula as a unit is based not solely on geographic considerations but, more importantly, on socioeconomic factors: throughout the Italian peninsula, "the Jews were ... organically involved on the socioeconomic level, playing an active role, with a specific function to perform, either as the instruments of power, or more simply as defenders of particular vested interests."[31]

The Jewish presence on the Italian peninsula is attested throughout the fourteenth and fifteenth centuries, though the evidence is spotty and a continuous Jewish presence in any one region can seldom be confirmed with certainty. The interactions between these primarily Ashkenazic Jews and their non-Jewish neighbors were often tense. However, after the expulsion of Iberian Jewry in the late fifteenth century, some rulers encouraged Jewish settlement; as Bonfil points out, this was largely due to the economic advantages that Sephardic Jews offered through their international connections in business and trade: these Jews "had already proved to be an economic force to reckon with. . . . Rulers therefore decided to integrate them into the local economy rather than continue to make use of them at the margins of society, where they had been relegated because of the despised roles they performed"—primarily, that is, moneylending.[32] As a result, Jews became increasingly concentrated within Italian cities, resulting in "intense social mixing between Jews of different backgrounds."[33] These Sephardic Jews joined the already established Ashkenazic communities in various regions across Italy, and the customs of these two populations merged with one another, mixing with their Christian neighbors and incorporating aspects of the broader Christian-dominated society in which they lived.

Jews from the Ottoman Empire likewise had a significant effect on Jewish communities of the Italian peninsula—especially in Venice; this is an area that has recently started to gain attention in the scholarly literature.[34] Dana E. Katz notes that the Venetian government consciously directed the influx of Jewish immigrants from the Levant to the city's Ghetto Vecchio in the mid-sixteenth century based on the role that they played in Venice's mercantile system.[35] As Edwin Seroussi has shown, the soundscape of the Venetian ghetto was shaped by a significant population of these Levantine Jews, for whom the Turkish system of musical modes known as *makam* was central. Seroussi demonstrates that Turkish cantors used this system frequently in synagogue worship, as documented in manuscript sources, and these sounds would have mixed with those of other Jewish musical systems on the streets of the ghetto.[36]

Religious and political pressures sometimes conflicted with the economically motivated openness of some rulers toward the Jewish presence. The Kingdom of Naples expelled its Jews in 1541; Jews were expelled from the Papal States in 1569 and from the Duchy of Milan in 1597. Yet other cities handled these pressures differently—especially through the advent of the ghetto, an institution that simultaneously separated the Jewish community and integrated it into the topography of a number of Italian cities. Complicating past studies that have painted the history of Renaissance Jews in Italy in broad strokes, Bonfil has demonstrated that, as long as Jews lived in a variety of locales across Italy, their encounters with Christians were neither entirely rosy nor entirely dark. He sheds new light on fundamental institutions of the Italian Renaissance, such as the ghetto and the *monte di pietà*, showing how such institutions reflect the complex and sometimes contradictory attitudes of non-Jews toward Jews and how Jews lived and worked within the constraints of their everyday experiences.[37] Bonfil shows that while the ghetto formalized the marginalization of Jews within Italian cities, it also allowed them to stay in those cities rather than face expulsion. Limited in their prospects for work, Jews were nevertheless viewed as necessary to the moral and economic well-being of Christians in Italian cities. Associated by necessity with the usurious practices of moneylending, Jews—along with prostitutes and the poor—were considered, in Bonfil's words, "'necessary' elements of society," objects against which Christians could define themselves, and on account of whom Christians could continue to exercise charity. In an age when the Roman church was under threat from reforming movements across Europe, the negative model of the Jews inspired continued loyalty.[38]

For Ruderman, the ghettos engendered a "complex dialectic between the conspicuous individuality of each ethnic subcommunity and its simultaneous connectedness to the larger public space within the ghetto walls."[39] More recently, Dana E. Katz has affirmed the connections between "urban segregation" as codified in ghettos and "stratifications of social status." For Katz, the ghetto in Venice constituted a "laboratory of the periphery."[40] And, importantly, Jütte has demonstrated that music played a significant role in the Venetian ghetto by "enabling and empowering Jews to define their own cultural space."[41]

Thus, despite the political diversity of the Italian peninsula, the socioeconomic factors that Bonfil identifies as consistent across the region—factors that affected the cultural situation of Jews with respect to their non-Jewish neighbors—mean that it is worthwhile considering the peninsula as a unit, and we do so in this volume. The authors here deal with situations in Venice and Mantua, where there were large concentrations of Jews and a flourishing of musical, artistic, and intellectual culture in the early modern era. In addition, we offer perspectives from Boccaccio's Florence, the Kingdom of Naples before the expulsion of Jews, and the court of Urbino. The case of Elye Bokher, discussed by Avery Gosfield, is perhaps emblematic of the larger migratory patterns that united Jews in Italy and beyond: born near Nürnberg, Bokher resided in Venice, Padua, and Rome; sojourned again in

Germany; and returned to Venice, and likewise, his musical poetry traverses linguistic borders.

Still, our effort to draw together the common threads of musical and cultural experiences of Jews should not be read as denying the importance of local experiences that separate Jews in these locales, and the authors attend to those local circumstances in their chapters. Indeed, that this book is intended as a contribution to the understanding of various aspects of the relationship between music and Jewish culture in early modern Italy is signaled by its subtitle: *New Perspectives*. This volume is not a comprehensive overview but a treatment of a series of case studies that shed light on a topic that has long fascinated scholars and that will doubtless continue to inspire new research and interpretations long into the future.

* * *

This volume explores the rich diversity of materials, topics, and approaches now possible within the study of music and Jewish culture in early modern Italy. Rather than imposing an unnecessary unity, much less an overarching project of apologetics, on the topics and methodologies now in use, the authors in this volume seek to highlight (1) the multifaceted experience of music within Jewish communities of early modern Italy; (2) the many ways that such communities conceived of music, both internally and as a bridge to their non-Jewish neighbors; and (3) reception of and responses to Jewish musical experiences and musical–material culture by non-Jews. The contributors to the volume—scholars in musicology and Jewish studies, as well as performers who specialize in early modern repertoire and performance practices—explore a range of topics that attest to the diversity of these experiences and understandings, shedding new light on the place of music in the complex cultural, political, and religious environments of early modern Italy.

In constructing the multiplicity of histories of music and Jewish culture in early modern Italy found in this volume, the contributors engage with both well-known historical figures, such as Rossi and Modena, and with the experiences of those whose work and practices have received less attention thus far. The authors consider music-theoretical writings in both Italian and Hebrew; vestiges of unwritten musical traditions that demonstrate the interrelationships between Jewish and non-Jewish musical practices; evidence of music making within particular Jewish communities; the role of Jews and Jewish converts to Christianity in musical practice, theory, and instrument building; and questions of performance practices and performance contexts. Drawing on a wide range of recent work in Jewish studies, history, philosophy, and the history of art and literature, in addition to the history of music, we seek to situate an array of musical experiences and expressions of musical thought within the complex landscape of early modern Jewish life.

This volume builds on recent work in the general history of Jews in early modern Italy that has attended to the specific experiences of communities and individuals. The authors seek to consider the social and religious factors that shaped or constrained musical experiences within Jewish culture and the encounters of Jewish and non-Jewish musicians. We engage with recent studies of cultural mediation and interreligious influence. Scholars such as Ruderman and Giuseppe Veltri have explored such learned topics as the position of Jewish philosophy within Italian humanism, the literary genre of the biography, and the genre of history writing, while Benjamin Ravid and Stefanie B. Siegmund, among others, have presented extensive archival documentation that illustrates the laws, political structures, economic restrictions, and religious environments (both Jewish and non-Jewish) that governed the lives of Jews in early modern Italy.[42] These social structures both shaped and were shaped by the understanding of Jews by their non-Jewish neighbors—understandings that found representation in the visual art of the period.[43] These new social insights have yet to be fully incorporated into studies of music—for understanding either the ways in which Christians represented Jews musically or the ways in which Jews actually participated in their musical environments.

This volume is about the intersections of music and Jewish culture in the broadest terms. The liminal position of musicians such as Rossi, Modena, and Guglielmo Ebreo was, it seems, common to Jewish musicians and musical thinkers. These individuals, by necessity, were required to negotiate the boundary between their status as Jews (which was, in most cases, marked through outward signs, such as a badge or special headgear) and their status as outward-looking people immersed in a diverse and polyphonic soundscape. Moreover, Christian thinkers, artists, and patrons—each group with more or less openness to Jews themselves—frequently peered into Jewish theological and philosophical texts, incorporating the ideas they read and calling to life the music that they heard or imagined to be associated with Jews. Music, then, worked as a mediator between these disparate worlds, sometimes engendering conflict and tension.[44]

The themes of mediation and interaction—with, by turns, resulting confluence and opposition—run throughout the present volume. After an opening chapter by Francesco Spagnolo that presents a broad overview of sources from throughout the early modern period, we have ordered the remaining chapters chronologically by subject, although themes will recur and build over the course of the volume. Above all, music and musicians emerge as mediators in a complex, multivocal world.

In the opening chapter, "Written in Italian, Heard as Jewish: Reconsidering the Notated Sources of Italian Jewish Music," Francesco Spagnolo presents a wide-ranging survey of notated musical sources and the residue of oral sources from Jewish history; the surviving evidence from the Renaissance through the nineteenth century, he shows, reflects a deep engagement between Jewish and Christian musicians and music theorists—an engagement manifested even within the walls of the synagogue itself. Despite whatever inclination modern theorists and historians might have to define Jewish music in a manner distinct from secular or Christian music, Spagnolo's chapter demonstrates that the lines among these categories cannot be clearly drawn; his work thus sheds new light on the historiography of Italian Jewry as a whole.

Chapter 2 reaches back to the dawn of the Renaissance. In "Miriam's Timbrel: The *Decameron* as Exodus," Aaron Beck presents an example of the incorporation of Jewish and Hebrew literary traditions by a Christian writer. Noting the innovative structure and contents of Boccaccio's fourteenth-century work, Beck argues that it is based heavily on the biblical Exodus story, which circulated in Boccaccio's world in both Hebrew and Latin versions. The ballatas contained in the *Decameron* strongly suggest musical performance—a circumstance that recalls Miriam's performance of the Song at the Sea in Exodus 15. Drawing on sources as disparate as Sephardic Haggadahs and the works of Saint Ambrose, Beck offers a nuanced reading of the *Decameron* that acknowledges the active interplay of Jewish and Christian interpretations.

Chapter 3, J. Drew Stephen's "Traces of Jewish Music and Culture at the Urbino Court of Federico da Montefeltro," shows how Jewish learning and Jewish culture were integrated into court culture and learning in fifteenth-century Urbino. The extensive patronage of arts and letters by Federico da Montefeltro, duke from 1474 to 1482, included support of Jewish musicians and, perhaps most famously, the Jewish dancing master Guglielmo Ebreo da Pesaro. In an era before the establishment of ghettos, Jews lived and worked within the city's population and were, Stephen shows, integrated into its learned and artistic culture. Although no notated evidence survives to attest to the precise ways in which music was made by Urbino's Jews, Stephen shows that a vibrant musical culture is likely to have existed and that traces of it may be seen in surviving evidence from the court.

The case of the musician and music theorist Pietro Aaron (ca. 1480–after 1545) forms the subject of chapter 4, Bonnie J. Blackburn's "The Peripatetic Career of a Converted Jew: The Music Theorist Pietro Aaron." Some years ago, Blackburn speculated that Aaron had converted from Judaism to Christianity; in this chapter, she provides newly discovered documentation that confirms her hypothesis. She shows, further, how the fact of Aaron's Jewish ancestry shaped his education and his career as a music theorist. Picking up on the apparently forced nature of a comment by one of his colleagues that he was loved "because of his priesthood," Blackburn elucidates the challenges that Aaron faced in forming a career in music—challenges apparently created by his status as a convert from Judaism—and his resourcefulness in negotiating those challenges. While Aaron left Judaism, Blackburn shows that his career was shaped in notable ways by his Jewish origins.

Chapter 5, Avery Gosfield's "A Fire, a Fight, and a Knight: Elye Bokher in Verse and Song," revives the sounds of musical–poetic recitation within the Jewish community of the early sixteenth century. Elye Bokher was a polymath and multilinguist who was widely known among non-Jewish intellectuals for his learned writings. However, he also wrote extensive poetry in Yiddish that was directed at what Gosfield describes as an "insider" readership; these poems make specific references to Jewish religious practices and cultural themes, and they are often parodic and even bawdy. Gosfield provides evidence that Bokher's lengthy epic poems in Yiddish were not just read but sung, and she locates specific "best-guess" melodies that match the poems and that function as *arie per cantar stanze* (melodies for the recitation of poetry), a common phenomenon in the Italian poetic tradition. Indeed, Gosfield's chapter draws on her performance-based research, bringing these poems to life in sound and enabling them to be heard again.

Chapter 6, Dongmyung Ahn's "The Bassanos at the Court of Henry VIII: A Story of Cooperation and Protection," brings the reader briefly outside Italy, addressing the case of the Jewish Bassano family of wind instrumentalists, some of whom left Venice for work at the court of Henry VIII of England in the 1530s. Ahn first considers factors related to economic and social conditions to explain why the Bassanos may have made this move. Despite the fact that Jews had been formally expelled from England in 1290, Henry was apparently willing to overlook that in order to secure these prized players for his court; nevertheless, Ahn argues that the religious dimension of the Bassanos' presence in England cannot simply be explained away through reference to Henry's self-serving needs. To elucidate this issue, she draws on John Foxe's *Acts and Monuments* (1570), which relates a story of interfaith cooperation situated in the 1530s. Ahn reads this story allegorically to understand the interfaith collaboration that led to Henry's patronage of the Bassanos.

In chapter 7, "Jewish and Converted Musicians and Musical Instrument Makers in Southern Italy in the Fifteenth through Early Seventeenth Centuries," Luigi Sisto presents new evidence about the extensive activity of Jews and Christians of Jewish descent in the rich tradition of instrument makers in the Kingdom of Naples and its environs. Sisto presents documents, including inventories of instruments and verbal descriptions of instrumentalists and builders, to show how deeply intertwined Jews were with non-Jews in the cultivation of instrumental practices and lutherie. That some of these documents were created at moments of interreligious tension or persecution—when, for example, the possessions of Jewish merchants were confiscated—underscores the difficulties and risks that Jews experienced in attempting to participate in Italian society.

In chapter 8, "Salamone Rossi's *Songs of Solomon*: The Pleasures and Pains of Marginality," Stefano Patuzzi reconsiders arguably the most widely known Jewish musician in early modern Italy, Salamone Rossi, and his Hebrew works, *Ha-shirim 'asher li-Shlomo*, the first polyphonic Hebrew music ever published. Patuzzi shows how Rossi acted as a "marginal mediator," someone who navigated the complex realities of the musical profession, moving among the soundscapes of the Mantuan ghetto, the active musical culture of the Gonzaga court, and the medium of printed music with Hebrew text. While Rossi is often venerated as the ancestor of synagogue composers of the nineteenth century, and thus someone who might seem to transcend history, Patuzzi shows that he is best understood as a man of his time. Far from adopting an assimilationist stance, loosening the distinctiveness of Jewish culture, Patuzzi shows that Rossi and his collaborator, Leon Modena, claimed polyphonic music as a fundamental component of Jewish practice. In contrast to studies that view Rossi, anachronistically, as an exceptional composer and a precursor to later developments, the *Shirim* form a written manifestation of the rich musical environments that Rossi encountered both inside and outside the ghetto on a regular basis.

In chapter 9, "Orality and Literacy in the Worlds of Salamone Rossi," Lynette Bowring and I view Rossi's volume of Hebrew compositions in a new light: as we argue, Rossi's notation and publication of Hebrew compositions in *Ha-shirim 'asher li-Shlomo* help to problematize the boundary between oral and written traditions in Jewish musical practice. Indeed, one of the features of the *Shirim* that Modena emphasizes in his preface is the very fact of their being written down, thus forming a written complement to the orally transmitted repertoire of Hebrew music. In fact, in his life as a composer and violinist at the Gonzaga court of Mantua, working in the most up-to-date styles of Italian vocal and instrumental music, Rossi was an accomplished composer as well as an improviser. Thus the incorporation of notated polyphony in his *Shirim* coincided with a shift from orality to literacy in the broader Italian musical environment—perhaps especially in instrumental music. Like Patuzzi in chapter 8, we seek to resituate Rossi within his broad musical environment, viewing him less as an exceptional figure than as a professional musician who dealt with all the complexities of musical and religious practice that characterized his everyday life.

In chapter 10, "L'Accademia degli Impediti: A Reevaluation," Liza Malamut picks up on the theme of mediation. She argues that the Academy of the Impeded Ones, active in early seventeenth-century Venice and led by the highly musical rabbi Leon Modena, occupies a paradoxical space in early modern Jewish culture. Drawing on Robert Bonfil's characterization of Qabbalah (literally "received tradition," referring to mysticism) as "a mediating element between opposites," Malamut shows that Modena positioned his musical academy as an "agent of modernity" that would bring Jewish musical practice in line with that of non-Jews.

As this volume shows, the diversity of political, social, and economic experiences of Jews throughout the Italian peninsula is mirrored in the wide range of ways in which they experienced music and of ways in which their musical cultures interacted with the cultures of non-Jews around them. We seek to explore that in this volume, pointing the way, in turn, toward further inquiry and discovery.

NOTES

1. Thomas Coryat, *Coryat's Crudities* (London: Stansby, 1611), 231–233.

2. Ruth HaCohen, *The Music Libel against the Jews* (New Haven, CT: Yale University Press, 2011).

3. "Che canta più forte degl'altri le orationi, detto canzan," Leon Modena, *Historia de' riti hebraici* (1637); I quote from the 1673 edition (Venice: Appresso il Miloco, 1673), 18. See Don Harrán, "'Dum recordaremur Sion': Music in the Life and Thought of the Venetian Rabbi Leon Modena (1571–1648)," *AJS Review* 23, no. 1 (1998): 17–61.

4. Leon Modena, *The Autobiography of a Seventeenth-Century Venetian Rabbi: Leon Modena's Life of Judah*, trans. and ed. Mark R. Cohen, with introduction and essays by Mark R. Cohen, Theodore K. Rabb, Howard E. Adelman, and Natalie Zemon Davis, with historical notes by Howard E. Adelman and Benjamin C. I. Ravid (Princeton, NJ: Princeton University Press, 1988), 86. A recent summary of Jewish participation in musical activities in early modern Italy is in Daniel Jütte, "The Place of Music in Early Modern Italian Jewish Culture," in *Musical Exodus: Al-Andalus and Its Jewish Diasporas*, ed. Ruth F. Davis (Lanham, MD: Rowman and Littlefield, 2015), 45–61.

5. Throughout this volume, the editors adopt the spelling of Rossi's given name that is most commonly used today: *Salamone*. However, Stefano Patuzzi points out that Rossi never used this spelling; he used *Salomone*, *Salomon*, or *Salamon* but never *Salamone*. If the final *e* was present, the only version attested in the historical sources was *Salomone*. Still, some Italian sources from the sixteenth and seventeenth centuries do use the spelling *Salamone*—for example, discussions of the biblical King Solomon. Thus, although the editors have made their choice based on pragmatic concerns—for the sake of consistency in citation of other modern scholars—there is some historical justification for this usage.

6. The literature on Rossi's *Shirim* and Modena's involvement in their publication is extensive. The relevant documents are transcribed and translated in Salamone Rossi, *Sacred Vocal Works in Hebrew: Hashirim 'asher lishlomo / "The Songs of Solomon,"* ed. with introduction and notes by Don Harrán, Complete Works, part 3, volumes 13a and 13b (s.l.: American Institute of Musicology and Neuhausen: Hänssler, 2003), and discussed, for example, in Don Harrán, *Salamone Rossi: Jewish Musician in Late Renaissance Mantua* (Oxford: Oxford University Press, 1999), 201–243; Joshua Jacobson, "Art Music and Jewish Culture before the Jewish Enlightenment: Negotiating Identities in Late Renaissance Italy," in *The Cambridge Companion to Jewish Music*, ed. Joshua S. Walden (Cambridge: Cambridge University Press, 2015), 143–155; and Stefano Patuzzi, "Music from a Confined Space: Salomone Rossi's *Hashirim asher lishlomoh* (1622/23) and the Mantuan Ghetto," in "Sacred Space," special issue, *Journal of Synagogue Music* 37 (Fall 2012): 49–69.

7. That Coimbram was citing the passage in Tractate *Gittin* is clear from his citation of the verse in the biblical book of Hosea (9:1) that is also cited there: "Rejoice not, oh Israel, to exultation like the [other] nations." The same listener might also have raised the objection that polyphonic music constituted an imitation of the customs of gentiles. The story of the

Talmudic heretic Aḥer (literally *Other*, a pseudonym for the rabbi Elisha ben Abuyya), about whom it was known that "Greek [i.e., vernacular] song never left his lips," serves as a case in point: the Talmud cites his engagement with non-Jewish music as a cause of his heresy. See Babylonian Talmud, Tractate Ḥagigah, 16a. Don Harrán has attributed Coimbram's objection to polyphony to the "proximity of the Sabbath to the doleful Ninth of Av" (the anniversary, according to tradition, of the destruction of both the first and second Temples in Jerusalem in 587 BCE and 70 CE, respectively), but this interpretation seems incorrect. See Harrán, "'Dum recordaremur Sion,'" 23.

8. See Harrán, "'Dum recordaremur Sion,'" 59.

9. Examples of this phenomenon in theoretical writings by Jewish scholars are discussed in Don Harrán, *Three Early Modern Hebrew Scholars on the Mysteries of Song* (Leiden: Brill, 2014). Compositions that adopt stylized "Hebrew" language in imitation of Jews' music making are discussed in Harrán, "Between Exclusion and Inclusion: Jews as Portrayed in Italian Music from the Late Fifteenth to the Early Seventeenth Centuries," in *Acculturation and Its Discontents: The Italian Jewish Experience between Exclusion and Inclusion*, ed. David N. Myers, Massimo Ciavolella, Peter H. Reill, and Geoffrey Symcox (Toronto: University of Toronto Press, 2008), 72–98. See also Emily Wilbourne, "Lo Schiavetto (1612): Travestied Sound, Ethnic Performance, and the Eloquence of the Body," *Journal of the American Musicological Society* 63, no. 1 (Spring 2010): 1–43.

10. Jütte, "The Place of Music," 55–57.

11. Cecil Roth, *The Jews in the Renaissance* (Philadelphia: Jewish Publication Society of America, 1959), chap. 12, "Music and the Dance"; Cecil Roth, *Personalities and Events in Jewish History* (Philadelphia: Jewish Publication Society of America, 1953), chap. 20, "When We Remembered Zion"; Israel Adler, "The Rise of Art Music in the Italian Ghetto," in *Jewish Medieval and Renaissance Studies*, ed. Alexander Altmann (Cambridge, MA: Harvard University Press, 1967), 321–364; Abraham Zvi Idelsohn, *Jewish Music: Its Historical Development* (New York: Henry Holt, 1929; New York: Dover, 1992/R), 196–203. These figures also contributed a great deal to the collation and presentation of primary materials; see, for example, Israel Adler, ed., *Hebrew Writings concerning Music in Manuscripts and Printed Books from Geonic Times up to 1800* (Munich: G. Henle, 1975).

12. For example, on the case of Doña Gracia Nasi, see Andrée Aelion Brooks, *The Woman Who Defied Kings: The Life and Times of Doña Gracia Nasi* (Saint Paul, MN: Paragon House, 2002). The tensions over the conversion of the Jewish musician Abramino dall'Arpa are discussed in Jütte, "The Place of Music," 53–54. For more on the relationships among Jews, Christians, and Muslims, see Alisa Meyuhas Ginio, ed., *Jews, Christians, and Muslims in the Mediterranean World after 1492* (New York: Routledge, 2013/R).

13. This is an approach taken, for example, in Harrán, *Salamone Rossi*.

14. Roth, *The Jews in the Renaissance*, 18.

15. Roth, 304.

16. Moshe Rosman, *How Jewish Is Jewish History?* (Oxford: Littman Library of Jewish Civilization, 2007), 112–113. Rosman's critique is directed, in particular, at Cecil Roth's volume *The Jewish Contribution to Civilization* (London: MacMillan, 1938). See also the essays in Jeremy Cohen and Richard I. Cohen, eds., *The Jewish Contribution to Civilization: Reassessing an Idea* (Oxford: Littman Library of Jewish Civilization, 2008).

17. Rosman, *How Jewish Is Jewish History?*, 113.

18. Rosman, 109.

19. See Harrán, *Salamone Rossi: Jewish Musician*, and Salamone Rossi, *Complete Works*, 13 vols. (S.l.: American Institute of Musicology and Neuhausen: Hänssler, 1995–). Harrán's

biography of Rossi contains methodological problems, however, some of which are explained in reviews by Tim Carter (*Journal of the Royal Musical Association* 125, no. 2 [2000]: 299–306) and Edwin Seroussi (in Hebrew) in the journal *Pe'amim* 93 (2003): 172–182; expanded English version as "In the Footsteps of the Great Jewish Composer," review of Harrán, *Salamone Rossi, Min Ad: Israel Studies in Musicology* 3 (2004): 14–20.

20. For example, Don Harrán, "As Framed, So Perceived: Salamone Rossi *Ebreo*, Late Renaissance Musician," in *Cultural Intermediaries: Jewish Intellectuals in Early Modern Italy*, ed. David B. Ruderman and Giuseppe Veltri (Philadelphia: University of Pennsylvania Press, 2004), 178–215. For more on Rossi, see Jacobson, "Art Music and Jewish Culture."

21. Don Harrán, "Madama Europa, Jewish Singer in Late Renaissance Mantua," in *Festa Musicologica: Essays in Honor of George J. Buelow*, ed. Thomas J. Mathiesen and Benito V. Rivera (Stuyvesant, NY: Pendragon, 1995), 197–231; Don Harrán, "Doubly Tainted, Doubly Talented: The Jewish Poet Sara Copio (d. 1641) as a Heroic Singer," in *Musica Franca: Essays in Honor of Frank A. D'Accone*, ed. Irene Alm, Alyson McLamore, and Colleen Reardon (Stuyvesant, NY: Pendragon, 1996), 367–422. Harrán transcribed and translated Sarra Copia Sulam's writings in Sarra Copia Sulam et al., *Jewish Poet and Intellectual in Seventeenth-Century Venice: The Works of Sarra Copia Sulam in Verse and Prose, along with Writings of Her Contemporaries in Her Praise, Condemnation, or Defense*, ed. and trans. with introduction by Don Harrán (Chicago: University of Chicago Press, 2009). For more on Sulam, see Lynn Lara Westwater, *Sarra Copia Sulam: A Jewish Salonnière and the Press in Counter-Reformation Rome* (Toronto: University of Toronto Press, 2020), and Umberto Fortis, *La "bella ebrea": Sara Copio Sullam, poetessa nel ghetto di Venezia del '600* (Turin: Silvio Zamorani editore, 2003). The spelling of Sulam's name (as well as that of her brother-in-law, Moses Sulam, who was the dedicatee of Rossi's *Ha-shirim 'asher li-Shlomo*) varies widely; we follow Westwater in adopting *Sarra Copia Sulam*.

22. See Harrán, *Three Early Modern Hebrew Scholars on the Mysteries of Song*, and Don Harrán, "In Search of the 'Song of Zion': Abraham Portaleone on Music in the Ancient Temple," *European Journal of Jewish Studies* 4, no. 2 (2010): 215–239.

23. Seroussi, "In the Footsteps of the Great Jewish Composer."

24. See, for example, Edwin Seroussi, "In Search of Jewish Musical Antiquity in the 18th-Century Venetian Ghetto: Reconsidering the Hebrew Melodies in Benedetto Marcello's *Estro poetico-armonico*," *Jewish Quarterly Review* 93, nos. 1–2 (July–October 2002): 149–199.

25. Jütte, "The Place of Music," 51–54.

26. Edwin Seroussi, "Music: The 'Jew' of Jewish Studies," *Jewish Studies* 46 (2009): 5.

27. David B. Ruderman, *Early Modern Jewry* (Princeton, NJ: Princeton University Press, 2010), 13.

28. Robert Bonfil, *Jewish Life in Renaissance Italy*, trans. Anthony Oldcorn (Berkeley: University of California Press, 1994), 20.

29. On literacy rates among Jews, see Bonfil, *Jewish Life in Renaissance Italy*, 147–148.

30. Ruderman, *Early Modern Jewry*, 17.

31. Bonfil, *Jewish Life in Renaissance Italy*, 11.

32. Bonfil, 62.

33. Ruderman, *Early Modern Jewry*, 38.

34. Yaron Ben-Naeh, "Research on Ottoman Jewish History and Culture: The State of the Art," *Revue Européenne des Études Hébraïques* 18 (2016): 77.

35. Dana E. Katz, *The Jewish Ghetto and the Visual Imagination of Early Modern Venice* (Cambridge: Cambridge University Press, 2017), 74.

36. Edwin Seroussi, "Ghetto Soundscapes: Venice and Beyond," in *Shirat Dvora: Essays in Honor of Professor Dvora Bregman*, ed. Haviva Ishay (Beer-Sheva: Ben Gurion University

in the Negev Press, 2019), 168–169. See also Edwin Seroussi, "The Turkish *Makam* in the Musical Culture of the Ottoman Jews: Sources and Examples," *Israeli Studies in Musicology* 5 (1989): 55–68.

37. Bonfil, *Jewish Life in Renaissance Italy*. One article that presents music in this nuanced light is Massimo Acanfora Torrefranca, "Sulle musiche degli ebrei in Italia," in *Gli ebrei in Italia*, vol. 1, *Dall'alto Medioevo all'età dei ghetti*, Storia d'Italia, Annali 11, ed. Corrado Vivanti (Turin: Einaudi, 1996), 478–493.

38. Bonfil, *Jewish Life in Renaissance Italy*, 44–50. For more on anti-Jewish sentiment, see Emanuele Ottolenghi, *Autodafé: l'Europa, gli Ebrei e l'antisemitismo* (Turin: Lindau, 2007), and, especially as it was manifested in blood libels in the Renaissance, see Ariel Toaff, *Pasque di sangue: ebrei d'Europa e omicidi rituali* (Bologna: Il mulino, 2008).

39. Ruderman, *Early Modern Jewry*, 40.

40. Katz, *The Jewish Ghetto and the Visual Imagination*, 29.

41. Jütte, "The Place of Music," 57.

42. See, for example, the collected essays in Benjamin Ravid, *Studies on the Jews of Venice, 1382–1797* (Aldershot: Ashgate, 2003); Stefanie B. Siegmund, *The Medici State and the Ghetto of Florence: The Construction of an Early Modern Jewish Community* (Stanford, CA: Stanford University Press, 2006); the essays in David B. Ruderman and Giuseppe Veltri, eds., *Cultural Intermediaries: Jewish Intellectuals in Early Modern Italy* (Philadelphia: University of Pennsylvania Press, 2004); the essays in David B. Ruderman, ed., *Essential Papers on Jewish Culture in Renaissance and Baroque Italy* (New York: New York University Press, 1992); Riccardo Calimani, *Storia degli ebrei italiani* (Milan: Mondadori, 2013); Roberto Salvadori, *Gli ebrei di Firenze: dalle origini ai giorni nostri* (Florence: Giuntina, 2000); and the essays in Myers et al., eds., *Acculturation and Its Discontents*.

43. See, for example, Dana E. Katz, *The Jew in the Art of the Italian Renaissance* (Philadelphia: University of Pennsylvania Press, 2008), and Vivian Mann, ed., *Gardens and Ghettos: The Art of Jewish Life in Italy*, art catalogue by the Jewish Museum, New York (Berkeley: University of California Press, 1989).

44. Jütte, "The Place of Music."

> REBECCA CYPESS is Associate Dean for Academic Affairs at the Mason Gross School of the Arts, Rutgers University, where she is also Associate Professor of Music. She is author of *Women and Musical Salons in the Enlightenment* and *Curious and Modern Inventions: Instrumental Music as Discovery in Galileo's Italy*, and she is editor (with Nancy Sinkoff) of *Sara Levy's World: Gender, Judaism, and the Bach Tradition in Enlightenment Berlin*.

1

Written in Italian, Heard as Jewish
Reconsidering the Notated Sources of Italian Jewish Music

FRANCESCO SPAGNOLO

Notated musical sources documenting the development of Jewish liturgical music in Italy prior to the emancipation in the nineteenth century are rare, precious, and extremely fragmentary.[1] Past scholarship focused on these materials as uncontested testimonies of the penetration of art music, ideas, and practices within the culture of Italian Jews, highlighting through them the emergence of Jewish musicianship in Europe.[2] My suggestion is to look at these sources once again in a new light. In spite of their fragmentary nature, they provide unexpected perspectives on the ongoing and consolidated musical, cultural, and personal relations and interactions between Jewish and non-Jewish musicians and intellectuals. These interactions centered on synagogue life within the confines of the Italian ghettos since their formation in the sixteenth century and bloomed throughout the emancipation three centuries later, waning with the rise of the Fascist regime and the ensuing persecutions in the twentieth century. For centuries, musical exchanges revolving around synagogue life impacted musical education and the framework of music historiography, life in and outside the ghettos, and the production of musical materials in both print and manuscript form.[3] While, for the most part, we can only speculate on the nature of these day-to-day exchanges among musicians of different faiths and social statuses, their nature and overall character emerge in stark contrast to previous interpretations of the materials under consideration. Such a new reading of these invaluable musical sources, written and oral, unveils their unique contribution to the study of

Italian Jewish cultural history. In turn, this reconsideration can also enhance the complexity and uniqueness of the historical narratives that have engendered a variety of debates within the field of "Jewish musicology" for the last 150 years, thus enlightening the general field of Jewish studies tout court from an unsuspected angle.

As stated by Edwin Seroussi, "Within the modern scholarly discourses on Jewish culture, from the nineteenth century German 'Science of Judaism,' via the Israeli *'mada'ei ha-yahadut'* to the more recent North American 'Jewish studies,' music emerges as a relatively minor field of inquiry in comparison to other disciplines. Comprehensive textbooks on Jewish culture of recent publication do not include the word 'music' in their index." Only in very recent decades have scholars from a variety of fields and disciplines "addressed music from very diverse angles, as a vital component of Jewish religious experience, reactions to social shifts, and constructions of memory, place, identity, and gender."[4] In spite of this rise in interest, it is safe to say that recent studies of Jewish music have neither touched on the liminal interactions between Jews and non-Jews that take place *inside* the synagogue nor explored the synagogue itself as an ever-challenging, and yet crucial, "shared sacred site."[5]

The notated sources discussed here are all well known to scholars of Jewish music. Many of the sources have been published, and occasionally performed, since the mid-nineteenth century. While their common denominator is to include both musical notes *and* Hebrew texts, the sources vary in how (and by whom) they were produced, their scope, the audience or readership at whom they were directed, and their specific musical and cultural content.

Among the sources that I will discuss are notations of music generated by synagogue cantors, such as Avraham Segre of Casale Monferrato (before 1670), who deployed his acquired skill in writing musical notation to commit to paper an orally transmitted repertoire; by Christian scholars like Giulio Bartolocci in Rome (1693), who, in researching the "music of the Jews," wished to notate what he had heard from the oral repertoires of Italian Jews he had encountered; and by Jewish and non-Jewish musicians, including Salamone Rossi (1622–1623) and Benedetto Marcello (1724–1727), who created new performance repertoires based on Hebrew texts.

In addition to their variety of origins, these materials also range in scope, as they served a host of diverse purposes. Their production aimed at documenting cantorial practice and passing it on to a new generation of synagogue musicians, at researching synagogue liturgy in order to identify the historical roots of Christian liturgical music, at creating a new corpus of polyphonic music based on Hebrew texts, or at regenerating the supposed musical "sacred bridge" between Jews and Christians in modern times.

These musical sources also vary in content and format. They include both manuscripts and printed music, created with different parameters aimed at balancing the graphic relationship between Hebrew texts—which, if not transliterated into Roman script, are written or printed from right to left—and musical notes, typically written or printed from left to right (unless set to match texts in Hebrew script). In these sources, the relationship between text and musical notes differs greatly and therefore ends up representing sounds (the sounds of both musical notes *and* Hebrew words) in radically different, and divergent, ways.

In spite of such substantive differences, all these sources stem from one basic experience: the encounter of Jewish and Christian musical cultures, and therefore of Jewish and Christian *musicians*, around the music of the synagogue and thus around their particular experiences of synagogue life.[6] In this respect, these sources should be compared with others that offer a wider picture of the role that music had in Italian synagogue life. This other category includes the scores, librettos, and historical descriptions of the kabbalistic ceremonies for the day of Hoshana Rabbah (the last day of the holiday of Sukkot) in Venice (before 1682) and Casale Monferrato (1732, 1733, and 1735), as well as the inauguration of the Synagogue of Siena (1786).[7] Past scholarship on Italian Jewish music, however, has more or less systematically avoided considering these musical testimonies as a place of Jewish-Christian interaction and has instead focused on creating a consistently Jewish historical narrative that surrounds their production.

For the sake of chronological consistency, I suggest excluding from this pool of sources a very important document in the history of Jewish music—one that could be otherwise used as a manifesto to demonstrate the cross-pollination between Jewish and Christian musical cultures in the documentation of Jewish music. I am referring to the musical notations produced in the twelfth century by Johannes, or Obadiah "the Norman Proselyte," a native of Oppido Lucano. These notations in diastematic Beneventan neumes (Fragment Cambridge TS. K 5/41 and Fragment Cincinnati ENA 4096b) were studied by Norman Golb, Hanoch Avenary, Israel Adler, and others and transcribed in modern notation by the latter.[8] Although they were created by a Christian native of Italy who had converted to Judaism, these sources do not seem to be linked to the musical cultures of the Jews of Italy.[9] As noted by Reinhardt Flender, they may instead be connected with the practice of Hebrew psalmody in North Africa and the Middle East.[10]

Even with the exclusion of Obadiah's manuscripts, we are looking at some of the earliest sources of Jewish musical culture produced in Italy, and we should therefore contextualize them within the musical cultures of Italian Jewry. As we know it through written and oral sources, Italian Jewish music comprises a vast corpus, consisting of numerous distinct liturgical and paraliturgical traditions of various origins, continuously in contact with a broad range of influences and in constant evolution over a long period of time. It developed in the many Jewish communities of the Italian peninsula and the areas in which Jews originating from the peninsula came to live. This complex and fascinating musical world remains one of the widest uncharted areas of Jewish music.

The study of Jewish musical cultures operates in a constant dialectic between oral and written sources, and it is based on the understanding that oral sources point to historical information that cannot be retrieved by relying on written sources alone—information that often sheds light on the cultural history of the Jews beyond the boundaries of "normative" Judaism. In other words, the orally transmitted musical repertoires of the present can offer an unprecedented view on Jewish life of the past beyond music, including daily life, intellectual and spiritual dimensions, economic and societal assets, family and gender roles, and Jewish-Christian relations. The study of Italian Jewish musical sources, past and present, written and oral, can best be conducted in conjunction with the reconstruction of Italy's diverse synagogue life. This perspective, which intersects the disciplinary arenas of musicology, history, and ethnography, prompts us to define Italian Jewish liturgical music as a hybrid of Ashkenazic, Italian, and Sephardic traditions, in constant cross-pollination with one another and in continuous interaction with the musical culture of the "other"—namely, of the Italian Christian majority.

The nature of this interaction needs to be assessed in the specificity of each local and chronological context. But it first needs, to put it bluntly, to be acknowledged. In order for the musical sources mentioned thus far to be produced, the interaction had to occur not only between Jewish and Christian musical cultures but also between Jewish and Christian musicians. This very basic fact has not been considered by the scholars of Italian Jewish music, with the exception of Edwin Seroussi's study of Benedetto Marcello's *Estro poetico-armonico* (Venice, 1724–1726).[11]

Israel Adler, the scholar to whom we owe the systematization and, in many cases, the gathering of almost all the sources of Italian Jewish music, in his seminal work devoted to the practice of art music among European Jews in the modern period, flatly denies the importance of the presence of non-Jewish musicians, as such, in the Jewish setting: "Under such conditions, one should not be at all surprised to see how some communities secured the collaboration of a non-Jewish composer for the celebration of their religious ceremonies. In terms of the value of these documents for the history of Jewish music, once their musical contents are not pulled from traditional Jewish song repertoires, whether their author is Jewish or not is of little importance. What matters is the intimately Jewish character of the ceremonies for which these works were conceived."[12] Instead, Adler focuses on emphasizing the role that segregation played in eliciting an artistic (thus de facto and broadly cultural) response from Jewish intellectuals and musicians: "It is not by chance that it is especially since this period that musical activity in Jewish contexts is known to us: forbidden to pursue an official musical career on the outside, Jewish musicians could only express themselves inside the ghetto."[13]

Don Harrán, whose portentous scholarly career was partly devoted to the study of the life and works of Salamone Rossi (ca. 1570–ca. 1630), focused greatly on Rossi's status as a Jewish musician in a gentile world. In Harrán's narrative (albeit not necessarily in his careful analysis of the materials themselves), Rossi appears less as a man of his time—someone whose professional and personal contacts were both outside and inside the ghetto and whose published works (including his Hebrew work, *Ha-shirim 'asher li-Shlomo*, published in Venice by the Bragadina press in 1622–1623) were the result of a Jewish-Christian partnership—and more like a timeless figure, a spiritual father to, or a prototype of, the stateless Jewish composers of postemancipation Europe:

> No other Jewish musician of [Rossi's] stature and accomplishments is known from ancient times to the early seventeenth century; he was described, in fact, as the first to have restored music to its splendor in the Ancient Temple and as having David the psalmist as his forebear. Nor can any later Jewish composer, of the same caliber, be found until the nineteenth and twentieth centuries. True, Mendelssohn and Mahler were Jewish-born, but

by converting [to Christianity] they masked their origins. Other composers, who were, in fact, preoccupied with their Jewish heritage, better qualify as Rossi's spiritual descendants, among them Ernest Bloch, Darius Milhaud, and Leonard Bernstein.[14]

Yet the question of *how* Jews acquired musical literacy—an ability that seems to characterize only a handful of Jewish intellectuals and entertainers in Italy and southern France since the sixteenth century—is only marginally asked by these scholars.

A possible answer to this question may come from considering the marginality of these early music literates within their society. For the musical notation of the Psalms in Casale Monferrato (MS 479, Montefiore Library, London; fig. 1.1) to be produced in the second half of the seventeenth century, several figures were needed.[15] First was a cantor (Avraham Segre), who wished to transmit his knowledge to his pupil. Second, there was the pupil, Ya'aqov Halewi Finzi, a student of Abraham ben David Provenzal and Samuel (Shemuel) Archivolti, defined in the manuscript as "sheliaḥtzibbur Ashkenazi," or "an Ashkenazic synagogue cantor," from Casale Monferrato; Finzi's desire was to write down the knowledge transmitted by his teacher. Third was the Jewish intellectual, rabbi, and grammarian Avraham Yosef Shelomoh ben Mordekhai Graziano (Pesaro, 1620–Modena, 1685), who inserted the pupil's annotations into his own compilations of glosses and notes on grammatical subjects.

The marginality of these characters and their deep relationship with music are epitomized by Graziano's nom de plume. Graziano signed himself emblematically, and puzzlingly, as "'ish ger 'anokhi ba-'aretz" (I am a sojourner in the land). This name may be, through Graziano's initials (the words *'ish ger* begin with the same Hebrew letters as *Avraham Graziano*), a pun on the figure of David as the father of Jewish music: the epithet interlaces 2 Samuel 1:13 ("ben 'ish ger 'amaleqi 'anokhi," I am the son of an Amalakite sojourner) and Psalm 119:19 ("ger 'anokhi ba-'aretz," I am a sojourner in the land). Thus, Graziano's epithet functions as a musical signature of estrangement, not unlike the notes fa-re-sol in the signature of the Italian scholar and geographer Abraham Farissol (1451–1525). It is, furthermore, a graphic marker of a marginality that betrays a closeness with the musical culture of the (Christian) other, as Graziano refers to himself as a sojourner in the land of Italy.

A more pronounced interaction between Jewish and non-Jewish music practitioners is also suggested by the typographic setting of Rossi's *Ha-shirim 'asher li-Shlomo*, perhaps the most famous and most performed Italian

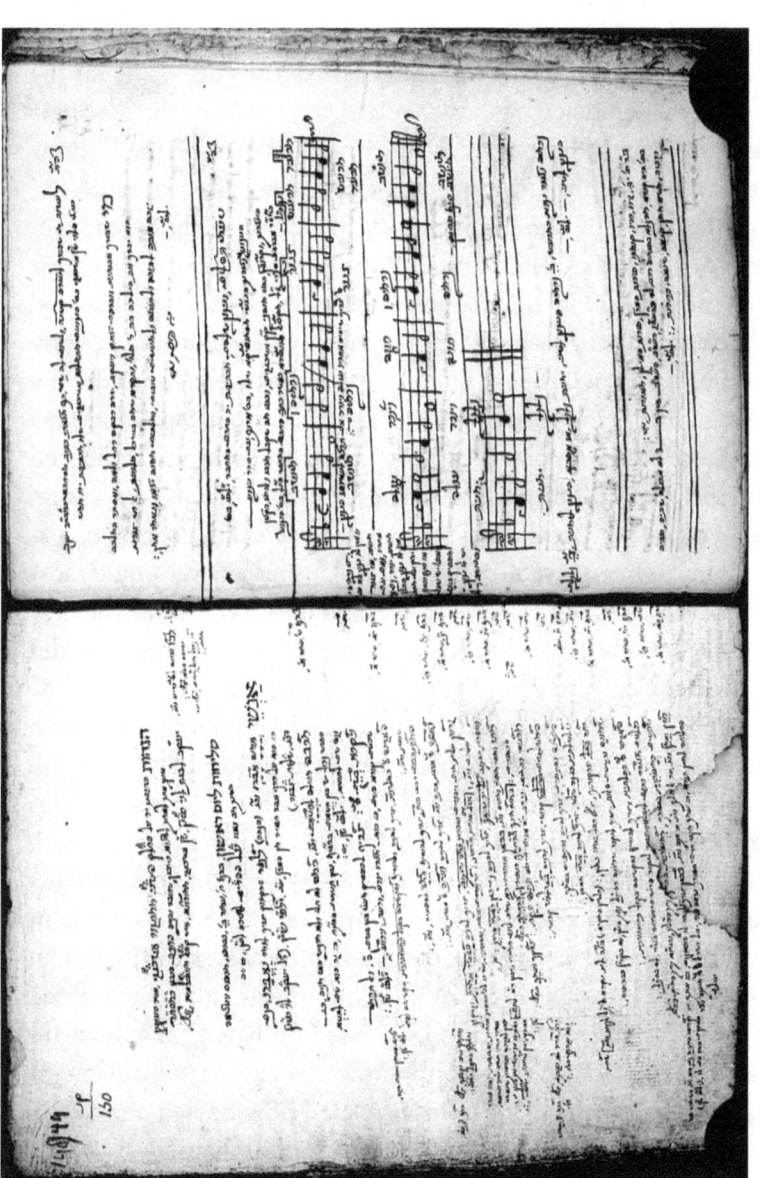

FIGURE 1.1.

Casale Monferrato, MS 479, Montefiore Library, London. The whereabouts of this manuscript are unknown at present, but a microfilm has been digitized at the National Library of Israel at https://web.nli.org.il/sites/NLI/Hebrew/digitallibrary/pages/viewer.aspx?presentorid=MANUSCRIPTS&docid=PNX_MANUSCRIPTS990001131470205171-1#|FL29607698 (accessed January 8, 2021), image no. 150.

Jewish musical work.[16] As a brief examination of its pages suggests, the Hebrew text of Rossi's settings was paginated following the left-to-right direction of the musical notes (fig. 1.2). Of the two languages that appear in the work—Hebrew, in Hebrew script, and music, in musical notation—the one that dominates the typographic architecture of the pages is by far the "Christian" one, the language of music. While the music of the *Shirim* is printed, as is customary in European culture, from left to right, the Hebrew words of the text (often drawn from biblical sources) are also printed, word by word, from the left to the right. This ends up forcing the Hebrew reader of the text to move against the customary right-to-left direction of the Hebrew script and makes establishing the connection between Hebrew syllables and musical notes extremely challenging. The creation of this publication clearly required a combination of different kinds of expertise, exercised under the roof of the Bragadina printing press, and careful collaboration among the author (Rossi), the editor (apparently Rabbi Leon Modena, who authored the preface to the publication), and the music printers. As far as I am aware, the question of who at the Bragadina press may have had the necessary expertise to print music has not yet been asked. A plausible answer would most likely point to other Christian printers active in Venice at the time, who may have had to be hired ad hoc by Bragadina, a printing firm that otherwise did not issue musical works.

The interaction between Jews and Christians in the production of Jewish musical sources comes into sharper focus in situations where the sources are the direct product of Christian authors, as is the case with transcriptions published by Giulio Bartolocci (1613–1687) in *Bibliotheca magna Rabbinica* (volume 4, 1693) and by Benedetto Marcello (1686–1739) in the context of his *Estro poetico-armonico* (1724–1726).[17] These Christian intellectuals, either in person or by way of an emissary, wrote down what they *heard* the Jews sing. In order to do so, they must have either gone into the ghetto (as suggested by Seroussi about how Marcello's transcriptions originated) or at least interviewed them at the Collegium Neophytorum (where Bartolocci taught Hebrew literature since 1651).[18] Bartolocci related how he had personally heard "with his own ears" the song of Sephardic and Italian Jews: "I have heard these [biblical] accents, which are common amongst the Spanish and Italian Jews, *with my own ears, sung from written text*, and have adapted them to the best of my knowledge of the art of music to our notes, Do, re, mi, fa, etc. overlaying them on the tenor part."[19] The practice of musical transcription requires solid musical skills (Bartolocci's disclaimer is that he did not

FIGURE 1.2.

Salamone Rossi, "'Ein kelohenu," Canto part of Choir II, from *Ha-shirim 'asher li-Shlomo* (Venice: Bragadini, 1622–1623). Image courtesy of the Bibliothèque nationale de France.

possess much of those) and also time: the time for the source to repeat, over and over again, the melody sung. It is not difficult for me to imagine how this may have happened then, without the assistance of recording devices: the source (a Jew, versed in synagogue song or in Torah reading) sings a melody, and the transcriber (a Christian, versed in music theory) jots down an initial melodic line and then asks his source to repeat it as many times as it is needed to ensure the accuracy of his transcription. In the case of Bartolocci (and of the Christian humanists who preceded and followed him but who do not explicitly mention the act of having heard Jews sing as the source of their transcription), this was done for the twenty-eight melodic formulas that represent the *te'amim* sung by Italian Jews (presumably of Roman tradition) in the reading of the *parashah* (the weekly reading from the Pentateuch) and the *haftarah* (the weekly reading from the books of the Prophets).[20] In the case of Benedetto Marcello's publication, this was done for the eleven melodies he included in it by interviewing two cantors representing the German and the Spanish traditions. Typographically, the publication of Marcello's melodies gave way to a solution in print different from Rossi's *Shirim*: here, in a source explicitly directed to a non-Jewish audience, both the Hebrew and the music layouts proceed together from right to left.

The very act of musical transcription of a Jewish oral source implies proximity: physical, professional, and intellectual proximity. We are left only to speculate about how this proximity may have been acted out in the seventeenth and eighteenth centuries: how sources were identified, how they were approached, how the fieldwork was conducted, and for what period of time it lasted. Edwin Seroussi, echoing a suggestion made by Pier Cesare Ioly-Zorattini, is the only scholar who actively described Marcello as a "proto-ethnomusicologist," successfully drawing the same picture I attempted to paint earlier, in which the knowledge of the details of fieldwork are brought into the reconstruction of historical events: "In order to make his transcriptions, which attained a remarkable degree of fidelity . . . Marcello needed much more than a glimpse of the sounds of the synagogue through the windows or adjacent houses. . . . He, or at least a (Jewish?) collaborator had to sit down with at least two synagogue cantors and to listen to repeated performances of each melody in order to write them down. This was a true situation of ethnomusicological fieldwork."[21]

While Seroussi's observations and mine match in terms of reconstructing the history of fieldwork—they are indeed based on firsthand experience drawn from our own research—I would like to carry these examples of Jewish-Christian proximity a bit further in the appreciation of the Italian context.

The musical production of the sources discussed here involved the transcription of melodies from the oral tradition through fieldwork, as well as the adaptation of Hebrew texts to music in manuscripts and print editions, but it also (and perhaps principally) touched on the *performance* and *reception* of the music itself inside the synagogue by Jews and Christians together. In other words, a final step in considering Jewish-Christian interaction implies also considering questions relating to the identity of the performers and the audience of these musical works: By whom and for whom was this music presented? If we begin to account for the presence of Christian musicians *and* listeners among the performers and the public in the synagogues of Italy at this time, our perception of the Italian Jewish soundscape, and thus the historical narrative that surrounds it, may change irremediably. These Christian presences in the synagogue are sporadically, albeit explicitly, documented in some contemporary sources from the early modern period and become more prominent in later times.

The role of non-Jewish musicians as performers of synagogue music before the nineteenth century can only be inferred from circumstantial evidence (such as the transliteration of the Hebrew texts into Roman script, as evidenced in musical scores from Mantua, Casale, and Siena mentioned previously). By the nineteenth century—but preceding the emancipatory edicts of 1848—the presence of Catholic choir directors and instrumentalists, whose task was to play the organs and harmoniums that by then had become a staple of most synagogues across the peninsula, was an essential component in the performance of synagogue liturgy. Non-Jews also played at Jewish weddings, as in Alessandria, where in 1835 the collapse of a building where a wedding reception was taking place killed several in attendance, including two musicians.[22]

As for listeners, the writings of Marino Sanuto, Leon Modena, and Giulio Morosini describe non-Jewish attendance of synagogue services by Catholic and Protestant synagoguegoers in Venice since the early sixteenth century.[23] The fact that the Hebrew librettos of the eighteenth-century musical ceremonies from Casale Monferrato and Siena were also made available in Italian translation suggests that these events may have been intended for an audience that also included non-Jews. Nineteenth-century testimonies are more numerous and clearly attest to the constant presence of non-Jews at synagogue celebrations. The consequences of these regular frequentations merit special attention, as they suggest that the commission of musical works by Catholic composers (or sometimes Jewish composers who could write like them) served precisely to create a corpus of musical liturgy that catered especially to non-Jewish audiences.

A multifaceted consideration of musical sources—creation, publication, performance, and reception—as the product of a Jewish-Christian interaction becomes particularly poignant once we consider a host of Qabbalah-inspired ceremonies, the music of which has been released numerous times in commercial recordings and recently even performed again in the original sites: the *Cantata hebraica in dialogo* by the Christian composer Carlo Grossi (Venice, before 1682); the anonymous cantatas-quasi-oratorios for Hoshana Rabbah in Casale Monferrato (1732, 1733, 1735), most likely composed by a Jewish-Christian team; and the music for the inauguration of the synagogue of Siena in 1786, which was the work of a Christian professional, Francesco Drei, and a Jewish amateur, Volunio (or Zevulun) Gallichi.[24] Each of these events, which marked religious and communal celebrations, indicates a cultural trend that points toward the collaborative efforts of Jews and Christians around synagogue liturgy, Jewish mysticism, Hebrew literature, and musical performance. Such a trend supports a reconsideration of the Italian Jewish ghettos and of the synagogues located inside them not only as sites of segregation and surveillance but also as porous spaces of cultural collaboration. While the close reexamination of these ceremonies as occasions for Jewish-Christian interaction remains to be explored, it is safe to assume that it is likely to change both our impression of the music itself and the weight of musical sources in our understanding of Italian Jewish cultural history.

NOTES

Previous versions of the ideas discussed here were presented, under different titles and in different forms, first as a paper discussed at the 39th Annual Conference of the Association for Jewish Studies (Washington, DC, 2008) and later as a short essay, in Italian, that appeared as "Scritto in italiano, ascoltato in ebraico: A proposito delle fonti scritte della musica ebraica in Italia," in *Ebraismo in musica: Da Mantova all'Europa e ritorno*, ed. Stefano Patuzzi (Mantua: Di Pellegrini, 2011), 87–101. I am grateful to several colleagues who provided feedback on the previous and current iterations of this work, especially Edwin Seroussi (who patiently read and corrected me on many an account), Francesca Bregoli, David Malkiel,

Stefano Patuzzi, and Sharon Bernstein. This essay is dedicated to the memory of the late Israel Adler (1925–2009), with whom I would have loved to argue about each word I wrote.

1. With the exception of the writings of Giulio Bartolocci, all sources discussed here have been previously gathered and described in Israel Adler, *La pratique musicale savante dans quelques communautés juives en Europe aux XVIIe et XVIIIe siècles*, 2 vols. (Paris and Den Haag: Mouton, 1966), and Israel Adler, *Hebrew Notated Manuscript Sources up to circa 1840: A Descriptive and Thematic Catalogue with a Checklist of Printed Sources*, with the assistance of Lea Shalem, 2 vols., RISM B/IX/1 (Munich: G. Henle, 1989).

2. For the notion of "penetration of art music," see Israel Adler, "La pénétration de la musique savante dans les synagogues italiennes au XVIIe siècle: le cas particulier de Venise," in *Gli ebrei a Venezia: secoli XIV–XVIII, Atti del Convegno Internazionale organizzato dall'Istituto di storia della società e dello stato veneziano della fondazione Giorgio Cini (Venezia 1983)*, ed. Gaetano Cozzi (Milan: Edizioni di Comunità, 1987), 527–535.

3. See Francesco Spagnolo, "La stampa periodica ebraica come fonte per la ricostruzione della vita sinagogale nell'Italia dell'emancipazione," *Materia Giudaica* 9, nos. 1–2 (2004): 265–273; Francesco Spagnolo, "Music and Synagogue Life" [in Hebrew], in *Jewish Communities in the East in the Nineteenth and Twentieth Centuries: Italy*, ed. Roni Weinstein (Jerusalem: Ben Zvi Institute, 2012), 143–150; and Francesco Spagnolo, "The Bimah and the Stage: Synagogue Music and Cultural Production in the Italian Ghettos," in *Venice, the Jews, and Europe*, ed. Donatella Calabi (Venice: Marsilio, 2016), 264–269.

4. Edwin Seroussi, "Music: The 'Jew' of Jewish Studies," *Jewish Studies* 46 (2009): 3–4.

5. For an illuminating, non-Eurocentric perspective on "shared sacred sites," see Elazar Barkan and Karen Barkey, *Choreographies of Shared Sacred Sites: Religion, Politics, and Conflict Resolution* (New York: Columbia University Press, 2016).

6. With the term *musician*, I designate within this context a variety of agents who are in active contact (as professionals or amateurs) with the world of sounds, including composers, performers, publishers, copyists, editors, and printers.

7. For a comprehensive survey, publication, and discussions of these sources, see Israel Adler, *La pratique musicale*, 9–109 (Venice) and 132–154 (Siena), as well as, for Casale Monferrato, Israel Adler, "Sheloshah teqasim musiqaliim lehosha'na rabah baqehilat qasale monferato (1732, 1733, 1735)," in *Yuval: Studies of the Jewish Music Research Center*, vol. 5, *The Abraham Zvi Idelsohn Memorial Volume*, ed. Israel Adler, Bathja Bayer, and Eliyahu Schleifer (Jerusalem: Magnes Press, the Hebrew University, 1986), 51–137 (Hebrew section).

8. Adler, *Hebrew Notated Manuscript Sources*, 550–553.

9. The only scholar to oppose this view and to suggest a specific Italian connection was Leo Levi, in "Le due più antiche trascrizioni musicali di melodie ebraico-italiane," in *Scritti sull'ebraismo in memoria di Guido Bedarida* (Florence: Tipografia Giuntina, 1966), 105–136.

10. Reinhard Flender, *Hebrew Psalmody: A Structural Investigation* (Jerusalem: Magnes Press, the Hebrew University, 1992).

11. Edwin Seroussi, "In Search of Jewish Musical Antiquity in the 18th-Century Venetian Ghetto: Reconsidering the Hebrew Melodies in Benedetto Marcello's *Estro poetico-armonico*," *Jewish Quarterly Review* 93, nos. 1–2 (July–October 2002): 149–200.

12. "Dans ces conditions on ne s'étonnera guère de voir certaines communautés s'assurer la collaboration d'un compositeur non-juif pour la célébration de leurs cérémonies religieuses. En ce qui concerne la valeur de ces documents pour l'histoire de la musique juive, à partir du moment ou leur contenu musical n'est pas puisé aux sources du chant traditionnel juif, il importe peu que leur auteur soit juif ou non-juif. Ce qui importe, c'est le caractère

intimement juif des cérémonies auxquelles ces œuvres étaient destinées," Adler, *La pratique musicale*, 39–40.

13. "Ce n'est peut-être pas un hasard si c'est surtout à partir de cette époque que l'activité musicale dans un cadre juif nous est connue: empêché de poursuivre une carrière musicale officielle à l'extérieur, le musicien juif devra désormais s'exprimer à l'intérieur du ghetto," Adler, 46.

14. Don Harrán, *Salamone Rossi: Jewish Musician in Late Renaissance Mantua* (Oxford: Oxford University Press, 1999), 2.

15. The current whereabouts of this manuscript, which was likely sold at auction, are unknown. A digital copy is available through the Institute of Microfilmed Hebrew Manuscripts of the National Library of Israel. I am grateful to my student Joseph Schindler for his assistance in gaining access to the digital copy and especially to Michelle Chesner, Norman E. Alexander Librarian for Jewish Studies at Columbia University, for pointing both of us in its direction.

16. On the technical (typographic) aspects of the *Shirim*, see Harrán, *Salamone Rossi*, 210–212.

17. Giulio Bartolocci, *Qiryat sefer. Bibliotheca magna Rabbinica de scriptoribus, et scriptis Hebraicis, ordine alphabetico Hebraicè, et Latinè digestis. . . . 4 partes*, ed. Carlo Imbonati (Rome: Typographia Sacrae Congregationis de Propaganda Fide, 1675–1693), and Benedetto Marcello, *Estro poetico-armonico: Parafrasi sopra li salmi* (Venice: Domenico Lovisa, 1724–1726).

18. Seroussi's view is articulated in Seroussi, "Music: The 'Jew' of Jewish Studies," 70–71.

19. "Hos Accentus ab Hebræis Hispanis, & Italis usitatos, *proprijs auribus ab ispis canere audivi*, qui à quodam Artis Musicæ perito, quanta fieri potuit proportione, nostris notis Ut, re mi, fa, &tc. adaptati, sunt suprascripti tenoris," Giulio Bartolocci, "De Hebræorum ΜΟΥΣΙΚΗ Musica Brevis Dissertatio," in *Qiryat sefer*, 4:441 (emphasis added).

20. Bartolocci, 440–441.

21. Seroussi, "In Search of Jewish Musical Antiquity," 170.

22. Aldo Perosino, "La comunità ebraica di Alessandria dal 1842 a oggi: indagine statistica," *Rassegna mensile di Israel* 68, no. 2 (May–August 2002): n68.

23. Benjamin Ravid, "How 'Other' Really Was the Jewish Other? Evidence from Venice," in *Acculturation and Its Discontents: The Italian Jewish Experience between Exclusion and Inclusion*, ed. David N. Myers, Massimo Ciavolella, Peter H. Reill, and Geoffrey Symcox (Toronto: University of Toronto Press, 2008), 19–55.

24. For more on these cases, see note 7.

> FRANCESCO SPAGNOLO is Curator of the Magnes Collection of Jewish Art and Life at the University of California, Berkeley, where he is also Associate Adjunct Professor in the Department of Music. He received his PhD from Hebrew University in 2007. Among his publications are *Italian Jewish Musical Traditions* and *The Jewish World: 100 Treasures of Art and Culture*.

2

Miriam's Timbrel
The Decameron *as Exodus*

AARON BECK*

The unique organization of Boccaccio's *Decameron*, in which ten people narrate one hundred stories over the course of ten days, has been the subject of much scholarly attention.[1] In the introduction to his 2015 translation, Wayne Rebhorn notes that while there is no antecedent in Italian literature for the *Decameron*'s structure, there are several non-Italian models for its use of a frame story. These include the *Panchatantra* (*The Five Heads*), which Boccaccio "probably knew ... although in a Latin translation based on a Hebrew version"; *The Seven Wise Masters* and *The Thousand and One Nights*, "which Boccaccio probably did not know"; and the eighth and ninth books of Apuleius's *Metamorphoses*, or *Golden Ass*, "which he certainly did."[2] Vittore Branca, on the other hand, cites Saint Ambrose's *Hexameron*, which describes the creation of the world in six days, as a possible inspiration for the *Decameron*'s title.[3] While the influence of Arab and Greek narratives on Boccaccio has been well established, I suggest that the Hebrew Bible also influenced the narrative structure of the *Decameron*. In particular, I argue that Boccaccio's introduction of dance songs brings together ancient Hebrew biblical traditions and Christian musical philosophy and that Boccaccio's ballata texts themselves, in addition to the implied musical performances, resonate strongly with the ritualic songs of the Hebrew Bible—in particular, the Song at the Sea, Miriam's song, in Exodus 15.

Don Harrán noted the connection between Boccaccio and Hebrew musical thought in his important book *In Search of Harmony: Hebrew and*

Humanist Elements in Sixteenth-Century Musical Thought, discussing Boccaccio's *Genealogy of the Pagan Gods* at the outset of the book. Harrán quotes the passage from book 14 where Boccaccio concludes that Moses is the inventor of poetry, or "heroic verse."[4] I will further illuminate the influence of Hebrew thought on Boccaccio's work by examining the relationship between the interpolation of Miriam's dance song in Exodus and the introduction of dance songs in the *Decameron*. The practice of singing responsorially is well attested in the ancient Hebrew musical tradition, and like Miriam's song in Exodus, several of Boccaccio's *Decameron* dance songs have refrains that the members of the *brigata* sing in a responsorial manner. I investigate how images of Miriam and her dancers found in Hebrew texts of Boccaccio's time relate to the dancers in the *Decameron*. Christian and Jewish sources intersected in Renaissance engagements with the Hebrew Bible, and Boccaccio most likely engaged with Christian interpretations of Hebrew biblical storytelling. I will juxtapose musical representations found in Saint Ambrose's *Hexameron* with the ballatas found in the *Decameron* to further illuminate the sacred nature of the *Decameron*'s implied music. I show that the ballatas in the *Decameron* imply musical performance that draws on literary-poetic traditions of both Judaism and Christianity.

THE EXODUS SONGS IN ICONOGRAPHY AND LITERATURE

Chapter 15 of the book of Exodus provides a harrowing description of the Israelites' escape from their Egyptian captors between walls of water in the Red Sea. After the Israelites reach dry ground, they turn to see the Egyptians drowned, their entire army devastated. The riveting action pauses in a most operatic manner: two songs are interjected, the first sung by Moses and the entire nation, the second by Miriam. Moses's song (Exodus 15:1–8), which I quote from an early translation of the Latin Vulgate, which Boccaccio would have known, begins:

> Let us sing to our Lord: for he is glouriously magnified, the horse and the rider he hath throwen into the sea.
> My strength, and my praise is our Lord, and he is made unto me a salvation: this is my God, and I wil glorifie him: the God of my father, and I wil exalt him.[5]

Following Moses's song, Miriam sings (Exodus 15:20–21), reiterating Moses's initial stanza. Although the complete text of Moses's song is included, it appears that only the refrain of Miriam's song is quoted in Exodus. The inclusion of only limited portions of her text may connect Miriam's song to some prominent performative rituals of Hebrew songs of praise—in particular, the ritual of responsorial performance, where a leader (Miriam) sings the first half of each line and a larger group completes the line. Miriam accompanies her song with a timbrel, and some other women join her in a dance. At this point, the inclusion of music produces a celebratory atmosphere:

> Marie [i.e., Miriam] therfore the Prophetesse, Aarons sister, tooke a tymbrel in her hand: and al the women went forth after her with tymbrels and dances,
> to whom she began the song, saying: Let us sing to our Lord, for he is gloriously magnified, the horse and his rider he hath cast into the sea.

Numerous scholars, both ancient and modern, have sought to imagine the performance of these songs. The responsorial aspect of the songs was observed by John Arthur Smith, who argues that Moses's song was likely a refrain that would have been repeated by the Israelites, or perhaps the first part of a phrase that would have been completed by the group.[6] He also postulates that these biblical songs and their narrative frameworks originated independently from one another and were only later combined: the songs are "set pieces that have been interpolated in the narrative," and "the prose text surrounding them . . . makes complete narrative sense without them."[7] Susan E. Gillingham similarly differentiates the songs from the framing narrative, writing that the "editor" (to use her language) who presumably put together the text of Exodus gave the song "a different theological emphasis in a narrative setting," which "limited its performative value to this context alone."[8]

The most noteworthy difference in the performance of the two songs is the fact that the text mentions Moses only singing, while Miriam is reported to sing, dance, and play. Dancing is an important activity in the Hebrew Bible and in its language, with twelve verbs in biblical Hebrew expressing the movement of the dance.[9] Alfred Sendrey notes the prominent role of dancing in the Hebrew Bible in his *Music in Ancient Israel*, writing that the timbrel "points unmistakably to the ritual dance as a complement to singing praises."[10] As one of his examples, Sendrey cites Psalm 149:3, "Let them praise his name in choir: let them sing to him with the timbrel and the psaltery."[11]

Christian images of women dancing while singing in the trecento, such as those underneath Giotto's Justice in the Scrovegni Chapel, often embody the Greek (and by extension Roman) concepts of justice and harmony, as is the case of the dancing figures in Ambrogio Lorenzetti's *Effects of Good Government in the City*.[12] It was in the Jewish culture of the time that the ancient Hebrew integration of poetry, music, and dance was strongly promulgated,[13] particularly in the Haggadah, a volume retelling the Exodus story that is used in the Jewish ritual of the Passover Seder. Originally bound with general prayer books, the Haggadah emerged as a separate book in the thirteenth century, first in Spain and subsequently in other parts of Europe.[14] Between 1280 and 1500, these volumes were accompanied by numerous illustrations in both the Sephardic and Ashkenazic traditions, with some Sephardic Haggadahs prefaced by full-page illuminations of biblical stories. Such books were likely made for affluent Jewish families with connections to Christian aristocrats.[15]

The relationship between the Haggadah and storytelling is integral, as the root of the noun *Haggadah* (נגד, which generates the verb form *higgid*) means "narrate" or "inform."[16] Raphael Loewe explains the complex nature of narrative in a Haggadah, which "is so called because it consists largely of the free elaboration ('information') of the biblical story, and of anecdotes based on it, in a manner calculated to make them the vehicles of a theological, ethical or aesthetic message."[17] Marc Epstein also challenges the reader to view the Haggadah's complex narrative organization as a series of clusters related to the pre-Exodus, Exodus, and post-Exodus stories.[18] He perceives the Haggadah as a Gesamtkunstwerk that interweaves narrative, image, and poetry, though he stops short of describing the role of music.[19]

Images of Miriam singing and dancing with other women were popular in late-medieval Haggadahs, as in the well-known image from a fourteenth-century Spanish Haggadah, known as the "Golden Haggadah," shown in figure 2.1.

The illumination embellishes the biblical story in fascinating ways. The illuminator includes seven women in the scene, five of whom play instruments. The cymbal, woodblock, lute, and timbrel are readily recognizable, while the second woman from the left holds a square object, identified by Judith Cohen as a *pandero cuadrado*.[20] Two women holding each other's fingers appear to be dancing on the right side of the picture.

In the Sarajevo Haggadah, shown in figure 2.2, Miriam strikes a timbrel while five women hold hands and accompany her with their dance. Miriam

FIGURE 2.1.

Miriam at the Sea (detail), full-page illumination in color and gold, Haggadah for Passover (the "Golden Haggadah"), 1320–1330, Add MS 27210, fol. 15r, British Library, London.

FIGURE 2.2.

Miriam and her timbrel (detail), Sarajevo Haggadah, ca. 1350–1360.
Courtesy of the National Museum of Bosnia and Herzegovina, Sarajevo.

is separated from the dancers by her white robe and headdress and by her position on the page: she faces the group of dancers. She is clearly the leader and accordingly is represented differently than she is in the Golden Haggadah, where it is difficult to identify her. Integral to these Haggadah images, as in the biblical text, is the fact that the action of Exodus stops as Miriam gathers the women to sing, a characteristic of the story that persists in other instantiations of this tale.

In addition to these iconographic representations of Miriam's song, the musical aspects of this portion of Exodus have also been represented in literary works. Even in writings from the Christian tradition, aspects of Hebrew performative practice show through revealingly. The fourth-century *Hexameron*, by Saint Ambrose, presents an interesting case study on this intersection of faiths. The name *Hexameron* was given to many medieval texts devoted to the six-day creation story told in Genesis. Ambrose's *Hexameron* was a popular book on a popular subject, the retelling of the Genesis story through a Greco-Christian lens.[21] While references to music do not appear in the biblical story of Genesis, they abound in Ambrose's *Hexameron*, as they do in the *Decameron*.[22] Boccaccio was clearly influenced by Ambrose in his choice of title and organization of narrative, thereby pinning his work to both the concept of Genesis and the idea of historical storytelling.

Music is first mentioned during the second day of the *Hexameron*. Ambrose describes David and his chorus, relating them to the Greek music of the spheres and, perhaps surprisingly, stating that the philosophers were imitating David. His description of the music of the spheres emphasizes their heavenly nature: "By the impact and motion of these spheres there is produced a tone full of sweetness, the fruit of consummate art and of most delightful modulation, inasmuch as the air, torn apart by such artful motion, combines in even and melodious fashion high and low notes to such a degree that it surpasses in sweetness any other musical composition."[23] Many more references to music are found in Ambrose's exegesis on the third day of the *Hexameron*, when he examines the biblical verse "Let the waters that are under the heaven be gathered together into one place" (Genesis 1:9). Here, he introduces the concept of the waters as a metaphor for community. The image of the Red Sea in Exodus exemplifies the connections among God's will, the waters, and the congregation: "The waters, then, know how to congregate, how to fear, and how to flee, when commanded to do so by God. Let us imitate these waters and let us recognize one congregation of the Lord, one Church."[24] He directly connects this sense of congregation to the music that they use, explaining that they "delight not in the baleful songs sung by theatrical performers, songs which lead to sensual love, but in the chants of the Church. Here we hear the voice of the people singing in harmony the praises of God."[25] This singing and Moses's verses are intrinsically related to God's melodious word, with Ambrose explaining that "in the people who are the instruments of the operations of God they [the pious] hear music which echoes from the melodious sound of God's word."[26] For Ambrose, the "people who are the instruments of the operations of God" are priests; Moses and Miriam are from the priestly tribe of the Levites, who would be tasked with making music in the Tabernacle and, later, the Temple in Jerusalem. While Ambrose does not mention Moses's or Miriam's song directly, the image of people coming together after a description of parting waters recalls the singing after the Israelites' escape from Egypt.

For Ambrose, the sound of the seas, too, is melodious. The splashing of waves on the shore is "pleasant and rhythmic," and the breaking of waves on an island has melodic qualities. His description of the sea emphasizes the "fond embrace of peace,"[27] tranquility, moderation, and prudence—qualities that are traditionally linked to harmony and music[28]—before directly connecting these sounds with the singing of hymns: "[The sea] provides an incentive to devout living for the faithful, so that they may rival the gentle sound of lapping waters with the songs of the psalms. Thus, the islands voice their approval with their tranquil chorus of blessed waters and with the singing of pious hymns resound."[29] He then solidifies this connection by specifying that it is the *responsorial* performance of Psalms that the waves evoke, an image that connects his writing directly to the Hebrew traditions depicted by Moses's and Miriam's songs in Exodus: "What else is that melodic sound of the waves if not the melody of the people? Hence, the sea is often well compared to a church which 'disgorges a tide' through all its vestibules at the first array of the approaching congregation; then, as the whole people unite in prayer, there is a hiss of receding waves; the echo of the psalms when sung in responsive harmony by men and women, maidens and children is like the sound of breaking waves."[30]

Earthly creatures also make beautiful music in the *Hexameron*. Descriptions of this appear in the fifth day, in response to Genesis 1:20: "And God said: 'Let the waters abound with life and above the earth let winged creatures fly below the firmament of the heavens.'" The close of Ambrose's exegesis of the fifth day is filled with a symphony of birdcalls, with Ambrose observing that "it is customary for the birds at nesting time 'to charm the sky with song,' in joy that their allotted task is done."[31] Ambrose's description highlights the "ritual pattern" of their songs, emphasizing that "the birds sing the praises of their Creator, at the moment of transition from day to night or from night to day."[32] Since Ambrose believes that the birds' songs are in praise of God, he notes their ability to prompt similar activities among the faithful; if the songs are not heard, people have "lost a mighty incentive for arousing our religious devotion."[33] This capability for resonance between birds and humans is heightened by birds who can imitate human sounds, "so that you would think a man, and not a bird, had spoken."[34] Overall, it is specifically the singing of Psalms that Ambrose draws connections to: "What person of natural human sensibility would not blush to terminate the day without a ritual singing of the psalms, since even the tiniest bird ushers in the approach of the day and night with customary devotion of sweet song?"[35] Ambrose uses the concept of birdsong to infuse his own text with musical implications, suggesting that his discussion should metaphorically "ring with the musical song of birds";[36] his suggestion that a religious text is inherently musical harks back to the Hebrew Bible, the text of which was sung. Like the text itself, the music serves as a reminder of the organization of God's universe, as well as a vehicle of praise. Although Ambrose's text is rooted in Christian traditions, he looks back at many aspects of Hebrew tradition in his conception of ritualistic praise through singing and music. His connection of these rituals of praise and the incorporation of music into the cycle of day and night set important precedents for Boccaccio, for whom the *Hexameron* was a vital inspiration.

JEWISH CULTURES IN BOCCACCIO'S LIFE AND WORKS

While generally not discussed in Boccaccio scholarship, Jewish culture was disseminated in late-medieval Italy through poetry and philosophy, and Hebrew manuscripts were composed and copied in various cities across the peninsula.[37] Boccaccio may have come into contact with Hebrew thought and tradition during his early years in Naples. Jews were present in the courts of Naples and other small towns throughout Italy, the only country in Europe where Jews did not suffer mass persecutions. Naples had a particularly strong connection to Jewish scholars. Of great importance in the century before Boccaccio was the contribution of Frederick II, king of Sicily and Holy Roman emperor (reigned 1220–1250), who enriched his Sicilian court with Christian, Muslim, and Jewish cultures and employed Jewish translators in Naples. He established the University of Naples in 1224, which included lectures in Hebrew, and invited Jacob Anatoli (ca. 1194–1256), a noted translator of Arabic texts into Hebrew. Charles of Anjou (reigned 1266–1285) followed this lead in employing Jewish translators, most notably Faraj of Girgenti (b. 1230), a Sicilian Jewish member of the royal household who also served as an expert on Jewish matters. Robert of Anjou, king of Naples from 1309 to 1343, was fascinated with Hebrew scholarship and is known to have studied the Hebrew Bible under the tutelage of the "Hebrew Schoolman" Judah Romano (b. 1290–after 1330). Robert's interest in and command of Hebrew is further evidenced by the fact that he had translated passages from Thomas Aquinas and Albertus Magnus into Hebrew.[38]

It was in this fertile environment of intersection between Hebrew and Christian cultures that Boccaccio spent his formative years. Born in Florence in 1313 to a mercantile father from Certaldo, Boccaccio spent the years 1328 to 1342 at the court of Naples, where his father worked for the Bardi banking family. There the Boccaccio family had contact with the Angevin family and its rich library and art collection.[39] The Angevin library was diverse and contained both secular and sacred texts in original Greek, Latin, and Arabic and in Hebrew translations. Evidence collected by Cornelia C. Coulter suggests that Boccaccio was familiar with Angevin library holdings; she writes, "His own monumental work on mythology, called *De Genealogia Deorum Gentilium*, makes use of just such genealogical trees as the *tabulae* of the descendants of Adam and Noah and the sons of Israel that were drawn for King Robert."[40] Coulter further elaborates, "In one of the final chapters of this great work Boccaccio speaks of the vast store of books that readers may consult, using phrases which might almost serve as an index to the contents of the royal library." Among these, she notes, are "texts of civil and canon law, with the commentaries written on them by learned men; the works of the philosophers, likewise annotated; writings on medicine, with notes that clear up all difficulties; the Sacred Scriptures and their interpretation." Although it is likely that Boccaccio encountered these texts through a Christian filter, Jewish and Christian sources cannot be easily disentangled. It is very possible, then, that Boccaccio would have been introduced to both Hebrew and Arabic theological and medical treatises while in Naples.

In his *Decameron*, Boccaccio presents rather sympathetic depictions of Jews in a time when they were dehumanized and expelled, their traditions shunned and feared. In day 1, second story, Boccaccio heaps praise on the Jewish merchant Abraam Giudeo, describing him as a "diritto e leale uomo assai" (an extremely upright and honest man). His friend, the merchant Giannotto di Civigní, who sees Abraam as honest and loyal, is concerned for Abraam's "anima d'un cosí valente e savio e buono" (soul of one so worthy, wise, and good) because he is not a Christian and his soul will be lost. To Giannotto's suggestion that he convert, Abraam responds respectfully that no faith is saintly or good outside of the Jewish one, and he intends to die in the faith that he was born into. Boccaccio calls Giannotto "dell'uomo idiota" (an idiot) in relation to the "sobrio e modesto" (sober and modest) Abraam, who is well schooled in Jewish law. While the story ends in Abraam's conversion, it is noteworthy that Boccaccio uses it to speak honestly and forthrightly about the bad behavior of a Christian and the good behavior of a Jew.

Further evidence of Boccaccio's exposure to Jewish culture comes in day 1, seventh story, in which he demonstrates his familiarity with celebrations at the Veronese court of Can Grande della Scala, which included Jewish and Muslim entertainers. Indeed, Boccaccio praises Can Grande, writing that he was one of the most outstanding princes since Frederick II; these two rulers were similarly reputed for the fluid cultural interactions within their courts. Boccaccio's story has Can Grande canceling a marvelous feast in Verona, which many people from different places were supposed to attend, especially courtly people of all types.

The descriptions of Jewish poet Immanuel Romano (ca. 1261–after 1328) vividly supplement Boccaccio's reference to Can Grande's court. Working in Verona during Can Grande's reign, Immanuel depicts the court in his poem "Bisbidis di Manoello Giudeo a magnificenza di Messer Cane de la Scala."[41] Using the metric structure of a lauda, Immanuel's poem describes "Egyptians, Romans, foreigners, Jews, Saracens, you will see."[42] He devotes a stanza to evoking the sounds of trumpets and later describes the music that could be heard in the court's celebration: "Guitars and lutes, viols and flutes, high and acute voices, you can hear singing."[43]

Boccaccio's writings, including his *Decameron* and *Genealogy of the Pagan Gods*, demonstrate that he was grappling with the issue of how to integrate musical performances within a prose context. In my previous work, I have argued that the *Decameron*'s ballatas were primarily secular insertions, or decorations, which reflected an Aristotelian view of music making as a pastime for educated citizens.[44] Indeed, for many scholars of the *Decameron*, these musical performances seem to be simply interesting corollary events, providing a needed reprieve from the storytelling. However, after tracing the origins of the ballatas back to songs of praise in the Hebrew Bible, I have come to a different and perhaps fuller picture of the reason for their presence. While the ballatas are certainly emblematic of the Platonic belief that music should be part of a well-rounded education and Aristotelian ideas regarding the uses of music during leisure time, they are also essentially songs of praise, which are foundational to narratives recounting a journey or an escape.

As Boccaccio was likely aware, words and music were closely intertwined in earlier biblical narratives—this was particularly the case in Hebrew chant traditions.[45] The Hebrew Bible is chanted according to the traditions of troping, making the separation between music and prose difficult to sustain. The text combines prose and poetic narratives: words repeat and alliteration is employed. The biblical King David was a musician and composer whose texts (with their musical implications) loom large in Jewish traditions; clearly, the singing of Psalms, many of which were attributed to David, was an essential part of life in Jewish practice.

Boccaccio demonstrates that he was familiar with poetical and musical traditions of the Hebrew Bible in his defense of poetry, book 14 of the *Genealogy of the Pagan Gods*.[46] When discussing the origins of poetry, he notes that some understand that poetry began with the holy rites of the "Ancients, that is among the Hebrews," and he lists the biblical tales for which poetry was written, including the stories of Cain and Abel and Noah's Ark. Boccaccio's philosophy of literary narrative, as presented in the *Genealogy*, places considerable importance on the Exodus story. In his account, the prayers and rites of Moses constitute the first flowering of poetry, tying its origins inextricably to Exodus and the establishment of these religious rites; he believes that Moses's "heroic verse" was a result of receiving God's word through poetry.[47] Boccaccio concludes, "It seems that poetry had its origin among the Hebrews not earlier than Moses, leader of the Israelites."[48] Although he discusses the hypothesis that poetry first arose with the Greeks, Boccaccio notes that "Moses was a master of poetry before either Babylonians or Greeks," and he concludes by writing, "I think the poets of the Gentiles in their poetry—not perhaps without understanding—followed in the steps of these prophets."[49] In light of Boccaccio's familiarity with Hebrew literary traditions, in which essentially prosaic texts are meant to be sung according to a traditional cantillation, his elevation of Moses to the position of first poet is extremely significant.[50] He does not accord Jesus the same honor, categorizing his words as "more history than fiction" and clearly differentiating the New Testament from the words of ancient poets such as Moses and Miriam.[51]

Boccaccio's defense of poetry in the *Genealogy* makes it clear that the Hebrew Bible is the realm of poetry, while the New Testament is the realm of prose. Perhaps as a nod to the importance of Hebrew poetical and devotional traditions, Boccaccio writes at the end of book 15, referencing Psalm 113:1, "It is my habit, at the conclusion of any honest labor, to utter with all devotion of which I am capable, that prayer of David's—Not unto us, O Lord, not unto us, but unto Thy name be the glory."[52] Boccaccio was clearly concerned with poetic musicality in storytelling; the differentiation between poetry and prose constitutes an important aesthetic underpinning the *Decameron*.

THE *DECAMERON* BALLATAS AS SONGS OF PRAISE

The religious resonances of the ballata, which were clearly known to Boccaccio, open the possibility that the ballatas in the *Decameron* are songs of praise, reflecting a complex web of Hebrew and Christian practices and writings through both their texts and their musical implications. Could they have their antecedents in the songs of the Hebrew Bible, in the book of Psalms or the Song of Songs? Do they relate to the role of music in Exodus and specifically to Miriam's dance song? This religious interpretation has previously been neglected, even though fundamental similarities to the genre of the lauda have been observed. Howard Mayer Brown, in his influential interdisciplinary article "Fantasia on a Theme by Boccaccio," alludes to the lauda repertory when discussing the genre of the inserted songs.[53] He notes that several of Boccaccio's stories include mentions of lauda societies. These include day 3, fourth story; day 7, first story; and that the group meets at the onset of the frame story at Santa Maria Novella, where Gianni Lotteringhi, the protagonist of day 7, first story, directs rehearsals. Brown suggests that perhaps the tunes that accompanied their ballata texts were closer in nature to syllabic lauda melodies, rather than melismatic melodies like those found in monophonic ballatas of the fourteenth century from the Rossi Codex. He does not consider the possible religious interpretations of Boccaccio's ballata texts, but I propose that the *Decameron* ballata texts themselves, in addition to their implied tunes, share qualities with laude; as such, they constitute songs of praise.

The lauda is an Italian musical form, a poem of praise that developed in the thirteenth century, specifically in Umbria, and was originally monophonic. The lauda-ballata is a hybrid genre of which we have only one polyphonic notated example, "Nel mio parlar" by Jacopo da Bologna, who was active in the eclectic court of the Scaligeri in Verona.[54] Its structure is similar to the Italian ballata, containing a ripresa (refrain), two piedi (rhythmic feet), and a volta (turn) and ending with a ripresa. In these genres, the importance of praising and the fact that the songs are primarily danced to suggest a connection to an earlier tradition. Arnaldo Bonaventura alludes to the ancient nature of the dance song tradition in his *Il Boccaccio e la musica*, pointing out that the dance song was used by the ancient Hebrews and by other eastern cultures; then by the Greeks; and in the Middle Ages, especially in the times of Lorenzo de' Medici.[55]

Before eating, dancing, and singing in the conclusion to day 1, Boccaccio provides a striking description of the brigata bathing in a stream—a point in his narrative that has evident biblical implications. The parting of the Red Sea is often understood in parallel Christian philosophy as a baptism, a washing away of sins, since the purifying power of water is central to Christian belief.[56] Before the first supper, the brigata travels to a stream of "crystal-clear water" and bathes before they return home to eat. The following paragraph begins with the queen (Pampinea) calling for "istrumenti" and demanding that a dance begin, led by Lauretta while Emilia sings and Dioneo accompanies on lute. Of note is that she asks for instruments, yet Boccaccio describes only the lute—perhaps the women accompany themselves with a drum or timbrel. As in the passage in Exodus, the dance is mentioned first: "No sooner did she hear the queen's command than Lauretta promptly began to dance, and she was joined by the others, whilst Emilia sang the following song in amorous tones: 'In mine own beauty take I such delight.'"[57]

Like in Exodus, Boccaccio introduces the poetry into his narrative. He exploits the visual characteristics of poetry on the page, separating the words into stanzas rather than allowing them to run into the end of the column. In early sources of the *Decameron*, each stanza is marked by a larger opening initial—for instance, in Cod. Hamilton 90, the second ballata (c. 32r).[58] The first poem is divided into four stanzas, the first of which is the refrain, or A. The second stanza begins with "Io veggio" and consists of two piedi (b, b) and a volta (a). One can imagine that women sang the opening refrain "Io son" after the volta and then continued to the next stanza, "Non fugge questo ben qualor disio" (b, b) and volta and so on. The poetical musical structure of the poem resembles an anonymous ballata from the Rossi

Table 2.1. Inset songs in Boccaccio's *Decameron*.

Group	Number of stanzas	Number of lines per stanza (not counting the *ripresa*)	Singer/dancer/musician
Group A:			
Ballata 1	3	7	Emilia/Lauretta/Dioneo
Ballata 2	3	8	Pampinea/Emilia/-
Ballata 3	5	9	Lauretta/Lauretta/-
Ballata 4	7	9	Filostrato/Filomena/-
Ballata 6	4	7	Elissa/Panfilo/-
Ballata 10	4	9	Fiammetta/Lauretta/-
Group B:			
Ballata 5	3	9	Dioneo/-/-
Ballata 7	4	9 (Dicesse)	Filomena/-/-
Ballata 8	3	9	Panfilo/-/-
Ballata 9	4	7	Neifile/-/-

Codex called "Lucente stella, che'l mio cor desfai," a song popular during Boccaccio's lifetime.[59]

I argue that there are in fact two types of ballatas performed by the brigata in the *Decameron*: those intended to be danced to (group A: 1, 2, 3, 4, 6, and 10) and those intended to be listened to (group B: 5, 7, 8, and 9). Table 2.1 displays the lengths of the songs and the names of the performers.

Several interesting observations may be made based on table 2.1. While all members of the brigata sing a ballata, not all dance a ballata: the ballata dancers are only Lauretta, Emilia, Filomena, and Panfilo. Absent from this list is the fun-loving Dioneo, who prefers to play an instrument. Also, Panfilo is the only male to be asked to dance a ballata—the women are much more prominent in the dancing. Lauretta seems to be the favored dancer, as she is asked to dance by the ruler of the day three times (days 1, 3, and 10) and is the only member of the brigade who sings and dances at the same time (day 4).

Like Miriam's song of praise, of which only the refrain is quoted in Exodus, several of Boccaccio's *Decameron* dance songs have refrains that the members of the brigata join in a responsorial manner. After the poetical text of day 1, Boccaccio adds, "This little ballata finished, they all joined cheerfully in the choruses," which we can only surmise to mean they sang the refrain.⁶⁰ As noted previously, this practice of a leader singing and a chorus responding was popular in Hebrew song, both sacred and secular.⁶¹ The manner of singing monophonically followed by a choir is also described in Dante's *Divina Commedia*, when a soul sings alone the words "Te lucis ante" (Purgatory, canto 8), answered by the others for the entire hymn, and Gabriel intones alone, "Ave gratia plena" (Paradise, canto 32), followed by the divine response of other angels.⁶²

Upon further examination, we see that the ballata text in day 1 itself has religious undertones. While on the surface the poem is merely about a woman looking at herself in the mirror and admiring what she sees, it can also be read as the woman looking into a mirror that reflects God. In this beauty, Emilia finds no parallel. The more she looks, the fiercer her love becomes. The idea that man was created in the image of God is found in Genesis 1:27; an allusion to the mirror appears in Exodus when the women supply mirrors for Bezalel to make a bronze pedestal and basin for the dwelling (tabernacle) (Exodus 38:8). This basin is used to cleanse oneself before entering, connecting this point back to the image of purifying water that prefaces the dancing in the *Decameron*.⁶³

The song introduced in the conclusion of day 2 also contains descriptions of dancing and a chorus, traditions that began, as Bonaventura writes, with "the ancient Hebrews."⁶⁴ We read that "at the queen's request Emilia began to dance whilst Pampinea sang the following song, the others joining in the chorus."⁶⁵ Here, Boccaccio calls the piece not a "ballata" but rather a "song," though it has the same refrain structure as the lauda-ballata and is clearly danced to. The refrain reads:

> If 'twere not I, what woman would sing
> Who am content in everything?

> Qual donna canterà, s'io non canto io,
> che son contenta d'ogni mio disio?⁶⁶

In the tradition of the Song of Songs, this poem is clearly about love. While it seems secular at the outset in its praise of "Amor," which may be translated as "Cupid," it turns decidedly sacred as Pampinea prays to God that this love will also be there for her in the next world:

> Within this world I have my bliss
> And I may in the next, entire,
> I love so faithfully,

If God who sees us from above
Will grant this boon upon our love.

Per che in questo mondo il mio volere
posseggo, e spero nell'altro aver pace
per quella intera fede
che io gli porto. Idio, che questo vede,
del regno suo ancor ne sarà pio.[67]

This song is followed by many others, as well as by dances with instrumental accompaniments, "piú altre se ne cantarono e piú danze si fecero e sonarono diversi suoni," as also occurred in day 1. While Boccaccio does not identify the players, one can imagine Dioneo on the lute and Fiammetta on the vielle, perhaps with another person on a timbrel or bagpipe. The story resumes again on Sunday, where at dawn the brigata walks through the most beautiful, lush countryside filled with birdsongs and reaches a garden, which the group declares to be like paradise on earth. There, both before and after breakfast, "they sang half-a-dozen canzonets and danced several dances." The third ballata, like the second, moves from the secular to a loftier place: Lauretta mourns the mistakes she has made and her unrequited loves before turning her gaze toward a higher love in the final stanza:

Oh, sweetest love, with whom
I once was so content!
From where you stand, with Him
To whom our souls are sent,
Ah, spare some pity for me
For I cannot remove
Your memory which burns me
With all the pain of love!
Ah, pray that I may soon return
To those sweet climes for which I yearn!

O caro amante, del qual prima fui
piú che altra contenta,
che or nel ciel se' davanti a Colui
che ne creò, deh! pietoso diventa
di me, che per altrui
te obliar non posso: fa ch'io senta
che quella fiamma spenta
non sia che per me t'arse,
e costà sú m'impetra la tornata.[68]

She speaks about a love who is now in heaven, "a Colui," to whom she prays to return soon. Lauretta's poem may have two meanings. First, it concerns a widow, which may relate to the widow in Lauretta's earlier story (day 3, eighth story). A second interpretation, albeit one with a Christian inflection, suggests Lauretta's longing to be united with God. Boccaccio notes that the brigata also comes to both lowly and lofty conclusions about the meaning of the song, though he is specific only about the more earthly interpretations: "Here Lauretta ended her song, to which all had listened raptly and construed in different ways. There were those who took it, in the Milanese fashion, to imply that a good fat pig was better than a comely wench. But others gave it a loftier, more subtle, and truer meaning, which this is not the moment to expound."[69]

Again, Boccaccio appears to infuse his ballatas with religious metaphors, while at the same time deflecting the praising nature of the lauda-ballata tradition. At one point, Boccaccio directly addresses readers about the Muses and his fear of criticism for not creating a work with significantly meaningful themes and symbolism. Perhaps this is a clever sleight of hand, in which he downplays the messages underlying his book. Or one could argue that trecento readers would have recognized the Old Testament allusions of the *Decameron* as part of a lush tapestry of different influences, as we have seen in the works of Immanuel Romano.

The text of ballata 6, as well as that of subsequent ballatas, includes more words relating to praying. This praying, or supplication, appears to become more intense in the ballatas of days 6, 7, and 8. Dancing also takes place on these days, but Boccaccio does not give precise indications about whether the songs themselves were accompanied by dance. He also omits any indication as to whether the rest of the brigata joined in the refrains for these songs. As in the previous poems, however, the most direct prayers to God are found in the last stanza. Elissa sings in her last stanza of day 6:

> I pray thee, Lord, at least to grant me this,
> For if thou dost, my faith is that at last
> I may regain that beauty
> That once I had by right
> And, sorrow banished, deck me
> With flowers of red and white.
>
> Deh! io ti priego, signor, che tu vogli;
> ché, se tu 'l fai, ancor porto fidanza

di tornar bella qual fu mia usanza,
e, il dolor rimosso,
di bianchi fiori ornarmi e di vermigli.[70]

In this case, dancing takes place before and after Elissa's song. Panfilo asks Tindaro to get his *cornamusa*, "the strains of which he caused several reels to be danced."[71]

A similar supplication occurs in Filomena's song in day 7. Similar to in day 6, before she starts to sing, Boccaccio notes that the brigata danced to Tindaro's bagpipes. He also adds that they were accompanied by other instruments: "They were dancing *caroles* beside the beautiful fountain, accompanied sometimes by Tindaro on the cornemuse and sometimes by the music of other instruments."[72] Just as with the previous song, there is no mention of dancing:

> Tell me what I should do, my dearest Lord;
> I dare ask none, nor know to whom to go
> To beg for hope and help except thyself,
> My soul is wounded so.
>
> Deh dilmi tu, ché 'l domandarne altrui
> non oso, né so cui.
> Deh, signor mio, deh fammelo sperare,
> sí ch'io conforti l'anima smarrita.[73]

Panfilo sings about a passionate love in day 8 and in so doing asks for salvation. Of all the ballatas in the *Decameron*, his is the fieriest and most exultative. Panfilo speaks directly about the act of singing, as Filostrato did on day 4. In Panfilo's song, there are echoes of singing praise aloud to God found in the Psalms—for instance, in Psalm 59:17. Panfilo exclaims, "I cannot sing aloud in song / Or sketch forth with my hand / The joy, Love, that I know." Panfilo convinces himself not to reveal the joy that he feels:

> Who is there who aright could guess
> My arms would find that place
> That they were clasped around?
> None would believe my happiness
> That I might bend my face
> Wither I did, and found
> Salvation sweet and grace.
> Hence I with burning joy conceal
> A rapture I may not reveal.

> Chi potrebbe estimar che le mie braccia
> aggiugnesser già mai
> là dov'io l'ho tenute,
> e chi'io dovessi giunger la mia faccia
> là dov'io l'accostai
> per grazia e per salute?
> Non mi sarien credute.[74]

Boccaccio describes dancing before Panfilo's song, "Love, I take such delight in thee," but does not indicate that this song was accompanied by a dance. He does, however, indicate that the brigata joined Panfilo in singing: "Thus did Panfilo's song come to an end... everyone had joined wholeheartedly in the refrain."[75]

Like the poem of day 8, the interpolated poem of day 9 is a song about singing. Still in the ballata form AbbaA (in which *A* represents the refrain), it begins, "I am so young I love to sing / And take delight in the early spring / Thanks to the sweet thoughts Love doth bring."[76] Neifile finds her love in the fields and flowers, and she picks a bloom, which recalls her love.[77] This also reads like a song of praise to God:

> That pleasure given by a flower
> To mortal eyes through Nature's power
> Is so bestowed on me that there
> I fancy my sweet love to be.
>
> E quel piacer che di natura il fiore
> agli occhi porge, quel simil mel dona
> che s'io vedessi la propria persona
> che m'ha accesa del suo dolce amore.[78]

Boccaccio does not indicate that the brigata danced to this song or sang its refrains.

The *Decameron*'s final song, sung by Fiammetta and danced to by Lauretta, is about jealousy. Fiammetta invokes God's name when asking women not to injure her by making her jealous. Again, the direct mention of God appears only in the last stanza, in a kind of final plea for help:

> But, in God's name, let every woman know
> Not to attempt such injury on me.
>
> Per Dio, dunque, ciascuna
> donna pregata sia che non s'attenti
> di farmi in ciò oltraggio.[79]

Once again, Boccaccio does not describe dancing or mention that the brigata sings the refrain. In fact, Boccaccio writes that Dioneo laughs at Fiammetta, asking her for the name of the person who makes her jealous. Upon completion of the ballata, Boccaccio simply states that the brigata sings a few other songs before he describes their return to Florence at the crack of dawn. In some ways, this last poem is the most earthly and the least evocative of praise. It symbolizes a return to the grim reality of life in Florence. While the brigata returns to an uncertain future in Florence, the Hebrews wander, uncertain of their home. The Hebrews walk through distant lands, tried and tested by God, led by Moses, the poet, his story told in heroic verse.

Scholarly appreciation of the *Decameron* has been principally focused through a secular lens, especially with regard to music, with the ballatas inserted into the narrative as decorative elements the way angels with instruments might decorate a ceiling. This chapter shines light on the sacred undertones of the narrative, especially with respect to its pervasive musical soundtrack in the form of interpolated poetry and descriptions of musical events. The presence of dance songs with refrains (performed predominantly by women) intertwined with the narrative of escape and journey conjures up Exodus and the image of Miriam and her timbrel. Through the course of the brigata's journey, Boccaccio includes representations of musical events that evoke biblical music making in the form of Miriam's song in Exodus. Through the interpolation of the musical women (Miriam's timbrel) and also in the juxtaposition of prose with poetry, I suggest that reading these added texts invokes a musical performance. A new reading of the *Decameron* as an Exodus story suggests that this foundational work should be read as a tapestry of different influences: Hebrew and Christian, sacred and secular.

NOTES

* formerly Eleonora M. Beck.

1. The ten young people in the *Decameron* retreated to the country for a period of isolation in order to avoid the plague. Much has been written on this frame story. See Joy Potter, *Five Frames for the Decameron: Communication and Social Systems in the Cornice* (Princeton, NJ: Princeton University Press, 1982), and Michelangelo Picone, "Il *Decamerone* come macrotesto: il problema della cornice," in *Introduzione al Decameron*, ed. Michelangelo Picone and Margherita Mesirca (Florence: Cesati, 2004), 9–34. Teodolinda Barolini interprets the presentation of stories in the *Decameron* as circular: see Teodolinda Barolini, "The Wheel of the 'Decameron,'" *Romance Philology* 36, no. 4 (1983): 521–539.

2. Giovanni Boccaccio, *The Decameron*, trans. and ed. Wayne A. Rebhorn (New York: W. W. Norton, 2015), xxxiii.

3. Giovanni Boccaccio, *Decameron*, ed. Vittore Branca (Turin: Einaudi, 1987), 3.

4. Don Harrán, *In Search of Harmony: Hebrew and Humanist Elements in Sixteenth-Century Musical Thought* (Amsterdam: American Institute of Musicology, 1988), 1, quotes Boccaccio's *Genealogy of the Pagan Gods*: "So it seems that poetry had its origin among the Hebrews not earlier than Moses." For the English translation, see Giovanni Boccaccio, *Boccaccio on Poetry: Being the Preface and the Fourteenth and Fifteenth Books of Boccaccio's* Genealogia deorum gentilium *in an English Version with Introductory Essay and Commentary*, trans. Charles G. Osgood (New York: Liberal Arts, 1956), 42.

5. I quote from the 1635 reprint of the 1609 Douay-Rheims Bible, which was translated from the Latin Vulgate Bible. Although elements of the Douay-Rheims translation are less accurate than direct translations from the original languages, the Douay-Rheims translation most closely represents the Vulgate Bible that Boccaccio would have known. The first-person plural, "Let us sing" (*Cantemus*), was introduced in the Vulgate, although this does differ from the first-person singular of the Hebrew. It is worth noting that Boccaccio would have known Miriam through the Latin *Maria*. See *The Holy Bible Faithfully Translated into English out of the Authentical Latin, Diligently Conferred with the Hebrew, Greek, & Other Editions in Diverse Languages*, trans. the English College of Doway (Rheims: John Cousturier, 1635).

6. John Arthur Smith, "Musical Aspects of Old Testament Canticles in Their Biblical Setting," *Early Music History* 17 (1998): 232–233.

7. Smith, 226.

8. Susan E. Gillingham, *The Poems and the Psalms of the Hebrew Bible* (Oxford: Oxford University Press, 1994), 145. Gillingham emphasizes the relationship between the biblical poetry and music throughout her study. She writes, "Biblical verse was heard as much as it was read" (44).

9. Alfred Sendrey, *Music in Ancient Israel* (London: Vision, 1969), 445. He writes, "Should we add to this the numerous terms found in the rabbinic literature pertaining to this occupation, it could be properly stated that no other ancient language possesses this wealth of expressions describing the various aspects of dancing" (445–446).

10. Sendrey, 451.

11. Sendrey, 451.

12. Eleonora M. [Aaron] Beck, *Singing in the Garden: Music and Culture in the Tuscan Trecento* (Florence: Libreria Musicale Italiana, 1998), 112. In this study, I note that the dancing figures in Ambrogio Lorenzetti's fresco suggest Miriam and her dancers in Exodus (112).

13. An early illumination of Miriam dancing that appears in an eleventh-century Byzantine Psalter (Biblioteca Apostolica Vaticana, MS Vat.gr.725, fol. 449v, digitized at DigiVatLib, accessed June 3, 2019, https://digi.vatlib.it/view/MSS_Vat.gr.725) is described by Tilman Seebass in "Iconography and Dance Research," *Yearbook for Traditional Music* 23 (1991): 33–51. András Borgó examines early iconography of Miriam's song in bibles and psalters in his "Miriam's Musical Instruments in Medieval Hebrew Representations," *Music in Art* 1–2 (2006): 175–193.

14. Katrin Kogman-Appel, "Portrayals of Women with Books: Female (Il)literacy in Medieval Jewish Culture," in *Reassessing the Roles of Women as "Makers" of Medieval Art and Architecture*, ed. Therese Martin, 2 vols. (Leiden: Brill, 2012), 2:525. I draw extensively on this source for information about the history of the Haggadah.

15. Bezalel Narkiss, *The Golden Haggadah* (Rohnert Park, CA: Pomegranate Artbooks, 1997), 55.

16. *The Rylands Haggadah: A Medieval Sephardi Masterpiece in Facsimile*, with introduction, notes on illuminations, transcription, and English translation by Raphael Loewe (London: Thames and Hudson, 1988), 11–12.

17. *The Rylands Haggadah*, 12.

18. Marc Epstein, *The Medieval Haggadah: Art, Narrative, and Religious Imagination* (New Haven, CT: Yale University Press, 2011), 77.

19. Epstein, 3.

20. Cohen argues that this instrument was played almost exclusively by women throughout its history; see Judith Cohen, "'This Drum I Play': Women and Square Frame Drums in Portugal and Spain," *Ethnomusicology Forum* 17, no. 1 (2008): 96. This is also called a "square frame drum" in Mauricio Molina, "Frame Drums in the Medieval Iberian Peninsula" (PhD diss., New York University, 2006), 73.

21. See Saint Ambrose, *Hexameron, Paradise, and Cain and Abel*, trans. John J. Savage (Washington, DC: Catholic University of America Press, 1961). The Latin edition referred to here is Ambrose, *Sancti Ambrosii Opera*, vol. 32, ed. Karl Schenkl (Vienna: F. Tempsky, 1897).

22. In contrast, representations of and metaphors related to music are few in Basil's and Augustine's exegeses of Genesis.

23. Ambrose, *Hexameron*, 50. "Motu ferri arbitrantur eoque inpulsu et motu ipsorum orbium dulcem quendam et plenum suavitatis atque artis et gratissimi modulaminis sonum reddi, quoniam scissus aer tam artifici motu et acuta cum gravibus temperante ita varios aequabiliter concentus efficiat, ut omnem supergrediatur musici carminis suavitatem," Ambrose, *Sancti Ambrosii Opera*, 45. In Latin transcriptions, where *u* functions as *v*, I have made this change silently.

24. Ambrose, *Hexameron*, 68. "Novit ergo aqua et congregari et timere et fugere, quando deus praecepit. hanc imitemur aquam et unam congregationem domini, unam ecclesiam noverimus," Ambrose, *Sancti Ambrosii Opera*, 60.

25. Ambrose, *Hexameron*, 69. "Quos non mortiferi cantus acroamatum scaenicorum, quae mentem emolliant ad amores, sed concentus ecclesiae, sed consona circa dei laudes populi vox et pia vita delectet," Ambrose, *Sancti Ambrosii Opera*, 61.

26. Ambrose, *Hexameron*, 70. "Populum hunc divinae operationis organum, in quo divini modulamen resultet oraculi et dei spiritus intus operetur," Ambrose, *Sancti Ambrosii Opera*, 61.

27. Ambrose, *Hexameron*, 83. "Sed velut pacificis ambit et salutat amplexibus," Ambrose, *Sancti Ambrosii Opera*, 73.

28. In his *De Republica*, Cicero makes a clear connection between peace and music in a just society. See Eleonora M. [Aaron] Beck, *Giotto's Harmony: Music and Art in Padua at the Crossroads of the Renaissance* (Florence: European Press Academic Publishing, 2005), 112.

29. Ambrose, *Hexameron*, 84. "Tum fidelibus viris atque devotis incentiuum devotionis, ut cum undarum leniter adluentium sono certent cantus psallentium, plaudant insulae tranquillo fluctuum sanctorum choro, hymnis sanctorum personent," Ambrose, *Sancti Ambrosii Opera*, 74–75.

30. Ambrose, *Hexameron*, 84. "Quid aliud ille concentus undarum nisi quidam concentus est plebis? unde bene mari plerumque comparatur ecclesia, quae primo ingredientis populi agmine totis vestibulis undas vomit, deinde in oratione totius plebis tamquam undis refluentibus stridit, cum responsoriis psalmorum cantus virorum mulierum virginum paruulorum consonus undarum fragor resultat," Ambrose, *Sancti Ambrosii Opera*, 75.

31. Ambrose, *Hexameron*, 192. "Quae cum eunt cubitum, quasi peracto laetae munere aethera cantu mulcere consuerunt," Ambrose, *Sancti Ambrosii Opera*, 170.

32. Ambrose, *Hexameron*, 192. "Quod velut sollemniter surgente et occidente die instaurare consuerunt, ut decursi vel adoriendi nocturni iuxta diurnique temporis laudes suo referant creatori," Ambrose, *Sancti Ambrosii Opera*, 170.

33. Ambrose, *Hexameron*, 192. "Magnum igitur incentiuum excitandae nobis devotionis amiseram," Ambrose, *Sancti Ambrosii Opera*, 170.

34. Ambrose, *Hexameron*, 200. "Ut hominem putes locutum, cum locuta sit avis," Ambrose, *Sancti Ambrosii Opera*, 177.

35. Ambrose, *Hexameron*, 192. "Qui enim sensum hominis gerens non erubescat sine psalmorum celebritate diem claudere, cum etiam minutissimae aues sollemni devotione et dulci carmine ortus dierum ac noctium prosequantur?" Ambrose, *Sancti Ambrosii Opera*, 170.

36. Ambrose, *Hexameron*, 193. "Canoris avibus resonet ac resultet," Ambrose, *Sancti Ambrosii Opera*, 171.

37. The following information about Jews in Italy is from Cecil Roth's seminal *The History of the Jews of Italy* (Philadelphia: Jewish Publication Society of America, 1946; repr. Farnborough: Gregg International, 1969). More recent studies of Jews in Renaissance Italy include David B. Ruderman and Giuseppe Veltri, eds., *Cultural Intermediaries: Jewish Intellectuals in Early Modern Italy* (Philadelphia: University of Pennsylvania Press, 2004); Robert Bonfil, *Jewish Life in Renaissance Italy*, trans. Anthony Oldcorn (Berkeley: University of California Press, 1994); and the essays in David B. Ruderman, ed., *Essential Papers on Jewish Culture in Renaissance and Baroque Italy* (New York: New York University Press, 1992).

38. Roth, *The History of the Jews*, 148.

39. Musical practice in the Angevin court in Naples has been recently reconstructed by Carla Vivarelli in "'Di una pretesa scuola napoletana': Sowing the Seeds of the *Ars nova* at the Court of Robert of Anjou," *Journal of Musicology* 24, no. 2 (2007): 272–296.

40. Cornelia C. Coulter, "The Library of the Angevin Kings of Naples," *Transactions and Proceedings of the American Philological Association* 75 (1944): 155.

41. Transcribed in Leonello Modona, "Una poesia inedita di Manuello, giudeo," in *Il vessillo israelitico: rivista mensile per la storia, la scienza e lo spirito del giudaismo*, ed. Flaminio Servi (Casale: Pane, 1885), 380–386. Nino Pirrotta includes lines from the poem in his discussion of music at the court of Can Grande della Scala in "Rhapsodic Elements of North-Italian Polyphony of the 14th Century," *Musica Disciplina* 37 (1983): 83–99.

42. "Quivi babuini / Romei et peregrini / Giudei et saracini / Vedrai capitare," transcribed in Modona, "Una poesia inedita," 385.

43. "Cithare Liuti / Viole et fiauti / Voce alti et acuti / Qui s'odon cantare," transcribed in Modona, 385.

44. Beck, *Singing in the Garden*, 35–50.

45. For more on Hebrew musical traditions, see Mark Kligman, "Jewish Liturgical Music," in *The Cambridge Companion to Jewish Music*, ed. Joshua S. Walden (Cambridge: Cambridge University Press, 2015), 84–103; Philip V. Bohlman, *Jewish Music and Modernity* (Oxford: Oxford University Press, 2008); and Sendrey, *Music in Ancient Israel*.

46. Book 14 of the *Genealogy of the Pagan Gods* is translated in Boccaccio, *Boccaccio on Poetry*, 14–101. For a Latin edition of book 14, see Giovanni Boccaccio, *In Defence of Poetry: Genealogiae deorum gentilium liber XIV*, ed. Jeremiah Reedy (Toronto: Pontifical Institute of Mediaeval Studies, 1978). For a discussion of Boccaccio's allusion to Moses, see Steven M. Grossvogel, "A Fable of the World's Creation and Phaeton (*Allegorica mitologica*)," in *Boccaccio: A Critical Guide to the Complete Works*, ed. Victoria Kirkham, Michael Sherberg, and Janet Smarr (Chicago: University of Chicago Press, 2013), 63–68.

47. Boccaccio, *Boccaccio on Poetry*, 46. "Heroico scriptsisse," Boccaccio, *In Defence of Poetry*, 40.

48. Boccaccio, *Boccaccio on Poetry*, 42. "Quibus inspectis videbitur non ante Moysis, ducis Israelitarum, tempus poesim apud Hebreos habuisse principium," Boccaccio, *In Defence of Poetry*, 36.

49. Boccaccio, *Boccaccio on Poetry*, 46. "Si vero Paulo fidem prestare velimus, sequetur Moysem primo quam Babilonios aut Grecos eiusdem fuisse magistrum . . . Quorum ego, nec forsan insipide, reor poetas gentiles in componendis poematibus sequutos vestigia," Boccaccio, *In Defence of Poetry*, 39–40.

50. Philo Alexandrinus recounts that Moses was well versed in music: "Arithmetic, geometry, the lore of metre, rhythm and harmony, and the whole subject of music as shown by the use of instruments or in textbooks and treatises of a more special character, were imparted to him by learned Egyptians." See Philo, *Philo*, vol. 6, *On Abraham. On Joseph. On Moses*, trans. Francis H. Colson (Cambridge, MA: Harvard University Press, 1966), 287.

51. Boccaccio, *Boccaccio on Poetry*, 48. "Hystorie quam fabule similis est," Boccaccio, *In Defence of Poetry*, 42.

52. Boccaccio, *Boccaccio on Poetry*, 142. "Cum ipse more meo semper post exactos quoscunque labores honestos consueverim, qua possum mentis devotione Daviticum illud dicere: Non nobis Domine, non nobis, sed nomini tuo da gloriam," from book 15 of the *Genealogy of the Pagan Gods*, accessed July 18, 2021, http://www.bibliotecaitaliana.it/testo/bibit000673.

53. Howard Mayer Brown, "Fantasia on a Theme by Boccaccio," *Early Music* 5 (1977): 324–339.

54. For more on the lauda-ballata, see Ross Duffin, *A Performer's Guide to Medieval Music* (Bloomington: Indiana University Press, 2000), 164–165.

55. Arnaldo Bonaventura, *Il Boccaccio e la musica: Studio e trascrizioni musicali* (Turin: Fratelli Bocca, 1914), 4.

56. See Corinthians 1:10, "For I would not have you ignorant, brethren, that our fathers were all under the cloud, and all passed through the sea. And all in Moses were baptized, in the cloud, and in the sea."

57. Giovanni Boccaccio, *The Decameron*, trans. George Henry McWilliam, 2nd ed. (London: Penguin Books, 1995), 68.

58. Giovanni Boccaccio, *Un autografo del Decameron (Codice Hamiltoniano 90)*, ed. Vittore Branca and Pier Giorgio Ricci (Padua: Casa editrice Dott. Antonio Milani, 1962), Tav. 11.

59. Nino Pirrotta, ed., *The Music of Fourteenth-Century Italy* (Amsterdam: American Institute of Musicology, 1960), 2:x.

60. "Questa ballatetta finita, alla qual tutti lietamente avean risposto," Boccaccio, *Decameron* (1987), 127; translation by the author.

61. For more on Jewish practices of singing, see Kligman, "Jewish Liturgical Music," 87.

62. Bonaventura, *Il Boccaccio e la musica*, 4–5.

63. Mirrors are often found in images of music making—for instance, in Lorenzetti's altarpiece in Palazzo Municipale in Massa Marittima. See Eleonora M. [Aaron] Beck, "Mirrors and Music in the *Decameron*," *Heliotropia* 7, nos. 1–2 (2010): 84–85.

64. Bonaventura, *Il Boccaccio e la musica*, 4.

65. Once again, Branca captures the idea of the choir singing in response to a leader in his note to this song, writing, "Cioè facendo coro per i due versi della ripresa," Boccaccio, *Decameron* (1987), 317.

66. Boccaccio, *The Decameron* (1995), 187. For the Italian, see Boccaccio, *Decameron* (1987), 318.

67. Boccaccio, *The Decameron* (1995), 188. For the Italian, see Boccaccio, *Decameron* (1987), 318.

68. Boccaccio, *The Decameron* (1995), 283. For the Italian, see Boccaccio, *Decameron* (1987), 455.

69. Boccaccio, *The Decameron* (1995), 283. "Qui fece fine la Lauretta alla sua canzone, la quale notata da tutti, diversamente da diversi fu intesa: e ebbevi di quegli che intender vollono alla melanese, che fosse meglio un buon porco che una bella tosa; altri furono di piú sublime e migliore e piú vero intelletto," Boccaccio, *Decameron* (1987), 456.

70. Boccaccio, *The Decameron* (1995), 483. For the Italian, see Boccaccio, *Decameron* (1987), 783.

71. Boccaccio, *The Decameron* (1995), 483. "Al suono della quale esso fece fare molte danze," Boccaccio, *Decameron* (1987), 784.

72. Boccaccio, *The Decameron* (1995), 549. "Intorno della bella fontana di presente furono in sul danzare, quando al suono della cornamusa di Tindaro e quando d'altri suon carolando," Boccaccio, *Decameron* (1987), 884.

73. Boccaccio, *The Decameron* (1995), 549. For the Italian, see Boccaccio, *Decameron* (1987), 885.

74. Boccaccio, *The Decameron* (1995), 646. For the Italian, see Boccaccio, *Decameron* (1987), 1027.

75. Boccaccio, *The Decameron* (1995), 646. "La canzone di Panfilo aveva fine, alla quale quantunque per tutti fosse compiutamente risposto," Boccaccio, *Decameron* (1987), 1028.

76. Boccaccio, *The Decameron* (1995), 700. "Io mi son giovinetta, e volentieri / m'allegro e canto en la stagion novella, / merzé, d'amore e de' dolci pensieri," Boccaccio, *Decameron* (1987), 1107.

77. This pastoral scene recalls the bucolic landscape of Psalm 23:2: "He hath set me in a place of pasture. He hath brought me up, on the water of refreshment."

78. Boccaccio, *The Decameron* (1995), 700. For the Italian, see Boccaccio, *Decameron* (1987), 1108.

79. Boccaccio, *The Decameron* (1995), 797. For the Italian, see Boccaccio, *Decameron* (1987), 1252.

AARON BECK is Professor of Music at Lewis & Clark College. He has published widely on the subject of Italian music and culture, including his books *Boccaccio and the Invention of Musical Narrative* and *Giotto's Harmony*.

3

Traces of Jewish Music and Culture at the Urbino Court of Federico da Montefeltro

J. DREW STEPHEN

Under the outstanding cultural leadership and astute political guidance of Federico da Montefeltro, count of Urbino from 1444 and duke from 1474 until his death in 1482, Urbino came to define what a prince could achieve within the intellectual humanist climate of the Renaissance. Although Federico earned his wealth through his military activities as one of the foremost condottieri (or mercenary captains) of his day, he spent it establishing his fame as an eminent patron of intellectuals and the arts. Historian Cecil Clough readily observes that during Urbino's golden age from 1468 to 1482, Federico "probably had more wealth to spend in patronage than any other prince in Italy, and perhaps even in western Christendom."[1] The fruits of this patronage are apparent in Baldassare Castiglione's *Il Cortegiano* (*The Book of the Courtier*), which celebrates the elegance and refinement of the Urbino court.[2] Castiglione defines Federico as the "lume della Italia" (the light of Italy) and praises him "della sua prudenza, della humanità, della giustitia, della liberalità, dell'animo inuitto e della disciplina militare" (for his prudence, humanity, justice, liberality, invincible spirit, and military discipline). Castiglione notes that Federico built in Urbino a place that is "secondo la opinione di molti, il più bello, che in tutta Italia si ritrovi, e d'ogni opportuna cosa sì ben lo fornì, che non un palazzo, ma una città in forma de palazzo esser pare" (according to the opinion of many, the most beautiful to be found in all Italy, and he took every opportunity to furnish it suitably so that it appeared not a palace but a city in the form of a palace). Castiglione makes particular note that Federico assembled "con grandissima spessa adunò un gran numero di eccellentissimi e rarissimi libri greci, latini, e hebraici, quali tutti ornò d'oro, e d'argento, estimando che questa fusse la suprema eccellenza del suo magno palazzo" (at grand expense a great number of exceptional and rare books in Greek, Latin, and Hebrew, all of which he decorated with gold and with silver, and considered to be the supreme excellence of his great palace).[3] Through his balance of military security, civic virtue, and artistic patronage, Federico achieved his vision of an ideal city that celebrated the values of early modern humanism.

Less apparent in the traditional accounts of Urbino is the presence of a stable Jewish community that both benefited from and contributed to Federico's policies and humanist environment. With numbers that, at one point, represented a third of the city's population, the Jewish community was well established in the financial sector and closely integrated into the larger community.[4] In this early period, prior to the establishment of ghettos in Italy, members of the Jewish community lived in all areas of the city; they served as advisers at court, where they were welcomed on the same footing as other courtiers, and engaged in religious and economic activities that were protected, or at least tolerated, by the duke.[5] Although the surviving records in Urbino do not convey information on Jewish musical activities, either at home or in religious services, the conditions were favorable for their production and were likely practiced in ways similar to those of other equivalent communities.

Given the lack of documentation, I will not attempt to reconstruct the musical practices of the Urbino community or justify the contributions of Jewish individuals in the context of the Christian values practiced at court. Instead, I examine the traces of Jewish music and culture that are reflected in Federico's court to demonstrate how open attitudes allowed for an intermingling of traditions and Jewish participation in the constructions of culture. Although this reveals less about the day-to-day activities of Jews in Urbino and more about Christian attitudes toward them, it allows for an examination of the Jewish presence in Federico's court, the symbolic value it represented for him, and the importance of a Jewish cultural presence within a courtly environment that was renowned as one of the most magnificent and elegant in all of Italy.

THE JEWISH COMMUNITY IN THE MONTEFELTRO ERA

Urbino's Jewish community was remarkable from the beginning for its coherence and for the freedoms and privileges it enjoyed. A stable Jewish presence was probably established near the end of the fourteenth century, around the same time as communities in Gubbio (1368), Fossombrone (1371), and Casteldurante (1387).[6] The earliest evidence of the Urbino Jewish community consists of documents from November 1, 1407, and April 1, 1409, that identify Isaia di maestro Daniele, "olim de Viterbo et nunc de Urbino" (once of Viterbo and now of Urbino), who had been living in Urbino since as early as 1389.[7] Around this time, Isaia di maestro Daniele was granted special privileges from Count Antonio II da Montefeltro to conduct activities as a merchant and moneylender. These privileges were passed on to Isaia di maestro Daniele's heirs, with the family ultimately holding exclusive rights to banking activities that continued throughout the fifteenth century.[8] Even as the community grew, the direct descendants of the original Isaia di maestro Daniele family remained central to the community. Although their main activity was pawnbrokerage, the community widened its activities to shelter itself from changes in attitude or policy that could result in expulsion or the revocation of privileges. Two of the sons of Isaia di maestro Daniele were involved in the practice of medicine, a traditional Jewish field in the Middle Ages, although it is clear that they did not limit their activities to this area alone.[9] Other areas included commerce of various types, including the trade of precious metals and fabrics, the design and marketing of garments, and the preparation and sale of leather and paper. By the time Federico da Montefeltro became count in 1444, the community was already well established in the city.

The lack or loss of documents from the first decades of the fifteenth century makes it impossible to know the precise conditions of property ownership, but it is clear that Jews were not forbidden from purchasing land or houses in the city or the countryside. Isaia di maestro Daniele owned a residence in a central area of the Pusterla district near the Piazza Maggiore, opposite the ducal palace, and many additional records show Jewish ownership of land and property throughout the city and its surroundings. Jews lived in all neighborhoods of the city but favored the Pusterla district, where the original synagogue was located. Although, as I explain in subsequent passages, the conditions would later change, members of the Jewish community were free at this time to practice banking activities in all their forms, engage in craft activities, live with Christians in neighborhoods they considered most beneficial to their activities, and keep Christians in their employment; they were not obliged to wear distinguishing badges.[10] The extent of Jewish banking activities in Urbino is apparent in an inventory of 1436 established on the death of a prominent Jewish lender. The list of nearly one thousand debtors who owed money to the banker and his family includes Jewish men, Christian men, Christian women, and even Federico's father, Count Guidantonio da Montefeltro. It is clear that Jewish bankers were an integral part of a credit market that crossed gender, class, and religious boundaries.[11] Under Federico da Montefeltro, the freedoms and economic opportunities granted to the Jewish community of Urbino created optimal conditions for Jews to actively participate in the creation of cultural works in the city and at court.

REFLECTIONS OF JEWISH CULTURE IN FEDERICO DA MONTEFELTRO'S COURT

Although the conditions in the Jewish community of Urbino were ideal for the creation of cultural works, the reality is that almost none survive from this era, because they were lost, destroyed, or created as part of oral traditions that were not preserved. What do survive are the reflections of Jewish culture from outside the community. While these reflections admittedly do not represent the Jewish community itself, they provide insight into the conditions under which the Jews of Urbino lived. As products of the social contexts and conditions in which they were created, they also demonstrate contemporary attitudes toward Jews that were formed by the larger social and historical events. In the case of Urbino, the defining events of the 1460s and 1470s were the foundation of a *monte di pietà* and the responses of the Italian papacy and princes, including Federico da Montefeltro, to the threats of Turkish invasion. The impact of both events is apparent in two significant Urbino artworks with substantial Jewish content.

As the Jewish population expanded in many Italian cities in the fifteenth century, resentment grew toward Jewish moneylenders who were perceived as an economic threat to local merchants. Religious orders, notably the Franciscans, capitalized on this situation by promoting rhetoric against Jews that focused on the sinfulness of usury. Fanatic friars, such as Giovanni da Capistrano, called for the immediate slaughter of Jews, while others, such as Bernardino da Feltre and his followers, proposed the establishment of a system of Christian banks called the *monti di pietà*. The banks were intended to operate on a nonprofit basis; they were administered by Christian organizations and served only Christians in order to allow cities to free themselves from the hold of Jewish bankers. The first monti di pietà appeared around 1460, and they quickly spread throughout central Italy. At the urging of Fra Domenico de Leonessa, a monte di pietà was founded in Urbino in 1468, with the original charter signed by Federico's wife, Contessa Battista Sforza. Although the establishment of the monte di pietà does not appear to have had a significant impact on Jewish moneylending activities in Urbino, its presence demonstrates local attitudes toward Jews.[12]

The anti-Jewish attitudes that led to the foundation of the monte di pietà in Urbino in 1468 found an explicit expression in Paolo Uccello's *Miracle of the Profaned Host* of the same year. The altarpiece and predella (fig. 3.1) were both commissioned by the major religious organization of Urbino, the Confraternity of Corpus Domini, and displayed prominently in the church of Corpus Domini in the Piazza di Pian di Mercato (now the Piazza della Repubblica) until the church was demolished in 1703.[13] Since the confraternity stood to benefit directly from the monte di pietà, it seems likely that the subject was selected to support the foundation.[14] The narrative of Uccello's predella is based on an event of host desecration that allegedly occurred in Paris in 1290. It was an unusual topic in Italy where there were few precedents and no recorded accusations.[15] According to the legend, a Jewish lender successfully tempted a Christian woman to procure a host obtained at mass in exchange for items of clothing that she had previously pawned. The Jew then attempted to injure the host with knives, fire, and boiling water, but it remained intact and bled to reveal the presence of Christ. On witnessing this miracle, the Jew's family converted to Christianity.[16] In Uccello's version, the legend is related in six continuous scenes. In the first, a Christian woman stands in the shop of a Jewish pawnbroker offering a host in exchange for unidentified items. The second panel moves the action to the Jew's home, where he attempts to cook the host. As his horrified family looks on, blood pours out and spills under the door to alert soldiers who stand ready to enter the house. The third scene shows a procession of religious

FIGURE 3.1.

Paolo Uccello, *Miracle of the Profaned Host*, predella of the Corpus Domini Altarpiece, 1468. With permission of Ministerio dei bene e delle attività culturali e del turismo—Galleria Nazionale delle Marche, Urbino.

figures returning the host to an altar. For residents of Urbino in the fifteenth century, this scene would clearly recall the annual Corpus Domini procession. The procession was the responsibility of the Confraternity of Corpus Domini and was the major religious event of the year in Urbino. "No other festival," notes Marilyn Lavin, "was so carefully prepared and solemnly carried out, nor did so much of the population take an active part." She further notes that "the annual procession involved decorating all the houses on the main streets, and illuminating the town with a stupendous quantity of wax candles. The participants in the march included the rulers of the town, the officials, the aristocracy, the citizens and all members of the religious orders, in proper dress, proper order, and proper decorum."[17] The final three panels show the consequences of host desecration for all participants. The Christian woman is hanged while a redemptive angel hovers overhead. At the moment of her death, two devils stand at her feet while two angels appear at her head ready to catch her soul as it emerges from her mouth. There is no chance of redemption for the Jew, who is burned at the stake along with his entire family.

The warnings against Jewish usury in Uccello's predella were clearly a response to the newly founded monte di pietà and a means of promoting its use among the local Christian population of Urbino. Although Uccello was originally considered to complete the main panel, he either did not take or was not offered the commission.[18] It went instead to the Flemish painter Joos van Ghent, who began work in 1473, five years after the completion of the predella.[19] The traditional topic of his *Communion of the Apostles*, with its veneration of the host, was well suited to the confraternity's mission (fig. 3.2). Jesus, who administers the host to the apostles surrounding him, is the focal point. Judas stands slightly apart, dressed in a traditional Jewish prayer shawl and clutching a purse of coins. The biblical scene is complemented by contemporary figures in the background, who engage in conversation. They include Duke Federico da Montefeltro and his courtiers, who converse with a bearded man in Eastern dress. The duke's recently deceased wife, Battista Sforza, and a crowned child—the duke's son and heir Guidobaldo—observe from a niche behind the group.[20] Marilyn Lavin has identified the bearded man as Isaac, a Jewish doctor from Spain serving as an ambassador for the king of Persia, Uzun Hasan.[21] Ambassador Isaac was in Italy as part of an extended campaign by Popes Pius II, Paul II, and Sixtus IV to unify the Italian

FIGURE 3.2.

Joos van Ghent, *Communion of the Apostles*, main panel of the Corpus Domini Altarpiece, 1474. With permission of the Ministerio dei bene e delle attività culturali e del turismo—Galleria Nazionale delle Marche, Urbino.

rulers in an alliance with Persia to defend Christendom against the Turks.[22] Court documents confirm that an unnamed Persian ambassador, likely Isaac, visited Urbino between September 1472 and January 1473, thus placing him in Urbino immediately before Joos van Ghent began work on the altarpiece in February 1473.[23] It also appears that Isaac, shortly before arriving in Urbino, was converted to Christianity and baptized by Pope Sixtus IV.[24]

The warmly sympathetic treatment of the Jewish ambassador in the altarpiece stands in contrast to the depiction of the Jews in the predella. Whereas the Jewish moneylender in the predella poses a threat that is quickly contained and eliminated through his execution, the Jewish ambassador is welcomed as a respected equal to engage in amicable conversation. He is even encouraged by the duke, who reaches out warmly to touch his arm. Lavin interprets the ambassador's distinctive gestures as a converted Jew's "profession of faith in the liturgical drama he sees enacted before him," whereas Dana E. Katz suggests that the duke and his visitor "perhaps discuss philosophical matters or, more convincingly, engage in a theological disputation, as each argues the merits of his position."[25] The placement of the altarpiece figures in relation to the scenes of the predella creates a direct correspondence between the two pieces that must have been intentional on the part of Joos van Ghent and possibly imposed by the confraternity. Judas appears directly above the scene in the pawnshop so that his distinctive Jewish clothing and coin purse connect him to the pawnbroker to emphasize the themes of avarice and betrayal. The host offered by Jesus to Peter appears directly above the procession that returns the host to the altar. Finally, Ambassador Isaac is placed above the execution of the Jewish family. This final juxtaposition contrasts the consequence of the transgressive Jew with the rewards to the Jew who embraces the faith. The placement of the ambassador horizontally opposite Judas and vertically above the execution emphasizes the differences on both axes. Judas is marginalized from the group and cut slightly out of the frame, and the Jewish pawnbroker is executed. The ambassador, by contrast, is accepted warmly into the group.

    A close examination of the predella and altarpiece reveals their multiple functions as well as the underlying assumptions that contribute to them. On the most basic level, the two works support and promote the mission of the Confraternity of Corpus Domini. Both paintings glorify the sacrament of the Eucharist and the miracle of transubstantiation. Whereas the theme of Jewish moneylending in the predella is a response to local conditions and a warning against the supposed evils of Jewish pawnbrokerage, the presence of contemporary figures in the altarpiece refers to broader political events. The fall of Constantinople, which had occurred just twenty years before the altarpiece was painted, brought the uncertainty and fear of a Turkish invasion. The visit of the Persian ambassador was part of a larger campaign to create political alliances that would protect Italy from this threat. The situation was clearly a pressing concern when the altarpiece was conceived as the duke had, in that year, demonstrated his support to the Pope's mission against the Turks by welcoming his leading cardinal. The duke offered further support by welcoming the Persian ambassador and writing a letter to the Persian sultan to express his loyalty and gratitude for the ambassador's visit.[26] The duke's presence in the painting is a demonstration of princely power that reinforces his role as a defender and protector of the Christian citizenry of Urbino. This, too, is the function of the predella, which essentially demonstrates how Urbino's secular authorities would avenge the blasphemous act of host desecration.

The subject matter of the altarpiece and predella must have been sanctioned by the court, yet both were obviously products of the confraternity and more directly represent its agendas and views. Although the duke contributed a small sum of 15 florins, it was the brotherhood that hired and paid both artists and determined the content.[27] Even though the works appear to support the duke's political causes and possibly appease radical religious attitudes, it is difficult to ascertain how much the views they express can be said to represent the policies and attitudes of the court. This is also the case with the monte di pietà. The original charter, which was overtly anti-Jewish in its conception, was signed, and presumably supported, by the duke's wife, Battista Sforza, and the duke himself made a gift of 350 florins to the fund when his son Guidobaldo was born on January 24, 1472. In practice, however, there was no impact on Jewish banking activities, which continued uninterrupted in the city, with the duke even maintaining the services of a Jewish moneylender named Solomon.[28] Despite the presence of anti-Jewish attitudes in the city at this time, evidence suggests that the duke remained largely supportive of the Jewish community and valued the products of Jewish culture.

A strong indication of the duke's appreciation of the value of Jewish culture is apparent in his renowned collection of Hebrew manuscripts. According to the duke's librarian, Vespasiano da Bisticci, the duke actively sought out "i libri ebrei, tutti quegli che si trovavano in quella lingua, cominciandosi alla Bibbia, e a tutti quegli che l'hanno comentata, Rabbì Moisè, e altri comentatori. Non solo vi sono libri ebrei nella Scrittura santa, ma in medicina, in filosofia e in tutte le facultà" (any books to be found in Hebrew, beginning with the Bible, and all those with remarks by the Rabbi Moses and other commentators. There were not only Hebrew books on the Holy scriptures but also on medicine, philosophy, and the other faculties).[29] Of the more than nine hundred manuscripts in the collection at the time of Federico's death, approximately eighty were in Hebrew.[30] One of the most impressive is a trilingual Psalter with parallel columns in Hebrew, Greek, and Latin. As Ingrid Alexander-Skipnes points out, "The strict paralleling of the text in three languages would be helpful to Federico in reading the familiar Latin and Greek, and comparing the languages to the unfamiliar Hebrew."[31] The elaborate decoration of the manuscript and the remarkable appearance of Federico's name in the Hebrew text suggest the high value he placed on the Hebrew language.

Another possible sign of the duke's support of the Jewish community is the magnificent Urbino Torah Ark that is now housed in the Jewish Museum in New York.[32] The ark was built specifically for the synagogue on the Via Veterani in the Pusterla district near the ducal palace in the late 1470s or 1480s. According to historian Maria Luisa Moscati Benigni, it was built in response to the anti-Jewish rhetoric in the predella and presented to the Jewish community by the duke as a reassurance of his support.[33] Stylistic similarities between the ark and the duke's private *studioli* suggest a personal connection to the duke. As Vivian Mann points out, the decorative system of the ark's doors and pilasters matches the inlaid wood paneling in the studiolo of the duke's palace in Gubbio, which was completed between 1479 and 1482, and also the more elaborate studiolo in the Urbino palace, which was completed in 1476.[34] In addition to the color scheme and design, there are also similarities in appearance between the Latin inscription of the Gubbio studiolo and the original Hebrew lettering on the ark.[35]

JEWS AND MUSICAL CULTURE IN EARLY MODERN ITALY

The duke's collection of rare Hebrew books and the stylistic elements that connect the Torah Ark to the duke's private studioli suggest that the duke was supportive and appreciative of the Jewish community and its culture. An even more tangible sign can be found in the significant role of dance and the status of the Jewish dancing masters at the Urbino court. For Jews living in Italy in the fifteenth century, music and dance were an integral part of their educational curriculum and social life. "It was in fact regarded as part of the duty of a Hebrew teacher in cultured households," notes Cecil Roth, "to give instructions to his pupils, not only in Bible and Talmud, but also in the allied subjects of singing, music, and dancing."[36] Dance played a central role within the Jewish community at weddings, *berit milah* (circumcision) festivities, and welcoming ceremonies. Still, it was outside the community that the Jewish musicians and dance instructors found the most promising opportunities. There is no clear explanation of how Jews established their expertise in dance and music, but Daniel Jütte suggests the origin may lie in the conditions of the Jewish *Tanzhaus* (dancing house) traditions in medieval Germany that were brought south as Jews from Germanic lands migrated in the fourteenth century. By the second half of the fifteenth century, Jewish musicians and dancing masters were active in nearly all Italian territories where Jews lived and were credited with introducing a dignified form of dance that Christian patrons and the nobility found appealing.[37] The high value placed on dance allowed Italian Jews to establish important points of contact between Jews and Christians. In fact, as Jütte advises, we should "approach Jewish musicians of this time as 'cultural intermediaries' in an environment in which music served as an important field of interaction and collaboration between Jews and Christians."[38]

Dance was integral to courtly Renaissance life and featured prominently at state functions and lavish entertainments. With spectacular costumes, masks, scenery, and special effects, these events were designed to flatter or idealize noble patrons or impress political allies and rivals.[39] An especially notable example occurred at the marriage of Costanzo Sforza and Camilla d'Aragona in Pesaro in 1475. The Jewish community took part throughout the festivities and was formally represented at key moments in the pageantry. The procession featured a queen of Sheba dressed in gold on a gilded chair riding a large wooden elephant that was cleverly maneuvered by men hidden inside so that it appeared to walk by itself. Upon reaching the bride and groom, she descended to deliver an address in Hebrew, which was then translated into Italian, comparing Costanzo to the wise King Solomon. Besides offering gifts and praise, the dancers solicited the favor of the ruling house for their Jewish subjects and requested permission to continue farming the land. The procession was followed by a *moresca*, a popular form of theater dance performed for the amusement of the spectators.[40] The moresca featured a Monte degli Ebrei (Mount of the Jews) from which a lion appeared to fight a wild man. In the following scene, twelve dancers emerged from the mount to perform representational actions depicting all phases of work related to farming the land, with wonderful jumps and gestures timed perfectly to the music.[41]

It is clear from the description of the 1475 wedding that the Jewish community of Pesaro had the resources, the personnel, and a sufficiently strong tradition to plan and stage such an elaborate presentation. This is an indication of the type of spectacle that was provided by the Jewish dancing masters and the reason why they were so highly valued among the Italian courts. It is also an indication of what the most famous dancing master of the day, Guglielmo Ebreo da Pesaro, was able to provide at many prestigious Italian courts, including Federico's court in Urbino.

GUGLIELMO EBREO DA PESARO

Of the many Jewish dancing masters who were active in fifteenth century, Guglielmo Ebreo da Pesaro is widely recognized as the most famous and successful. In addition to writing an influential treatise on the art of dancing in 1463, he taught dancing, choreographed spectacles, and organized festivities at most major Italian courts, including the Aragon court in Naples, the Montefeltro court in Urbino, and the courts of Francesco Sforza in Pavia and Milan.[42] He was also conferred the title of Knight of the Golden Spur by the Holy Roman emperor Frederick III. Still, it was his association with his two main patrons—Alessandro Sforza, lord of Pesaro, and Federico da Montefeltro, duke of Urbino—that defines his career. Based on the biographical information conveyed in the 1463 version of his treatise, it appears that Guglielmo was born in Pesaro around 1420. Very little is known of his father, Musetto or Moysè de Cicilia (Moses of Sicily), except that he served as dancing master to the Malatesta family in Pesaro and was held in sufficiently high esteem to receive a "warm letter of recommendation" from his employer's wife, Camilla Sforza, when he went to San Marino in 1429 to claim his dowry.[43] Guglielmo's brother, Giuseppe, was also a successful dancing master, and he was employed by Lorenzo de' Medici and, along with his Christian partner, operated a music and dancing school in Florence.[44]

Guglielmo states in his treatise that he was present at the wedding of Federico da Montefeltro and Gentile Brancaleone in Urbino in 1437, although it is unknown in what capacity or in whose retinue. He likely began his professional career when he entered the service of Alessandro Sforza shortly after

Alessandro became lord of Pesaro in 1444. Guglielmo maintained a close relationship with his patron until Alessandro's death in 1473. Although it has been generally assumed that Guglielmo was briefly employed by the Sforza family in Milan, it is more likely that he remained in Alessandro's service throughout this time. The duke of Milan, Francesco Sforza, was Alessandro's brother, and although Guglielmo was present at multiple events at the Milanese court during Francesco's reign as duke (1450–1466), he attended almost all of them in the company of Alessandro or Alessandro's son Costanzo.[45] Likewise, Guglielmo probably remained in Alessandro's service during his two years of residency at the court of Naples (1465–1467). Alessandro was an ally of the king of Naples with strong ties and an official position at court. He was probably engaging in a common practice that saw rulers lend members of their retinue to other courts to teach the young princes or organize special festivities.[46] It is also possible that Guglielmo played an integral role in designing the dances for the Jewish presentation at the Pesaro wedding in 1475, although there is no existing evidence of his presence or participation.[47]

Guglielmo's activities in the years immediately following the death of his patron, Alessandro Sforza, in 1473, are unknown, although it seems likely that Guglielmo entered the service of Federico da Montefeltro around this time. Guglielmo clearly admired Federico and had enjoyed repeated professional contact with him since their first encounter at Federico's wedding in 1437. Moreover, there were deep ties between the Montefeltro court in Urbino and the Sforza court in Pesaro. Guglielmo was present when Alessandro married Federico's half sister Sveva Colonna da Montefeltro in 1448 and again when Federico married Alessandro's daughter, Battista, in 1460. Guglielmo was also present in Urbino as a member of Alessandro's retinue when Federico held a reception for the visit of Alfonso d'Avalos in 1460 and again when, in 1471, Guglielmo arranged a suite of *moresche* for the betrothal celebrations of Federico's daughter Elisabetta to Roberto Malatesta, lord of Rimini. The first evidence of Guglielmo's official association with the Urbino court is a letter from Guglielmo to Lorenzo de' Medici dated May 29, 1476, in which Guglielmo identifies himself as being "in the retinue of the Duke of Urbino." Guglielmo and his son, Pietro Paolo, are also listed as the "ballerini" (dancing masters) in an undated document created sometime after 1474 that lists the courtiers and retinue attached to the duke's court.[48]

Guglielmo published the first edition of his dancing treatise in 1463 under the name of Guglielmo Ebreo da Pesaro. Within three years of its completion, Guglielmo converted to Catholicism and took the name Giovanni Ambrosio. In a subsequent redaction of the treatise, made between 1471 and 1476, his Christian name is substituted consistently for the original Jewish name. Although a motive for Guglielmo's conversion has not emerged, there are several possibilities. There is no evidence that Guglielmo was hindered in his career as a Jew, but he may have been pressured to convert by his patron. Alessandro Sforza turned to religious piety in the 1460s by founding charitable institutions, giving himself to the care of the Franciscans, and adopting a more devout mode of living. Since his newfound spirituality extended to his mistress, it may have influenced his dancing master as well.[49] There may also have been professional motivations for the conversion. Guglielmo took the name Ambrosio after the patron saint of Milan and was baptized in that city, with Duke Francesco and Bianca Maria Sforza serving as his godparents. This may have been an attempt by Guglielmo to strengthen his connections to the Sforza court in Milan, where he had made repeated applications for an engagement.[50] Even though he was unsuccessful in gaining an appointment in Milan, his conversion made possible his knighthood shortly afterward, which was probably procured for him by Alessandro Sforza.[51]

Whatever the reason for his conversion, Guglielmo clearly saw it as a means to promote his services. The topic of conversion came up again, this time concerning Guglielmo's brother, Giuseppe, in two letters sent from Urbino by Guglielmo and Federico da Montefeltro on April 13, 1469. Both letters are addressed to Lorenzo de' Medici and solicit his help in realizing Giuseppe's conversion to Christianity. Guglielmo asserts that he is "certain this would happen if I were to come there" and notes that "if this were the case, we, that is he and I, could be together and could do such pleasant and novel things that I am certain would please Your Magnificence to the utmost."[52] Given the date and the promise of "pleasant and novel things," it seems likely that Guglielmo was hoping to work with his brother to provide the dances for Lorenzo's wedding in June of that year.[53] Both letters state that Giuseppe had originally planned his conversion to coincide with an earlier wedding celebration in Milan,[54] but he was prevented from attending because of an outbreak of the plague, so there was certainly good reason to suggest Lorenzo's wedding as an alternative event for the conversion.[55]

Guglielmo's conversion did not gain him favor with everyone. In 1469, when Federico da Montefeltro sent Galeazzo Sforza, the duke of Milan, a recommendation on Guglielmo's behalf, Galeazzo responded that Federico should "give no hearing to that Ambrosio, alias Jew, who has said certain things against Camillo, but treat him for what he is."[56] Guglielmo was also associated with Judaism well after his conversion. A 1481 letter reveals that the six-year-old Isabella d'Este "danced twice with Ambrosio, formerly a Jew, and [who] is with the most illustrious lord Duke of Urbino as his dancing-master."[57] This may also account for Guglielmo's placement on the hierarchical lists of courtiers and retinue attached to the duke of Urbino's court. The dancing masters are named well down on the list, after the princes, counts, knights, gentlemen, councillors, squires, kitchen stewards, pages, and other servants. A similar inventory list from around the same time lists the dancing masters as 183 and 184 of the 203 members of the household.[58] Barbara Sparti points out that the status of the dancing master was generally low in Renaissance Italy, but it is still surprising to see Guglielmo, given his reputation and accomplishments, at the bottom of these lists and well below the other five Knights of the Golden Spur, who are listed after the princes and counts.[59]

GUGLIELMO EBREO AND MUSIC AT THE COURT OF URBINO

Guglielmo may have held an ambiguous status within the hierarchy of the Urbino court, but his symbolic value and contributions as dancing master, musician, and converted Jew were certainly much greater. As a contributor to the elaborate court spectacles, he brought the skills and traditions necessary to promote the duke's image at court events with an unmatched visual prominence. Moreover, dance, which harmonized sound, movement, body, space, and time, was perceived at the Urbino court as a manifestation of the harmony of the world and particularly valued in an environment that promoted a humanistic reinterpretation of classical ideas.[60] Guglielmo may not be acknowledged directly, but traces of his symbolic value are apparent in the artistic products that define and promote the duke. Ultimately these reveal the subtle yet significant presence and importance of Jewish culture at the Urbino court.

The key to understanding Guglielmo's symbolic importance is found in his treatise, *De pratica seu arte tripudii* (*On the Practice or Art of Dancing*). As noted before, the original document was completed in 1463, and it was dedicated to Galeazzo Maria Sforza, then count of Pavia. Several additional presentation copies were made, including one, unfortunately now lost, for the duke of Urbino, Federico da Montefeltro.[61] More than just an instruction book on dancing, the treatise argues for the moral and ethical worth of dance and establishes Guglielmo's credentials as a dancing master, musician, and theorist. In the theoretical introduction, Guglielmo affirms the place of dance within the liberal arts by claiming for it the status enjoyed by music in fifteenth-century Italy, where it was recognized as both an art and a science. The concluding section includes a laudatory poem by the poet and humanist Giovanni Mario Filelfo that celebrates Guglielmo's musical skills and agility as a dancer by comparing him to the champions of antiquity.[62] Guglielmo's elevation of dance in humanistic terms was clearly well suited to the values of the Urbino court, where the ideals of harmony dominated. As Sparti observes, "It is harmony—the source and sustenance of the dance—that dominated the introductory sonnet and the preface of *De practica*."[63]

Guglielmo's status as a musician is apparent in Filelfo's descriptions in the laudatory poem as well as in the treatment of musical issues in the body of the treatise. Guglielmo focuses on musical problems in ten of the sixteen introductory chapters and offers detailed instructions on composing the dances and their music. Moreover, of the thirty-one dance melodies included in the practical part of the treatise, fourteen were composed by Guglielmo. For Guglielmo, dance without music was inconceivable. As Nicoletta Guidobaldi has demonstrated in her detailed study of musical imagery at the court of Federico, Guglielmo's music, as much as his dance, provided the material that celebrated the duke's image, supported his political goals, and promoted his vision of the ideal city.[64] In a court that recognized both music and dance as reflections of worldly harmony, Guglielmo was the ideal individual.

Evidence of Guglielmo's presence in the imagery celebrating Duke Federico can be found in the duke's private studiolo in Urbino. The studiolo's location between the duke's private apartments and his audience room suggests that favored guests may have been allowed to admire it, but it was essentially a space for solitary meditation and study. "More than any other part of the palace," observes June Osborne, "it seems to reflect Federico's taste and character."[65] The space displays an elaborate scheme of armor, scientific and musical instruments, books, and even musical scores. "However," writes Jean Castex, "beyond displaying perspective perfection, the marquetry panels also trained the eye and the mind to envision the ideal city that the palace was promoting."[66]

While the musical instruments in the studiolo marquetry represent the Renaissance ideal of harmonious proportion, Guidobaldi argues that the two song manuscripts convey political significance, with the song on the west wall, "Bella gerit," containing a possible allusion to Guglielmo.[67] Although the authorship and circumstances of its first performance are unknown, the text clearly glorifies Federico and celebrates his deeds as military captain, patron of the arts, and leader: "Bella gerit musasque colit / Federicus / omnium maximus Italorum dux foris atque domi" (He captained wars and cultivated arts, / Federico / the great, leader of Italians abroad and at home). Federico's dual role as military leader and patron of the arts is apparent in the text but also supported through allusions in the music. Guidobaldi identifies similarities between the tenor voice in the opening section of "Bella gerit" and the *L'homme armé* melody. The *L'homme armé* melody, of course, was part of an established tradition in military and anti-Ottoman contexts as well as in initiatives supporting the Crusades. The allusion clearly supports Federico's accomplishments and interests in these areas.[68] The military allusions of the first part of the chanson are complemented in the final section by figurations that are typical of dance music. According to Guidobaldi, this section refers to a well-known basse danse by Guglielmo Ebreo, "Falla con misuras." The allusion establishes a direct connection between the chanson and the musical environment at Federico's court, where Guglielmo was already well known. Guidobaldi also notes that the proportions of the three sections of the chanson, including the middle section, which evokes Federico's name, follow the structural principals of the golden ratio to suggest a sense of balance and proportion between Federico's military and artistic imagery and serve as a reflection of the perfect harmony he sought to attain for the duchy.[69]

Guglielmo's music may have provided the symbolic content for the "Bella gerit" chanson, but it was Guglielmo himself who provided the model for the allegorical *Music* panel by Joos van Ghent (fig. 3.3). The painting was part

FIGURE 3.3.

Joos van Ghent, *Music*, oil on poplar, ca. 1470s. © The National Gallery, London, reproduced with permission.

of a series of liberal arts panels personifying rhetoric, music, dialectic, and astronomy that were completed in the late 1470s or early 1480s and intended for either the duke's library in Urbino or his studiolo in Gubbio.[70] Each of the four panels represents a man, seen either from the rear or in profile, kneeling on steps in front of a female personification of a liberal art seated on a throne. Although the only male figure to be identified definitively is Federico da Montefeltro, who appears in the *Dialectic* panel, the other three have sufficiently distinct features to suggest that they represent specific people, presumably specialists in the fields of liberal arts they represent, with a significant connection to the Urbino court.

Although it was previously believed that the figure in the *Music* panel might be Costanzo Sforza, lord of Pesaro and the son of Guglielmo's former patron, Guidobaldi argues that the panel more plausibly represents Guglielmo.[71] Guglielmo's connection to the Urbino environment spanned multiple decades: he had a stable position at court, and a dedication copy of his treatise was held in the duke's library. Moreover, of Federico's court musicians at this time, Guglielmo was the only one whose professional standing in the realm of music justified his inclusion in the series.[72] The visual details of the painting appear to point to Guglielmo as well. Each of the panels depicts the male figure with distinctive professional instruments and clothing that enhance the association to the particular liberal art. The subject of the *Music* panel is clearly defined by the small portative organ on the steps that provides the focal point for the gaze of both figures. The clothing of the male figure, however, is more typical of a dancer than a musician. The blouse that extends only to the waist, the tight-fitting socks, and even the beret placed on the stairs are all typical of the dress of dancing masters from this era. They correspond to the style that Guglielmo prescribes in his treatise (so as not to impede the virtuosity of the execution) and are identical to the clothing worn by the unidentified male dancer depicted in Guglielmo's treatise.[73] While the personification of music gestures toward the organ, the male figure places his hands in a distinctive gesture of counting similar to the pose of Federico's courtier in the Corpus Domini Altarpiece, which was, of course, also painted by Joos van Ghent. While the figure in the altarpiece appears to be marking the points made during discourse, Guidobaldi suggests that the gesture in the *Music* panel is that of a dancing master marking tempo, steps, and space.[74]

A peculiar element of the *Music* panel, and one not found elsewhere in the series, is the Kufic inscription on the arch and columns behind the throne. This script was developed in the seventh century and employed in Islamic texts, including the earliest copies of the Koran. Guidobaldi suggests that the script and its placement recall the remote origins of music and its foundations in both Islamic and Jewish traditions. The placement of the inscription on two columns refers first to Jubal, who is celebrated in the Hebrew Bible as the inventor of music. According to tradition, Jubal preserved his knowledge of music on two pillars, one made of brick and the other of marble, so that when the world was destroyed by fire and water, his art would not be lost.[75] The use of Kufic refers to Barbad, a musician at the court of the Sassanian king of Persia, Khosrow II, who ruled from 591 to 628. Barbad was active as a performer, composer, and music theorist. Like Jubal, he is considered the founder of an early system of music used in Persia. The allusion to Barbad celebrates the remote foundations of music but also suggests a comparison between the court of Federico in Urbino and the ancient Persian court. Khosrow II was a cultured and enlightened ruler and patron of the arts who oversaw the greatest expansion of the empire. "Within the rhetorical scheme of comparison with an authoritative example of the past," notes Guidobaldi, "it would have been difficult to select a more splendid or pertinent model on which to base the eulogy of the Duke of Montefeltro."[76] Since Khosrow fought with the Byzantines against the Turks, the allusion establishes an additional connection between the panel and the contemporary political campaign celebrated in the Corpus Domini Altarpiece.

CONCLUSIONS

Guglielmo's presence in the *Music* panel suggests his varied roles in a web of symbolic cultural meanings within the environment of the Urbino court. As a dancing master, he was recognized as an expert in a field that harmonized sound, movement, body, space, and time in a way that was understood as a complete manifestation of universal harmony. As the representative of the liberal art of music, he embodied both the practical and theoretical realizations of the art. As a Jew, Guglielmo was doubly connected to the art of music: he was associated with Jubal, the inventor of music as conveyed in biblical sources and referred to in the *Music* panel, and he was also part of the tradition of Jewish dance that was highly valued in Italian courts. Although Sparti notes that there do not appear to be any differences in style or content between the music and choreography created by Jewish dancing masters such as Guglielmo and their non-Jewish counterparts, the high quality of Jewish dancing masters was recognized by both Jews and Christians.[77] Finally, as a converted Jew, Guglielmo is connected to the Persian ambassador in the Corpus Domini Altarpiece and seems to have fulfilled a similar symbolic function in Federico's court. In the same way that the rare Hebrew books were highly prized among the duke's collection, Federico seems to have embraced the aspects of Jewish culture embodied by Ambassador Isaac and Guglielmo when they served to support and promote his political and aesthetic aims.

As a tolerant ruler who valued the arts highly, Federico da Montefeltro fostered conditions that allowed the Jewish community to thrive and Jewish artists such as Guglielmo Ebreo to maintain an important role at court. Although these policies were largely preserved by Federico's son and successor, Guidobaldo, the situation changed with Guidobaldo's death in 1508 and the succession of his nephew, Francesco Maria della Rovere. There were immediate and significant changes for the Jewish community. Within a month of assuming power, the new duke issued a decree annulling all previous concessions and limiting the rights and prerogatives of Jews. All forms of moneylending were prohibited, the purchase of real estate was forbidden, men were required to wear distinguishing yellow badges and women yellow veils, food could not be purchased before sunset, Jews were obliged to live in the district known as the "Androne delli giudei" (gateway of the Jews) in the area around the synagogue in the Pusterla district, and Jews were prohibited from employing Christian women.[78] Despite the severity of the decrees, they do not appear to have been applied rigorously. Jewish banks continued their operations, Jews were able to purchase and possess property, and Jews continued to live among Christians rather than being restricted to a single neighborhood. Unlike in the previous century, there was now less certainty and consistency of policy, not only from the first della Rovere duke but from his successors as well. Guidobaldo II banned all loan activities in 1548 but reinstated them the following year. In 1553, he ordered all Talmudic texts confiscated and destroyed but then, between 1556 and 1565, issued a series of edicts favorable to Jews and their activities.[79] The inconsistent policies, along with external events, also had an impact on the demographics of the Jewish community. When the ducal court was moved from Urbino to Pesaro in 1523, many Jews followed or moved to Ancona, where they had access to flourishing markets, trade centers, and better schools. They were replaced in Urbino by an influx of Jews from the expulsions in Spain and Portugal or Jews leaving areas under papal control for more hospitable environments. Whereas the Jewish community of Urbino was coherent in the fifteenth century, there was now a greater diversity and less solidarity. When Guidobaldo II discreetly opted to accept new Jewish refugees in 1556, a letter from local Jews warned against this policy from either fear of competition or worry that a larger community would attract the attention of the ecclesiastical authorities.[80]

Despite the changes and uncertainties, members of the Urbino Jewish community continued their professional activities in banking and trade in quality fabrics, and they were valued as tailors, even supplying quality clothing to the dukes. Under the final duke of Urbino, Francesco Maria II, the Jewish community enjoyed a period of relative tranquility. When the duke died without an heir in 1631, the duchy was annexed to the Papal States, all rights were unambiguously revoked, and restrictions were rigorously enforced. In 1633, all Jews were ordered into the newly established ghetto near the Porta Valbona, where a new synagogue was established and curfews enforced.[81] This marked a long period of decline for the city but especially for the Jewish community. Although the forced segregation of Jews in the seventeenth century seems to have allowed art music traditions to flourish in some Jewish communities, there do not appear to have been any musicians of stature living in Urbino who rose to prominence.[82] Urbino has recently regained some of its former splendor through restoration projects that have revitalized the city as a thriving university town with an active artistic community, but the vibrant Jewish community that participated in the establishment of the city's initial glory is no longer present.

NOTES

1. Cecil H. Clough, "Federigo da Montefeltro's Artistic Patronage," *Journal of the Royal Society for the Encouragement of Arts, Manufactures and Commerce* 126 (1978): 719.

2. Baldassare Castiglione, *Il libro del Cortegiano* (Venice: Gabriel Giolito di Ferrarii, 1544). The intent of Castiglione's book is to define the behaviors of the perfect courtier and to

celebrate the excellence of the Urbino court under the Montefeltro dukes. It consists of a series of fictional conversations among the courtiers of the Duchy of Urbino under Federico's son and heir, Guidobaldo, in 1507, when Castiglione was a member at court. Although not published until 1528, the book was written partly in Urbino and partly in Rome between 1508 and 1516, after the dukedom passed from the house of Montefeltro to the della Rovere family. The 1544 edition is the earliest to survive in the Urbino libraries; translations from this edition are my own.

3. Castiglione, *Il libro del Cortegiano*, 10–11.

4. The population statistics are in Annie Sacerdoti, *Guida all'Italia ebraica* (Genova: Casa Editrice Marietti S.p.A, 1986), 245.

5. The relative status of Jewish advisers and other courtiers is discussed in Maria Luisa Moscati Benigni, *Marche itinerari ebraici: i luoghi, la storia, l'arte* (Venice: Marsilio, 1996), 175.

6. The existence of transient Jewish settlements seems likely because of Urbino's proximity to the Via Flaminia—an ancient Roman road leading from Rome to Fano and then along the Adriatic coast to Rimini. See Moscati Benigni, *Marche itinerari ebraici*, 165.

7. Sezione di Archivio di Stato di Urbino, Quadra di Pusterla, n. 1 (1407–1408), cc. 13v–14r; n. 2 (1408–1409), cc. 200v–200r. See Alessandra Veronese, "La presenza ebraica nel ducato di Urbino nel Quattrocento," in *Italia Judaica: Gli ebrei nello Stato pontificio fino al Ghetto (1555): Atti del VI Convegno internazionale, Tel Aviv, 18–22 giugno 1995* (Rome: Ministero per i beni culturali e ambientali ufficio centrale per i beni archivistici, 1998), 257–258.

8. Gino Luzzatto, *I banchieri ebrei in Urbino nell'età ducale* (Padua: Arnoldi Forni, 1902), 30–31; Veronese, "La presenza ebraica," 258.

9. Veronese, "La presenza ebraica," 272.

10. Alessandra Veronese, "Gli ebrei nel ducato di Urbino tra cinque e seicento: insediamenti, economia e societa," *Materia giudaica: Rivista dell'associazione italiana per lo studio del giudaismo* 10, no. 1 (2005): 112–113.

11. Dana E. Katz, "The Contours of Tolerance and the Corpus Domini Altarpiece in Urbino," in *The Jew in the Art of the Italian Renaissance* (Philadelphia: University of Pennsylvania Press, 2008), 19–20.

12. On the establishment of the monte di pietà in Urbino, see Marilyn Aronberg Lavin, "The Altar of Corpus Domini in Urbino: Joos Van Ghent, Piero della Francesca," *Art Bulletin* 49, no. 1 (1967): 9; Luzzatto, *I banchieri ebrei*, 39–42. On the general impact of the monti di pietà on Jewish moneylending, see Nicola Lorenzo Barile, "Renaissance Monti di Pietà in Modern Scholarship: Themes, Studies, and Historiographic Trends," *Renaissance and Reformation / Renaissance et Réforme* 35, no. 3 (2012): 91–94; Maristella Botticini, "A Tale of 'Benevolent' Governments: Private Credit Markets, Public Finance, and the Role of Jewish Lenders in Medieval and Renaissance Italy," *Journal of Economic History* 60, no. 1 (2000): 173. Battista's signature is found within the Liber Capitoli del Monte della Pietà d'Urbino. Urbino, Bibl. Università.

13. After the demolition of the church, the altarpiece was transferred to Sant'Agata and then to the Collegio dei R.P. Scolopi. The altar was moved to its present location in the Palazzo Ducale in 1861, with the predella following in 1881. See Lavin, "The Altar of Corpus Domini in Urbino," 1.

14. On the relationship between the monte di pietà and the Confraternity of Corpus Domini and the ways the confraternity stood to benefit from the foundation of this institution, see Lavin, "The Altar of Corpus Domini in Urbino," 9–10.

15. Katz, "The Contours of Tolerance," 28; Lavin, "The Altar of Corpus Domini in Urbino," 8–9.

16. An extensive summary of the original legend and literary sources can be found in Lavin, "The Altar of Corpus Domini in Urbino," 2–8; a survey of the pictorial traditions can be found in Katz, "The Contours of Tolerance," 22–33.

17. Lavin, "The Altar of Corpus Domini in Urbino," 10.

18. Lavin, 10.

19. Katz notes that it was unusual to commission the predella before the altarpiece, but this may have been related to the founding of the monte di pietà. See Katz, "The Contours of Tolerance," 20.

20. On the identity and placement of the woman, see Lavin, "The Altar of Corpus Domini in Urbino," 18–19.

21. See Lavin, 14. Although the bearded man was previously thought to have been a Venetian nobleman, Lavin asserts that he is more likely Ambassador Isaac, who is known to have been in Italy in 1472–1473. On the distinctive Jewish appearance and clothing of this figure, see Joseph Hoffman, "Piero della Francesca's 'Flagellation': A Reading from Jewish History," *Zeitschrift für Kunstgeschichte* 44, no. 4 (1981): 345–348.

22. For details of the campaign, see Katz, "The Contours of Tolerance," 37, and Lavin, "The Altar of Corpus Domini in Urbino," 14–16.

23. Lavin, "The Altar of Corpus Domini in Urbino," 16.

24. Lavin, 15.

25. Lavin, "The Altar of Corpus Domini in Urbino," 16; Katz, "The Contours of Tolerance," 36.

26. Federico demonstrated support of the Pope's mission by welcoming Cardinal Bessarion to Urbino and also wrote a letter to the Persian ruler Uzun Hasan describing his loyalty to the sultan and expressing gratitude for the Persian ambassador's visit. The duke's letter to the Persian ruler can be found in Federico da Montefeltro, *Lettere di stato e d'arte (1470–1480)*, ed. Paulo Alatri (Rome: Edizioni di Storia e Letteratura, 1949), 78–79.

27. Katz, "The Contours of Tolerance," 37.

28. Lavin, "The Altar of Corpus Domini in Urbino," 9n50; Luzzatto, *I banchieri ebrei*, 42.

29. Vespasiano da Bisticci, *Vite di uomini illustri del secolo XV*, ed. Paolo d'Ancona and Erhard Aeschlimann (Milan: Ulrico Hoepli, 1951), 211.

30. Delio Proverbio, "Notes on the Diaspora of the Hebrew Manuscripts: From Volterra to Urbino," in *Federico da Montefeltro and His Library*, ed. Marcello Simonetta (Milan: Y-Press, 2007), 51–52.

31. Ingrid Alexander-Skipnes, "'Bound with Wond'rous Beauty': Eastern Codices in the Library of Federico da Montefeltro," *Mediterranean Studies* 19 (2010): 79–80. The trilingual Psalter manuscript is Vatican City, Biblioteca Apostolica Vaticana. Psalterium David secundum traductionem Septuaginta interpetrum [sic] a beato Hieronymo ex Greco in Latinum traductum. MS Urb.lat.9. Digitized at DigiVatLib, accessed January 30, 2019, https://digi.vatlib.it/view/MSS_Urb.lat.9. The duke's collection consisted of about 600 manuscripts in Latin, 180 in Greek, 80 in Hebrew, 70 in the vernacular, and a few in Arabic and Coptic. At the end of the reign of the last duke of Urbino, Francesco Maria II della Rovere, an agreement was achieved with Pope Alexander VII to move the treasured collection to Rome. In 1657, the entire collection was transferred to the Vatican Library. It is one of the few instances of a library remaining intact since the Renaissance. The literature on the library is substantial, including Marcella Peruzzi, *Cultura, potere immagine: La biblioteca di Federico di Montefeltro*, Collana di Studi e Testi 20 (Urbino: Accademia Raffaello, 2004), and Marcella Peruzzi, Lorenza Mochi Onori, and Claudia Caldari, eds., *Ornatissimo codice: La biblioteca di Federico di Montefeltro* (Milan: Skira, 2008).

32. "The Jewish Museum—Collection—Torah Ark," Jewish Museum, accessed January 30, 2019, https://thejewishmuseum.org/collection/22237-torah-ark. The ark was redecorated in 1623–1624 and moved to the new synagogue upon the establishment of the Urbino ghetto in the 1630s. The ark was sold to an art dealer in 1906 so that the community could raise money for restoration and conservation work. See Vivian B. Mann, "The Recovery of a Known Work," *Jewish Art* 12–13 (1986–1987): 271; Moscati Benigni, *Marche itinerari ebraici*, 170. A precise date of completion has not been determined. It was initially given a date of 1451 in a sales catalog of 1916, but stylistic studies suggest it could have been built as late as 1488. For more on the date of completion, see Mann, "The Recovery of a Known Work," 269.

33. Moscati Benigni, *Marche itinerari ebraici*, 174.

34. Luciano Cheles, "The Inlaid Decorations of Federico da Montefeltro's Urbino Studiolo: An Iconographic Study," *Mitteilungen des Kunsthistorischen Institutes in Florenz* 26, no. 1 (1982): 2.

35. Mann, "The Recovery of a Known Work," 269.

36. Israel Adler, "The Rise of Art Music in the Italian Ghetto," in *Jewish Medieval and Renaissance Studies*, ed. Alexander Altmann (Cambridge, MA: Harvard University Press, 1967), 328–329; Cecil Roth, *The Jews in the Renaissance* (Philadelphia: Jewish Publication Society of America, 1959), 275.

37. Daniel Jütte, "The Place of Music in Early Modern Italian Jewish Culture," in *Musical Exodus: Al-Andalus and Its Jewish Diasporas*, ed. Ruth F. Davis (Lanham, MD: Rowman and Littlefield, 2015), 48–49.

38. Jütte, 46.

39. Barbara Sparti, "Dancing in Fifteenth-Century Italian Society," in Guglielmo Ebreo da Pesaro, *De pratica seu arte tripudii: On the Practice or Art of Dancing*, ed. and trans. Barbara Sparti (Oxford: Clarendon, 1993), 56.

40. The moresca was a mimed or danced theatrical work that was very popular in Italy in the fifteenth century. It often served as an interlude at larger events and often had a mythological theme. For more on the fifteenth-century moresca, see Sparti, "Dancing in Fifteenth-Century Italian Society," 53–54, and Barbara Sparti, "The Moresca and Mattaccino in Italy—circa 1450–1630," in *Proceedings of the Symposium "Moreska: Past and Present,"* ed. Elsie Ivancich Dunin (Zabreb: Institute of Ethnology and Folklore Research, 2002), 129–142.

41. The entire wedding festivities are described in a detailed anonymous account. A copy made five years later by Leonardo da Colle and enriched with thirty-two illustrations is housed in the Biblioteca Apostolica Vaticana as Codice Urb.lat.899. The manuscript is available online in a digitized version at https://digi.vatlib.it/view/MSS_Urb.lat.899 (accessed January 30, 2019); see pages 88r and 91r for the illustrations of the queen of Sheba on her elephant and the Mount of the Jews. For a full English-language description of the event, see William A. Smith, "Jewish Dancing in Wedding Pageantry at Pesaro, Italy in 1475," *Israel Dance Annual* (1987–1988): 11–24. A shorter summary of the Jewish contributions is in Roth, *The Jews in the Renaissance*, 277–278.

42. For an extensive survey of Guglielmo's life, see Barbara Sparti, "Guglielmo's Life," in Ebreo da Pesaro, *De pratica seu arte tripudii*, 23–45.

43. Roth, *The Jews in the Renaissance*, 275. On the lack of information concerning Moses of Sicily, see Alessandra Veronese, "Una societas ebraico-christiana *in docendo tripudiare ac cantare* nella Firenze del Quattrocento," in *Guglielmo Ebreo da Pesaro e la danza nelle corti italiane del XV secolo: Atti del Convegno Internazionale di Studi, Pesaro 16/18 luglio 1987*, ed.

Maurizio Padovan (Pisa: Pacini, 1990), 51. The letter of recommendation is reproduced in Amy A. Bernardy, "Les juifs dans la république de San Marin du XIV au XVII siècle," *Revue des études juives* 48 (1904): 246.

44. Timothy J. McGee, "Dancing Masters and the Medici Court in the 15th Century," *Studi Musicali* 17 (1988): 204–205. McGee points out on page 209 that it would seem that "at the end of the 1460s Giuseppe was at least as well-known as his brother." On Giuseppe's activities as a dance instructor in Florence, see Veronese, "Una societas ebraico-christiana *in docendo tripudiare ac cantare* nella Firenze del Quattrocento."

45. Sparti, "Guglielmo's Life," 30–31.

46. Sparti, 32.

47. Although Roth casually credits Guglielmo with creating all the dances at the Pesaro festivities, Sparti has questioned this assumption. See Roth, *The Jews in the Renaissance*, 277–278; Barbara Sparti, "Questions concerning the Life and Works of Guglielmo Ebreo," in *Guglielmo Ebreo da Pesaro e la danza nelle corti italiane del XV secolo: Atti del Convegno Internazionale di Studi, Pesaro 16/18 luglio 1987*, ed. Maurizio Padovan (Pisa: Pacini, 1990), 40–41; Barbara Sparti, "Jewish Dancing-Masters and 'Jewish Dance' in Renaissance Italy: Guglielmo Ebreo and Beyond," in *Seeing Israeli and Jewish Dance*, ed. Judith Brin Ingber (Detroit: Wayne State University Press, 2011), 240.

48. Guglielmo's letter to Lorenzo quoted in McGee, "Dancing Masters and the Medici Court," 209–210. The inventory is discussed on page 217. Since Federico is identified with the title of *duke* in the document, it could not have originated earlier than 1474.

49. Sparti, "Guglielmo's Life," 34.

50. Sparti, "Jewish Dancing-Masters and 'Jewish Dance' in Renaissance Italy," 237.

51. Sparti, "Guglielmo's Life," 35.

52. "El quale mi rendo certo che venendo io là, haveria a seguire et sequendo noi, cioè lui et io, porrimmo essere inseime et fare cose si legiadre et nove che mi rendo certo piaxeriano summamente ala Magnificentia vostra," McGee, "Dancing Masters and the Medici Court," 203 and 220. Both letters are published in Italian and English in this article.

53. Lorenzo was married to Clarise Orsini by proxy in February 1469, with the marriage in person taking place on June 4, 1469.

54. The wedding of Galeazzo Maria Sforza, duke of Milan, to Bona of Savoy. See McGee, "Dancing Masters and the Medici Court," 204.

55. It is unknown whether Giuseppe converted. See Sparti, "Guglielmo's Life," 36.

56. Sparti, 35. It seems likely that *Camillo* refers to Camillo Borzi, the ambassador of Urbino at the court of Milan. Sparti notes that it is impossible to know if the statement is an example of Galeazzo's arrogance or his contempt for dancing masters, for Jews, or for Guglielmo in particular.

57. Quoted in Sparti, 38.

58. McGee, "Dancing Masters and the Medici Court," 213; Sparti, "Guglielmo's Life," 39. The document referred to by Sparti is held in the Biblioteca Apostolica Vaticana, codice Urb. lat.1204, accessed January 30, 2019, https://digi.vatlib.it/view/MSS_Urb.lat.1204. The dancing masters are found on page 110r.[02.mn.0000]. The document referred to by McGee is held in the Biblioteca Universitaria in Urbino.

59. On the low social status of dancing masters, see Sparti, "Dancing in Fifteenth-Century Italian Society," 49–51.

60. Nicoletta Guidobaldi, *La musica di Federico: Immagini e suoni alla corte di Urbino* (Florence: Leo S. Olschki, 1995), 85.

61. The various copies are discussed in Barbara Sparti, "Status and Description of *De pratica*," in Ebreo da Pesaro, *De pratica seu arte tripudii*, 16.

62. The poem is reproduced Otto Kinkeldey, "A Jewish Dancing Master of the Renaissance (Guglielmo Ebreo)," in *Studies in Jewish Bibliography and Related Subjects, in Memory of Abraham Solomon Freidus (1867–1923)* (New York: Alexander Kohut Memorial Foundation, 1929), 368–370.

63. Sparti, "Status and Description of *De pratica*," 11.

64. Guidobaldi, *La musica di Federico*.

65. June Osborne, *Urbino: The Story of a Renaissance City* (Chicago: University of Chicago Press, 2003), 87.

66. Jean Castex, "Ducal Palace, Urbino," in *Architecture of Italy* (Westport, CT: Greenwood, 2008), 47.

67. The song on the north wall, "J'ay prins amour," was sung and danced to at the festivities celebrating the visit of Federico of Aragon in 1474 and is tied to imagery recognizing Federico da Montefeltro for his defense of Christianity from the Ottomans. See Guidobaldi, *La musica di Federico*, 50–61.

68. Guidobaldi, *La musica di Federico*, 63–65; Lewis Lockwood, "Aspects of the 'L'homme armé' Tradition," *Proceedings of the Royal Musical Association* 100, no. 1 (1973): 105–106.

69. Guidobaldi, *La musica di Federico*, 66–68. It is actually a modified Fibonacci series based on the numbers 23, 58, and 61.

70. The provenance and attribution to Joos van Ghent has not been definitively established, although the attribution to Joos van Ghent is widely accepted. See Marcin Fabiański, "Federigo da Montefeltro's 'Studiolo' in Gubbio Reconsidered. Its Decoration and Its Iconographic Program: An Interpretation," *Artibus et Historiae* 11, no. 21 (1990): 201–204. The *Rhetoric* and *Music* panels are now in the National Gallery in London. The *Dialectic* and *Astronomy* panels were destroyed in Berlin in the Second World War.

71. Fabiański, 211n31. Guidobaldi discusses the identity of the figures in the four panels and argues that each is an accomplished individual in his respective area of specialization in the liberal arts. See Guidobaldi, *La musica di Federico*, 79–85.

72. Guidobaldi, 85.

73. Guidobaldi, 96. For Guglielmo's reference to dress and the illustration, see Sparti, "Status and Description of *De pratica*," 8 and 14.

74. Guidobaldi, *La musica di Federico*, 96. For the interpretation of the hand gesture in the Corpus Domini Altarpiece, see Katz, "The Contours of Tolerance," 36.

75. Howard Mayer Brown, "St. Augustine, Lady Music, and the Gittern in Fourteenth-Century Italy," *Musica Disciplina* 38 (1984): 101; Guidobaldi, *La musica di Federico*, 27–28.

76. "Entro lo schema retorico del confronto con un esempio autorevole del passato, sarebbe stato difficile scegliere un modello più splendido e più pertinente su cui basare l'elogio del duca di Montefeltro," Guidobaldi, *La musica di Federico*, 105.

77. Sparti's observations can be found in Sparti, "Jewish Dancing-Masters and 'Jewish Dance' in Renaissance Italy," 245.

78. Luzzatto, *I banchieri ebrei*, 43.

79. For a detailed account of the situation for Jews in Urbino during the della Rovere era, see Veronese, "Gli ebrei nel ducato di Urbino tra cinque e seicento," 113–118.

80. Veronese, 118.

81. On the establishment of the ghetto, see Maria Luisa Moscati Benigni, "Urbino 1633: nasce il ghetto," in *La presenza ebraica nelle Marche: secoli XIII–XX*, ed. Sergio Anselmi and Viviana Bonazzoli (Ancona: Proposte e ricerche, 1993), 121–138.

82. On the flourishing of music in other Jewish communities as a possible result of forced segregation, see Adler, "The Rise of Art Music in the Italian Ghetto."

> J. DREW STEPHEN is Associate Professor of Musicology at the University of Texas at San Antonio. He is a regular participant in the cultural activities in Urbino, Italy, where he leads a study-abroad program for music students from the University of Texas at San Antonio, performs with regional music ensembles, and devotes his attention to research projects.

4

THE PERIPATETIC CAREER OF A CONVERTED JEW
The Music Theorist Pietro Aaron

BONNIE J. BLACKBURN

"We love him because of his priesthood." This is a curious remark to make in Catholic Italy in 1516. It is one of a trail of hints that suggest the reason for the unusual career of the Florentine music theorist Pietro Aaron (ca. 1480–after 1545). The hypothesis that he was of Jewish origin, proposed in 1991, can now be confirmed with near certainty. No contemporary source known so far, however, alludes to Aaron as Jewish; perhaps it was obvious from his name. As I will show in this chapter, Aaron's early education and his peripatetic career were shaped in significant ways by his status as a convert from Judaism to Christianity.

All we know about Aaron's early life is what he himself tells us. He took great pride in being a native of Florence, as he states on the title pages of all his treatises; moreover, he gave his second treatise the title *Thoscanello de la musica di Messer Pietro Aaron fiorentino canonico da Rimini* (Venice, 1523) "in grateful homage to my homeland and place of birth."[1] In his dedication to the Venetian patrician Sebastiano Michiel, the grand prior of the Knights of Saint John of Jerusalem in Venice, Aaron explains the desire of many gifted people of his time to seek the patronage of princes to further their studies. Since Pope Leo X greatly favored music (and was himself Florentine), Aaron put himself forth as one among the many who sought to receive his patronage, for "having been one who was born in tenuous circumstances, and seeking an honest way to support my lowly status in the study of music, I exerted not a little effort, if not so happily as I would have wished, at least as much as my ingenuity and efforts made possible."[2] But the unfortunate death of the pope in 1521 dashed his hopes. Thus he is grateful to Michiel for rewarding his efforts by accepting the dedication of the *Thoscanello*. Perhaps Aaron had originally intended to dedicate his book to Leo X; he was probably jealous of his contemporary, the Florentine music theorist Pier Maria Bonini, who dedicated his *Acutissime observationes nobilissime disciplinarum omnium musices* to Pope Leo X in 1520.

Unlike many music theorists and composers, Aaron never mentions with whom he studied. A single incidental remark in his first treatise, *Libri tres de institutione harmonica*, published in Bologna in 1516, reveals those whose modern style in composition he imitated: Josquin, Obrecht, Isaac, and Agricola, "with whom," he says, "I had the greatest friendship and familiarity in Florence."[3] When could that have been? Alexander Agricola was in Florence from September 1491 to June 1492 and Henricus Isaac from July 1485 to approximately 1495, returning in the second decade of the sixteenth century. Both were singers at the cathedral and at SS. Annunziata. There is no record of either Jacob Obrecht or Josquin des Prez in Florence, but each could have passed through on his way to Rome from Ferrara and Milan, respectively. Since there were many northern singers in Florence, both would have found congenial company there and perhaps former colleagues. The most likely time for Aaron to have met these composers was before March 1493, when the two chapels were dissolved at the time of the increasing influence of Girolamo Savonarola; the Medici were forced to flee Florence in 1494.

It is unlikely that Aaron studied formally with any of these composers; rather, he admired their music and learned from it. For a young music lover growing up in Florence, the rich tradition of music not only at these two chapels but also at the Medici court under Lorenzo de' Medici would have made a great impression, especially if Aaron was not from a Christian family and had not experienced Catholic ritual from a young age. Thus he would have missed the first step on the ladder to becoming a professional musician: singing as a choirboy in a church or cathedral, which would have included formal instruction in music and grammar, ensuring knowledge of Latin. From there, the normal progression, as we can document in the lives of most composers, would have been to adult singer (perhaps with university education intervening, especially in the north), then maestro di cappella, and, for those so inclined, composer or author of treatises on music. Aaron evidently missed out all the preliminary stages, but he reached the top of the profession as the author of four well-regarded publications, an exceptional accomplishment in the first half of the sixteenth century; the *Toscanello* alone went through no fewer than four editions, from 1523 to 1562.[4] He published only one composition, the frottola "Io non posso più durare," in a volume published by Ottaviano Petrucci, *Frottole libro quinto* (Venice, 1505), under the name Aron. However, we know from his correspondence that he composed masses, motets, and madrigals; none have survived.

Judging from his early treatises, Aaron's musical education was spotty; it seems he was self-taught. From that point of view, the *Toscanello* lays out the rudiments of music for beginners in a logical and straightforward way. Written in Italian, it would have appealed to those who could not afford a teacher. Aaron is in fact to be their teacher: the woodcut shows him *in cathedra*, surrounded by young and old men, with two books (one surely of theory, the other of practical music), a lute, a recorder, and a lira da braccio on a table before him (see fig. 4.1). The pose implies a much more formal position than he held; he was certainly not a university professor.[5] As befits a manual of instruction, the first book of the treatise, after the obligatory praise of music and its inventors, covers musical notation; the second book is dedicated to the intervals, the chromatic and enharmonic genera, and precepts on composition, closing with a description of proportions and their practical use in composition, with the relevant mensuration signs, and finally proportionality, which, as purely mathematical, is rather superfluous in the context of a practical treatise, but Aaron evidently did not feel he could leave it out. The final two chapters take up a demonstration of the division of the monochord, the one-string instrument used to demonstrate intervals by stopping the string at certain points, and the method of tuning the organ. Up to this point, there are few differences between the 1523 and 1529 editions. The later edition then continues with a ten-folio supplement, "Aggiunta del Toscanello a complacenza de gli amici fatta" (Addition to the *Toscanello* made to satisfy his friends). Here Aaron takes up questions that he had not anticipated earlier and that require more extended comment: his friends must have asked him about these problems. A pressing question was the use of the sharp and flat signs, since the pitches were often expected to be raised or lowered without being so indicated (for example, from F-natural to F-sharp at a cadence; the practice is commonly called *musica ficta*, "feigned

FIGURE 4.1.

Pietro Aaron as teacher in the *Toscanello in musica* (Venice: Bernardino & Matheo de Vitali, 1529). Photo: author.

music"). Here Aaron shows how thoroughly he had studied the publications of Ottaviano Petrucci, for he refers to specific pieces and even includes music examples.[6] Then Aaron turns to a topic he had not discussed earlier and was to ignore thereafter: the plainchant intonations (with music examples) of the Ordinary of the Mass and the Te Deum and their tones, with reference to other chants. By the time Aaron had completed the 1529 edition, he had been in an ecclesiastical environment for at least fifteen years and now was in a position to discuss the choices clerics had to make in singing plainchant.

Between Aaron's youth in Florence and the publication of his first book in 1516, his life is a total blank. The prefatory material to this volume, however, is informative about his situation at that time and hints at problems he had encountered in trying to make a living as a musician. Unusually, on the title page, the book is billed as a joint publication: *Libri tres de institutione harmonica editi a Petro Aaron florentino interprete Io. Antonio Flam. Forocornelite.* The *interpres*, the translator, was the humanist Giovanni Antonio Flaminio, then living in Imola, and he played a much larger part in this production than one might assume, including arranging for the publication in Bologna; he fully deserves, as will become clear, to have his name on the title page. Aaron acknowledges the eloquence of Flaminio's Latin style in the book's dedication to the *cavaliere* Girolamo San Pietro, to whom Aaron taught music and who was perhaps a patron who supported him. Divided into three books, the *Libri tres* covers the same main topics as the *Toscanello*: the Guidonian hand, mutation, the intervals, and the modes; counterpoint, again mutations, the three genera, and notation; and cadences and proportions. It suffered, however, from a lack of music examples, which his Bolognese publisher, Benedetto di Ettore, was not able to provide.[7]

In addition to translating the *Libri tres*, Flaminio provided a five-page preface to the work and substantial prefaces to all three books, cast in the form of a dialogue between himself and Aaron. In a charming and personal way, Flaminio explains how the *Libri tres* came about. At the time of publication in 1516, Aaron was a priest in Imola and evidently had been there for some time, since Flaminio speaks of their long acquaintance. Aaron had seen a copy of Flaminio's recently published book of poetry (*Sylvarum libri II*, of 1515), and he admitted his envy. Flaminio asked Aaron why he didn't bring out his own work, which was already completed. But Aaron had held back because his Latin, as he confessed, was inadequate, and for the circles in which he moved, the prestige of Latin was expected. Flaminio then offered to translate the work, and so it came about. This explains the high level of the Latin but also the difficulty in comprehending the text, because Flaminio was not familiar with musical terminology; on the other hand, he knew Greek, so much is added on ideas of music in ancient Greece. Flaminio's offer also pleased the illustrious community of humanists in Imola, in whose discussions Aaron participated; they all lauded this offer since they loved Aaron "because of his priesthood and virtue."[8] This is the remark that raises a red flag about Aaron's origin: there is nothing unusual about being a Catholic priest in sixteenth-century Italy or even a priest who could not competently write Latin. This comment not only suggests that Aaron had converted from Judaism (a subject on which I will present new evidence in the following pages) but also makes clear that he had become a priest.

The normal age for a person to become a priest at this time was twenty-five, though there are instances in which elevation to the priesthood occurred earlier. For Aaron, this must have been a big leap: familiarizing himself with Catholic theology and ritual, as well as learning Latin and Gregorian chant. As of now, we do not know how and when this came about. Aaron must have been older than twenty-five, however, in order to have been familiar with musicians in Florence in the early 1490s; it is assumed that he was born around 1480. He would then have been thirty-six in 1516.

Thanks to the research of nineteenth-century historians, we know something about Aaron's career in Imola.[9] In the *Libri tres*, nothing is said about Aaron's having an official position; if he did, it would surely have been stated on the title page. Thus it is unclear why he was in Imola and how he made his living, except perhaps through private patronage. By 1520, he had been hired as "Cantor" in the cathedral, San Cassiano, with the obligation of "being present at the Divine Office and occupying himself on solemn and festal days for the year beginning on 1 March of next year (1521)" (at the end of the document, it is stated that it is in fact a renewal of the previous year's contract).[10] At that time, he was living in the house of the Preposito della Volpe, as we learn from the first extant letter to him, dated March 7, 1521, from the Bolognese music theorist Giovanni Spataro, his long-standing friend and sometime adversary.[11] "Cantor" might indicate the official position of the cleric in charge of supervising the liturgy, but more likely, it is a simple singer. Aaron was designated as "Cantor Musicus" when he was hired by the city to "teach poor clerics gratis, as well as all others serving in the church" and to "conserve and augment the practice of music in the city and community of Imola," and for this, he was to be paid 60 Bolognese lire.[12] The document states that Aaron had been offered a higher salary elsewhere, and the present offer was intended to keep him in Imola. Further emoluments followed: in October 1521, he was appointed chaplain of the altar of the Assumption in the cathedral, "with the obligation to say three masses a week."[13]

Less than a year after he achieved this promotion, the first of several disasters befell Aaron. In May 1522, a ferocious battle broke out between the Guelf and Ghibelline factions in the city, causing many houses to be destroyed and eleven churches to be sacked, including Aaron's altar in San Cassiano.[14] Aaron himself was wounded.[15] On June 19, 1522, he resigned his benefice in the cathedral and shortly thereafter must have left Imola.[16] There is no indication that Aaron was targeted; he simply happens to have been mentioned in the chronicle because he had achieved some fame in the city.

In an abrupt and surprising change of career, Aaron found a new position in Venice under the protection of Sebastiano Michiel, the grand prior of the Knights of Saint John of Jerusalem in Venice, to whose sons he functioned as tutor of some sort, as we know from a letter by Spataro; perhaps he taught them music. We do not know how this arrangement came about—perhaps his friends in Imola had connections in Venice, but if so, they were not able to obtain a post for him as singer in a church, which one might have expected at this stage in Aaron's career. Aaron was in his new post by February 1523, as we know from a letter written to him by Spataro, who corresponded with him regularly until 1533, mostly on matters of mensural notation.[17] Aaron must have been content with his position, which apparently was not onerous, and he had the time to write and publish the *Toscanello*, followed by the treatise on the modes in polyphonic music in 1525 and then the augmented version of the *Toscanello* in 1529. However, he was totally dependent on the generosity of the grand prior.

Aaron's second period of employment likewise suddenly came to grief: Sebastiano Michiel died in 1534, and Aaron discovered that he had not been left the promised inheritance. What developed into a long-standing dispute between the order and Michiel's heirs stood in the way of Aaron's receiving the 50 ducats bequeathed to him, as he bitterly reported in a March 13, 1536, letter to the Venetian theorist Giovanni del Lago.[18] As Aaron was at the age of about fifty-five, it was too late to find another post, and having no means of supporting himself, he depended on friends. He was briefly in Padua in 1535, hosted by the captain Giacomo Cornaro, but his experience with patrons must have made him wary of entering into another such relationship.[19] In another abrupt change of career, in 1536, he shocked his friends by becoming a friar, entering the Order of the Crociferi (Crutched Friars) and settling in the convent of San Leonardo, near Bergamo (now within the city; only the church remains). He was quite defensive about this move, claiming in a letter to Del Lago that he was much better off than he had been with "Monsignore": not only did he have a beautiful, clean room, but he also had meals, a doctor, medicine, a barber, a boy to serve him, and twenty ducats a year for clothing, in addition to a benefice in a confraternity. Moreover, upon taking the habit, he proudly related, he was honored by the maestro di cappella of the musically famed confraternity of Santa Maria Maggiore in Bergamo, Gasparo Alberti, who came with twenty-two of his singers to sing Vespers for double choir and all the antiphons in counterpoint. After the reception, the singers performed a six-voice madrigal in his honor.[20]

Aaron continued corresponding with Del Lago, whom he had known since his arrival in Venice, until early July 1540, when his six-folio bruising critique of the latter's *Breve introduttione di musica misurata*, published in that year, put paid to their friendship.[21] Aaron was not one to mince words, and he could be shockingly frank. He faulted Del Lago for not consulting him before publication: "First that you trusted yourself alone, something certainly no one praises because no one is so wise that consultation with others on one's work is useless, whence if you had thought to send it to me first, the wound could have been healed better, which I am sure would have satisfied everyone, and because you have always esteemed yourself too highly and printed the work without consulting others—or perhaps you thought no criticism was possible."[22] No further letters by Aaron are known.

The leisure of the convent near Bergamo allowed Aaron to complete his last major treatise, *Lucidario in musica*. It was published in Venice in 1545 with a privilege from the Venetian Senate, which appears in the preliminary matter of the edition.[23] He dedicated the book to Count Fortunato Martinengo of Brescia, with whom he had spent a happy month making and discussing music in 1539, as he reported in a letter to Del Lago on October 7 of that year.[24] The *Lucidario*, structured as a series of ancient and modern opinions and their oppositions and resolutions, some of which surely arose during his conversations in Brescia,[25] continues a thread that runs through Aaron's treatises from the very beginning: the desire to uncover secrets of the art that so far had not been revealed. On the title page, he states, "Con molti altri secreti appresso, & questioni da altrui anchora non dichiarati" (with many other secrets thereof, and questions not yet considered by others). In his earliest treatise, the *Libri tres*, he proposes to reveal "many secret chambers of the art."[26] The title page of the *Trattato della natura et cognitione di tutti gli tuoni di canto figurato* promises that what he will say is new: "non da altri più scritti" (not written by any others). Only the *Toscanello* remains wedded to the essentials. The eagerness to learn, rather than being content with the conventional, must have characterized Aaron from his youth; as a Jewish convert, he had much to absorb not only about music and music theory but also about the Christian religion.

The strange trajectory of Aaron's career becomes more comprehensible in light of his conversion from Judaism. In the introduction to *A Correspondence of Renaissance Musicians*, I developed Edward Lowinsky's hypothesis of his Jewish origin, but I did not have any firm evidence. In 2012, I contacted the preeminent scholar of fifteenth- and sixteenth-century Italian Jews, Professor Michele Luzzati of the University of Pisa. He responded that Aaron might be the son of Buonaventura (or Ventura) di Aronne di Buonaventura da Este, who converted between 1493 or 1494 and approximately 1501, and possibly his son did so at the same time. To my surprise and gratitude, Luzzati sent me all the information he had collected on that family.[27] The sequence of given names is suggestive, since Ashkenazic sons were conventionally named after a deceased grandfather. Moreover, in an October 10, 1489, document, Buonaventura is called "il Fiorentino" (see subsequent discussion). What follows is based on Luzzati's notes and his references to the relevant literature.

The earliest document Luzzati discovered about the family dates from June 5, 1437, when Aronne di Buonaventura da Este, then living in Siena, named as his procurators the Jews Salomone di Manuele da Montagnana (not far from Padua and Este) and Abramo "teutonico," apparently living in Fermo, to recuperate the money owed him by the Paduan Jew Musetto di Buonaiuto, living in the Marche.[28] Four years later, on January 16, 1441,

Aronne, in an act notarized in Florence, named as his procurators a Sienese notary and two Jews, Manuele di Guglielmo da Asciano Senese and Manuele di Iochanan da Perugia. From this document, it is evident that Aronne had married Perna, daughter of the Jewish lender Dattilo di Angelo da Corneto (now Tarquinia), with the substantial dowry of 340 gold florins. The dowry was deposited in the Jewish bank in Siena owned by Jacob di Consiglio da Toscanella (today's Tuscania, in the province of Viterbo).[29] Aronne appears to have continued living in Siena, where on June 30, 1457, with his "famiglia," he was included among the Jewish beneficiaries of the "condotta" stipulated with the Comune di Siena.[30] The owner was again Jacob di Consiglio. Luzzati suggests that he was the reason for Aronne's transfer to Tuscany.

From 1458 to at least 1463, Aronne di Buonaventura da Este administered the Jewish bank in San Gimignano, whose "padrona" was Jacob di Consiglio's wife, Dolce di Daniele di Vitale da Pisa, first cousin of one of the major Jewish bankers at the time, Vitale di Isacco da Pisa. The Comune of San Gimignano accused Aronne of not respecting the terms of the "condotta," but the difficulty was overcome, probably with the intervention, in Florence, of the son of Cosimo de' Medici the elder, Giovanni, to whom Jacob had appealed.[31] In her last testament, Dolce gave a full quittance to Aronne relative to his role in the bank.[32]

After this, we lose sight of Aronne but have notice of his son, named after his grandfather, mentioned on October 10, 1489, as Ventura di Aronne da Este, called "il Fiorentino." He was named procurator by Lazzaro di Emanuele da Volterra, living in Rieti, with the task of liberating a slave, who presumably lived with the family, at Florence or Volterra.[33] On May 12, 1492, the magistrates of the Otto di Guardia and Balìa in Florence ordered that Ventura be arrested and forced to pay a debt of 12 gold florins to the Bolognese Jew Abramo di Assalonne and to appear before the magistrates to "stare ad ragione et paghare il giudicato."[34] As of September 5 of that year, the debt had not been paid, though the Otto di Guardia prohibited Abramo from pursuing the case against "Buonaventura di Aronne, detto Ventura, ebreo fiorentino" (Buonaventura di Aronne, called Ventura, a Florentine Jew).[35] Finally, on October 24, 1492, Buonaventura or his guarantor, Buonaventura di Emanuele da Volterra,[36] was ordered to pay Abramo 17½ florins plus 8 florins for the expenses of the proceedings.[37]

It is very likely, Luzzati believes, that Buonaventura di Aronne da Este is identical with the Giovanni Battista, son of the late Aronne da Este, "olim"

Jew and now a Christian, mentioned in a Ferrarese document of February 11, 1502, a witness statement by Simone di Noé da Norcia, or Norsa. According to Simone, nine years earlier (thus in 1493), Buonaventura, then still a Jew, had arranged the marriage, which eventually took place in 1501, of Bellafiore, stepdaughter of Manuele di Isacco da Fano, and Jacob, son of Buonaventura di Emanuele da Volterra, who, as mentioned previously, in 1492 was a guarantor of Buonaventura da Este.[38] It was probably thanks to this statement that in Florence on April 27, 1502, the decision was made and then ratified on April 29 to resolve the quarrel between Emanuele di Buonaventura di Emanuele da Volterra and Giovanni Battista, "olim hebreus, hodie vero christianus" (formerly a Jew, now, however, a Christian), son of the late Aronne di Buonaventura da Este.

Before the arrival of Charles VIII in Italy, and therefore before autumn 1494, Giovanni Battista was "sensalis et mezanus" (marriage broker) between Buonaventura di Manuele da Volterra, on behalf of his son Jacob, and Dolce, on behalf of her daughter Bellafiore, born around 1480 from her previous marriage to Abramo di Davide dei Galli da Tortona. Since the marriage had now been celebrated and consummated, Giovanni Battista requested that he be paid the "senseria" (his fee) by Buonaventura di Emanuele da Volterra, as was approved by the judges.[39]

A few months later, on August 3, 1502, Giovan Battista del fu Aronne da Este, now living in Siena, received the proxy from Emanuele di fu Angelo da Volterra left him by Anna di Vitale di Isacco da Pisa, widow of Lazzaro di Emanuele da Volterra.[40] Buonaventura alias Giovanni Battista was thus related to the principal Jewish families, predominantly bankers, active in Tuscany in the fifteenth century.[41]

Bellafiore was about the same age as Pietro Aaron, and after her mother, Dolce or Dolcetta, having been widowed, married the banker Vitale di Isacco da Pisa, they lived in Pisa and Florence. Dolce, widowed again in 1490, then married Manuele di Isacco da Fano; he was guardian of Bellafiore at the time when Buonaventura di Aronne arranged her marriage. The family, including Vitale's two sons, subsequently moved to Bologna, and they paid part of her dowry to Emanuele di Buonaventura da Volterra (250 gold ducats) in 1501.[42]

According to Luzzati, the continuing relationships between the converted Buonaventura and the Jewish community did not entail particular tensions, especially during a period of great uncertainty for the status of the Jewish community in the Florentine state.[43] Curiously, by the time of the judgment in favor of payment to Giovanni Battista olim Buonaventura of his marriage broker fee, Bellafiore's marriage had become invalid because of the recent conversion of her husband Jacob; she declined to convert.[44]

Aaron's name at birth was surely the Hebrew Aharon, that of his grandfather Aronne. For civil purposes, it was necessary to have a Christian name, which was usually related to the Hebrew name in some way.[45] The biblical Aaron, the brother of Moses, was the first high priest of the Jews. I hypothesized that the name Pietro was chosen for Aaron at an early age, even before conversion, because it was the name of the Christian equivalent, the first pope, Peter. He probably retained the name Aaron because Jews, in common with many nonnoble Italians, did not have surnames. Some Jews took the Christian names of their sponsors in baptism; in Aaron's case, this is unknown.

Aaron would have grown up in the Florence of Lorenzo de' Medici in an atmosphere that was largely benevolent toward Jews.[46] Lorenzo, however, had to contend periodically with the hatred spread by the friars. In 1488, Fra Bernardino da Feltre, in his Lenten sermons in Florence, urged the expulsion of the Jews and the setting up of a *monte di pietà*, which would obviate the need for Jewish moneylenders. Lorenzo had to call out the soldiers to quell the antisemitic mob. After Lorenzo's death, the situation changed for the worse. In March 1493, the Otto di Guardia decided to expel the "ebrei forestieri"—that is, those Jews who were not Florentine natives. In 1496, a proclamation was issued forbidding Jews to lend money, and they were given one year to leave Florence. The decree was suspended, however, until all the money owed to the bankers was repaid, which did not happen until 1508. This was a period of great uncertainty for Jews, and it is not surprising that many left the city and some converted.[47]

Conversion was promoted by Christians. Marino Sanuto's Venetian diary relates a number of conversion ceremonies, sponsored by the doge and other patricians, in San Marco and in other Venetian churches. The ceremony could be quite grand for rich Jews.[48] In Ferrara, too, Ercole d'Este and his wife, Eleonora, sometimes acted as godparents for Jewish converts—for example, on Sunday, October 9, 1491: "There were baptized on a large tribunal in the cathedral two male Jews, father and son, and a beautiful Jewish woman, in the presence of the most illustrious duchess our lady Eleonora with her sons and all the court."[49] This was too early, however, to think that it might be Buonaventura and Aaron.

If Aaron had not converted, whether because his father did or it was at his own initiative, what possibilities were there in the fifteenth century for a Jew with musical interests? The main examples that spring to mind are the Jewish dancing masters, indispensable for dancing on grand occasions in the noble courts. The best-known example is Guglielmo Ebreo da Pesaro, author of *De pratica seu arte tripudii*.[50] His autobiography recounts his professional life from the wedding in Ferrara in 1444 of the marquis Leonello d'Este to Maria, daughter of King Alfonso of Aragon, through many other noble weddings and social events, to a joust in Naples 1474.[51] His brother, Giuseppe, likewise a dancing master, signed a contract in Florence in May 1467 with a Christian establishing a partnership in which they would teach dancing, singing, and instrumental music. Two years later, Giuseppe was in the employ of Lorenzo de' Medici, by which time his brother, Guglielmo, had converted (before 1465), taking the name Giovanni Ambrosio, and urged Giuseppe to convert. Guglielmo reached illustrious heights, being made a Knight of the Golden Spur by the Holy Roman emperor Frederick III in Venice in 1469.[52]

The other famous Florentine musician who was a Jewish convert was Giovan Maria Hebreo, or Johannes Maria de Medicis, a lutenist at the court of Leo X, who became count of Verucchio. In his earlier life in Florence, but after conversion, he was notorious for having killed a man in a brawl in 1492, for which reason he entered the court records. He fled the city before being condemned and disappears from the records until 1510,[53] when he surfaces as a lutenist at the court of Urbino; he then moved to the service of Cardinal Giovanni de' Medici, who later became Pope Leo X. He is first called *de Medicis* in Rome in 1516. His life, too, fell apart when his patron Leo X died, though he remained in Rome, forming part of a quartet of lute players.[54] It is claimed that he committed suicide.[55]

Finding employment as a converted Jew seems not to have been difficult for practical musicians. Their current or former religion would have made no difference. The same was not true for a musically talented Jew who wanted to become a teacher of music theory and a scholar. This was clearly Aaron's overriding ambition, and he must have cast about for a way to achieve it. First, he had to acquire the skills he had missed in his youth: knowledge of Latin, facility in composition, and familiarity with music theory. He probably took as his models the church musicians he had known in Florence, seeing how easily the talented ones could move from one position to another.

I do not know how he was able to acquire this education, but judging from his early treatises, we know that he studied on his own and learned by talking with singers and listening to performances in church. Not all church musicians were priests, though that qualification led to the possibility of extra income through benefices. There was much that Aaron had to learn before he could be promoted to the priesthood, and he had to find a bishop to achieve his elevation. We have no idea when and where this happened. His motivation for such a move appears to have been purely personal, not a wish to prove that Jews could equally contribute to a society dominated by Christians. Whatever influence he felt from his Jewish background he kept to himself; none of his acquaintances ever refer to it.

As difficult as Pietro Aaron's career was, in the end, he achieved his dearest wish, recognition by his contemporaries. The *Lucidario* includes on the first page a woodcut medallion of his head, crowned with laurel and with the superscription "Virga Aron refloruit" (Aaron's rod will flower again), an allusion to the flowering of the rod of Aaron in Numbers 17:23: "Behold, the rod of Aaron for the house of Levi was budded, and put forth buds, and bloomed blossoms, and bore ripe almonds."[56] That verse might have been chosen only because of his name, but it perhaps hints at his Jewish origin. It was, however, uncannily fitting for Aaron's career, which did indeed blossom. Today he is remembered as one of the major theorists of the first half of the sixteenth century. Underneath the inscription is a poem by the Mantuan poet Niccolò d'Arco, who was Fortunato Martinengo's son-in-law and a friend of Giovanni Antonio Flaminio's son Marc'Antonio. Aaron may have met him in Brescia in 1539. It accurately anticipates Aaron's fame:

> NICOLAI COMITIS ARCITENENTIS EXASTICHON IN P. ARON LAVDES
> Vivat Aron, saeclo sua virgo refloreat omni,
>   Per quem, obscura olim, Musica nunc rutilat.
> Ergo digna feret tantorum dona laborum:
>   Praemia quis tanto digna neget capiti?
> Vos vivum, vates, statua et decorate corona:
>   Post obitum sidus, dii, facite esse novem.
>
> Long live Aaron; may his rod reblossom in every generation;
>   Through whom Music, once obscure, now shines.
> Thus shall he receive gifts worthy of such great labours:
>   For who would deny fitting rewards to so great a man?
> In life, you poets, honour him with statue and laurel wreath;
>   After death, o gods, fashion of him a new constellation.[57]

NOTES

1. "Il nostro Toscanello, che così ho voluto fargli il titolo in gratia de la terra patria et nativa," book 1, chap. 6. A second edition was published in 1529 with the slightly different title: *Toscanello in musica di Messer Piero Aron fiorentino del ordine Hierosolimitano et canonico in Rimini* (Venice: Bernardino & Matheo de Vitali, 1529; repr. with preface by Willem Elders, Bologna: Forni, 1969). On Aaron's life and works, see Ed Peter Bergquist, "The Theoretical Writings of Pietro Aaron" (PhD diss., Columbia University, 1964), and, with additional documentation, Bonnie J. Blackburn, Edward E. Lowinsky, and Clement A. Miller, eds., *A Correspondence of Renaissance Musicians* (Oxford: Clarendon, 1991), especially chap. 4. This publication includes all his extant letters and letters written to him. I have considered Aaron's theoretical writings in several articles; in this essay, I concentrate on his personal life and professional life.

2. *Thoscanello de la musica*, dedication: "Io sono stato uno, il quale in tenue fortuna nato ricercando per alcuna honesta via di sostentare la mia tenuità negli studii di Musica mi sono non poco affaticato, se non così felicemente, come harrei uoluto, almeno quanto l'ingegno, et la industria mia ha potuto." The dedication remained the same in the 1529 edition, except that the remark on the lamentable death of Leo X is omitted. It is difficult to be sure of the meaning Aaron attaches to *tenuità*. He had just used the word *tenue* to describe the circumstances of his early life, and must mean something like "fragility," but it is probably a trope of modesty; it appears that he does not have the means on his own to study to improve his knowledge.

3. He remarks that the modern style of composition, rather than writing one voice after another, is to take all four voices into account when composing, "quod nos quoque crebro facimus: summos in arte viros imitati praecipuae [sic] vero Iosquinum. Obret. Isaac. et Agricolam: quibus cum mihi Florentiae familiaritas: et consuetudo summa fuit"; *Libri tres de institutione harmonica editi a Petro Aaron florentino interprete Io. Antonio Flam. Forocornelite* (Bologna: Benedetto di Ettore, 1516; facs. ed. New York: Broude Brothers, 1976), fol. 39v.

4. Aaron's second treatise was the *Trattato della natura et cognitione di tutti gli tuoni di canto figurato* (Venice: Bernardino de Vitali, 1525; repr. Utrecht: Joachimsthal, 1966, with a preface by Willem Elders). He again emphasizes his identity as "musico fiorentino" (Florentine musician) but now specifies his occupation as "maestro di casa del reverendo et magnifico cavaliere hierosolimitano messer Sebastiano Michele, priore di Vinetia" (master of the household of the reverend and magnificent Knight of Saint John of Jerusalem, *messer* Sebastiano Michele, prior of Venice). The last treatise is the less didactic *Lucidario in musica di alcune oppenioni antiche, et moderne con le loro Oppositioni, & Resolutioni ... dall'eccellente, & consumato Musico Pietro Aron del Ordine de Crosachieri, & della città di Firenze* (Venice: Girolamo Scotto, 1545; facs. ed. Bologna: Editrice Forni, 1969). A further treatise was published under Aaron's name by the Milanese publisher Giovanni Antonio Castiglione (repr. Bologna: Editrice Forni, 1970). It is undated (1550 is estimated), and the title suggests that it was posthumous: *Compendiolo di molti dubbi, segreti et sentenze intorno al canto fermo, et figurato, da molti eccellenti & consumati Musici dichiarate, Raccolte dallo Eccellente & scienzato Autore frate Pietro Aron del ordine de Crosachieri & della Inclita Città di Firenze*. The printer's mark is followed by the epigram "In memoria ęterna erit Aron, Et nomen eius nunquam destruetur" (Aaron will be remembered in eternity, and his name will never be destroyed). The last sentence in the treatise (which has no colophon) reads, "Et se nell'avenire altro di me, non si vedrà, senza Disdegno tuo, farò il fine. Vale" (And if in the future nothing more will be seen of me, without your disdain, I shall end). I am inclined to believe that the book

was put together by his friends from material left in his study after he died. It is relatively short and quite elementary. It cannot date before 1549, when the dedicatee, Monsignor Traiano da San Celso, Traiano Alicorni, became connected with the abbey of San Celso in Milan (Bergquist, "The Theoretical Writings," 43). The dedication is probably by the publisher.

5. The same woodcut reappears in all editions of the *Toscanello* and the treatise on the modes.

6. On this part of the treatise, see Margaret Bent, "Accidentals, Counterpoint, and Notation in Aaron's *Aggiunta* to the *Toscanello*," *Journal of Musicology* 12 (1994): 306–344. On Aaron's engagement with Petrucci's editions, see Cristle Collins Judd, *Reading Renaissance Music Theory: Hearing with the Eyes*, Cambridge Studies in Music Theory and Analysis (Cambridge: Cambridge University Press, 2000), chap. 3.

7. On the intemperate reaction to this book by the Milanese theorist Franchino Gaffurio, see Bonnie J. Blackburn, "Publishing Music Theory in Early Cinquecento Venice and Bologna: Friends and Foes," in *Music in Print and Beyond: Hildegard von Bingen to the Beatles*, ed. Craig A. Monson and Roberta Montemorra Marvin, Eastman Studies in Music (Rochester, NY: Rochester University Press, 2013), 37–40.

8. "Docti viri qui te simul amant & ob sacerdotium ac virtutem colunt" (learned men who both love you and admire you because of your priesthood and virtue), *Libri tres de institutione harmonica*, fol. 5v.

9. I initially found the documentation among the papers of the librarian Gaetano Gaspari (d. 1881) in the then Civico Museo Bibliografico Musicale in Bologna, now the Museo Internazionale e Biblioteca della Musica di Bologna. They had been copied by Gaspari's friend Antonio Gabriele Zardi from notarial acts in Imola. I republished them in *A Correspondence of Renaissance Musicians*, 96–100, and subsequently have been able to check most of them against the originals in Imola.

10. "Promisit in Choro divinis interesse et cantu se occupare diebus solemnibus et festivis per annum incipiendum in Kalendis Martii proxime futuris . . . intelligatur perserverare eo modo et forma quo anno tunc preterito" (the document is dated February 15, 1521).

11. Blackburn, Lowinsky, and Miller, *A Correspondence of Renaissance Musicians*, letter 4.

12. "Dictus Cantor teneatur et obligatus docere gratis clericos pauperes, nec non omnes alios sotios et servientes ipsi Capellę . . . pro virtute dicti Cantus musices conservandi, et augendi in ipsa Civitate, quoniam est decoris et honoris dictę Civitati et comunitati Imolę," Blackburn, Lowinsky, and Miller, 98–99 (I did not find the unnamed and undated source of this document in Imola). Such an arrangement was not uncommon in smaller Italian cities.

13. "Cum onere trium missarum pro qualibet hebdomada," Blackburn, Lowinsky, and Miller, 99.

14. Sanzio Bombardini, *Il diavolo nel tamburo: Lotte e tragedie nella storia di una città romagnola e nel diario di un guelfo imolese (1500–1525)* (Bologna: University Press, 1982), 43.

15. Grazia Agostini and Claudia Pedrini, eds., *Innocenzo da Imola: Il tirocinio di un artista* (Imola: Trafis, 1993), 42n38, exhibition catalogue.

16. On his resignation, see Blackburn, Lowinsky, and Miller, *A Correspondence of Renaissance Musicians*, 99–100.

17. Blackburn, Lowinsky, and Miller, letter 5. Unfortunately, all of Aaron's letters to Spataro are lost, though one can discern their main contents from Spataro's replies.

18. Blackburn, Lowinsky, and Miller, letter 62.

19. On his stay in Padua, see Blackburn, Lowinsky, and Miller, letter 61.

20. Blackburn, Lowinsky, and Miller, letter 62. Unfortunately, the madrigal appears not to have survived.

21. *Breve introduttione di musica misurata, composta per il venerabile Pre Giovanni del Lago Venetiano: scritta al Magnifico Lorenzo Moresino patricio Venetiano patron suo honorendissimo* [sic] (Venice: Brandino and Ottaviano Scotto, 1540; facs. ed. Bologna: Forni Editrice, 1969). Much of the short treatise (43 pages) is based on his correspondence with Spataro and Aaron and other theorists. On this, see Blackburn, Lowinsky, and Miller, *A Correspondence of Renaissance Musicians*, 135–142.

22. "Primo che di voi solo vi siate confidato, cosa non certo da nessun laudata, perché non è sì sapiente che ad altri non conferisca le fatiche sue, onde se a me prima vi confidavi mandarle, più rettamente si sanava la piaga, la qual mi rendo certo satisfaceva a tutti, et perché voi sempre troppo vi siate reputato, senza altro parere l'opera havete impressa, et perché forse a voi è parso non si potere opponergli," Blackburn, Lowinsky, and Miller, *A Correspondence of Renaissance Musicians*, letter 66, 728. Interestingly, Aaron himself received much the same reaction from Spataro when he published his *Trattato della natura et cognitione di tutti gli tuoni* in 1525. In a letter to Del Lago on August 23, 1529, Spataro says that Aaron sent him the manuscript before publication but then ignored his two-hundred-page critique and his attempt to persuade Aaron to withdraw it from publication (letter 27). In the *Trattato*, Aaron mentions Del Lago a number of times but not Spataro. (And in the *Lucidario*, he mentions Spataro but not Del Lago.)

23. Both editions of the *Toscanello* carry the words *Con privilegio* (with privilege) on the title page, and in the *Trattato* following the colophon, but do not include a transcription. The privilege for the 1523 *Toscanello* is one of the few noted by the Venetian diarist Marino Sanuto: "Fu posto, per li Consieri, concieder una gratia a domino Piero Aron musicho far stampar una opera sua ditta el *Toschanello*" (it was proposed, by the Councillors, to grant a favor to don Pietro Aaron, musician, to have his work entitled *Toschanello* printed). The proposal was passed with 154 votes in favor, 8 against. Marino Sanuto, *I diarii di Marino Sanuto*, ed. Rinaldo Fulin et al., vol. 34 (Venice: F. Visentini, 1892), col. 287. The *Libri tres* and the *Compendiolo* were not eligible for a Venetian or papal privilege.

24. Blackburn, Lowinsky, and Miller, *A Correspondence of Renaissance Musicians*, letter 64. Still defensive about becoming a friar and the status that implied for his friends, he boasts that Count Martinengo treated him like a brother and sent him back to Bergamo on a noble steed, inviting him to return for Carnival.

25. On Fortunato's interest in music and his circle, see Bonnie J. Blackburn, "Cipriano de Rore's Early Italian Years: The Brescian Connection," in *Cipriano de Rore: New Perspectives on His Life and Music*, ed. Jessie Ann Owens and Katelijne Schiltz (Turnhout: Brepols, 2016), 29–74, and Bonnie J. Blackburn, "Fortunato Martinengo and His Musical Tour around Lake Garda: The Place of Music and Poetry in Silvan Cattaneo's *Dodici giornate*," in *Fortunato Martinengo: Un gentiluomo del Rinascimento fra arti, lettere e musica*, ed. Elisabetta Selmi and Marco Bizzarini, Annali di Storia Bresciana (Brescia: Morcelliana, 2018), 181–211.

26. "Plurima ex intimis artis penetralibus quae a nullo ad hunc vulgata fuissent," *Libri tres de institutione harmonica*, fol. 7r.

27. The world of Jewish studies suffered a great loss at his death in 2014, but his extraordinary generosity, shared in an email on July 25, 2012, has made it possible for me to make a more cogent case for Aaron's origins.

28. Archivio di Stato di Siena, Notarile Antecosimiano, no. 361, 1436–1439, ser Cristoforo Marri, fols. 35v–36. I have not checked the primary sources Luzzati cites but include them here as a record.

29. Archivio di Stato di Firenze (hereafter ASFi), Notarile Antecosimiano, no. 17996, *olim* R 189, 1440–1442/1443, ser Verdiano Rimbotti, fol. 36v.

30. Sofia Boesch Cajano, "Il Comune di Siena e il prestito ebraico nei secoli XIV e XV: Fonti e problemi," in *Aspetti e problemi della presenza ebraica nell'Italia centro-settentrionale (secoli XIV e XV)*, Quaderni 2 (Rome: Istituto di Scienze Storiche dell'Università di Roma, 1983), 216 and 221.

31. Maria Emilia Garruto, "Ebrei in Valdelsa nel Quattrocento: Una storia di famiglia (I Poggibonsi)" (doctoral thesis, Università degli Studi di Pisa, Dottorato in Storia, ciclo XVI, 2001–2003), 55, 63, 65–67, 72–72, 75–77, and 82.

32. ASFi, Notarile Antecosimiano, no. 10198, olim G 619, 1456–1496, ser Simone di Jacopo Grazzini da Staggia, fols. 70r–71.

33. Vincenzo Di Flavio and Alessandro Papò, *Res publica hebreorum de Reate* (Rieti: Comune di Rieti, 2000), 170.

34. ASFi, Otto di Guardia e Balìa della Repubblica, no. 92, fol. 70r.

35. ASFi, fol. 80r.

36. This Buonaventura undertook a voyage to Israel in 1481, of which he left a diary in Hebrew. It has been translated by Alessandra Veronese and published as Mešullam da Volterra, *Viaggio in Terra d'Israele* (Rimini: Luisè, 1989).

37. ASFi, Otto di Guardia e Balìa della Repubblica, no. 92, fol. 124rv.

38. Archivio di Stato di Ferrara, Antichi Notai, matr. 283, ser Bartolomeo Codegori, pacco 21, 1502–1503, under February 11, 1502.

39. ASFi, Notarile Antecosiminiano, no. 16838, olim P 356, 1499–1502, ser Piero di Antonio da Vinci, fols. 386v–388v. See also Alessandra Veronese, *Una famiglia di banchieri ebrei tra XIV e XVI secolo: I da Volterra. Reti di credito nell'Italia del Rinascimento* (Pisa: Edizioni ETS, 1998), 51–52 and 219, though, Luzzati remarks, she confused Bellafiore's husband with his father.

40. Veronese, *Una famiglia*, 219.

41. Luzzati gives more details of family relationships, which I omit here.

42. Archivio di Stato di Bologna, Rogiti del notaio Melchiorre Zanetti, busta III, 1499–1508, August 22, 1503, cited in Michele Luzzati, *La casa dell'ebreo: Saggi sugli ebrei a Pisa e in Toscana nel Medioevo e nel Rinascimento* (Pisa: Nistri Lischi, 1985), 248.

43. See Michele Luzzati, "Una 'condotta' con divieto di prestito e con scadenza *sine die*: Gli Alpilinc e altri sefarditi nello Stato fiorentino agli inizi del Cinquecento," in *Studi sul mondo sefardita in memoria de Aron Leoni*, ed. Pier Cesare Joly Zorattini, Michele Luzzati, and Michele Sarfatti (Florence: Leo S. Olschki, 2012), 13–21.

44. Veronese, *Una famiglia*, 219–20.

45. See Umberto Cassuto, *Gli ebrei a Firenze nell'età del Rinascimento* (Florence: Galletti e Cocci, 1918), 233–235.

46. The following account is based on Cassuto, *Gli ebrei a Firenze*, 51–81, and Cecil Roth, *The History of the Jews of Italy* (Philadelphia: Jewish Publication Society of America, 1946; repr. Farnborough: Gregg International, 1969), 166–190.

47. On this period, see Jean-Marc Rivière, "Les Juifs florentins dans l'espace politique republicain (1494–1496)," in *Ebrei migranti: Le voci della diaspora*, ed. Raniero Speelman, Monica Jansen, and Silvia Gaiga, Italistica Ultraiectina 7 (Utrecht: Igitur, 2012), 14–30.

48. For example, on August 24, 1521, Sanuto reports the baptism in San Marco of a fifteen-year-old Jew, David, grandson of Cervo di Verona, who received the name Constantin Marco. Among his godparents was Marco Grimani, nephew of the doge, and twenty gentlemen, who gave a ducat each. Then a collection was taken in the church, which netted 51 ducats.

Sanuto remarks that nevertheless he was rich and was moved by the Holy Spirit to be baptized and would stay with the prior of San Giovanni del Tempio. This is Sebastiano Michiel, Aaron's patron, and shows that Michiel was hospitable to converted Jews. Sanuto, *Diarii*, vol. 31, col. 291.

49. "A dì 9 [Oct. 1491], de domenega. Se baptizòno suxo uno tribunale grande in domo, a l'intrare del choro, dui Zudei maschi, padri e fioli, e una Zudea bella, in presentia de la illustrissima duchessa nostra madona Eleonora con li soi fioli e con tuta la Corte," Bernardo Zambotti, *Diario ferrarese dall'anno 1476 sino al 1504*, ed. Giuseppe Pardi, Rerum italicarum scriptores XXIV, parte VII (Bologna: Nicola Zanichelli, 1934), 223.

50. For his treatise and biography, see Guglielmo Ebreo da Pesaro, *De pratica seu arte tripudii: On the Practice or Art of Dancing*, ed. and trans. Barbara Sparti (Oxford: Clarendon, 1993).

51. Ebreo da Pesaro, 248–254.

52. Sparti, "Guglielmo's Life," in Ebreo da Pesaro, *De pratica seu arte tripudii*, 33–34. Other Jewish dancing masters are discussed in Barbara Sparti, "Jewish Dancing-Masters and 'Jewish Dance' in Renaissance Italy: Guglielmo Ebreo and Beyond," in *Seeing Israeli and Jewish Dance*, ed. Judith Brin Ingber (Detroit: Wayne State University Press, 2011), 235–250. For more on Guglielmo Ebreo da Pesaro, see J. Drew Stephen's contribution to the present volume.

53. Though he is likely to be the "Giovanni Maria Alemagna musico" and "Giovanni Maria Zudeo sonador," among the musicians who served Cardinal Ippolito I d'Este in Ferrara in 1503 and 1506–1507. See Lewis Lockwood, "Adrian Willaert and Cardinal Ippolito I d'Este: New Light on Willaert's Early Career in Italy, 1515–21," *Early Music History* 5 (1985): 111.

54. On him, see H. Colin Slim, "Some Fifteenth- and Sixteenth-Century Namesakes," *Musical Quarterly* 57 (1971): 562–574.

55. Domenico Gnoli, *La Roma di Leon X* (Milan: Hoepli, 1938), 335. No source is given.

56. I am grateful to Rebecca Cypess for reminding me of this passage.

57. The poem is taken from an eighteenth-century edition of Niccolò d'Arco's verse, *Hieronymi Fracastorii Veronensis, Adami Fumani canonici Veronensis, et Nicolai Archii comitis Carminum editio II*, 2 vols. (Padua: Giuseppe Comino, 1739), 2:240, printed in Blackburn, Lowinsky, and Miller, *A Correspondence of Renaissance Musicians*, 92, with translation. In the *Lucidario*, line 3 reads, "Ergo pulchra ferat." (In the Bologna 1969 facsimile, the preliminary pages are out of order; the title page is page 3 in the original.) For another poem to Aaron, by the Bolognese humanist Achille Bocchi, a member of the humanist circle in Imola, see Blackburn, Lowinsky, and Miller, *A Correspondence of Renaissance Musicians*, 93–94.

BONNIE J. BLACKBURN is an Oxford-based musicologist and editor who specializes in music and music theory of the fifteenth and sixteenth centuries, with a particular interest in compositional process, early printing, notation, and canons. She is editor (with Edward E. Lowinsky and Clement A. Miller) of *A Correspondence of Renaissance Musicians*, which includes many letters to and from the music theorist Pietro Aaron.

5

A Fire, a Fight, and a Knight
Elye Bokher in Verse and Song

AVERY GOSFIELD

Elye Bokher (1468 or 1469–1549), also known as Eliyahu ben Asher HaLevi Ashkenazi, Elia Bachur Levita, or Elijah Levita, was one of the most highly regarded Hebrew scholars of his era, as well as a poet. Although he clearly wrote other works, only three Yiddish-language poems that can definitely be attributed to him have come down to us. The earliest is the chivalric poem *Bovo d'Antona* (Padua, completed in 1507, published in 1541), based on an Italian model but completely transformed according to German-Jewish tastes and tenets and his own artistic vision. It was a work that would, in addition, become one of the bulwarks of Yiddish culture, surviving in prose versions into the twentieth century.[1] Transformed, it also gave birth to the Yiddish expression *Bubbe Mayses* (grandmother's tales) that is still used to describe a tall tale today.[2] The two other works are based on German-Jewish metric models (the first with some Italian influence); however, they are firmly anchored on Italian soil: *Dås lid ouf di śèrèfè ṽun Wènèdig* (*A Song about the Fire in Venice*, henceforth known as *Śèrèfè lid*, Venice, 1514) is a parody, an account of a fire on the Venetian Rialto, while *HaMaṽdil lid* (*The One Who Distinguishes*, Venice, 1514), a mocking account of a certain Hillel Cohen's wrongdoings, is clearly set in northern Italy.

For all three poems, some kind of melodic recitation-formula model has survived. The musical recitation of poetry—especially in Italy but also elsewhere throughout Europe—was a long-standing tradition that manifested itself both in folk practices and in elite, courtly performance. Standard musical formulas, often consisting of both melodies and accompanying harmonic progressions, were used to facilitate the oral performance of poetry in a wide range of social situations. Poets in Jewish communities were familiar with the recitation formulas used by their Christian neighbors, and such formulas often permeated religious boundaries, becoming embedded in Jewish communal practices. That all three of Elye Bokher's known poems survive with references to such specific recitation formulas enables us to construct a best-guess melody for the performance of each one, although from different kinds of musical data.

The aim of the present essay is to arrive at such a best guess for two of these poems, demonstrating the powerful link between song and poetry in Italian Jewish communities and in Elye Bokher's work in particular. In sources, the Śĕrēfẹ lid is described as "ain lid bénigu` Tzur mi-shelo" (a song sung to the tune of *Tzur mi-shelo*), a late-medieval *piyyut* (postbiblical poem in Hebrew) traditionally sung during Sabbath festivities. Almost miraculously, a transcription of a contemporary South German *Tzur mi-shelo 'okhalnu* (Rock from Whom [i.e., from Whose Beneficence] We Have Eaten) has survived.³ Elye Bokher's *HaMavdil lid* is also based on a sung piyyut: *Hamavdil bein qodesh le-ḥol* (The One Who Distinguishes between Sacred and Profane). Here, too, a melody has survived, albeit one dating from more than two hundred years after Elye wrote the original parody: in the third volume of Benedetto Marcello's *Estro poetico-armonico* (1724–1726), transcribed as sung by the Ashkenazic community of Venice.⁴

Although the aim of this essay is to discuss two specific cases in which actual Jewish melodic models have survived, this should be seen against the background of the widespread adoption and transformation of Italian verse forms by the Jews living on the Italian peninsula. During his lifetime, Elye Bokher played a dual role—as ambassador to the Christian intellectual world and as an influential member of the Jewish community—so it is inevitable that the dynamics between Jew and gentile in late fifteenth- and early sixteenth-century Italy shaped his poetry. In turn, the poems themselves, with their mixture of Italian, Jewish, and German traits, give important insights into the mechanics of cultural crossover during the same period.

I have already proposed a musical setting for Elye Bokher's *Bovo d'Antona* (henceforth referred to as the *Bovo Bukh*) elsewhere, so I will not include it here.⁵ However, the poem deserves to be mentioned because it is the most widely known, ambitious, and celebrated example of Elye Bokher's hybrid artistic output. Furthermore, the author's choice of subject matter, an epic poem drawn from the "Matter of France,"[6] and poetic form, the ottava rima,[7] both demonstrate the deep penetration of mainstream Italian culture into the lives of the German Jews living there. *Buovo d'Antona*, the story on which Elye Bokher's *Bovo Bukh* is based, is first found in Italy as a rhymed epic together with other poems dedicated to the Carolingian canon, one of the pillars of Italian culture, in a Franco-Venetian source from the fourteenth century, the so-called *Geste Francor*.[8] Elye's probable model comes from a later source, an Italian edition in ottava rima published in 1497 by Caligola de' Bazalieri.[9]

The ottava is considered the vehicle par excellence for communication and is used for sung improvisations and storytelling, in particular the recitation of epic poetry. Dating back to Boccaccio's time, if not earlier, it has been linked to vocal performance since its origins[10] and was used extensively by *cantastorie*.[11] Almost incredibly, it is still sung in parts of Italy today, an art form that never really died out,[12] but lives on between tradition and folk revival in central Italy.[13] Those who sing it today are roughly divided between *interpreti*—artists who perform written poetry (although usually memorized and in some cases learned orally), drawn from classic works such as the *Orlando furioso* and *Gerusalemme liberata*—and the *poeti*, capable of improvising verses.[14] With his use of ottava rima, and indications that it was to be "sung to an Italian tune," Elye Bokher seems to point toward a mode of performance modeled on Italian practices. In the search for a plausible melody and singing style for the *Bovo Bukh*, one path to follow could be that of the current experiments aimed at a reproposal of the performance of narrative verse in early modern Italy.[15] The usual point of departure is musical settings of the *strambotto*, a form in vogue from the late fifteenth to early seventeenth century that used the same rhyme scheme as the Tuscan ottava rima. As a short art song transmitted in written form, it fulfilled a function different from—and was performed in contexts different from—those of the sung narratives of the cantastorie. However, in some cases, the strambotto might have been set to melodies inspired by the oral tradition. Indeed, some even share certain characteristics with the traditional ottava rima performances of today, as well as with similar forms of folk performance, such as the *Maggio drammatico*.[16] This has led to performances based on a comparative study of both historical sources and modern orally transmitted practices.[17] Furthermore, the study of enduring traditions, such as the ottava rima and Maggio drammatico—their context and reception, as well as the aesthetics, melodies, and practices of their performers—could be valuable tools for singing narrative verse, including the *Šèrèfe lid* or the *HaMavdil lid*, today.

Elye Bokher grew up in Neustadt an der Aisch near Nuremberg[18] and moved to Italy around 1492.[19] He lived between Mestre and Venice until around 1496,[20] when, perhaps driven by the growing restrictions on Jews living in the Venice area[21] or simply attracted to the better living conditions and larger German Jewish population in Padua, Elye moved to that historical center of learning, home to several yeshivas[22] and one of the oldest and most important universities in Europe.[23] It was in Padua that he would write the *Bovo Bukh*. In 1509, a war between the Venetian Republic and the League of Cambrai saw much of the Veneto and neighboring territories overrun by their enemies. As a result, the government of the Serenissima issued a *condotta* (legal contract) allowing refugees to reside in the city, including, essentially for the first time, Jews. The government was particularly interested in admitting German Jewish bankers and moneylenders in order to protect their capital and to make sure that the poor would have access to economic relief. Elye Bokher, after losing everything he owned in Padua, and probably following on the coattails of the wealthy banker Anselmo Meshullam, also fled to the Serenissima. In Venice, he probably worked for the printer Gershon Soncino, writing commentaries on Hebrew publications and Yiddish poems, including the two lampoons mentioned previously.[24]

Around 1514, Elye left Venice, moving to Rome, where the "Pope's Jews" lived under conditions better than those in much of the rest of Italy.[25] He worked for Giles of Viterbo, who was named cardinal in 1518, living in Giles's palace for more than a decade. He taught Christian intellectuals about Hebrew, Jewish learning, and Jewish mysticism, in particular the Qabbalah. In addition to Elye being held in high regard rather than being vilified for his religious affiliation, this might have also been the only period in which he lived with any kind of economic security. This all came to an abrupt end in 1527 with the Sack of Rome. Elye again lost everything, including his entire library, which was destroyed by fire. The last decades of his life (1527–1549) were spent in the Venetian ghetto (established in 1516), except for a sojourn in Germany (1540–1541 or 1542), where he worked as a proofreader for Paul

Fagius; while in Germany, he also published a number of his works for the first time, even some that had lain in manuscript for decades, such as the *Bovo Bukh* (published 1541).[26]

At least during his lifetime, Elye Bokher was most known for his Hebrew writings, and his fame as a scholar, teacher, author, and editor went far beyond the Jewish community: he was held in the highest regard by Christian humanists from all over Europe, to the point where he was often criticized by Jews for fraternizing excessively with Christians. His works in *loshen qodesh* (Hebrew, the Holy Tongue) and *mama-loshen* (Yiddish, the Mother Tongue) differed from one another on multiple levels, in terms of subject matter, style, form, context, and target market. In addition, it would be fair to say that they also expressed different aspects of his personality. This is also the opinion of the anonymous author of the introduction to the Yiddish epic poem *Paris un Wiene* (whether the poem itself was written by Elye or one of his followers has long been a subject of disagreement among Yiddish scholars), who writes:

> Elje Beher,
> may his name live on forever and never perish:
> these are the books, that he brought into being.
> In the Holy tongue, he had
> six truly fine ones printed ...
> ... how dear do many hold his *sèforim* ...[27]

> I'm afraid I'm talking too much,
> so I will put down his *sèforim*,
> to talk about German things.
> And thus must reiterate—
> who will now create Purim plays,
> or stories,[28] or wedding songs?[29]
> Who will make whole books rhyme, and write
> so that we can, with laughing, make the time go by?[30]

While his works in Hebrew were intended for a crossover market of observant Jews and Christian intellectuals, all educated to the highest level and almost all, if not exclusively, male, his Yiddish works were a kind of insider literature, written in a language and alphabet only an Ashkenazic Jew could understand, and often dealt with specifically Jewish situations. They were destined for both men and women but especially the latter because they did not require fluency in Hebrew or much of a formal education. The separation between high and low, between serious and funny, between sanctity and obscenity, were emblematic of the two sides of Elye Bokher.

In passing, it should be noted that there are also instances of Bokher using Yiddish in a more serious context: many of his Hebrew works had glosses or commentaries in Yiddish (and other languages), and 1545 saw the publication of his translation of the Psalms.[31] However, it should be pointed out that these were not, strictly speaking, examples of original artistic creativity in the same sense as the other works considered here. He certainly wrote more Yiddish poems, but these did not survive. Many might have been composed for single occasions, hence their disappearance, although one, *Dȧs bukh der shonen Glukėn* (The book of good luck), is documented in other contemporary sources.[32] As noted earlier, *Paris un Wiene*, although not attributed to Elye in the original, is held to be his by certain scholars on stylistic grounds.[33]

Elye Bokher's surviving (and reliably identifiable) original artistic Yiddish productions can all be dated to a period spanning less than a decade, from the *Bovo Bukh*'s completion in 1507 to 1514, years spent in Mestre, Padua, and Venice, where, as in most of the north of Italy, German Jews made up the majority of the community.[34] Indeed, while Elye lived there, it was one of the most important European centers of Yiddish literary production and publishing.[35] His surviving Yiddish poems were written while he was living in a stimulating environment, surrounded by his countrymen, where he could produce insider works that would be read, appreciated, disseminated, and engaged through criticism. While in Rome, he lived in far better circumstances but probably did not have daily contact with a community of Ashkenazim: in any case, he does not seem to have produced many Yiddish works while there.

THE TEXT SOURCES

The *Sėrėfę lid* and *HaMavdil lid* are both found in the same two sources. The first, Oxford, Bodleian Library, MS Canonici Or. 12, fols. 203r–207r and 258r–261v (fig. 5.1 and fig. 5.2), was a manuscript given by Menahem Katz to his twenty-one-year-old daughter, Serlina (note the Italianate diminutive of *Sarah*), on the occasion of her marriage (the source indicates that she was "born in Venice"). Copied by Kalonimus ben Shimon and other scribes during a period dating from 1553 to at latest 1561, it contains a miscellany of

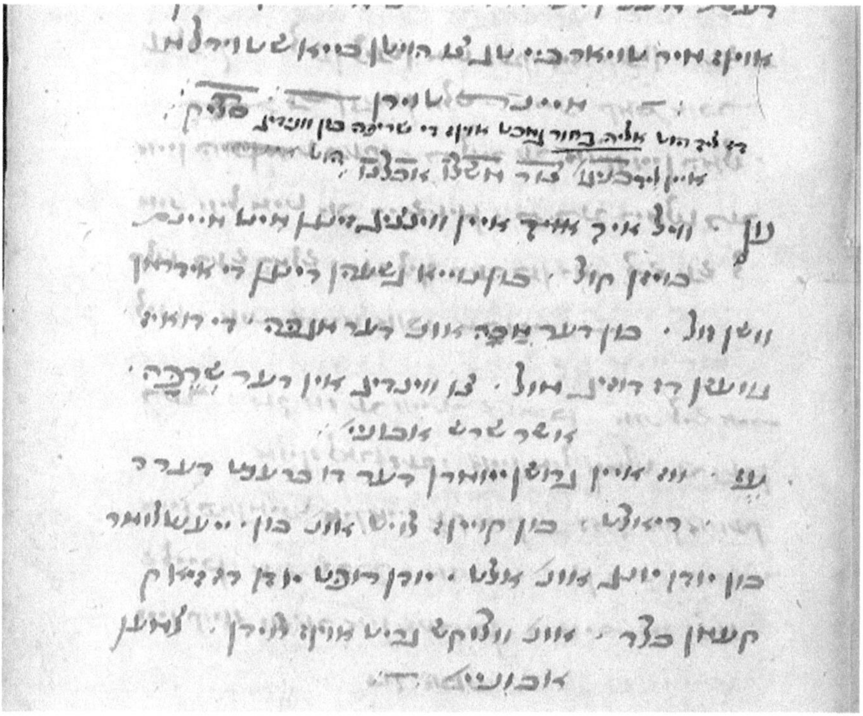

FIGURE 5.1.

"Śe'réfẹ lid." Oxford, Bodleian Library, MS Canonici Or. 12, fol. 258r. Reproduced with permission from the Bodleian Libraries, the University of Oxford.

items: a Yiddish translation of the Pentateuch, a book of minhag (a guide to Jewish observances), stories, and poems, including Elye's irreverent songs.[36] Incidentally, Serlina's father's interest in her intellectual development is demonstrated by a considerable use of Hebrew and its lack of focus on women's issues: only 18 of the 274 folios in the book are dedicated to *mitzvot nashim*, the traditional women's guide to keeping an observant household. In the other source, Cambridge, Trinity College Library, MS F.12.45, fols. 4r–9v, copied around 1530, the two *pasquinate* (a form of public social commentary, often with slanderous intentions, that were hung up on the walls for all to see) found in the opening folios are the only poems, followed by three *mayses* (literally "happenings," or stories in prose), Jewish versions of mainstream tales, with a widespread use of Italian words.[37]

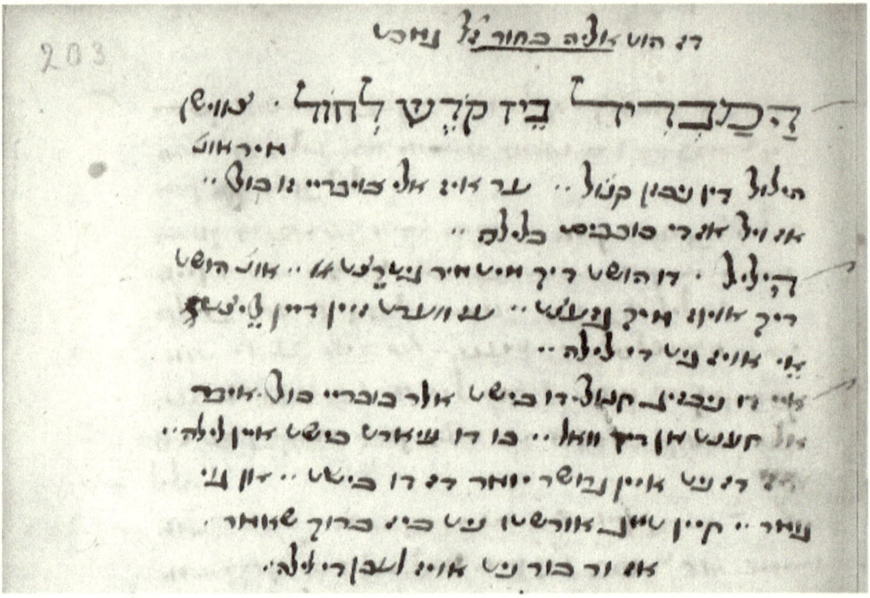

FIGURE 5.2.

"HaMav̆dil lid." Oxford, Bodleian Library, MS Canonici Or. 12, fol. 203r. Reproduced with permission from the Bodleian Libraries, the University of Oxford.

MUSIC

At more than five hundred years' distance, it is difficult to decipher the signs that could point to a poem being primarily read (silently or out loud), recited, or performed musically. While the line between poetry and song might seem clear to twentieth- and twenty-first-century readers, early modern usage of the terms *shir* (in Hebrew), *lid* (in Yiddish), and *canto* (in Italian) encompassed both meanings. Accounts of the *Orlando furioso* being sung to improvised melodies coexist with those about it being read, even, in at least one example, by Jewish girls: in his *Precetti d'esser imparati dalle donne hebree*, Italian translator Giacob Alpron writes, "Ariosto, the centenovelle, and Amadis of Gaul, or similar profane books, should not be read [by Jewish girls] during Shabbat, as our teacher Moses states, in order to avoid their learning about lechery or vain things from them."[38]

It has already been pointed out that, in the postlude to the *Bovo Bukh*, Elye Bokher writes, "I sing it [the *Bovo Bukh*] to an Italian tune, he who finds a better one will find thanks." This should be seen not as a specific reference to the melody of a specific poem but as a demonstration of a widespread aesthetic value system (which is certainly not limited to the early modern period) that gave prominence to the expression of the text, and where setting a particular text to a particular tune was not an essential element to its performance. This is also attested to by the wide dissemination of songs in text-only transmission, with and without named melodic models, together with the numerous musical sources of generic *arie per cantare*.[39]

Indeed, as mentioned earlier, there have been numerous studies about the art of the cantastorie, declamation, and an entire repertoire of partially or wholly orally transmitted song that flourished next to the music that survived in notation.[40] There are many references in Jewish writings that demonstrate participation in the practice of singing poetry, such as the statement of Mordechai Dato in his poetic translation in ottava rima of the biblical book of Esther:

> Because I know you ladies,
> Are all kind and devout,
> I'm sure you'll have prepared choice dishes . . .
> There will be sweets, nut brittle and candied almonds,
> Malvasia and Muscat wine:
> But let me remind you: make sure they're well chilled—
> I'm dying of thirst after all this singing.
>
> (E per che so che voi donni in effetto,
> tutti benigni e devote seti,
> so che avereti fatti vivandi eletti, arrosto
> e a lesso apparecchiato aveti,
> zuccarini, nociata e confetti,
> malvasia e moscatel teneti,
> ma vi raccomondo che sia rinfrescato,
> che de seta me moro tant'ho cantata.[41])

Gumprecht von Szczebrszyn likewise left a description of musical–poetic recitation in a poem written for Purim:

> And I set it to a lovely melody,
> so that no one should get bored.
>
> (Auch hab ich's gėmacht ouf ain hipsh gėsank,
> dås ainėm di' wail doriber nit sol werdėn lang.[42])

And the introduction to Lazzaro da Viterbo's adaptation of Moses da Rieti's *Il Tempio* (known in Hebrew as *Me'on ha-sho'alim*) likewise refers to sung recitation:

> And so, I hope you will accept, with the usual gratitude of your heart, this small gift, that with respect and humility I give to you, with the pledge, however, that, when the time comes ... if it pleases you, you will let me hear you sing some of its verses.
>
> (Accetti adunque V.S. con la solita gratitudine dell' animo suo il picciol dono, quale da me, con riverenza, & humiltà segli porge, con patto però, che quando sera tempo ... li piacci, che gliene senti cantare qualche verso.[43])

Although these comments could be simply rhetorical (except perhaps the last), they do point toward an awareness of singing poetry within the Jewish community. Some of the characteristics that could suggest the sung performance of a given poem, roughly in order of completeness of data (but not necessarily of probability), are as follows:

1. A version of the text is found complete with musical notation in another source. The largest example in this category stemming from the Jewish community is an early seventeenth-century source known as the Wallich manuscript.[44]
2. The poem names a melodic model (like the *Tzur mi-shelo* in the *Śĕrĕfẹ lid*).
3. The poem is a parody of a known song (like *HaMav̄dil lid*).
4. References to singing are found in the title or text.
5. The poem is found in a source containing the texts of known songs—again, like the Wallich manuscript.
6. The poem's meter is that of a form that was normally sung, such as the ottava rima (the *Bovo Bukh*, the book of Esther in ottava rima), terza rima (*Me'on ha-sho'alim/Il Tempio*), sonnets (in some cases), or the so-called *Shmuel Bukh* and *Bovo Bukh* tunes.

I have included two tables here that give examples of the crossover that went on in the Italian Jewish community during the sixteenth century (table 5.1) and examples of evidence of sung performance (table 5.2).

Returning to the two Venetian poems, there are, as often, conflicting signals about reading and singing. Claudia Rosenzweig gives a convincing argument that they were originally pasquinate or *katoves*, which, as noted previously, were poems containing social commentary posted on walls in

Table 5.1. Selected examples of linguistic crossover by Jewish poets in sixteenth-century Italy.

Author	Work	Form/model	Language/translation	Subject matter / notes
Josef Tzarfati	*Ieshena 'at, 'ani ne'or ve-nodad*	strambotto	Italian to Hebrew, close to literal translation	Love poem (from Italian original)
Elye Bokher	*Dás lid ouf di śerefe vun Wenedig*	ottava rima with girdle rhyme	Yiddish, original poem	Events in Jewish community of Venice; stress based, irregular number of syllables
Elye Bokher	*Bovo d'Antona*	ottava rima	Italian to Yiddish, free adaptation	Situations added / transformed according to Jewish practices and points of view; stress based, irregular number of syllables
Elye Bokher	*Hamavdil lid*	quatrains with girdle rhyme	Yiddish, parody of Hebrew piyyut *Ha-mavdil bein kodesh le-ḥol*	Set in northern Italy; stress based, irregular number of syllables
Mordechai Dato	*Megillat 'Ester in ottava rima*	ottava rima	Hebrew to Italian (written in Hebrew characters)	Free translation of Megillat Ester into Italian, with midrashic and popular additions
Zatri di Cuneo(?)	*la cansonetta di Purim*	octosyllabic quatrains	Italian dialect (written in Hebrew characters) with Hebrew inserts	Popular (style?) retelling (third-person narrative) of Purim story
Lazzaro da Viterbo	*Il Tempio*	terza rima	Hebrew to Italian (in Latin characters)	One of the many translations of Moses of Rieti's *Mikdash me'at*, which was in turn inspired by Dante's *Divine Comedy*
Leon Modena	*Parashim klei zain ve-nashim*	ottava rima	Hebrew to Italian, exact translation	Translation of Ariosto's *Orlando Furioso*
Anonymous	*Dás mensh geglichen*	quatrains	Yiddish and (corrupt) Italian dialect (in Hebrew characters) with Hebrew titles, probably original composition	Only known poem in Yiddish and Italian: author was probably German Jew living in Italy

Table 5.2. Selected examples of evidence for the sung performance of poems written by Jewish authors in sixteenth-century Italy.

Author	Work	Form/model	Indications of possible sung performance
Josef Tzarfati	*Ieshena 'at, 'ani neor ve-nodad*	strambotto	Translation of a strambotto that has survived with musical notation. A separate parody also survives with notation.
Elye Bokher	*Dås lid ouf di śėrėfę yun Wėnėdig*	ottava rima / *Tzur mi-shelo*	"A song sung to the tune of *Tzur mi-shelo*."
Elye Bokher	*Bovo d'Antona*	ottava rima	Indication in postscript: "I sing it to an Italian tune."
Mordechai Dato	*Megillat 'Ester in ottava rima*	ottava rima	Narrator speaks of singing in body of poem.
Lazzaro da Viterbo	*Il Tempio*	terza rima	Author/translator tells dedicatee he would like to hear her sing his verses.
Leon Modena	*Parashim klei zain ve-nashim*	ottava rima	Translation of a poetic work that has traditionally been sung and is still sung in central Italy today.

public.[45] Were these wall poems recited, sung aloud, or read silently? The answer is probably all the above, given that these were forms of expression that coexisted. In any case, the juxtaposition of elements taken from the pious original, like verse form, rhymes, and melody, with a humorous, often disconcertingly vulgar text, would have meant that even imagining the original melody (and context) while reading would have enhanced the comic effect.

The Cambridge collection is mostly made up of reading material, with stories following the poems. The Oxford miscellanea was destined for a young lady, perhaps as Shabbat reading material, perhaps for singing, perhaps for both. The surprising superimpositions of its content—ranging from biblical translations to poems that talk about carnal relations with children and animals—are neither what we in the twenty-first century would see as coherent or unified nor what would we consider an appropriate gift from a pious father to a young Jewish girl. Yet these factors were obviously not at issue for the compilers and owners of the manuscript, and they thus attest to the enormous gaps in attitude and mentality that lie between the early modern era and our own.

As an argument for singing, even if *HaMavdil lid* and the *Śėrėfę lid* have come down to us in reader-oriented sources, they are called songs and have named melodic models that, as part of the weekly devotional cycle, would have been familiar to all. Rosenzweig writes, "Few texts have survived from the period in which these two songs were written. The fact that both songs have been preserved in two manuscripts, and that these were copied after Elye Bokher's death, suggests that they must have been quite popular."[46] This said, the once commonly held supposition that Elye Bokher earned part of his living as a *spilman* (minstrel)[47] has since come under criticism.[48] However, there is the possibility that his statement "I sing it to an Italian tune" is not completely rhetorical and that he, like his fellow Venetian, the highly respected rabbi, poet, and scholar Leon Modena, also sang on occasion for financial reward, especially considering his (and Leon Modena's) often precarious financial situations. In any case, evidence points to the two poems being widely disseminated, with well-known melodic models, during an era in which poetry was consumed and expressed in many different fashions.

THE POEMS AND THEIR MUSIC

In *Dås lid ouf di śėrėfę ṽun Wėnėdig*, Elye portrays the looting that went on in Venice after a fire on the Rialto—in particular, the crimes of a certain Hillel Cohen—with the last strophe identifying it as a song for Purim (the occasion indicating that the stories it relays were parodic and cannot be taken at face value).[49] Claudia Rosenzweig, citing an article by D. Jacoby that pinpoints the date of the fire as January 10, 1514, hypothesizes that the poem could well have been in defense of the son of his probable patron, Anselmo Meshullam, who was accused of participating in the robbery.[50]

The work is thirty-five stanzas long in the Oxford source, while sixteen stanzas survive (some are missing from the middle and end) in the Cambridge manuscript. In his *Early Yiddish Texts, 1100–1750*, Jerold C. Frakes points out that two mostly concordant sources have made it possible to put together a critical edition, a rarity with early Yiddish texts.[51]

It is written in ottava rima, a form with which Elye was certainly familiar. In fact, the influence of the ottava rima transcended communal lines, with examples surviving from the Italian, Sephardic, and Ashkenazic communities. These include Mordechai Dato's epic poem-style setting of the *Megillat 'Ester in ottava rima* (Italian in Hebrew characters);[52] Leon Modena's juvenile translation of selected *stanze* of the *Orlando furioso* into Hebrew;[53] an anonymous, undated Hebrew-letter transcription of Jerónimo de Urrea's (1510–ca. 1570) Spanish-language translation of *Orlando furioso*;[54] and Elye Bokher's own *Bovo Bukh*.

THE ŚĒRĒFE LID

The *Śērēfe lid* does not use the classic Tuscan ottava rima rhyme scheme (*abababcc*), instead employing a hybrid form—*ababcbcx* (followed by *cdcdcdcx*, etc.), with the *x* rhyme ("Abonai") repeated in the last line of every stanza.[55] This kind of girdle rhyme, called *muwashshah*, was adopted by Jewish poets from Spanish-Arabic poetry. In fact, the vast majority of piyyutim written in Europe actually followed the Arab-Andalusian tradition.[56] However, there are also many examples of European fusion forms that combine Eastern and Western practices: in this case, the girdle-form last-line repetition is grafted onto a typical Italianate form.

In the introduction to the poem, Elye Bokher calls it "ain lid bēnigu' Tzur mi-shelo 'okhalnu": "A song sung to the tune of *Tzur mi-shelo 'okhalnu*." The *Tzur mi-shelo*'s rhyme structure is as follows: that of the ritornello, which is sung twice and repeated after every strophe, is *axax*, while the strophes are *bcbcbccx*, with the same rhyming syllables (moh/aynu/nay) repeated in the first four stanzas with a variation, *dbdbdbbx* (dosh/loh/nay), in the fifth and last one. Even if the rhyme scheme is not glaringly different from that of the *Śērēfe lid*, its even syllabic count contrasts with Elye's poem, which is based on accent patterns (and therefore has a syllabic count that varies considerably), as is true of all his poems, most Yiddish poetry, and much German poetry of the era.

THE MUNICH *TZUR MI-SHELO*

A German *Tzur mi-shelo* with music that could be a plausible melodic model was discovered by the musicologist Israel Adler in the Bavarian National

Library in 1984 (Munich, 4° Cod. MS 757); the manuscript is a Hebrew exercise book compiled and copied by Johannes Renhart, finished at some time between 1510 and 1511 in Esslingen (fig. 5.3 and fig. 5.4).[57] Its structure is made up of a ritornello, where the first four lines (eight hemistiches) of text are repeated twice to different tunes, followed by five stanze, each with its own music. This through composition is unusual, if not unique, because the normal practice at the time was to set only one strophe to music and to write the rest of the strophes down in text-only form, presumably under the assumption that a singer would understand how to set the rest of the text from the model provided.

In the Munich manuscript (transcribed in ex. 5.1), each strophe has its own melody, and all are interrelated, with small but significant differences related to text and function. In my opinion, this and other considerations point toward it being an early example of ethnomusicological fieldwork, reflecting actual performance practice; this notion, furthermore, might call for a reconsideration of how strophic song was actually performed.[58] The added or subtracted notes according to accent and syllabic count (compare stanza 1, "'Al ken nodo li-shmo"; stanza 2, "Mozon ve-tzedoh"; and stanza 3, "U-Ben Dovid 'avedekho"), changing contour and final tone in the second line in the internal strophes (see stanza 1, "ve-yeyno shosinu": *f*; stanza 2, "she-hinḥil lavoyseynu": *g*; stanza 3, "zevul beys tif'arseynu": *d*; and stanza 4, "yisborakh ve-yis'aleh": *f*; see ex. 5.1), and distinctive structure (using pre-existent melodic elements) of the final strophe, which probably heralded the arrival of the last repetition of the ritornello, are all consistent with the kinds of changes made during actual performance, as opposed to a transcription made according to the usual constraints of written transmission.[59] In fact, the same kind of melodic transformations can be observed in performances of the piyyut, which has remained in the Jewish tradition, from across the globe.[60]

The unique aspects of the music for the stanze (as opposed to that of the ritornello) of the Munich *Tzur mi-shelo*—the way in which melodies bend and change according to text, function, and context, creating a total fusion of poetry and music—also render them unsuitable for setting Elye's text. This is why, after much experimentation, I have chosen the ritornello, which is straightforward, simple, and unchanging and, in turn, easily altered to fit the Yiddish text, to set the *Śėrėfę lid*.

In the two charts that follow, the ritornello of the *Tzur mi-shelo* and the first two strophes of the *Śėrėfę lid* are compared.[61] In the Hebrew model,

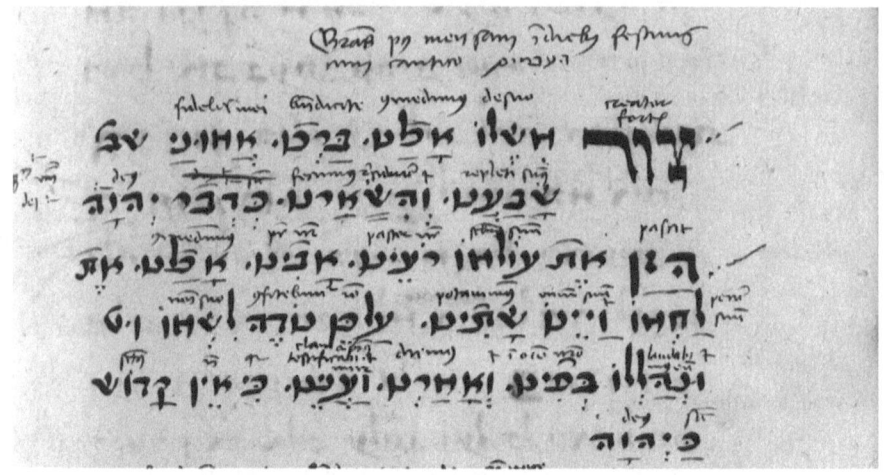

FIGURE 5.3.

"Tzur mi-shelo" (text). Munich, Universitätsbibliothek der Ludwig-Maximilians-Universität München, 4° Cod. MS 757, fol. 96r, upper page.

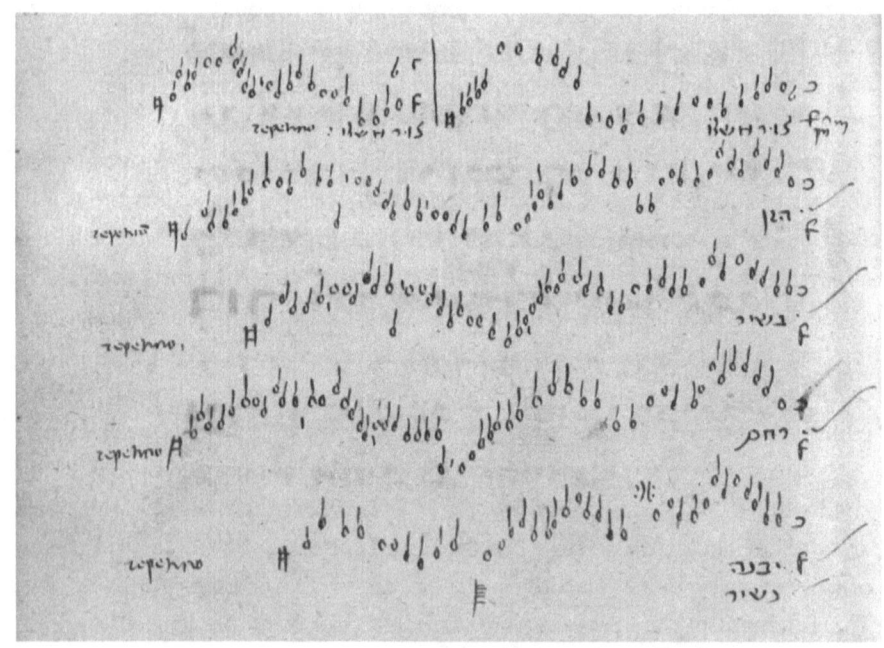

FIGURE 5.4.

"Tzur mi-shelo" (music). Munich, Universitätsbibliothek der Ludwig-Maximilians-Universität München, 4° Cod. MS 757, fol. 95v, lower page.

EXAMPLE 5.1.

Transcription of "Tzur mi-shelo 'okhalnu." Munich, Universitätsbibliothek der Ludwig-Maximilians-Universität München, Cod. MS 757 (40), fol. 95v–96r. Transliterations to the Roman alphabet follow Ashkenazic pronunciation.

EXAMPLE 5.1. *(Continued)*

Transcription of "Tzur mi-shelo 'okhalnu." Munich, Universitätsbibliothek der Ludwig-Maximilians-Universität München, Cod. MS 757 (40), fol. 95v–96r. Transliterations to the Roman alphabet follow Ashkenazic pronunciation.

the lines are regular, each having seven (first hemistich) plus five (second hemistich) syllables. By contrast, the Yiddish poem is irregular and organized according to stress (here marked with bold type), with three to each line.

Tzur mi-shelo

Tzur mi-shelo 'okhalnu	7a
borekhu 'emunai	5x
Sova'nu ve-hosarnu	7a
kidvar 'Abonai	5x

(The Lord, Our Rock, whose food we have eaten,
let us bless Him.
We are satiated and there is still food left over,
as G*d has instructed.)

[The text is repeated to new music.]

Śėrėfę lid
Nun wil **ich** ain **win**zig **sing**ėn	8a
Mit **meinėm bösėn kòl**	6b
V̄un **nöü̇'** gėsche̊hėn **ding**ėn	7a
Di idėrmȧn **w[i]**ßėn **sòl**	7b
V̄un der **makę** un' der ma**gefę**	8c
Di dȯiṣ gėwesėn dȧṣ **dȯ**sig **mȯl**	10b
Zu Wėnėdig in der śėrėfę	8c
Ašer śor[ef] abȯnai'	7x

Eṣ **wȧṣ** ain **grö́**ßėn **jo**mėrn	7d
Der **dȯ** brent **der** Ri**alt**	6e
V̄un köüf-**löut** un' v̄un jjentė**lȯmėr**[n]	9d
V̄un **judė**n **jung** un' **alt**	6d
Judėn **ruft ju**dėn	5d
Dȧṣ si' **kemėn bȧld**	5e
Un' **vvluks** gėrėt ouf-lüdėn	7d
Lėma'an abȯnai'	5x

(I would like to sing to you a bit,
With my poor voice,
About some things seen recently
That everyone should know about:
About the scourge and the plague
That happened at the time,
When there was a fire in Venice,
[That came] by G*d's hand.

There was a great outcry
As the Rialto burned:
From merchant and gentleman,
And from Jews young and old.
Jew called out to Jew
To come right away,
And, quickly, a cry rang out:
"For G*d!")

EXAMPLE 5.2.

Text: Elye Bokher, "Dās lid ouf di śėrėfę v̄un Wėnėdig," written ca. 1512. Oxford, Bodleian Library, MS Canonici Or. 12, fols. 258r–261v (based on a transcription by Simon Neuberg). Music: "Tzur Mi-shelo 'okhalnu." Munich, Universitätsbibliothek der Ludwig-Maximilians-Universität München, Cod. MS 757 (40), fol. 95v.

A comparison with my attempt at a musical setting of the first four stanzas of the Śėrėfę lid with the original Tzur mi-shelo reflects the consequences of this irregularity, such as added and subtracted notes and multiple syllables added before the first stress (see ex. 5.2).[62]

HAMAV̄DIL LID

As noted previously, the poem is found in two manuscripts: Oxford, Bodleian Library, MS Canonici Or. 12, with fifty-five stanzas, and Cambridge, Trinity College Library, MS F.12.45, with sixty-eight and a half, because of a missing folio at the end.[63] HaMav̄dil lid is written in quatrains, with a rhyme scheme of aaax, bbbx, a girdle rhyme like that of the Śėrėfę lid. In this case, the final word of each group of four is lajlę (night). It uses exactly the same rhyme structure as its model, *Ha-mavdil bein qodesh le-ḥol*, a piyyut traditionally sung at the end of the Sabbath to signify the symbolic separation between the holy (the Sabbath day) and the profane (the other days of the week). Of uncertain authorship, it is still sung today, for the same occasion, throughout the Jewish world.[64] In contrast to *Tzur mi-shelo*, its syllabic count fluctuates from hemistich to hemistich, illustrating the wide variety of meters, styles, and origins found in the piyyutim that circulated during Elye Bokher's era.

> ***Ha-mavdil bein qodesh le-ḥol***
> Ha-mavdil bein qodesh le-ḥol,
> Ḥatoseinu [Hu] yimḥol,
> Zarʻeinu ve-ḥaspeinu yarbeh ka-ḥol,
> ve-kha-kokhavim ba-laylah.

(He who makes a distinction between the holy and the profane,
May he nullify our sins.
May he multiply our offspring and our wealth,
like the sand and like the stars in the night.)

> ***HaMav̌dil lid***
> HaMav̌dil bên kodeš léḥòl
> Zwischén **mir** un' Hillel, **dèn** nibsén **knòl**,
> **Er** iṣ alé bübèrei **sò v̌òl**
> Aṣ **vil** aṣ di *còchov̌ˈim balajlẹ*

> Hillel, du **hòst** dich mit **mir** gètrèzt
> Un' hòst **dich** ouf **mich** gèsetzt;
> **Eṣ** wert **sein dein** lèzt
> Ê ouṣ-gèt di *lajlẹ*.[65]

(That which differentiates the holy from the profane,
Stands between me and Hillel, that naughty rascal.
He that is as full of stupidity,
As there are stars in the night.

Hillel, you have fought [?] with me,
And have pitted yourself against me:
It shall be your last
Night's end.)

The pasquinata was supposedly written in response to a poem by Hillel Cohen, which was, in turn, written in response to Elye's *Śèrèfẹ lid*. In it, Cohen is accused of numerous sins, including being ignorant and unworthy of teaching, being a glutton unable to satisfy any of his three wives (all of whom divorce him), molesting children and animals, having a brother who is a priest, and being like a gentile (although Elye uses another word) himself. The verses mention cities throughout northern Italy—Cividale del Friuli, Udine, Portogruaro, Ferrara, Padua, and of course Venice—painting the picture of an environment that was no longer foreign but at home in a fusional German-Italian-Jewish culture.

As far as melodic models are concerned, we are not as fortunate as in the case of the *Śėrėfe lid*, where a geographically and temporally appropriate model has survived. Here, although the tune transcribed is indicated as one sung at the German Synagogue in Venice, the model dates from 1724, more than 150 years after Elye Bokher's death and the compilation of the poem's surviving sources.

With aspects resembling Gregorian chant, vocal and instrumental repertoire from the late fifteenth and early sixteenth centuries, and orally transmitted *Chazzonos*, the Munich *Tzur mi-shelo* is an exceptional relic, as well as one with the right pedigree: "Made in 1510." In comparison, the *Ha-Mavdil* tune transcribed by Benedetto Marcello (see fig. 5.5 and ex. 5.3), although it is an uncomplicated and, to use a dangerous adjective, "folklike" tune, without any glaringly baroque traits, does not have a clear heritage, and we cannot place it exactly just by analyzing or listening. Curiously enough, it is one of the examples transcribed by Marcello that remained in the Jewish-Italian oral tradition until well into the twentieth century.[66] Unfortunately, this does not give us any information about at what point prior to the 1720s this particular tune was composed or adopted. However, whatever its origins, it does express and follow the line, syntax, accent, and pitch height of the text perfectly. The music of the Munich *Tzur mi-shelo* is syllabic, with psalmodic text repetitions on single notes and fixed modal cadential formulas. This is not the case of the *Ha-Mavdil*. In addition, its embellishments, although quite basic, are organized at different points of the phrase, which means that they do not have the kind of repetitive function—of opening the phrase or heralding the cadence—common to declamation, both in sixteenth-century *arie per cantare* and in the modern orally transmitted tradition.[67] Although it is always dangerous to trust our ears in such matters, the melody of *Ha-Mavdil* seems to have been created around a simple harmonic framework—in any case, we can easily imagine a subdominant-tonic-dominant-tonic

FIGURE 5.5.

Salmo decimosettimo a tre "Diligram te Domine": "Intonazione degli Ebrei Tedeschi sopra המבדיל וגו'." Benedetto Marcello, *Estro poetico-armonico* (Venice: Domenico Lovisa, 1724–1726), vol. 3, unpaginated.

* dotted half note in original

EXAMPLE 5.3.

Salmo decimosettimo a tre "Diligram te Domine": "Intonazione degli Ebrei Tedeschi sopra המבדיל וגו'." Benedetto Marcello, *Estro poetico-armonico* (Venice: Domenico Lovisa, 1724–1726), 3:94. Transliterations to the Roman alphabet follow Ashkenazic pronunciation.

progression under the melody (the bars have also been kept here for reference, the melody has also been slightly altered from the original) for Ḥatoseinu yimḥol (mm. 6–8) or a dominant chord under the repeated Ds on the "*kha-kokhavim*" before the final cadence (mm. 15–16), which could point toward a possible seventeenth- or even eighteenth-century origin for the melody. However, my attempts at modifying the tune in order to make

EXAMPLE 5.4.

Text: Elye Bokher, "HaMavdil lid." Oxford, Bodleian Library, MS Canonici Or. 12, fols. 203r–207r (based on a transcription by Simon Neuberg). Music: "Intonazione degli Ebrei Tedeschi sopra המבדיל וגו׳." Benedetto Marcello, *Estro poetico-armonico* (Venice: Domenico Lovisa, 1724–1726), 3:94.

EXAMPLE 5.4. (*Continued*)

Text: Elye Bokher, "HaMavdil lid." Oxford, Bodleian Library, MS Canonici Or. 12, fols. 203r–207r (based on a transcription by Simon Neuberg). Music: "Intonazione degli Ebrei Tedeschi sopra המבדיל וגו׳." Benedetto Marcello, *Estro poetico-armonico* (Venice: Domenico Lovisa, 1724–1726), 3:94.

it conform better in modal structure, cadences, and ornamental style to the Munich *Tzur mi-shelo* led only to an incohesive and unconvincing line that did not match the pitch height or syntax of the text, which is why, with the reservations mentioned previously, the tune transcribed by Marcello was deemed the best one to use. My reconstruction is shown in example 5.4.[68]

With the two settings presented here, together with a version of the *Bovo Bukh* included in an earlier publication and another version recorded for the label K617, the surviving Yiddish poems of Elye Bokher have now been published or released together with a best-guess melody.[69] The road to constructing a performable edition, and to performance itself, saw countless choices, governed by artistic, aesthetic, practical, and commercial and politically motivated concerns, made by myself and the other performers involved. There is no doubt that the vibrations produced by our voices and instruments, as well as our audiences' ways of hearing them, are completely different from the way they would have been transmitted (or perceived) in the sixteenth century. Of course, this is true of any music, whether it has survived complete with musical notation or not, when it is performed in a totally different context, for a totally different set of ears, after a major time gap. Despite the inherent imperfections that come from performing material based on incomplete data, the importance of respecting one of its modes of transmission should also be considered: much of the poetry of the era was meant to be sung and heard, not only to be read in silence. Data from the early modern period points to the relative unimportance, in some circumstances (especially in pieces focused on the text), of singing a specific poem to a specific tune. Indeed, there is an argument against applying twentieth- and twenty-first-century values and priorities to material for which these considerations might have been irrelevant. Performing Elye Bokher's works in public, even in a fashion largely shaped by twenty-first-century creativity, is a way of letting the significant role he played in Jewish-Christian (as well as Italian-German) cultural exchange become known outside scholarly circles and, by extension, letting lesser-known voices be heard today, audibly demonstrating the deep roots of a multicultural Europe.

NOTES

This chapter could not have been written without the benefit of a Sassoon Fellowship at the Centre for the Study of the Book at the Bodleian Library. During the month I spent there, I had access to almost unlimited sources and was able to hold the main source for this chapter, Oxford, Bodleian Library, MS Canonici Or. 12, in my hands, just as Serlina did more than 450 years ago. Many thanks to Alexandra Franklin and Rachel Naismith, who provided me with everything I could have possibly needed while there, and to César Merchán-Hamann and Bonnie J. Blackburn for their precious advice. My dear friend Dr. Diana Matut was an invaluable help with the Old Yiddish texts, while Simon Neuberg kindly gave me access to his unpublished transcriptions of Canonici Or. 12. It goes without saying that any errors found in the translations and transcriptions are my own responsibility, not that of the scholars kind enough to help a musician who sometimes struggles with the texts. Many thanks to Richard Barrett, who was my writing coach for this chapter in its original form (as an individual writing project for the docARTES program), and to Julia Kursell, my supervisor at the University of Amsterdam. The support of my family, in particular my son Justin Biggi, was precious throughout. Last but not least, I would like to thank the editors of the present volume, Lynette Bowring, Rebecca Cypess, and Liza Malamut, for their astute observations and editorial suggestions. Yiddish transliterations were made according to the indications found in the introduction to *Das schwedesch lid: ein westjiddischer Bericht über Ereignisse in Prag im Jahre 1684*, ed. Simon Neuberg (Hamburg: H. Buske, 2000), 1–2; this is the system used by numerous scholars, such as Erika Timm, Wolf-Otto Dreessen, and Maria Fuchs.

1. See the appendix, "Later Transformations of the *Bovo d'Antona*, 17th–20th Centuries," in Elye Bokher, Bovo d'Antona *by Elye Bokher: A Yiddish Romance: A Critical Edition with Commentary*, ed. Claudia Rosenzweig (Leiden and Boston: Brill, 2016), 503–531.

2. Sol Liptzin, *A History of Yiddish Literature* (Middle Village, NY: Jonathan David, 1972), 7.

3. Munich, Universitätsbibliothek der Ludwig-Maximilians-Universität München, 4° Cod. MS 757, fols. 95v–96r.

4. Benedetto Marcello, *Estro poetico-armonico: Parafrasi sopra li salmi* (Venice: Domenico Lovisa, 1724–1726), vol. 3, unpaginated. Called "Intonazione degli Ebrei Tedeschi sopra

"המבדילוגו," it is the model for the melody of "Salmo decimosettimo a tre 'Diligram te Domini.'"

5. Avery Gosfield, "I Sing It to an Italian Tune ... Thoughts on Performing Sixteenth-Century Italian-Jewish Sung Poetry Today," *European Journal of Jewish Studies* 8, no. 1 (June 2014): 9–52.

6. The "Matter of France," or Carolingian cycle, is a series dedicated to Charlemagne and his followers with roots in the chanson de geste genre, transposed into Italian ottava rima at the end of the fifteenth century.

7. A poem made up of eight-line stanzas, with each line containing eleven syllables. The most widely used form, the Tuscan ottava, has the rhyme scheme *abababcc*.

8. Venice, Biblioteca Marciana, Fr. XIII, a collection of eight rhymed Carolingian epics written in Franco-Venetian, including "Karleto" and "Orlandino." See Leslie Zarker Morgan, "*Bovo d'Antona* in the *Geste Francor* (V 13): Unity of Composition and Clan Destiny," *Italian Culture* 16, no. 2 (1998): 15–38. See also Daniela Delcorno Branca, "Fortuna e trasformazioni del *Buovo d'Antona*," in *Testi, cotesti e contesti del franco-italiano*, ed. Gunter Holtus, Henning Krauss, and Peter Wunderli (Tubingen: Max Niemeyer, 1989), 285–306. For a complete edition, see Aldo Rosellini, ed., *La "Geste Francor" di Venezia. Edizione integrale del Codice XIII del Fondo francese della Marciana*, Centro di Linguistica dell'Universita Cattolica, Saggi e monografie 6 (Brescia: La Scuola, 1986).

9. *Buovo di Antona di Guidone Palladino, Rezunto e Revisto* (Bologna: Caligola de' Bazalieri, 1497). See Erika Timm, "Wie Elia Levita sein Bovobuch für den Druck überarbeitete: ein Kapitel aus der italo-jiddischen Literatur der Renaissancezeit," *Germanisch-romanische Monatsschrift* 41, no. 1 (1991): 61–81; Claudia Rosenzweig, "From the Square and the Court to the Private Room: Some Remarks on the Yiddish Version of the Chivalric Poem *Bovo d'Antona*," *Zutot: Perspectives on Jewish Culture* 5, no. 1 (2008): 51–52; and Claudia Rosenzweig, "Introduction," in Bokher, Bovo d'Antona, 29–39. For an annotated modern edition drawn from an earlier source, see Daniela Delcorno Branca, ed., *Buovo d'Antona: cantari in ottava rima (1480)*, Biblioteca medievale 118 (Rome: Carocci, 2008).

10. See Nino Pirrotta, *Li due Orfei* (Turin: Einaudi, 1975); Nino Pirrotta, "Tradizione orale e tradizione scritta nella musica," in *L'Ars Nova italiana del Trecento* 3, ed. F. Albert Gallo (Certaldo: Centro di studi sull' Ars Nova italiana del Trecento, 1970), 431–441; Elena Abramov-van Rijk, *Parlar cantando: The Practice of Reciting Verses in Italy from 1300 to 1600* (New York: Peter Lang, 2009); Don Harrán, "Doubly Tainted, Doubly Talented: The Jewish Poet Sara Copio (d. 1641) as a Heroic Singer," in *Musica Franca: Essays in Honor of Frank A. D'Accone*, ed. Irene Alm, Alyson McLamore, and Colleen Reardon (Stuyvesant, NY: Pendragon, 1996): 367–422; James Haar, "*Improvvisatori* and Their Relationship to Sixteenth-Century Music," in *Essays on Italian Poetry and Music in the Renaissance, 1350–1600* (Berkeley: University of California Press, 1986): 76–99; James Haar, "Arie per cantar stanze ariostesche," in *L'Ariosto: la musica, i musicisti: Quattro studi e sette madrigali arioschi*, ed. Maria Antonella Balsano, Quaderni della Rivista Italiana di Musicologia 5 (Florence: Leo S. Olschki, 1981), 31–46; Maria Antonella Balsano and James Haar, "L'Ariosto in musica," in Balsano, *L'Ariosto: la musica, i musicisti*, 47–88; Maurizio Agamennone, "Cantar ottave. Una introduzione," in *Cantar ottave: Per una storia culturale dell'intonazione cantata in ottava rima*, ed. Maurizio Agamennone (Lucca: Libreria Musicale Italiana, 2017), VII–XXVI; Francesco Saggio, "Improvvisazione e scrittura nel tardo-quattrocento cortese: lo strambotto al tempo di Leonardo Giustinian e Serafino Aquilano," in Agamennone, *Cantar ottave*, 25–47; and Brian Richardson, "The Social Connotations of Singing Verse in Cinquecento Italy," *Italianist* 34, no. 3 (2014): 362–378.

11. Literally, a "singer of stories." In a largely illiterate society, like that of early modern Italy, cantastorie played an important role as disseminators of culture. One of the mainstays of their repertoire was epic poetry, in particular the poems in ottava rima dedicated to the aforementioned "Matter of France." Their art was one that cut across social levels, with many performing in both courtly and popular milieus. Blake Wilson, "The *Cantastoria/Canterino/Cantimbanco* as Musician," *Italian Studies* 71, no. 2 (2016): 154–170; Blake Wilson, "Dominion of the Ear: Singing the Vernacular in Piazza San Martino," *Tatti Studies in the Italian Renaissance* 16, no. 1/2 (September 2013): 273–287; Rosa Salzberg and Massimo Rospocher, "Street Singers in Italian Renaissance Culture and Communication," *Cultural and Social History* 9 (2012): 9–26; Rosa Salzberg, "In the Mouths of Charlatans: Street Performers and the Dissemination of Pamphlets in Renaissance Italy," *Renaissance Studies*, 24 (2010): 638–653; and Blake Wilson, "*Canterino* and *improvvisatore*: Oral Poetry and Performance," in *The Cambridge History of Fifteenth-Century Music*, ed. Anna Maria Busse Berger and Jesse Rodin (Cambridge: Cambridge University Press, 2015), 292–310.

12. For a history of the sung ottava tradition from the fifteenth century until the present day, see Maurizio Agamennone, dir., *APORIE (Archivio e Portale informatico sulla Poesia in Ottava Rima Estemporanea)*. It offers information on ottave in notation (such as Rousseau's *Tasso alla Veneziana* and *Ottave alla Fiorentina*), artists' biographies, and a lengthy bibliography, as well as links to media, archives, etc. Accessed December 28, 2019, http://www.aporie.it.

13. See Giovanni Kezich and Maurizio Agamennone, *I poeti contadini: introduzione all'ottava rima popolare: immaginario poetico e paesaggio sociale* (Rome: Bulzoni, 1986), and Maria Elena Giusti, "Scrittura e oralità nell'ottava toscana," in *L'albicocco e la rigaglia. Un ritratto del poeta di Realdo Tonti*, ed. Pietro Clemente and Antonio Fanelli (Siena: Edizioni Gorée, 2009). For more than twenty pages of transcriptions of ottava melodies from the last century, see Maurizio Agamennone, "Cantar l'Ottava," in Kezich and Agamennone, *I poeti contadini*, 171–218. See also Francis Biggi, liner notes for Ensemble Lucidarium, *Una musa plebea: Everyday Music from Renaissance Italy*, audio recording (Raumklang, RK 2410, 2011).

14. There are few recordings or films of interpreters (although there are numerous examples of transcribed melodies in Kezich and Agamennone, *I poeti contadini*). Some examples are Dolando Bernardini singing stanze from *Orlando furioso*, released on Ensemble Lucidarium, *Una musa plebea*, track 19, https://soundcloud.com/ensemble-lucidarium/ottave-from-orlando-furioso; *L'Orlando innamorato di Gelasio Spadi*, October 25, 2016, Banca della Memoria del Casentino, https://www.youtube.com/watch?v=4B5hTcluyEQ; and *Ottava di Morgana, dall'Orlando Innamorato per Flavia Buzzetta*, January 4, 2013, https://www.youtube.com/watch?v=elFosR9pw4M. In contrast, numerous videos of improvisers can be found on YouTube and elsewhere: *Borbona—Festival di canto a braccio 2009—Ottave di saluto*, June 23, 2010, https://www.youtube.com/watch?v=iwGCCx9Po5A; *Cantar l'ottava: Progetto pilota per un documentario sui poeti in ottava rima realizzato da Leonardo D'Amico*, July 27, 2016, https://www.youtube.com/watch?v=bMXdDJzfomw; and numerous videos on the YouTube channel of the Banca della Memoria del Casentino. See also the filmography page of the Aporie website, http://www.aporie.it/filmografia.html; all accessed December 28, 2019.

15. See Wilson, "The *Cantastoria*," 167–170, and Harrán, "Doubly Tainted, Doubly Talented," 392–422.

16. See Maria Elena Giusti, "Etnografia sul teatro dei Maggi. Un bilancio degli ultimi 30 anni," in *Progetto Incontro. Materiali di ricerca e analisi*, ed. Ignazio Macchiarella and Duilio

Caocci (Isre: Nuoro, 2011), 440–461, and Mariano Fresta, "Il teatro popolare tradizionale nel Sud della provincia di Siena," in *La Val d'Orcia di Iris. Storia, vita e cultura dei mezzadri*, ed. Mariano Fresta (Montepulciano: Le Balze, 2003), 13; see also Mariano Fresta, "Glossario del teatro popolare tradizionale," in *Guida al Museo Te.Po.Tra.Tos.—Scene del teatro popolare tradizionale toscano* (Siena: Protagon, 2010). For some examples of performances of the Maggio drammatico, see the audio/video page of the website of the Centro Tradizioni Popolare della Provincia di Lucca, accessed December 28, 2019, http://www.centrotradizionipopolari.it/index.php?id=1&lang=it. Many other examples can be found on YouTube by searching for "Maggio drammatico."

17. See Francis Biggi, "La *Fabula di Orpheo* d'Ange Politien ou comment rendre une oeuvre à l'espace de l'interprétation?" in *La Musique ancienne entre historiens et musiciens*, ed. Xavier Bisaro and Rémy Campos, Musique & Recherche 3 (Geneva: Droz, Haute Ecole de musique de Genève, 2014), 491–512, and Alexandre Traube, "Traces de déclamation dans les recueils de frottole à la fin du XVe siècle: Quelques pistes pour une recherche," in *La Musique Ancienne entre historiens et musiciens*, 513–520; see also La Compagnia dell'Orpheo, Francis Biggi, dir., Angelo Poliziano, *La fabula di Orpheo*, audio recording (Sarrebourg: K617, 2007), and Ensemble Lucidarium, *Una musa plebea*.

18. Rosenzweig, "Introduction," in Bokher, Bovo d'Antona, 3.

19. A handwritten note by Elye Bokher in the margins of the *Qimḥi* talks about his first son being born in Venice on 9 Elul 5255. See Gérard Weil, *Élie Lévita: humaniste et massorète*, Studia Post Biblica 7 (Leiden: E. J. Brill, 1963), 6 and 29, and Rosenzweig, "Introduction," in Bokher, Bovo d'Antona, 3.

20. Weil, *Élie Lévita*, 6–8 and 30; Rosenzweig, "Introduction," in Bokher, Bovo d'Antona, 3.

21. In his *Sefer HaTishbi* (*The Tishbite's Book*), he complains about Jews being forced to wear yellow hats. See Paolo Nissim, "Le tappe del soggiorno in Italia di Elia Levita," *La Rassegna mensile di Israel* 32, no. 8 (1966): 359–364, 360, and Weil, *Élie Lévita*, 30.

22. Educational institutions that specialize in the study of Jewish religious texts. Their main focus is on the Torah (the first five books of the Jewish Bible) and especially the Talmud, the collection of the rabbis' writings dating from before the Common Era to the fifth century that is the basis of Jewish law.

23. Weil, *Élie Lévita*, 53–57.

24. Rosenzweig, "Introduction," in Bokher, Bovo d'Antona, 5.

25. Claudia Rosenzweig, "Elia Levita," in Elye Bokher, *Due canti yiddish: rime di un poeta ashkenazita nella Venezia del Cinquecento*, trans. Claudia Rosenzweig and Anna Linda Callow, Quaderni di traduzione 4 (Arezzo: Bibliotheca Arentina, 2010), 20.

26. Rosenzweig, "Introduction," in Bokher, Bovo d'Antona, 9.

27. The term *sèforim* is used here to indicate holy texts.

28. *Ṣpruch*, which, according to Erika Timm, means "short [rhymed] stories that are not sung"; see Elia Levita [a.k.a. Elye Bokher], *Paris un Wiene: Ein jiddischer Stanzenroman des 16. Jahrhunderts*, trans. and ed. Erika Timm and Gustav Adolf Beckmann (Tübingen: M. Niemeyer, 1996), 4–5.

29. "Bridal songs" (*Kale* means "bride").

30. Levita [Bokher], *Paris un Wiene*, 4–5, stanza 3, lines 6–8; stanza 4, lines 1, 2, and 7; stanza 5, lines 1–8. Translations are mine unless otherwise indicated.

31. See Jerold C. Frakes, ed., *Early Yiddish Texts, 1100–1750* (Oxford: Oxford University Press, 2008), 179–180—for example, *Sefer HaTishbi* (*The Tishbite's Book*, 1541), 189–192; *Nomenclatura Hebraica* (1542), 254–259; etc. The translation of the Psalms published by Conrad Adelkind was a particularly good seller and was reprinted numerous times.

32. According to Claudia Rosenzweig, its upcoming publication is mentioned in the colophon of the published version of *Bovo Bukh*. It is also found in the lists of books given by Jewish families to the censorship authorities in Mantua in 1595 and is given as an example of one of the books not to be read in the introduction to Elye's own Psalm translations. See Rosenzweig, "Introduction," in Bokher, Bovo d'Antona, 21; for an English translation of the actual quote, see Rosenzweig, 81–82.

33. Levita [Bokher], *Paris un Wiene*, cxxxvi–cxxxvii; Bokher, *Due canti yiddish*, 27–28.

34. Moses A. Shulvass, "The Jewish Population in Renaissance Italy," *Jewish Social Studies* 13, no. 1 (1951): 3–24.

35. Chava Turniansky and Erika Timm, eds., with the collaboration of Claudia Rosenzweig, *Yiddish in Italia: Yiddish Manuscripts and Printed Books from the 15th to the 17th Century* (Milan: Associazione Italiana Amici dell'Università di Gerusalemme, 2003). They state that the around eighty Yiddish documents, including minhagim (instructional books about Jewish customs), letters, literature, and Passover Haggadahs, written in Italy that have come down to us are only a small proportion of the thousands (if not tens of thousands) that were probably produced there between the late fifteenth and early seventeenth centuries.

36. Bokher, *Due canti yiddish*, 32–33; Turniansky, Timm, and Rosenzweig, *Yiddish in Italia*, 96–99.

37. Bokher, *Due canti yiddish*, 146; Turniansky, Timm, and Rosenzweig, *Yiddish in Italia*, 108–109.

38. "L'Ariosto le cento novelle, Amadis di Gaula, e simil libri profani, che non è lecito leggerli al שבת come dice רבנו משה è che da quelli non s'imparase non lascività, e cose vane," Benjamin Aaron ben Abraham Slonik, *Precetti d'esser imparati dalle donne hebree*, trans. Giacob Alpron (Venice: Gioanni de' Paoli, 1710), iii. On the reading (as opposed to singing) of Ariosto, see Michel Montaigne, *Journal du voyage en Italie, par la Suisse & l'Allemagne en 1580 et 1581. Avec des notes-par M. de Querlon* (Paris: Le Jay, 1774), 2:292 ("Di veder questi contadini il liuto in mano, e fin alle pastorelle l'Ariosto in bocca. Questo si vede per tutta Italia.").

39. Some examples are Giovanni Maria Nanino, "Aria di cantar sonetti," from *Il primo libro delle canzonette a tre voci* (Venice: Angelo Gardano, 1593), and Cosimo Bottegari, "Aria di Sonetti," from "Arie e Canzoni in musica di Cosimo Bottegari" (Modena, Biblioteca Estense, MS C 311, 1574). Alternatively, the melody of one of the many sonnet settings of the era, especially those with a generic declamatory framework, can be used as a basis for a contrafacta, such as one of the *sonetti* from *Strambotti, ode, sonetti et modo de cantar versi latini e capituli, Libro quarto* (Venice: Petrucci, [1505]).

40. See notes 10 and 11.

41. From Mordechai Dato, "Megillat Ester in Ottava rima," in *La Istoria de Purim io ve racconto ... Il Libro di Ester secondo un rabbino emiliano del Cinquecento*, ed. Giulio Busi (Venice: Luis Editore, 1987), 107.

42. Gumprecht von Szczebrszyn, MS, Budapest, Akademie der Wissenschaften, Kauffman Collection, No. 397, written in Venice, probably 1553–1554, verses 491–492. From Moritz Stern, ed., *Die Lieder des venezianischen Lehrers Gumprecht von Szczebrszyn* (Berlin: Hausfreund, 1922), 18.

43. From the dedication to Donna Corcos in Lazzaro da Viterbo, *Il Tempio di M. Moise di Riete, trasportato in vulgare Italiano* (Venice: Giovanni De Gara, ca. 1585). See also Alessandro Guetta, "Le opere italiane e latine di Lazzaro da Viterbo, ebreo umanista del XVI secolo," in *Giacobbe e l'angelo. Figure ebraiche alle radici della modernità europea*, ed. Emilia D'Anruono et al. (Rome: Lithos libri, 2012), 33–34, 46–63. A facsimile of Lazzaro's *Tempio*

can be found at Hebrew Books, accessed April 10, 2019, http://www.hebrewbooks.org/pdfpager.aspx?req=42193.

44. The Wallich manuscript, likely compiled by or for Isaac Wallich (Eisak Wallikh), is held by the Bodleian Library, Oxford; for a model example of song reconstruction of this important source of early modern Jewish music, see Diana Matut, *Dichtung und Musik im frühneuzeitlichen Aschkenas* (Leiden: Brill, 2011).

45. This tradition goes back to at least the Roman Empire. See Claudia Rosenzweig, "Rhymes to Sing and Rhymes to Hang Up," in *The Italia Judaica Jubilee Conference*, ed. Shlomo Simonsohn and Joseph Shatzmiller, Brill's Series in Jewish Studies 48 (Leiden and Boston: Brill, 2012), 149–153. Using evidence from Elye's *Sefer Ha-Tishbi*, studies by Maks Erik, and the poem itself, Rosenzweig places the poems in the pasquinata / *katovah* tradition.

46. Rosenzweig continues by saying that because manuscripts were usually produced for local use, "Nokhum Shtif argues that they became a kind of *folks-lider*, folk songs"; see Rosenzweig, "Rhymes to Sing and Rhymes to Hang Up," 148–149, and Nokhum Shtif, "Naye materialn tsu Elye Halevi's *Hamavdil-lid*," *Shriftn* 1 (1928): 154.

47. See Maks Erik, *Di geshikte von der yidisher literature fun di eltste tsaytn biz der Haskoletkufe* (Warsaw: Furlag Kultur-lige, 1928; repr. Publications of the Congress for Jewish Culture, New York: Shulsinger Bros., 1979), 179–202: page numbers same in original and reprint.

48. See "An Old *querele*," in Rosenzweig, "Introduction," in Bokher, Bovo d'Antona, 64–70, in particular 64–65.

49. The holiday celebrates the Jews' salvation at the hands of Queen Esther, wife of King Ahasuerus, and her uncle Mordechai. It is an occasion for drinking, celebration, and theatrics—often (but not exclusively) retellings of the Esther story in the vernacular—and is one of the most important days of the year for Jewish creativity.

50. Bokher, *Due canti yiddish*, 46–48; citing David Jacoby, "New Evidence on Jewish Bankers in Venice and the Venetian Terraferma (ca. 1450–1550)," in *The Mediterranean and the Jews*, ed. Ariel Toaff (Ramat-Gan: Bar-Ilan University Press, 1989), 151–178.

51. Frakes, *Early Yiddish Texts*, 140–141.

52. There is a transcription of the entire poem in both Hebrew and Latin letters in Busi, "La Istoria de Purim," 32–107.

53. Oxford, Bodleian Library, MS Michael 528, fol. 55. See Leon Modena, *The Divan of Leo de Modena: Collection of His Hebrew Poetical Works, Edited from a Unique MS in the Bodleian Library*, ed. Simon Bernstein (Philadelphia: Jewish Publication Society of America, 1932), 33–35.

54. Oxford, Bodleian Library, MS Canonici Or. 6. See Laura Minervini, "Una versione giudeospagnola dell'*Orlando Furioso*," *Annali di Ca'Foscari* 32, no. 3 (1993): 35–45. Adolf Neubauer listed it as "Italian transcribed in Hebrew characters," in Adolf Neubauer, *Catalogue of the Hebrew Manuscripts in the Bodleian Library and in the College Libraries of Oxford* (Oxford: Clarendon, 1886), 687. In his *The Jews in the Renaissance* (Philadelphia: Jewish Publication Society of America, 1959), 307, Cecil Roth theorized that it belonged to a Sephardic Jew living in Venice. Since then, in Adolf Neubauer, *Catalogue of the Hebrew Manuscripts in the Bodleian Library: Supplement of Addenda and Corrigenda to Vol. I (A. Neubauer's Catalogue)*, ed. Malachi Beit-Arié and Ron A. May (Oxford: Clarendon, 1994), 364, Malachi Beit-Arié has confirmed that it was probably compiled in Turkey. The manuscript can be found at the Digital Bodleian, accessed April 10, 2019, https://digital.bodleian.ox.ac.uk/inquire/p/bcf48b43-f81c-4dce-9aa5-f33d3ad079b9. It is a transcription of Ludovico Ariosto, *Orlando Fvrioso di M. Ludovico Ariosto*, trans. Jeronimo De Urrea (Venice: Gabriel Iolito di Ferrari,

1542). However, Minervini states that the second edition, *Orlando Furioso ... traduzido en Romance Castellano por Don Ieronimo di Vrrea* (Antwerp: Martin Nuncio, 1549), was the probable model for the Oxford transcription, while Malachi Beit-Arié writes that it was based on the 1556 Lyons edition; see Neubauer, *Catalogue of the Hebrew Manuscripts in the Bodleian Library*, 364.

55. The poet uses the word *Abonai* instead of *Adonai* to avoid writing the name of the Lord.

56. T. Carmi (pseudonym of Carmi Chamay), ed., *The Penguin Book of Hebrew Verse* (London: Penguin Books, 2006), 61–65. The Arab-Andalusian compositions are much more numerous than any poems based on Western models. Although we know they were sung, no notated melodic models from the era have survived.

57. See Israel Adler, "The Earliest Notation of a Sabbath Table Song (ca. 1508–1518)," *Journal of Synagogue Music* 16, no. 2 (1986): 17–37. For more information on the musical notation of the Christian Hebraists in Caspar Amman's circle, see Hanoch Avenary, "The Earliest Notation of Ashkenazi Bible Chant," *Journal of Jewish Studies* 26 (1975): 132–150. The information and entire manuscript are on the website of the Universitätsbibliothek der Ludwig-Maximilians-Universität München, accessed April 10, 2019, https://epub.ub.uni-muenchen.de/22791/. The extracts reproduced here appear with the permission of the Universitätsbibliothek.

58. Avery Gosfield, "Gratias post mensam in diebus festiuis cum cantico העבריים: A New Look at an Early Sixteenth-Century *Tzur Mishelo*," in *Revealing the Secrets of the Jews: Johannes Pfefferkorn and Christian Writings about Jewish Life and Literature in Early Modern Europe*, ed. Jonathan Adams and Cordelia Heß (Berlin: De Gruyter, 2017), 275–296.

59. For more information about the melodic variations, see Adler, "The Earliest Notations of a Sabbath Table Song," and Gosfield, "Gratias Post Mensam." They are also clearly visible in the melodic example given here.

60. See http://web.nli.org.il/sites/nlis/he/song/pages/results.aspx#query=any,contains, משלשו%20צור; see also Gosfield, "Gratias Post Mensam," 287–289.

61. The texts used here for both the *Šérėfę lid* and the *Hamavdil lid* were kindly provided by Dr. Simon Neuberg from his unpublished transcriptions of Oxford, Bodleian Library, MS Canonici Or. 12. It should be noted that the *o* for *qamatz* and *s* for *tav* used in the Latin-letter transcriptions of Hebrew here are not the result of an error but consistent with transcriptions made in German-speaking areas in the sixteenth century. For more information, see Gosfield, "Gratias Post Mensam," 281–284. MS Canonici Or. 12 has been digitized at the Digital Bodleian, accessed July 19, 2021, https://digital.bodleian.ox.ac.uk/objects/2303b438-073b-4e0e-81b6-4955acffb6b0/.

62. Two recordings of this piece that draw on my research are available: "Dos lid fun der sreyfe in Venedig," on Ensemble Lucidarium, *La Istoria de Purim: Musique et poésie des Juifs en Italie à la Renaissance*, audio recording (Sarrebourg: K617, 2005), with Enrico Fink, Gloria Moretti, and Viva Biancaluna Biffi, voices; Avery Gosfield and Marco Ferrari, recorders; Francis Biggi, cetra; Viva Biancaluna Biffi, vielle; and Massimiliano Dragoni, hammer dulcimer. "Tzur mi-shelo," live performance at the Musica Cortese Early Music Festival, Gorizia, 2011, by Ensemble Lucidarium with Enrico Fink, Gloria Moretti, and Marie-Pierre Duceau, voices; accessed January 17, 2021, https://www.youtube.com/watch?v=uim-XWuj8MQ&list=FLe6CoIDQQfEZsxvCN90qtpw&index=7&t=0s.

63. Frakes, *Early Yiddish Texts*, 149–150.

64. Because of an acrostic reading of "Isaac the Younger," the poem's authorship has been tentatively attributed to Isaac Judah ibn Ghayyat (Spain, 1030–1089) by some scholars (see

Frakes, 150). For audio examples of settings of this poem, see the piyyut database hosted by the National Library of Israel at http://web.nli.org.il/sites/nlis/he/song/pages/results.aspx#query=any,contains,המבדיל&indx=21 (accessed May 22, 2019).

65. Transcription from Oxford, Bodleian Library, MS Canonici Or. 12, provided by Simon Neuberg.

66. Edwin Seroussi, "In Search of Jewish Musical Antiquity in the 18th-Century Venetian Ghetto: Reconsidering the Hebrew Melodies in Benedetto Marcello's *Estro poetico-armonico*," *Jewish Quarterly Review* 93, nos. 1–2 (July–October 2002): 179–180. The informant is Leo Levy.

67. There is an extensive literature dedicated to declamation—for example, Kezich and Agamennone, *I poeti contadini*. For more than twenty pages of transcriptions of ottava melodies from the last century, see Agamennone's appendix to *I poeti contadini*, 171–218. See also Giusti, "Scrittura e oralità nell'ottava toscana," 277–306.

68. An audio recording incorporating my research is forthcoming: "HaMavdil lid," on Ensemble Lucidarium, *Sounds from Shylock's Venice*, audio recording (Abbaye de Bonmont: Ramée / Outhere, in production), with Enrico Fink, voice; Dana Howe, lute; and Avery Gosfield, recorder.

69. Gosfield, "I Sing It to an Italian Tune," and Ensemble Lucidarium, *La Istoria de Purim*.

AVERY GOSFIELD is Director of Ensemble Lucidarium, an early music group based in Italy and Switzerland. She has published numerous articles, chapters, and recordings dedicated to Jewish music in the Renaissance.

6

The Bassanos at the Court of Henry VIII
A Story of Cooperation and Protection

DONGMYUNG AHN

In 1290, the Jewish community was expelled from England and not officially readmitted until 1606, yet in the 1520s and 1530s, Henry VIII initiated two important cultural exchanges with Venetian Jews. The first, his consultation of Venetian rabbis about his divorce from Catherine of Aragon, is well known.[1] The second was his invitation to a Venetian Jewish wind-instrument family, the Bassanos, to join his court in the 1530s. In this chapter, I consider the Bassanos' move to England through the lens of an intriguing story of interfaith friendship that took place in England in 1539, related in the second edition of John Foxe's *Acts and Monuments* (1570).

Just as this friendship between a Jewish child and a Christian child in Foxe's story ostensibly promotes a message of tolerance, I argue that Henry's patronage of the Bassanos could also have been received as a message of tolerance, even if a self-serving one, because he seemingly sidestepped religious differences and protocol in his desire to elevate the musical aspect of the court. John Foxe's work, also known as the *Book of Martyrs*, becomes a useful tool for understanding the religious implications of this musical event. Ultimately, I propose that Foxe's story can be interpreted as a parable for the relationship between Henry VIII and the Bassanos, an interpretation that can illuminate the musical, political, and religious significance of their partnership.

Foxe's very brief story, which claims to recount events that took place in England in 1539, follows a Jewish child and a Christian child, "playfellow[s]," into a church and up to the altar.² At the altar, they happen on an instance of transubstantiation: however, rather than the traditional bread and wine becoming the body and blood of Christ, they see a child "broken and torn in pieces ... to be distributed among the people." Upon hearing that the Jewish boy witnessed transubstantiation, the Christian townspeople burn his house down. Miraculously, the boy survives, without even a single strand of singed hair. He claims it is because the mother of the child from the altar protected him. Set against this backdrop of transubstantiation (which, as I will argue, may be understood as an allegory for the Bassanos' creative process), I propose that the characters and scenario of the story can be useful models for understanding the relationships between the figures in the Bassano–Henry VIII story. By analyzing the story according to three methods of biblical exegesis—historical (literal), tropological (moral), and allegorical—I seek to demonstrate how this story indeed can function as a parable for the Bassanos and Henry VIII.

The details of Henry's invitation to the Bassanos have been explored by scholars such as Roger Prior, David Lasocki, and Alessio Ruffatti, but I propose that the invitation's significance has yet to be fully understood in its religious, political, cultural, and musical contexts.³ I will weave the Bassanos' story into the general history of Jews in England and Italy in order to give religious and economic context to the Bassanos' decision to leave Venice for England, allowing for the application of the Foxe story to this event.⁴

THE JEWS OF VENICE AND THE BASSANO FAMILY

In the past, some doubt has been cast on the Bassanos' status as Jews. However, Lasocki and Prior have provided ample circumstantial evidence to suggest that they were indeed Jewish, even if their professional obligations at the Scuola di San Marco required them to conceal their religion and live as Christians in Venice rather than as Jews in the ghetto.⁵ Though it was common for working-class Christians to take the name of their town as their surname (the Bassanos were from the town of Bassano), Lasocki and Prior point out that the surname Bassano was associated with rabbis in many cities of Italy.⁶ That the Bassanos married Jews is also a strong indicator of their Jewishness: Alvise, son of the family patriarch, had a daughter who married the younger son of Ambrose Lupo, the Spanish Iberian viol player whose Jewish name was Almaliach, while Jacomo and Anthony I Bassano married sisters whose surname was Nasi, a Sephardic family name.[7] Lasocki and Prior also note that the Bassanos' coat of arms—three silkworm moths and a mulberry tree—suggests that the family was connected to Jewish silk farming at one point in their family history.[8] According to Lasocki, the Bassanos' banishment from Bassano del Grappa (presumably for being Jewish) during the War of the League of Cambrai left them essentially as exiles in Venice, thus implying that they "had less to lose from the move to England."[9] Moreover, Prior and Lasocki postulate that "their readiness to conform with whatever society they happened to be in [Catholics in Venice and Protestants in England] agrees with the hypothesis that the family was at some stage Jewish."[10] For Jews living in hostile environments, the tendency to take on the religion or culture of their adopted country would not have been unusual.

What could life have been like for a Jew in Venice in the sixteenth century? On the cultural front, on April 11, 1443, Jewish schools for singing, instrument playing, dancing, and drawing were prohibited in Venice, and anyone who broke this law was subject to a fine of 500 ducats and six months in jail.[11] At the same time, Robert Bonfil notes that Jewish dancing masters were prevalent during this period and would have served both Jewish and Christian communities.[12] While Jews were permitted to reside in Venice, their residency was accompanied by a myriad of restrictions. For instance, in 1496, legislation by the Venetian Senate adjusted an earlier dress code that required Jews to wear yellow signs on their chests to a more prominent requirement—the wearing of *berete* or yellow head coverings in the summer and winter months. This was to prevent them from circumventing the earlier legislation and to make their otherness much more apparent to Venetians.[13] Though Venice allowed Jews to "stay, dwell, leave, and return as they wished," restrictions were placed on synagogue worship.[14] These kinds of restrictions could have driven Jews to a reclusive existence, at least religiously.[15]

On the other hand, Jews' occupation as moneylenders had protected them, to a certain degree, from being shut out from Venetian society. But these privileges did not protect them from intensifying persecution. Proposals to set up Christian banks—*monti di pietà*—that would replace Jewish moneylenders were intended to restrict contact between Jews and

Christians. Apparently, they were spearheaded by the rhetoric of Franciscan friars; as Bonfil notes, these friars dwelled on the "rhetorical image of the blood sucked by Jewish moneylenders."[16] In a sermon by friar Bernardino of Siena (1380–1444), Jews were cast as "leeches who ask for nothing better than the opportunity to devour an ailing member, whose blood they suck with insatiable ardor."[17] However, while monti di pietà were established in other cities in Italy, they developed less of a stronghold in Venice. Instead, as Brian Pullan notes, Jewish moneylenders were forced to charge extremely low interest rates, making it difficult for them to earn a living from this profession at all: "Incapable of making a profit if they observed the rules, the Jewish banks offered a public service that was, in effect, a fiscal burden laid on the Jewish community."[18]

Politically, by 1516, Venice had suffered a number of disappointing defeats in the War of the League of Cambrai. Complaints against the Jews escalated during this period: Franciscan friars "assaulted the alien minority with accusations of blasphemy, treachery, and hereditary guilt."[19] The city had become particularly vulnerable, as Brescia and Verona had fallen to Emperor Maximilian. Because the Venetian mentality was such that "military encounters ... were framed by eschatology," Robert Finlay argues that the ghetto's "segregation of the Jews ... was an attempt to regain God's favor at a critical time by expiating a sin."[20] On March 29, 1516, the Senate passed legislation approving the foundation of the Venetian ghetto.[21] A sermon given at the Basilica of San Marco on March 31, 1516, stated that "if the government acted against the sins of the city, the foremost of which was the freedom of the Jews, then 'God will prosper this Republic against its enemies.'"[22] Finlay theorizes that Maximillian's retreat from Milan two days later was interpreted as sign of God's intervention.[23]

On the other hand, Robert Bonfil argues for a more nuanced interpretation of the ghetto as a "halfway house between acceptance and expulsion" that "led to the crystallization of the Jewish presence within the city's topography."[24] He theorizes that the Jews did not leave the city en masse after the establishment of the ghetto because it was a place of tolerance. As he argues, "The overall attitude towards the Jews was in fact far more liberal during the period of the ghettos than it had been before. Accusations of ritual murder disappeared almost completely and the frequency of attacks and pogroms declined markedly, as did the tendency to expel the Jews."[25]

In fact, these two readings are compatible; as Bonfil writes, "Did not the continued presence of the Jews in the bosom of the Christian world present itself as necessary to the spiritual economy of Christianity?"[26] The continued Jewish presence in a Christian-dominated environment provided a "foil to Christian ... spiritual wealth."[27]

If life in Venice was indeed tolerable, albeit troubled, for the Jews, what other factors could have contributed to the Bassanos' move to England? After all, Jews were not officially permitted to reside in Tudor England, making the Bassanos' move to England particularly dependent on royal patronage and protection. Ruffatti has claimed that the superiority of economic circumstances and working conditions at the royal court in England to those at the Scuola di San Marco of Venice, where the Bassanos had been employed, could have contributed to their decision to leave.[28]

These difficult economic circumstances are reflected in the documentation concerning their employment in Venice. The Bassanos are found in Venetian records as early as 1512. Jeronimo Bassano, the patriarch of the family, is known to have played trombone for the Doge's *trombe e piffari* in 1512; his name is also found among musicians for the Mariegole of the Scuola della Misericordia.[29] The first record of a Bassano in service at the Scuola di San Marco (1515) is Jeronimo's son, Alvise, in the Notatorio. This entry describes the role the trumpets and shawms played in processions and the mass:

> (Reg. 17, Notatorio, 1498–1530)
> In the procession is carried, as was said, the aforesaid most Holy Wood under a small canopy with the umbrella, illumined by candles and accompanied by our singers, as far as the great altar of the said church.... The aforesaid Guardian and companions have resolved that whenever the said procession is done according to the forms written above, the above named singers must sing, accompanied by the trumpets and shawms. They must play at the going from the Scuola and at the returning at this solemnity, and also at all of the mass. Not only the trumpets and shawms, but also the flutes and cornets [must play]. The said trumpets and shawms must have for every such occasion 2 small lire, that is at the rate of 4 ducats a year. Thus we are in accord with the aforesaid players, who promise to attend, and not be absent, and do their duty.
>
> The trumpets and shawms are the following:
> Ser Bernardin son of Ser Bortolomeo, piffaro of the Serenissimo
> Ser Gasparo son of Ser Bernardo da Toregni
> Ser Alvise da Bassan di maestro Jeronimo
> Ser Yipolito de Ser Salvador[30]

Alvise's name is also found in membership lists of the Scuola di San Marco, as part of the Doge's trombe e piffari.[31] He served, too, in the Concerto Palatino in Bologna in 1519–1520.[32]

Players in these ensembles were not employed on a full-time basis, and Ruffatti suggests that this inconsistent employment and the resulting low morale probably factored into the Bassanos' decision to leave Venice.[33] In the period from 1526 to 1534, right around the time when the Bassanos were considering their move to England, the Scuola di San Marco experienced a period of acute financial difficulty. A document arguing for restricted hiring of trumpets and shawms testifies to the low regard the Scuola had for wind players, at least in those lean times:

> (Reg. 19, Notatorio 3, 1526–1538)
> We find in our Scuola many expenses that are superfluous and of little value to the Scuola, such as the trumpets and shawms, that misser Vetor Ziliol, during his first term as Guardian, chose for the first Sundays of the month only, with an expense of 4 ducats a year ... such expense for *cantadori solenni* is superfluous to the Scuola, because in times of procession, for 2½ ducats per occasion, we can have three singers alongside Lorenzo who will do the same as was done by those salaried permanently and perhaps better.... In that way we will come to save 16 ducats in singers and 4 ducats in instrumentalists, that in all makes 20 ducats a year, which is something certainly to do, especially in these evil times that we now find ourselves in.[34]

Given this information, perhaps it should not be surprising that despite being "esteemed above all," the Bassanos were poor and needed funds to complete their journey to England. This was noted in a letter to Thomas Cromwell from Edmund Harvell, the English ambassador to Venice who arranged for their passageway.[35] It is also telling that Harvell comments that the Bassanos left Venice without waiting for permission. Had working conditions and remuneration in Venice been favorable, would the Bassanos have made such a hasty departure?[36] Perhaps it was also a curiosity that compelled the Bassanos to set off for England, similar to the curiosity that compelled the Jewish boy in Foxe's story to dare accompany his Christian friend to a church.

THE STATUS OF JEWS IN ENGLAND

What kind of religious and cultural environment would Jews have found in sixteenth-century England? The well-documented inclusion of anti-Jewish stories in John Foxe's *Book of Martyrs* demonstrates the desire to perpetuate and solidify anti-Jewish sentiment within the Protestant martyrology, pointing to the potential that the Bassanos faced a hostile climate working at the English court, with royal protection or without it. Foxe's inclusion of four anti-Jewish stories that predate the Jews' expulsion from England testify to the history of anti-Jewish sentiment in England. The first story, dating from 1189, tells of the discovery of a false conversion of a Jew.[37] This discovery led to such hatred among the English that house burnings and general destruction of Jewish property ensued. As a result, fifteen hundred Jews took refuge in a castle and, seeing "no other remedy," took part in mass suicide.[38] Foxe's anti-Jewish sentiments are displayed in his justification of the event: he writes that "neither was this plague of theirs undeserved; for every year commonly their custom was, to get some Christian man's child from the parents, and on Good Friday to crucify him, in despite of our religion."[39] The next two stories involve children. The first, from 1235, tells of the circumcision and detention of a child by Jews in Norwich, in the aftermath of which eighteen Jews were hanged.[40] The second recounts a story of a nine-year-old child named Hugo who was crucified and left in a pit.[41] The thirty "abominable" Jews held responsible were executed. Finally, a story dating to 1257 that tells of a "wretched superstitious" Jew who fell into a privy and who "for the great reverence he had to his holy sabbath, would not suffer himself to be plucked out" conveys Foxe's prejudices against Jewish legalism.[42] The Jew in that story was found dead on Monday. In her analysis of this story, Sharon Achinstein comments that "with a whiff of *foetor judaicus*, this passage makes a strong correlation between Jew and excrement, pointing to the sewer as the place where a Jew can be found."[43] These stories display a general anti-Jewish bias that, as I will show, contrasts sharply with the story of the friendship between the Jewish and Christian children that Foxe recounts.

The expulsion of Jews from England commenced on July 18, 1290. They were given until November 1, 1290, to leave England. The Statutum de Judaismo (1275) had already forbidden Jews (and Christians) from practicing usury, one of the primary sources of income for Jews, as well as one of the few professional paths open to them, so this extreme measure of expulsion indicates the English escalation against Jews.[44] Their subsequent absence in England is reflected in Foxe's *Book of Martyrs*, which lacks stories of Jews from 1290 until the Tudor era.

Some Jews migrated to England in the late fifteenth century when Ferdinand and Isabella expelled Jews from Spain. As Cecil Roth noted, this migration created a small refugee crisis in England as Marranos—"crypto Jews who, under an outward guise of Catholicism, remained faithful at heart to the religion of their fathers"—made their way there.[45] A Marrano community in London discovered by one Gracia, widow of Francisco Mendes (a prominent pepper merchant), in 1535 on her way to Antwerp was eventually persecuted by the Inquisition in the early 1540s for false Christianity. Records from the Milan Commission of 1540 reflect the presence of sixty-nine Marrano Jews in England—including physicians; a merchant who was "a tall Jew with one eye, a master of Hebrew theology"; a perfumer with a wife and six children; and one who maintained a synagogue in his home.[46] Not all investigations into suspected Marranos revealed false Christianity, though. An account from the Acts of the Privy Council from 1545 to 1546 relates an incident of a Portuguese man by the name of Henry Alvaros who was examined to verify his Christian faith. In the end, after it was determined that he was of "Christes profession and no Jewe," Alvaros's goods and money were restored.[47]

Why would the Bassanos want to relocate to a place where Jews were not openly or legally welcomed? Could it be their status as exiles in Venice that drove them to England, as Lasocki posits? Or was it the unique situation of a monarch willing to protect the musicians just as the mother in the Foxe story protects the Jewish boy from the flames of anti-Judaism? Perhaps Henry VIII's interaction with Venetian rabbis concerning his divorce reveals that he, at least, had an open, though solipsistic, attitude toward Jews.[48] In 1527, Henry VIII's request for a divorce from Catherine of Aragon, his late brother's widow, was rejected by Pope Clement VII. Henry decided to consult Venetian rabbis to support his claim that the Leviticus 20:21 passage—"He that marrieth his brother's wife, doth an unlawful thing: he hath uncovered his brother's nakedness"—would release him from any marital obligation to Catherine. (While this biblical passage refers to cases in which the brother is alive, Henry applied it to his own situation.) Another passage in question, Deuteronomy 25:5–6, presents the opposite position and hence the debate: "When brethren dwell together, and one of them dieth without children, the wife of the deceased shall not marry to another; but his brother shall take her, and raise up seed for his brother." In a letter from John Casale to the duke of Norfolk on April 5, 1530, Casale assures the duke that "we shall have many of our side, and two Jews, to one of whom Croke has already spoken, and the other is my great friend, who translated for the Pope and the bishop of Verona certain parts of the Old Testament from Hebrew to Latin."[49] These two Jews were Elijah Menahem Halfan, an Italian rabbi and physician, and Marco Raphael, a Venetian convert to Christianity. Both agreed that the passage in Leviticus trumped the passage in Deuteronomy. But by October 1530, further controversy ensued over the Levitical stipulations in Jewish circles. Miguel Mai, imperial ambassador, wrote to Emperor Charles V in a letter on October 2, 1530, that a Jew in Rome had been "obliged to take the widow of his brother, who had died without children—a thing which is not only not prohibited, but actually enjoined by their law."[50] Even as Henry VIII's hopes of convincing Rome of the dissolution of his marriage weakened, Marco Raphael continued to advise the king. Ultimately, though Henry VIII's appeal to the Venetian rabbis was not successful, his willingness to work with Jews is notable when considered within the anti-Jewish climate of England.

It should be noted that Edmund Harvell, the ambassador who was instrumental in granting the Bassanos' passage to England, was also tangentially involved in this endeavor of Jewish-Christian cooperation. He furthered Henry's campaign for his divorce through the raising of funds from the University of Padua.[51] Perhaps his involvement in this situation and the Bassanos' situation suggests his amenability not only to cross-cultural interactions (obviously as the English ambassador to Venice) but also to interfaith interactions.

Another incident that could also be seen as evidence of Henry VIII's advocacy for Jews, even if only for self-serving and convenient reasons, is his defense of Diego Mendes. Mendes was a Marrano from Portugal, the brother-in-law of Gracia Mendes, who resettled his pepper trade business in Antwerp in 1512 after being expelled from Portugal. He was charged by the Inquisition with Judaizing.[52] Henry VIII's intervention in Mendes's case may have only been because Mendes was involved in loan transactions for the English treasury, yet his efforts seem unusual and point again to his engagement with Jews, albeit for personal gain.

ENGLISH COURT MUSICIANS

While wind players were undervalued in Venice, life as a court wind musician in England appears to have been stable and profitable. Victor Coelho and Keith Polk note that "an essential feature of English court music [was] that it was part of a large bureaucratic machine that tended to grind away on its own regardless of changes at the top," indicating that players at the bottom of the food chain, the Bassanos among them, could have expected their positions to be retained through regime changes.[53] Eileen Pearsall notes that "Tudor trumpeters were appointed for life," and there is nothing in the court records indicating otherwise for other players.[54] Thus, it appears that, economically, life as a court musician in England could be auspicious.

A group of Flemish sackbut players appears in the English court records starting in 1516, yet they gradually disappeared starting in around 1531. This suggests that room was being made for the Bassanos.[55] Two documents place the Bassanos in England in 1531: the first is a payment in September of that year to "a sackbut consort + Loyses de Jeronom" and Jasper and John "de Jeronimo," and the second is a payment in November to "Antony the Sagbut" for his trip to Southampton with new sagbuttes.[56] Lasocki notes that the duration of the Bassanos' initial stay is unclear.[57] It was their second foray into England in 1539—a stay that included all four Bassano brothers—that was more celebrated and lasting. While Lasocki argues that the Bassanos were part of a recorder consort, Coelho and Polk posit that they were "omnibus musicians, capable of performing on a variety of instruments as desired, including bowed strings."[58] In any case, their presence—even celebrity—in a country that had formally expelled the Jews centuries earlier is noteworthy and curious, and, I argue, it cannot be adequately explained through economic pressures alone. Here, a new interpretation of this historical event becomes possible through reference to the story of interfaith tolerance recounted by John Foxe.

JOHN FOXE'S *ACTS AND MONUMENTS* AND THE ALLEGORY OF THE BASSANOS AND HENRY VIII

I propose to read the story from Foxe's *Book of Martyrs* as an allegory for the Bassanos in the court of Henry VIII. In this allegory, the Bassanos are protagonists, but the figure of Henry VIII and the context of Tudor England loom large. Superimposed onto the story's Jewish-Christian binary are the Protestant-Catholic tensions that characterized sixteenth-century England, a layer that can complicate the understanding of the parabolic story but that I will untangle in my exegetical reading.

The Protestant bias on which Foxe's work is based is established in his preface, where he condemns papists, calling them "persecutors of God's truth" whose "handy work" sought "so many silly, simple lambs of Christ ... whose bodies you have slain, racked, and tormented."[59] John Foxe was steeped in Reformation theology from his years at Oxford. According to the Reverend George Townsend's *Life of the Martyrologist* (1841), Foxe had suffered much as a student at Oxford because of the passing of the Act of the Six Articles (what Foxe calls the "Whip of Six Strings"), legislation passed during Henry VIII's reign (1539) that advanced Catholicism; its first article mandated transubstantiation. Townsend recounts Foxe's response to this:

> A visible change had come over John Foxe. He was not the man to conceal his convictions and his emotions. Spies and informers were ready to seize upon any peculiarities in his behaviour.... He soon found that if he followed his convictions, he should suffer persecution. He never wavered, however, but passed through a conflict, which served only to deepen and strengthen his Christian character.... The dogma of transubstantiation and the idolatry of the mass having become odious to him, he avoided attendance as much as possible both at the College chapel and at the University Church.[60]

By the 1550s, Foxe left England to escape Catholic dogma. He began work on the *Acts and Monuments* in Basel on the urging of Grindal, one of Bishop Ridley's chaplains (Ridley was later burned at the stake during the Marian persecutions). The book, a compendium of stories of Christian martyrs from the early church to the present time, was first printed in Latin in 1554; the first English printing was in 1563. Townsend characterizes this work as the "last book which was commanded by the sovereign, sanctioned by the bishops, and ordered by a canon of the Anglican Convocation to be placed in the hall of every episcopal palace in the land."[61] Foxe himself equated his martyrology with that of the histories found in the Bible—Judges, King, Maccabees, Acts—pleading, "May it redound to no small use in the church, to know the acts of Christ's martyrs now, since the time of the apostles."[62]

Included in this martyrology is the unusual story of interfaith friendship.[63] This extraordinary instance of Jewish-Christian cooperation may have been subsidiary to the Protestant-Catholic tensions inherent in this work. John Foxe characterizes the story as one of the "lying miracles of transubstantiation," suggesting that Foxe intended the story to disabuse the reader of the notion of transubstantiation. He included it in a section titled "Allegations against the Six Articles," following Elfric's tenth-century sermon against transubstantiation and a synopsis of eleventh-century councils against Berengarius, who was called a heretic for his stance against transubstantiation.

What was a "lying miracle"? In sixteenth-century Protestant Christianity, saintly miracles, past and present, were reexamined, reassessed, and reinterpreted as "fraud, sleight of hand, or diabolical manipulation" in order to claim that the Roman church, in fact, was the false church.[64] William Tyndale, a leading sixteenth-century Protestant theologian, quotes from scripture to argue for this perspective on miracles, equating "lying miracles and wonders" with the Antichrist as Saint Paul does in 2 Thessalonians 2.[65] Tyndale also paraphrases Matthew 24:24 to state that even the "very elect" can be led astray by these "lying miracles."[66] This disbelief in miracles bled over into the question of transubstantiation during the Eucharist.[67] Tyndale accuses Thomas More, the Catholic apologist who was executed for refusing to pledge allegiance to Henry VIII, of "mischief and pernicious perverting of God's holy word" for taking Jesus literally at his word in John 6:55 ("He that eateth my flesh and drinketh my blood hath everlasting life").[68] An example of a "fayninge and counterfeyting ... miracle" that Protestants relished was the story of a priest in 1545 at Paul's Cross who "pricked his finger, that the bloude dropped on the corporasse and aulter, so that he woulde have made men beleve that the hoste of the body of Christe, by him consecrated, had bledde."[69]

I will apply three of the four senses of biblical exegesis—historical, tropological, and allegorical—in order to understand the light that they shed on the curious history of the Bassanos and Henry VIII and how they bring the Jewish-Christian exchange to the foreground. I begin with the historical or literal sense. In this story, a Jewish boy and a Christian boy enter a church. We may deduce that the Christian boy was Catholic, since the story, for Foxe, is an indictment of transubstantiation. Foxe describes the two boys as "playfellow[s]," though the veracity of this scenario seems highly unlikely given that Jews were not readmitted to England until 1606. While Foxe's characterization of the boys' relationship could, perhaps, be understood as a utopian gesture, I suggest that the alliance of Catholics and Jews should not be surprising, as both were considered opponents to the Protestant faith. Sharon Achinstein concludes that Foxe's treatment of Jews and Catholics in the *Acts and Monuments* accuses both of excessive ceremonialism and concern with law over faith.[70] From Foxe's perspective, however, the boys' friendship could simply have been part of the "lying" aspect of the story.

While this story features a Christian boy leading an apparently curious and willing Jewish boy into a church, in reality, Christian scholars have sought out Jewish texts and spirituality since the Middle Ages. Known as Christian Hebraism, this type of inquiry uses the Jewish language and culture as a conduit for the deepening of the Christian's faith. In some cases, it has led to conversion. Christian Hebraism's influence has also been felt in the gradual "minimizing [of] the role of Christ in the redemptive process," ultimately promoting "a more tolerant and open version of Christianity that blurred the boundaries between Catholics and Protestants, and between Christians and Jews."[71]

Christian scholars have also sought out Jewish scholars in matters outside religion. For instance, in the fifteenth century, Venetian scholar Marco Lippomano's inquiry of Rabbi Isaac ha-Kohen about Arabic grammar is an example of this kind of Jewish-Christian exchange.[72] While their religious differences are clear—Rabbi Isaac is referred to as "the Jew" and Lippomano as the "uncircumcised" in two of the manuscripts of the Hebrew letter—their spirit of collaboration is undeniable.[73] The letter's final benediction from Rabbi Isaac to Lippomano—"may [God] place you upon the seat of the exalted"—according to Daniel Stein Kokin, "reflects clear awareness of Lippomano's political career and ambition."[74] It is also evidence that this relationship was, at the very least, cordial.

Foxe relates that the two boys go to the altar and see a "little child broken and torn in pieces . . . to be distributed among the people." There is no mention of priests, congregation, or liturgy. But it still appears that the two boys witnessed some element of transubstantiation, with Christ himself taking the form of a child. That this miracle occurred outside the sanctity of the mass perhaps compounds its "lying" miraculousness. Upon telling his father what he saw, the Jewish boy is condemned to be burned by the townspeople (Foxe does not relate how the townspeople discovered the news). The townspeople's anti-Jewish response seems like the most realistic aspect of the story. The Christian boy is not heard of again.

What follows can be categorized as a bizarre display of interfaith goodwill. After the Jewish boy is locked in his house to be burned, the Christians check to see that he has perished. The boy is alive, with not even one singed hair. He explains it this way: "'There appeared,' said he, 'to me, a beautiful woman sitting on a chair, whose son the child was, which was before divided and distributed in the church among the people; who reached to me her hand in the burning flame, and with her gown-skirts kept the flame from me, so that I was preserved thereby from perishing.'"[75]

On the tropological level, Foxe's story seems to have more than one moral. As stories often allow their readers to imagine a world outside conventions, this story's presentation of a Christian-Jewish friendship imparts a message of religious tolerance and cooperation. In addition, the mother's protection of the Jewish boy with her gown skirts could be understood as a directive to model one's behavior after such magnanimous actions; the mother, after all, purportedly saved the Jewish boy despite his faith. This compassionate mother appears to represent the Virgin Mary, an inadvertently pro-Catholic gesture in an otherwise anti-Catholic story. Ultimately, the Virgin Mary transcends the religious divide between Christians and Jews in this story.

It must be noted that Foxe's story bears an uncanny resemblance to a story from Gregory of Tours's *Glory of the Martyrs* (sixth century) in which a Jewish boy is thrown into a fire for "happily" partaking in the Eucharist.[76] In Gregory's story, it is the boy's father, "an enemy of Christ the Lord and his law"—not a group of marauding Christians, as in Foxe's story—who throws him into a fire. But, as in Foxe's story, the Jewish boy survives the flames, "reclining as if on very soft feathers," because "the woman who was sitting on the throne in that church where [he] received the bread from the table and who was cradling a young boy in her lap covered [him] with her cloak, so that the fire did not devour [him]." Gregory notes that "there is hence no doubt that the blessed Mary had appeared to him."[77] While some details of Foxe's story are different from those of Gregory's well-known centuries-old legend, the striking similarities between the stories perhaps reinforce an understanding of Mary's compassion for the Jew.

For Foxe, however, the moral of the story is quite different. At the outset, by calling the story a "lying miracle of transubstantiation," the Protestant Foxe insinuates the moral that Catholics should not lie about such serious religious matters as transubstantiation. Foxe chastises Catholics for "borrow[ing] such figments of the Jews, to prove their feigned transubstantiation." In this case, the Jewish boy provided a witness for the transubstantiation he and the Christian boy saw.

It is at the allegorical level that this tale, a "lying miracle of transubstantiation," can be transformed into a parable about Henry VIII and the Bassanos. There is no evidence that Foxe had this story in mind—or even that he knew of it—but it emerges from the context of Tudor England as a powerful tool for understanding Henry's inclinations in bringing the Bassanos to his court. Indeed, the moral discussed previously—that readers should not believe Catholic lies about transubstantiation (lies in which Jews are also implicated)—is subverted in my allegorical reading of the story, for Henry VIII *does* borrow from the musical and artistic gifts of the Jewish Bassanos, not to prove transubstantiation but to elevate the musical culture at his court.

In my reading, the Jewish boy may be taken to represent the Bassano family, and the Christian boy may be understood as serving the same function as Edmund Harvell, the envoy who recruited the Bassanos to work at Henry VIII's court. In this scenario, the church may be taken to represent England, as both entities were governed by laws and societal norms, and the altar, the heart of the church where the liturgy culminates, may represent Henry VIII's court. The little child "broken and torn in pieces," Foxe's representation of Jesus, may be understood as the cultural aspect of the court. As the French ambassador Marillac writes to Montmorency in 1539, Henry VIII wanted to secure artists of all kinds to elevate the culture of his court: "The King, who in some former years has been solitary and pensive, now gives himself up to amusement, going to play every night upon the Thames, with harps, chanters, and all kinds of music and pastime. He evidently delights now in painting and embroidery, [having sent men to France, Flanders, Italy, and elsewhere for masters of this art, and also for musicians and other ministers of pastime.]"[78]

In a sense, Henry VIII becomes the bishop or custodian of the "flock" of artisans whom he invites from all over Europe. From Italy, in addition to the Bassanos, Henry recruited sculptors such as Pietro Torrigiano (Florence) to design a tomb for Henry VII and Elizabeth of York in 1511 and the painter Vincenzo Volpe (Naples) to paint maps.[79] Hans Holbein the younger, from Basel, became the king's painter, painting portraits of members of Henry's court.[80] Jewelers from Antwerp designed Henry's jewelry, and tailors also came from Flanders to serve the king.[81] While the collection of Flemish tapestries is known to have begun with Edward IV, by the time of Henry VIII, the court had more than two thousand tapestries.[82] The Horenbouts,

Flemish illuminators, came to the court in the 1520s; in addition to illuminating liturgical manuscripts, they also painted portrait miniatures.[83] In this context, Foxe's narrative of transubstantiation may be taken as a metaphor for the creative process of these artisans. Just as the priest takes and transforms the materials of the Eucharist (the bread and the wine), these artisans also take materials with no intrinsically divine properties (paint, clay, canvas, stone, string, wood, and musical notes) and transform them into art.

The final (and perhaps the most ludicrous) analogy to be drawn is that Henry himself can be likened to the Virgin Mary in Foxe's story. If this comparison seems implausible, the relationship between the two as manifested in the stories I am considering is uncanny. Just as Mary protects the Jewish child from the fire set by his would-be murderers in Foxe's story, it is Henry who protects the Bassanos from the fire of the Inquisition, as well as from the locals who were resentful of foreigners working in the court. Even when the Jewish Portuguese viol players were imprisoned in January 1542 for being Marranos, the Bassanos were left alone.[84] Thus, although Henry's tolerance obviously had limits and he did not extend it to those Portuguese viol players, he was willing to ignore the Bassanos' Jewish heritage apparently because their presence in his court was of benefit.[85] Indeed, Henry's "gown-skirts" of patronage allowed the Bassanos to flourish in England for three generations, as they eventually acquired titles of gentlemen.[86]

While my usage of Foxe's anti-Catholic story of a "lying miracle of transubstantiation" may seem unusual in its correlation to the Bassanos and Henry VIII, I propose that it is particularly constructive in teaching us how to understand afresh the connections among musicians, rulers, and their emissaries. A close reading of this story also sheds light on the distinctive religious aspects of the situation, which not only include the religious protection Henry seemed to offer to the Bassanos but also extend to the esteem that Henry gave to the arts—an esteem bordering on worship.

NOTES

1. For a more detailed discussion of the inner workings of these negotiations, see David S. Katz, *The Jews in the History of England, 1485–1850* (Oxford: Clarendon, 1994), 1–48.

2. This story is related in John Foxe and George Townsend, *The Acts and Monuments of John Foxe: With a Life and Defence of the Martyrologist, by the Late Rev. George Townsend*, 8 vols. (London: G. Seeley, 1870), 5:295. Curiously, this story is not discussed in Sharon Achinstein, "John Foxe and the Jews," *Renaissance Quarterly* 54, no. 1 (Spring 2001): 86–120.

3. See Roger Prior, "Jewish Musicians at the Tudor Court," *Musical Quarterly* 69, no. 2 (Spring 1983): 253–265; David Lasocki with Roger Prior, *The Bassanos: Venetian Musicians and Instrument Makers in England, 1531–1665* (Aldershot: Scolar and Brookfield, VT: Ashgate, 1995); and Alessio Ruffatti, "Italian Musicians at the Tudor Court," *Jewish Historical Studies* 35 (1996–1998): 1–14. Peter Holman also discusses the Bassanos within the context of the string players at the English court in Peter Holman, *Four and Twenty Fiddlers: The Violin at the English Court, 1540–1690* (Oxford: Clarendon, 1993).

4. My objective is not to understand the Bassanos' contributions to either Venetian or English musical life but rather to explore the complexities of their situation in these two environments with very different religious profiles and professional opportunities. On the contribution discourse, see Moshe Rosman, *How Jewish Is Jewish History?* (Oxford: Littman Library of Jewish Civilization, 2007), 111–130.

5. By contrast, Alessio Ruffatti calls their Jewish heritage into question, arguing that before they moved to Venice, the Bassanos' surname was actually Piva, a name "that does not *seem* Jewish at all" (italics added). He questions that the Bassanos lived as crypto-Christians, as none of the customary evidence citing their Jewish origins (particularly important for those who converted) appears in any documents. See Ruffatti, "Italian Musicians at the Tudor Court," 6.

6. Lasocki and Prior, *The Bassanos*, 92.

7. See Lasocki and Prior, 94; Prior, "Jewish Musicians at the Tudor Court," 257–258.

8. Lasocki and Prior, *The Bassanos*, 93.

9. Lasocki and Prior, 93.

10. Lasocki and Prior, 96.

11. See Benjamin Ravid, "The Legal Status of the Jews in Venice to 1509," *Proceedings of the American Academy for Jewish Research* 54 (1987): 186.

12. See Robert Bonfil, *Jewish Life in Renaissance Italy*, trans. Anthony Oldcorn (Berkeley: University of California Press, 1994), 135.

13. Ravid, "The Legal Status of the Jews in Venice to 1509," 192.

14. Ravid, 196.

15. On the other hand, earlier in 1464, Pope Pius II actually protected Jewish freedom of religion, stipulating that Jews be permitted to "practice their religion and threatened with excommunication anyone who forbade them from doing so." Ravid, 188.

16. See Bonfil, *Jewish Life in Renaissance Italy*, 23.

17. Bonfil, 24.

18. Brian Pullan, "Jewish Banks and Monti di Pietà," in *The Jews of Early Modern Venice*, ed. Robert C. Davis and Benjamin Ravid (Baltimore: Johns Hopkins University Press, 2001), 60. See also Brian Pullan, *Rich and Poor in Renaissance Venice: The Social Institutions of a Catholic State, to 1620* (Cambridge, MA: Harvard University Press, 1971), 449–452.

19. See Robert Finlay, "Foundation of the Ghetto: Venice, the Jews, and the War of the League of Cambrai," *Proceedings of the American Philosophical Society* 126, no. 2 (April 1982): 140.

20. Finlay, 145.

21. Asher Meshullam, leader of Jewish community, was consulted over the foundation of the ghetto—he worried that this segregation would result in a pogrom—but the proposal was still set forth. Finlay, 151.

22. Finlay, 152.

23. Finlay, 152.

24. See Bonfil, *Jewish Life in Renaissance Italy*, 72–74.

25. Bonfil, 72.
26. Bonfil, 45.
27. Bonfil, 45.
28. See Ruffatti, "Italian Musicians at the Tudor Court."
29. See Jonathan Glixon, "Music at the Venetian Scuole Grande, 1440–1540" (PhD diss., Princeton University, 1979), 1:155.
30. Translated from Glixon, 1:94–95. The original Italian (Glixon, 2:34) reads as follows:

> In la qual procession vi è portado, come è ditto, el prefato sanctissimo legno suso uno soleretto con la ombrella aluminato de cere et acompagnato cum i cantadori nostri fina al'altar grando di ditta Giesia . . . El preditto Vardian et compagni hano terminato che sempre che ditta procession se farà neli soprascritti zorni, aventi i cantadori sopranominati debi chanto acompagnarne i trombetti et piffari. I qual al andar et al tornar dela Scuola tal solmenità, ac etiam a tutta la Messa debano sonar. Si de trombe e piffari haver debiano per ogni fiada in simel caxo lire do di pizoli, che serà a raxon de anno ducati quatro al'anno. Et così sono rimasti d'acordo con i soprascritti piffari. I qual promettino attendar, et non mancar, et farà el debito suo.
>
> I trombi e pifari sono li infrascriti:
> Ser Bernardin fio de Ser Bortolomeo, pifaro del Serenissimo
> Ser Gasparo fio de Ser Bernardo da Toregni
> Ser Alvise da Bassan di maestro Jeronimo
> Ser Yipolito de San Salvador

31. Glixon, 1:104.
32. See Jeffrey Kurtzman, "Instruments, Instrument Makers, and Instrumentalists in the Second Half of the Sixteenth Century," in *A Companion to Music in Sixteenth-Century Venice*, ed. Katelijne Schiltz (Leiden: Brill, 2018), 310.
33. Six players were hired to play for the vigil and feast of San Marco as well as the feast of Sant'Agnese. See Glixon, "Music at the Venetian Scuole Grande," 1:92 and 1:48. See also Ruffatti, "Italian Musicians at the Tudor Court."
34. Translation from Glixon, "Music at the Venetian Scuole Grande," 1:98. The original Italian (Glixon, 2:37) is as follows:

> Ritrovandosi nella Schuola nostra molte spese superflue e di poco frutto a quella, come è gli trombi et pifferi, che misser Vettor Ziliol nel suo primo guardianato tolse per li prime Domeneghe del meze solamente, con spesa di ducati 4 all'anno . . . .
> Par che tal spesa di cantadori solenni sia superflua alla Schuola, perchè nel tempo delle procession con ducati 2 ½ per volta si haverà 3 cantadori apresso Lorenzo, che faranno quello istesso che fanno questi salariati de fermo, et forse meglio . . . dove a questo modo si vegnerà a sparagnar ducati 16 de cantadori et ducati 4 de sonadori, che in tutto farà ducati xx all'anno: cosa certo da far, et massime ne gli tempi senestri, che hora si ritroviamo.

35. See entry 280 in *Letters and Papers, Foreign and Domestic, of the Reign of Henry VIII: Preserved in the Public Record Office, the British Museum, and Elsewhere in England*, arranged and catalogued by J. S. Brewer (London: Longman, Green, Longman, and Roberts, 1862–1932), vol. 14/2: 106.
36. See also Ruffatti, "Italian Musicians at the Tudor Court."
37. See Foxe and Townsend, *The Acts and Monuments of John Foxe*, 2:277.

38. Foxe and Townsend, 2:277.
39. Foxe and Townsend, 2:277.
40. Foxe and Townsend, 2:534.
41. Foxe and Townsend, 2:534.
42. Foxe and Townsend, 2:535.
43. See Achinstein, "John Foxe and the Jews," 86.
44. See Cecil Roth, *A History of the Jews in England* (Oxford: Clarendon, 1941), 70.
45. Roth, 135.
46. See Lucien Wolf, "Jews in Tudor England," in *Essays in Jewish History*, ed. Cecil Roth (London: Jewish Historical Society of England, 1934), 78–79.
47. *Acts of the Privy Council of England*, vol. 1, 1542–1547 (London: H. M. Stationery Office, 1890), 305–306.
48. David Lasocki and Roger Prior note the "welcome extended him [Mark Raphael, one the king's Venetian Jewish advisors] would obviously smooth a path for other Jews." See Lasocki and Prior, *The Bassanos*, 94.
49. See entry 6310 in *Letters and Papers*, vol. 4/3: 2835.
50. See entry 6661 in *Letters and Papers*, vol. 4/3: 3002.
51. See Robert Barrington, "Two Houses Both Alike in Dignity: Reginald Pole and Edmund Harvell," *Historical Journal* 39, no. 4 (December 1996): 904.
52. See Roth, *A History of Jews in England*, 135. See also Katz, *The Jews in the History of England*, 3–6.
53. See Victor Coelho and Keith Polk, *Instrumentalists and Renaissance Culture, 1420–1600: Players of Function and Fantasy* (Cambridge: Cambridge University Press, 2016), 28.
54. See Eileen Sharpe Pearsall, "Tudor Court Musicians, 1485–1547: Their Number, Status and Function" (PhD diss., New York University, 1986), 124.
55. Pearsall, 128.
56. See the entry for September 30, 1531, in Andrew Ashbee, *Records of English Court Music*, vol. 7, 1485–1558 (Aldershot: Scolar, 1993), 368–369.
57. Lasocki and Prior, *The Bassanos*, 7.
58. See Coelho and Polk, *Instrumentalists and Renaissance Culture*, 30.
59. Foxe and Townsend, *The Acts and Monuments of John Foxe*, 1:xii.
60. Foxe and Townsend, 1:7.
61. Foxe and Townsend, 1:3.
62. Foxe and Townsend, 1:viii.
63. Foxe and Townsend, 5:295.
64. See Helen Parish, *Monks, Miracles, and Magic: Reformation Representations of the Medieval Church* (London: Routledge, 2005), 46.
65. William Tyndale, *Doctrinal Treatises and Introductions to Different Portions of the Holy Scriptures*, ed. Henry Walter (Cambridge: Parker Society, 1848), 286–287.
66. See William Tyndale, *The Works of English Reformers: William Tyndale and John Frith*, ed. Thomas Russell, 3 vols. (London: Ebenezer Palmer, 1831), 2:95.
67. As Helen Parish has written, "The rhetoric of novelty, fraud, and feigned miracle that had been directed against the cult of the saints was also turned against the central rite and sacrament of the church and used to justify the rejection of traditional teaching on the theology of the Eucharist." See Parish, *Monks, Miracles, and Magic*, 63.
68. See William Tyndale, *An Answer to Sir Thomas More's Dialogue, the Supper of the Lord after the True Meaning of John VI and 1 Cor. XI* (Cambridge: Cambridge University Press, 1850), 229.

69. Story from Charles Wriothesley, *A Chronicle of England during the Reigns of the Tudors, from A.D. 1485 to 1559*, ed. William Douglas Hamilton, 2 vols. (London: Camden Society, 1875–1877), 1:152. This story is discussed in Peter Marshall, "Forgery and Miracles in the Reign of Henry VIII," *Past and Present* 178 (February 2003): 66.

70. See Achinstein, "John Foxe and the Jews," 93–94.

71. See David B. Ruderman, *Early Modern Jewry: A New Cultural History* (Princeton, NJ: Princeton University Press, 2010), 176.

72. See Daniel Stein Kokin, "Isaac ha-Kohen's Letter to Marco Lippomano: Jewish-Christian Exchange and Arabic Learning in Renaissance Italy," *Jewish Quarterly Review* 104, no. 2 (Spring 2014): 192–233. Also, a series of Hebrew letters that were exchanged between Marco Lippomano and Jewish scholar Crescas Me'ir were published by Adolf Neubauer in 1886. See Adolf Neubauer, *Catalogue of the Hebrew Manuscripts of the Bodleian Library and in the College Libraries of Oxford* (Oxford: Clarendon, 1886), cols. 751–752, no. 2174. See also Kokin, "Isaac ha-Kohen's Letter to Marco Lippomano," 193n3.

73. As Kokin points out, "Though the term 'uncircumcised'... might appear derogatory, it appears to have functioned as a neutral designation for Christians." Kokin, 203.

74. Kokin, 217.

75. Foxe and Townsend, *The Acts and Monuments of John Foxe*, 5:295.

76. See Gregory of Tours, *Glory of the Martyrs*, trans. Raymond Van Dam (Liverpool: Liverpool University Press, 1988), 29–30. Margot Fassler notes that Fulbert of Chartres (twelfth century) refers to Gregory of Tours's story of the Jewish boy in his prayer found in the sermon *Approbate consuetudinis* attributed to him: "May you be gentle and merciful, as you were to the little Jewish boy, so that just as you freed him from the furnace of glowing fire, so may you free me from the seasurge of carnal desires with your intercessions and holy prayers." Margot Fassler, *The Virgin of Chartres: Making History through the Arts* (New Haven, CT: Yale University Press, 2010), 88–89.

77. Gregory of Tours, *Glory of the Martyrs*, 30.

78. See entry 1092 in *Letters and Papers*, vol. 14/1, 498.

79. Carol Galvin and Phillip Lindley, "Pietro Torrigiano's Portrait Bust of King Henry VII," *Burlington Magazine* 130, no. 1029 (December 1988): 892–902; Peter Barber, "England I: Pageantry, Defense, and Government: Maps at Court to 1550," in *Monarchs, Ministers, and Maps: The Emergence of Cartography as a Tool of Government in Early Modern Europe*, ed. David Buisseret (Chicago: University of Chicago Press, 1992), 33.

80. Susan Foster, "Holbein as Court Painter," in *Henry VIII: A European Court in England*, ed. David Starkey (London: Collins and Brown, 1991), 58–63.

81. Alison Weir, *Henry VIII: King and Court* (London: Jonathan Cape, 2001), 192 and 188.

82. David Starkey, *Henry VIII: A European Court in England* (London: Collins and Brown, 1991), 8. See also Theodor Dumitrescu, *The Early Tudor Court and International Musical Relations* (Burlington, VT: Ashgate, 2007), 6 and 16.

83. Janet Backhouse, "Illuminated Manuscripts and the Development of the Portrait Miniature," in *Henry VIII: A European Court in England*, 88–93.

84. For a closer look at the Jewish Portuguese viol players in England in the 1540s, see Roger Prior, "A Second Jewish Community in Tudor England," *Jewish Historical Studies: Transactions of the Jewish Historical Society of England* 31 (1988–1990): 137–152.

85. Roger Prior suggests that Jewish employment could have been precisely because they were Jewish. He writes, "Despite official ban and some popular prejudice against Jews... their employment must have been a deliberate act of policy.... It was doubtless realized...

that Jews would make reliable servants precisely because they owed loyalty neither to the Pope nor to Luther. Indeed, in a curious way their independence from both camps was a reflection of Henry's own attitude. And in the event, their loyalty to the Crown was amply proved." See Prior, "Jewish Musicians at the Tudor Court," 262–263.

86. Lasocki and Prior, *The Bassanos*, 86.

> DONGMYUNG AHN teaches music history at Queens College and is Director of the Queens College Baroque Ensemble. She received her PhD in musicology at the Graduate Center, CUNY, and has published an article on medieval liturgy in the Rodopi series Faux Titre.

7

Jewish and Converted Musicians and Musical Instrument Makers in Southern Italy in the Fifteenth through Early Seventeenth Centuries

LUIGI SISTO

The migration of Iberian Jewish and converted musicians to Italy following the Sephardic expulsions from Spain (1492) and Portugal (1497) had a strong impact on Italian culture—both Jewish and non-Jewish—at the turn of the sixteenth century. A rich array of sources reveals the importance of Jewish and converted musicians and makers of musical instruments within the Kingdom of Naples. Specifically, an exploration of materials preserved in the State Archive of Palermo (1513) reveals an indelible link between Sephardic migrant musicians and Neapolitan musical life. This connection runs deep enough that it directly affected the evolution of musical instrument design, as demonstrated by accounts in theoretical treatises, iconography, and evidence recovered from the shops and residences of Jewish and converted instrument makers in the sixteenth century. These findings provide an opportunity to retrace the paths of Jewish and converted musicians from Spain to Naples, illuminating the extensive participation of Iberian Jews in Italian musical culture.

From a conceptual standpoint, the purposes of studying the participation of migrating Jews and converts in the cultures of musical instrument design and manufacture run well beyond identifying the so-called contributions of Jews to European civilization. Indeed, as historian Moshe Rosman has noted, the historiographical urge to account for Jews' "contributions" to society seems to accept the premise that such contributions are a prerequisite for scholarly attention and study.[1] By contrast, I view the Jews and converts who migrated to the Italian peninsula as agents of musical culture whose artisanship and commercial networks facilitated innovative ideas and practices.

For David B. Ruderman, mobility was a defining feature of early modern Jewry with far-reaching social and cultural consequences.[2] Indeed, Ruderman hypothesizes (admitting that this cannot yet be demonstrated definitively) that migration such as those caused by the expulsions from the Iberian Peninsula may have led to "cultural productivity" and innovation, including in "itinerant professions such as medicine, performing arts, the rabbinate, and trade."[3] Migration—whether forced or voluntary—brought together individuals from disparate backgrounds, and the presence of Sephardic Jews and converts on the Italian peninsula had a marked impact on both Jewish communities and the wider cultural landscape. Moreover, Ruderman argues, it is logical and worthwhile to consider Jews and converts away from Judaism together, since many Sephardic Jews viewed their religious affiliation flexibly and "pragmatically," with converts often playing a "mediating role" between Jews and Christians.[4] The effect of Jewish and converted instrument builders on instrumental culture at a revolutionary moment in Italian musical history demonstrates the extent to which Jews and converts interacted with their Christian-born neighbors. Although such interactions were often uneasy and sometimes led to persecution and even violence (examples of which I discuss in subsequent passages), such tensions did not prevent these individuals from dramatically reshaping the practices of musical instrument manufacture—and, by extension, musical practice— in early modern Italy.

THE EXPULSION FROM IBERIA (1492 AND 1497)

With the election of Alonso Borgia as pontiff Callistus III in 1455, the Borgia dynasty—originally from Játiva and Gandia, two small towns south of Valencia—emerged from anonymity. The rise of this powerful Valencian family to the papal throne opened a path for the inclusion of a large number of Catalans in the papal court, which in turn led to accusations of nepotism.

The strength of these claims was reinforced by Callistus's appointment of his nephew Rodrigo Borgia to the post of bishop of Valencia. Rodrigo assumed that role shortly before his uncle's death in 1458, settling in Italy and embarking on a career that would eventually lead him to the papacy in 1492. Now known as Alessandro VI (1492–1503), the new pope encouraged the settlement of Catalans throughout Rome and the Papal States. This migration included musicians and makers of musical instruments. Indeed, as Ian Woodfield rightly asserts, "The Borgia family played a vital, if inadvertent, role in the dissemination of these [Valencian] instruments on the Italian mainland."[5]

Closely linked to the dominion of the Borgias was the Kingdom of Naples, which was under Aragonese rule during this period. Ferrante d'Aragona (1423–1494) succeeded his father, Alfonso d'Aragona, in 1458 and was thereafter known as Ferdinando I. Ferdinando's passion for music and the arts attracted a multitude of musicians and musical instrument makers from across Europe. Eyewitness accounts confirm this influx of musicians; the orator Raffaello Lippo Brandolini, writing at the turn of the sixteenth century, observed, "It is true that Ferdinando inherited the Neapolitan Kingdom from his father Alfonso. He governed with moderation for about 37 years. He dedicated himself greatly to the study of the discipline of music, both in public and in private, not only practicing it often, harmoniously, during his leisure, but also attracting men from all over Europe who were highly skilled in the discipline [of music] and expert craftsmen of musical instruments, with the promise of great rewards."[6]

Ferdinando also demonstrated a notable tolerance toward foreigners. This can be seen in the 1469 decree *Prammatica super immunitatibus exterorum*, which granted a series of privileges to foreigners residing in the Kingdom of Naples, allowing them to become integrated into the population.[7] Together with Naples's geographic location, this tolerance encouraged a large number of Sephardic Jews to migrate to the region, which included Sicily and Palermo, following their expulsion from Spain in 1492 and Portugal in 1497.[8] As a result, many Sephardic musicians—including musical instrument makers—settled in those territories. The Kingdom of Naples thus joined the Papal States in becoming a privileged place for the circulation of musical sources and, above all, one of the most important sites of convergence for musical instruments and building traditions.[9]

New instrument technologies emerged as a result of the convergence of diverse peoples in this relatively friendly atmosphere. The development of the viola da gamba particularly aroused the interest of the Flemish theorist Johannes Tinctoris, who resided in the region in 1472.[10] During his time in Naples, Tinctoris witnessed one of the most significant innovations in the construction of stringed instruments, the invention of the arched bridge: "But there is *another viola* [which Tinctoris understood to have come from the Mediterranean area], which differs from the lute not only in shape (as did the last-mentioned) but also in stringing and method of playing. For it has either (1) three simple strings tuned to a pair of fifths, which is the most usual, or (2) five strings tuned unevenly in fifths and unisons. These are stretched in a protuberant manner so that the bow (which is strung with horse-hair) can touch any one string the player wills, leaving the others untouched."[11]

Although Tinctoris hypothesized an Eastern origin for this type of instrument, the Sephardic musicians who joined the flourishing Aragonese court of Naples at the end of the century were likely involved in these developments. Among the builders active at his court (not all of Jewish origin) were Antonio Ferrer (a member of a Christian religious order), who received payments for building musical instruments for Ferdinando;[12] Sebastiano de Martino, a luthier and (likely) maker of violas; and the young Raffaele Massa of nearby Sorrento, who had clearer Jewish origins and who became Martino's apprentice on November 16, 1486.[13]

Evidence of Sephardic involvement in the development of musical instruments is also extant in Neapolitan iconography. New types of musical instruments of clear Spanish origin may be seen in paintings produced in Naples at this time. Around 1500, the painter Cristoforo Scacco depicted *The Coronation of the Virgin*, now housed at the Museum of Capodimonte in Naples. Among the musician angels above the painting's protagonists, some appear to be playing the *viola d'arco* (*vihuela de arco*) and the *viola da mano* (*vihuela de mano*) (fig. 7.1). Indeed, ample evidence of the widespread use of these instruments survives in later sources. The first testimony in Italy of the use of a viola da mano appears in the musical works of Francesco Canova da Milano (1497–1543), a Milanese lutenist working in Naples. In 1536, Francesco published his *Intavolatura per viola overo lauto*.[14] His work preceded Bartolomeo Lieto's 1559 treatise, *Dialogo quarto de musica per intavolare con viola da mano over lauto*, also printed in Naples.[15] Both works have profound

FIGURE 7.1.

Cristoforo Scacco, *L'incoronazione della vergine coi Ss Marco e Giuliano* (ca. 1500), Museum of Capodimonte, Naples (tempera and gold on wood). With permission of the Ministry for Cultural Heritage and Activities and for Tourism—Museo e Real Bosco di Capodimonte.

significance for musical instrument development in Naples: they not only attest to the interchangeability between the lute and the viola da mano but provide unequivocal evidence of the viola da mano's proliferation in those territories over the course of these decades.

Sicilian Jews and recent converts from Judaism played a leading role in the distribution of these musical instruments, serving as agents in the spread of Renaissance artistic culture in the territories they reached. This must surely be due, in part, to the networks of trade that they established throughout the Italian peninsula and across parts of Europe.[16] Their stories, and those of their musical instruments, emerge through documentary evidence dating to the early sixteenth century.[17]

As noted by Nadia Zeldes, some of these stories can be discerned from the records of the Inquisition, which confiscated and catalogued the property of recent Sicilian converts: "Since most of these inventories were made in the first decade of the sixteenth century it is reasonable to suppose that they reflect the existing cultural trends among the Jews rather than new tastes of the recently converted."[18] One of these recent converts from Judaism was the fabric merchant Matteo Porto in Messina.[19] Among Porto's possessions were a "violecta" and a "cornecto di caccia" (hunting horn).[20] Another case that Zeldes has discussed is that of Matteo Sansone, a musician in Palermo, whose goods were also confiscated by the Inquisition. Among his property, "contained within the church of San Sebastiano and the marina," were twenty-eight music books, four violas, five "hand viols" (*viole de mane*), and strings for the viola d'arco. The list also includes paintings, objects of amber and coral, nautical charts, fabrics, and texts by Virgil, Ovid, and Petrarch:

> Macteo sansonj Musico / Inventarium bonorum repertorum in domo Mactey De sansono De panhormo
> De mandato R.mj Dominj Alfonsi / bernal Inquisitoris
> Apud f<idelissimam> u<rbem> panhormj die X marcij prime jnd<ictionis> 1513 . . .
> Im primis la casa undi ipso habita existenti in ditta citate di palermo confinata cum la eclesia di santo Sebastiano et la marina
> In una saletta suso di la ditta casa
> Item XXVIII peze di libre
> Item uno Virgilio et uno Ovidio
> Item un petrarca y otro libro tuscano
> Item uno letillo di tenere libre de musica pinto pichulo . . . Item quattro viole di arco cum soi arcque . . .
> Item v [cinque] viole di mane dissero essere de prestare . . . Item quattro liutj grande et mezane
> Item una caxa di viola di arco
> Jn una cassa blanca usata pichula . . .
> Item una viola grande vecha con sua caxa . . . In uno scrigno barrato . . .
> Item una gitarra seu violecta spagnola[21]

The extent of Matteo Sansone's confiscated property leaves no doubt about his flourishing musical activity. He owned fifteen exemplars of violin manufacture, together with a keyboard instrument ("clavabuena") noted in a separate inventory written in Spanish; that same Spanish inventory indicates that some of these instruments were meant to be loaned.[22] Indeed, ownership of such a substantial collection by a Sephardic musician suggests that he managed these instruments in a business capacity, perhaps renting them to other musicians.

The inventory of Sansone's property offers interesting terminological details. The distinctions between "viole di mane" and "viole di arco" are to be expected, since the term *viola*—even during the second half of the fifteenth century—signified what Woodfield describes as "two manifestations of the one basic type," as demonstrated by the terms *viola cum arculo* and *viola sine arculo*.[23] In light of this, the presence of a "gitarra seu violecta spagnola"—an instrument clearly differentiated from others included in the inventory—takes on particular significance. The noun *violecta*, when modified by the Spanish adjective *spagnola*, designates a type of musical instrument closer to the lute than to a bowed string instrument. In fact, there is no doubt that this instrument derived from the lute, as reflected in its smaller dimensions, its tortoise-shaped box, and its similar arrangement of strings. Here, apparently for the first time, the term *violecta* is used as a synonym for *gitarra*, the guitar.

A description of this instrument appears in Tinctoris's treatise *De inventione et usu musicae*. Calling it the "ghiterra" or "ghiterna," he specifies that it was invented by the Catalans themselves: "In addition, the instrument invented by the Catalans: some call it *ghiterra*, others *ghiterna*: it derives from our lyra. Indeed, this [instrument] is like the lute (though much smaller) and has the form of a tortoise shell, and the touch and the disposition of the strings derive from it."[24] The characteristics of this instrument are also known thanks to its iconographic representation in Sebastian Virdung's *Musica getutscht* (1511), published only two years before the requisition of Matteo Sansone's property (see fig. 7.2).

The terminological clarifications that appear in Sansone's inventory add nuance to the term *viola*, a complex word applied to a wide array of musical instruments in the fifteenth and sixteenth centuries.[25] These include the "lute, *viola da mano, viola d'arco*, violin, *lira da braccio* and perhaps also *ribeca*."[26] This diversity of meanings is confirmed by a Ferrarese inventory of 1511, which appears in the correspondence between Isabella d'Este (1474–1539) and the *strumentaio* (instrument maker) Lorenzo Gugnasco, in which

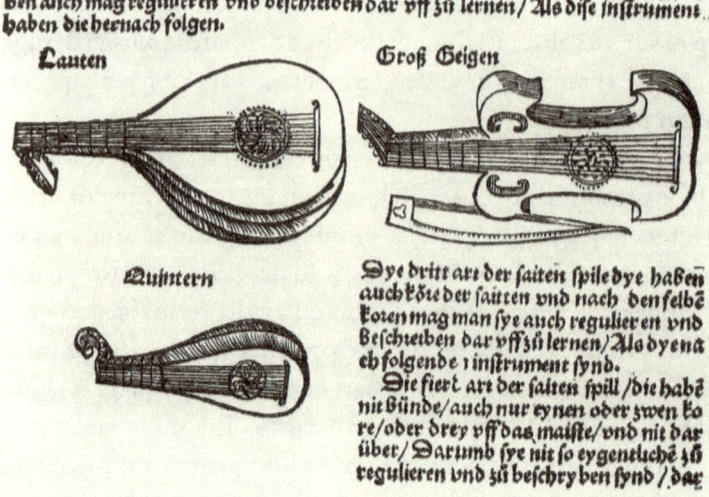

FIGURE 7.2.

Sebastian Virdung, *Musica getutscht* (Basel: M. Furter, 1511), fol. Bij.
Image courtesy of the Bibliothèque nationale de France.

"Quattro violoni alla napolitana" are listed under the entry entitled *lauti*.[27] Previously, the term *violetta*, as a diminutive of *viola*, had been associated with small bowed instruments; think of the violetta of Santa Caterina de' Vigri (before 1463), kept at the Convent of Corpus Domini in Bologna, or the typology depicted by Benvenuto Tisi in the frescoes in the Sala del tesoro (1508–1512) at Palazzo Costabili in Ferrara.[28] The terminological clarification presented in the Sansone inventory confirms that the modifiers *spagnola* and *alla spagnola* not only refer to plucked instruments coming from or closely linked to Spain—thus referring to its place of origin—but were also used to highlight typological features of the instruments.[29]

It is noteworthy that so many of Matteo Sansone's instruments indicate that he was at the forefront of musical instrument culture on the Italian peninsula. His case appears to be an instance in which his network of contacts positioned him as an agent of musical culture who helped to shape the practices of others around him. And yet his status as a convert from Judaism led to the confiscation of his property. We do not know Sansone's fate; it is likely that he emigrated to the more open and tolerant courts of northern

FIGURE 7.3.

Giovanni Battista (Sansone) known as "Il Siciliano / Ciciliano" (Lat. *Siculus*) from Nikolaus Reusner, *Icones sive imagines vivae* (Basel: Conr. Valdkirch, 1589). Image courtesy of the Bibliothèque nationale de France.

Italy, or to those of Henry VIII of England, where numerous Sephardic Jews migrated during the Inquisition, despite the official ban on Jews there.[30]

Incidentally, migrants to northern Italy included the viol player Messer Giovanni Battista Sansone (fig. 7.3), known as Il Siciliano or Ciciliano. It is unknown whether he was related to Matteo Sansone, but again, the last name suggests a Jewish lineage, and it is possible that he moved to northern Italy in search of a more tolerant environment. The son of Antonio I, Il Siciliano was in the employ of Cardinal Ippolito de' Medici and was referred to as a "peritissimo di tal istromento dirò del violon" (virtuoso of this instrument called the viola) by Silvestro Ganassi in the second volume of his *Regola Rubertina*.[31]

At first, many Jewish migrants merely stopped in Naples, where the Sephardic population was temporarily safe—at least until their expulsion in 1544. The young Antonio Catalano of Palermo, whose surname is of evident Judeo-Spanish origin, was active in the Spanish-ruled city of Naples (Spain having ruled the region from 1503 onward) starting in the 1540s.[32] As documented in a contract dated October 6, 1544, Antonio Catalano was an apprentice in the workshop of the Neapolitan *violaro* (viola maker) Jacopo Antonio Cuccurullo.[33] Other apprentices active in the same workshop during those years include the Neapolitan Giangiacomo de Rosa, who was apprenticed there for eight years beginning on October 7, 1545, and Marco de Callo, who hailed from Mormanno in the territories of the Vicereign and was apprenticed to Cuccurullo by a six-year contract on March 6, 1546.[34]

It is quite probable that the Neapolitan violin makers active during the second half of the sixteenth century included descendants of converted Jews who had been established in Naples for several generations. Jewish ancestry may be hypothesized for the violaro Giovanni Tommaso Matino, whose partnership with Orazio Albanese is documented in 1578.[35] Although we do not know the family origins of these violin makers with certainty, the term *Ebreo neofito* or *Levante* was often refined to the surname Matino, and the name Albanese may be associated with populations from the Apulian region of Italy.[36] These populations may have been Jewish or Arbëreshë (a group of Italian-Albanians descended from the Albanian refugees who immigrated to the Apulian region of southern Italy following the Ottoman invasion in the fourteenth century). In fact, the partnership between the two violin makers could point to connections between the Arbëreshë and Jews from the Spanish Kingdom of Naples. Such a partnership would be characteristic of Jews and converts during this period of migration and the forging of international networks of community and trade.

It is fascinating to contemplate these builders' activities, which likely contributed to the survival of certain musical instruments, including the viola d'arco, notably used in Naples at the end of the sixteenth century. It is no accident that Scipione Cerreto highlights players of this instrument in his *Della prattica musica vocale, et strumentale* (1601), calling them "excellent players of *viola d'arco* from the city of Naples, who [still] live today." Among these, he mentions Enrico Francese, Francesco di Paola, Ottavio Cortese, and Antonio Miscia.[37] Table 7.1 presents the names of string players and their specific instruments as outlined in Cerreto's treatise. In addition to providing the players' names, this table illustrates the most commonly used string instruments by musicians in Naples during this time period. Some of the names, such as Montella and di Paola, were common among recent converts.

Given Cerreto's extensive musical knowledge, it is likely that he used instrumental terminology such as *viola d'arco* precisely, referring to a specific type of musical instrument later referred to as the "viola tastata."[38] Even more certain is that this precise terminology was used to provide a necessary clarification that distinguished the viola d'arco "from its new competitor, the violin."[39]

FROM THE COURT OF GESUALDO DA VENOSA TO THE TOLERANCE OF THE GONZAGAS

Openness toward converted Jews grew in the late sixteenth and early seventeenth centuries, providing professional opportunities for a significant number of musicians. Many of these were active at the court of Carlo Gesualdo, prince of Venosa, of whom Cerreto noted, "Everything current, it seems to me, you may see in the figure of the illustrious Signor Don Carlo Gesualdo, Prince of Venosa ... to this Prince it is not enough to take delight in music; in addition, for his pleasure and entertainment, he keeps many excellent composers, performers, and singers at his court."[40]

Among these musicians were certainly Scipione "Pietro Paolo" Stella, priest of Theatine and author of the dedications in Gesualdo's first and

Table 7.1. Instruments and musicians in Naples before and in 1601, as described in Scipione Cerreto, *Della prattica musica vocale, et strumentale* (Naples: G. G. Carlino, 1601), 3:154–160.

		Ante 1601		
liuto	viola d'arco	chitarra a sette corde	lira da gamba	arpa
Giovanni Antonio Severino	Herrico Francese	Fabio Caltelano	Antonio Miscia	Giovan Leonardo dell'Arpa
Giovan Domenico Montella	Francesco di Paola	Antonio Miscia	Martio Cortese	Ascanio Maione
Camillo Lambardi	Ottavio Cortese	Giovan Battista di Nicola	Domenico Gallo	
Luca Bolino	Antonio Miscia	Ottavio Cortese		
Prospero Staivalo				

		In 1601		
liuto	viola d'arco	chitarra a sette corde	lira da gamba	arpa
Fabrizio Dentice	Orazio del Violone	Ottavio Miroballo		
Vicencello Severino	Andrea Romano	Vito Antonio, *per antichità napolitano*		
Giulio Severino	Bartolomeo Roy			
Pompeo Severino	Annibale Bolognese			
Garzia e Luise Maglione	Prospero Planterio			
A. Bolognese				
G. C. Stellatello				
F. Cardone				
Luise Caso				

second books of madrigals for five voices (Ferrara, 1594); the composer and organist Pomponio Nenna; the Flemish composer Jean de Macque, who had been in the service of the prince since 1585 following nearly twenty years in Rome (he was also master of the Royal Chapel in Naples from 1599 to 1614); de Macque's pupil Giovanni Domenico Montella; and the keyboardist and composer Scipione Dentice. (Some of these musicians likely had Jewish origins, as I will discuss in the following pages.) In the same circle as these figures were Ascanio Mayone and Giovanni Maria Trabaci; since 1601, Trabaci had been organist of the Royal Chapel, and he was then promoted to master, serving as a substitute for de Macque. Mayone and Trabaci were not in the direct service of Gesualdo, but they understood Gesualdo's tastes and innovations. This was evident in their production of music for *cimbalo cromatico* (chromatic harpsichord), an instrument dear to Gesualdo and present in his castle in southern Italy.[41]

The list may be completed with the name of another musician of Jewish origin, of whom little biographical information is known: Mutio Effrem (*de effrem, de fremma*), who was born in Bari on November 4, 1549, and died in Naples after 1640 and whose name apparently derives from the biblical name Efraïm. Effrem was in Gesualdo's service from about 1591 until at least 1609. During this time, Effrem came into contact with many musicians from the Apulia area; most prominent among these was Stefano Felis, and others included Rocco Rodio, Giovanni Massa, Diego Perfino, Luigi Rossi, and Pomponio Nenna. These names attest to Gesualdo's influence among musicians from southern Italy, as well as those with apparent eastern origins—origins that are evident despite the names that these musicians gave to their children. Effrem, for example, baptized his eldest son Giovan Battista in 1601:

> Act 45. May 2 (1601)
> Giovan Battista, son of Mutio Effrem and Vittoria de Donatellis, was baptized by me, the archpriest, and named after his godfather Giovanni Battista de Paola.[42]

Despite the use of such obviously Christian names as Giovanni Battista, the court of Gesualdo, at its moment of greatest splendor—the end of the sixteenth century and the beginning of the seventeenth—was one of the foremost Italian courts for the reception of musicians and instrument builders with clear Jewish origins.

Clues indicating the Jewish origins of Gesualdo court artisans can be found in their surnames. Widely documented in southern Italian communities, surnames such as Stella, De Paula, and Montella point to a clear Jewish derivation.[43] In addition to its biblical Hebrew association, the name Effrem was also the name of the Syriac patron saint of singers and musicians; in the case of Mutio Effrem, it assumes an almost prophetic character. If Mutio was the first in his family to convert, his surname may indicate a transparent underlining of his origins and craft. The slippage between Jewish and Christian identity evident in the case of the Effrem family is characteristic of early modernity, as Ruderman has argued, since converts often served as bridges between Jewish and Christian communities and cultures.[44]

Such connections can be seen at the court of Ferdinando Gonzaga, duke of Mantua, which was considered one of the most open and tolerant in Renaissance Italy—the Jewish composer and violinist Salamone Rossi spent his entire career at the Mantuan court, and the city was home to a robust Jewish community that was actively engaged in music and theater. Ferdinando hired Effrem in 1615 and paid his considerable travel expenses from Naples.[45] Compositions by Effrem survive alongside those of Salamone Rossi and the Christians Claudio Monteverdi and Alessandro Ghivizzani in the music for Giovan Battista Andreini's *La Maddalena*, a *sacra rappresentazione* likely staged for the wedding of Ferdinando Gonzaga and Caterina de' Medici in 1617.[46]

Indeed, Effrem was almost certainly one of the many converts in Mantua who practiced the crafts of music and musical instrument making. Members of other families with Jewish origins who were involved in these endeavors include the d'Aponte dynasty, active in Naples at the end of the sixteenth century, and the organ builder Geronimo d'Amato, whose surname was particularly widespread in the sixteenth-century Italian Jewish communities.[47] Indeed, the name d'Amato has a close affinity with that of the most famous violin makers in Brescia, the Amati family, whose surname also has an apparent Hebrew origin meaning, "of my nation."[48]

Undoubtedly, the presence and skills of these Jewish and converted musicians enriched not only the Italian courts of the Renaissance but also courts and musical establishments across Europe. One thinks, for example, of the exodus of Italian musicians, with their consort of violins, toward the court of Henry VIII. As Meucci has argued, the migration of Jewish or converted string players from Italy to England may have included others in addition to the Bassano family, who were specialists in wind instruments. The Bassanos had moved to England in 1539 despite the official prohibition on Jews in England.[49]

Even so, their long-standing presence in Venice became emblematic, representing a diverse musical and cultural environment that included musicians of both Jewish and non-Jewish origins. Important figures in that city range from Giovanni Battista Sansone (Il Siciliano), discussed previously, to Ventura Linarol, a violin maker and a talented musician. In the late fifteenth and early sixteenth centuries, Venice was also the home of Lorenzo Gugnasco, trusted instrument maker to Isabella d'Este (1474–1539). Gugnasco built many types of instruments for Isabella, and their correspondence (1496–1515) demonstrates the typical versatility of these makers.[50] Other figures include Giovan Maria of Brescia, an instrument maker and bass violin player active between 1573 and 1601 at the Scuola Grande di San Rocco, and Bernardino "dalli violini" (of the violins), another musician and instrument maker active in Venice at the same time.[51] The last name Bernardino suggests a connection (not just a symbolic one) to Jewish culture.[52]

It is evident that the participation of these musicians in the cultures of musical instrument manufacture on the heels of their migration led to the birth or transformation of certain types of musical instruments. Related, and equally noteworthy, was their participation as musicians and composers, through which they apparently helped to drive cultural innovations. Despite the wishes of the Catholic rulers of Spain in the late fifteenth century, their influence persisted even though they sometimes chose—or were forced—to convert to Christianity from Judaism. Working within the highest levels of early modern courts and societies, Sephardic Jews had a marked impact on the spread of innovations in musical culture of southern Italy, one of the centers of the Renaissance.

NOTES

1. Moshe Rosman, *How Jewish Is Jewish History?* (Oxford: Littman Library of Jewish Civilization, 2007), 109–130.
2. David B. Ruderman, *Early Modern Jewry: A New Cultural History* (Princeton, NJ: Princeton University Press, 2010), 23–55.
3. Ruderman, 55.
4. Ruderman, 35, 180–186.

An initial discussion of this topic is in Luigi Sisto, "La confisca dei beni di Matteo Sansone, musico sefardita (Palermo 1513). Considerazioni sull'introduzione della violecta spagnola in Italia," in *Musica tra storia e filologia*, ed. Federica Nardacci (Rome: Istituto Italiano per la Storia della Musica, 2010), 1–12.

5. Ian Woodfield, *The Early History of the Viol* (Cambridge: Cambridge University Press, 1984), 81; I also cite the Italian translation, Ian Woodfield, *La viola da gamba dalle origini al Rinascimento*, trans. Cristiano Contadin and Alberto Ponchio, ed. Renato Meucci (Torino: EDT, 1999), 94. See also Renato Meucci, ed., *Un corpo alla ricerca dell'anima: Andrea Amati e la nascita del violino 1505–2005*, 2 vols. (Cremona: Ente Triennale Internazionale degli Strumenti ad Arco, 2005); Luigi Sisto, *I liutai tedeschi a Napoli tra Cinque e Seicento. Storia di una migrazione in senso contrario* (Rome: Istituto Italiano per la Storia della Musica, 2010).

6. "Ferdinandus vero qui neapolitanum Regnum ab Alphonso patre acceptum septimum circiter ac.xxx. um pacatissime gubernavit et privatim et publice musicam disciplinam tanto fuit studio prosecutus ut non modo sese in ea privato ocio sepe numero exerceret: sed ab universa europa viros eius disciplinæ doctissimos solertissimos atque instrumentorum artifices summis ad se premijs avocaret." See Raffaello Lippo Brandolini, *De musica et poetica opusclum*, Roma Biblioteca Casanatense, MS 805, 1513, cc. 16v–17r. My translation.

7. Among these was the possibility for a foreign-born man to marry a Neapolitan wife and obtain citizenship. The *Prammatica* was published in the late eighteenth century as *Prammatica super immunitatibus exterorum (1469)*, in *Capitula regni utriusque Siciliae*, ed. Antonio Cervoni, Constitutionum Regni Siciliarum Libri III 2 (Naples, 1773), 278–279.

8. On the Jewish converts who established themselves in Sicily in the fifteenth and sixteenth centuries, see Nadia Zeldes, "The Converted Jews of Sicily before and after the Expulsion (1460–1550)" (PhD diss., Tel Aviv University, 1997), and Nadia Zeldes, *"The Former Jews of This Kingdom": Sicilian Converts after the Expulsion, 1492–1516* (Leiden and Boston: Brill, 2003).

9. See Woodfield, *La viola da gamba*, 94. An important confirmation also comes from the Neapolitan printing of works (mainly intended for the viola da mano) by Francesco Canova da Milano and Bartolomeo Lieto. See also Renato Meucci, "Alle origini della liuteria classica italiana: come in una gara ad ostacoli . . . / The Origins of Italian Violin Making: Rather like an Obstacle Course," in Meucci, *Un corpo alla ricerca dell'anima*, 1:24.

10. On music at the Aragonese court of Naples, see Allan William Atlas, *Music at the Aragonese Court of Naples* (Cambridge: Cambridge University Press, 1985).

11. "Alia tamen viola est: a grecis (ut ajunt) comperta: non solum forma (sicut illa) differens a leuto: sed etiam chordarum dispositione ac pulsatione. Enimvero: sive tres ei sint chorde simplices ut in pluribus: per geminam diapentem: sive quinque (ut in aliquibus) sic et per unisonos temperate: inequaliter. hoc est tumide sunt extente: ut arculus (quom chorda ejus pilis equinis confecta: sit recta) unam tangens: juxta libitum sonitoris: alias relinquat inconcussas," Johannes Tinctoris, *De inventione et usu musicae* (Naples, ca. 1497), ed. Karl Weinmann as *Johannes Tinctoris (1445–1511) und sein unbekannter Traktat,"De inventione et usu musicae"* (Regensburg: F. Pustet, 1917; repr. Tutzing: Wilhelm Fischer, Schneider, 1961), 42. Translated in Anthony Baines, "Fifteenth-Century Instruments in Tinctoris's *De Inventione et Usu Musicae*," *Galpin Society Journal* 3 (March 1950): 22–23. On the descriptions of musical instruments, see Baines, 19–26.

12. See Edmond Van der Straeten, *La musique aux Pays-Bas avant le XIXe siècle*, 8 vols. (Brussels, 1867–1888), 4:32.

13. On the Jewish origins of the name Massa, see Samuele Schaerf, *I cognomi degli ebrei d' Italia* (Florence: Casa Editrice "Israel," 1925). The surname De Martino (as well as its

variants Di Martino and Martino), attested in all the viceregal territories, also displays a clear Jewish derivation, as evidenced by the analysis of archival documents presented in Michele Sisto, "Presenze multietniche in Irpinia: Cristiani novelli ed altre minoranze etniche nell'età Moderna," *Grammata* 2 (2000): 141–185; in particular, "L'onomastica di derivazione ebraica a Gesualdo," 159–169. On Raffaele Massa as apprentice to Sebastiano de Martino, see State Archive of Naples (ASNA), Notai del '400, lawyer Giovanni de Carpanis, 1486–1487, c. 65, cited in Gaetano Filangieri, ed., *Documenti per la storia delle arti e le industrie delle province napoletane raccolti e pubblicati*, 6 vols. (Naples: Tipografia dell'Accademia Reale delle Scienze, 1883–1891), 6:138.

14. Francesco da Milano, *Intavolatura per viola overo lauto* (Naples, 1536; repr. Geneva: Minkoff, 1988).

15. Bartolomeo Lieto, *Dialogo quarto di musica* (Naples, 1559; repr. ed. Patrizio Barbieri, Lucca: Libreria Musicale Italiana, 1993).

16. Ruderman discusses these networks of Sephardic Jews and *conversos* and their role in disseminating ideas and goods. See Ruderman, *Early Modern Jewry*, 36–37 and passim.

17. On Sicily and Spain, see David Abulafia, "The Diffusion of the Italian Renaissance: Southern Italy and Beyond," in *Palgrave Advances in Renaissance Historiography*, ed. Jonathan Woolfson (Houndmills, Basingstoke: Palgrave Macmillan, 2005), 27–51.

18. See Zeldes, *"The Former Jews of This Kingdom,"* 245–246 and 251–252, and Nadia Zeldes, "Dress, Dancing and Music: Aspects of Renaissance Culture among Sicilian Jews and Converts," in *Le usate leggiadrie. I cortei, le cerimonie, le feste e il costume nel Mediterraneo tra XV e XVI secolo*, ed. Gemma T. Colesanti (Montella: Edizioni Dragonetti, 2009), 230; this discussion draws on 230–231.

19. On the Spanish Inquisition in Sicily, see Francesco Renda, *L'Inquisizione in Sicilia* (Palermo: Sellerio, 1997).

20. State Archive of Palermo (ASP), Tribunale del Santo Uffizio, Ricevitoria, reg. 8 bis, c. 251v (Matteo Porto).

21. ASP, Tribunale del Santo Uffizio, Ricevitoria, reg. 8 *bis*, cc. 58v–161v ("Inventarium bonorum repertorum in domo Mactei De sansono De panhormo").

22. In fact, the Spanish inventory is almost identical to the one presented previously. See ASP, Tribunale del Santo Uffizio, Ricevitoria, reg. 9, c. 93r–v.

23. See Woodfield, *The Early History of the Viol*, 96, and Woodfield, *La viola da gamba*, 111.

24. "Quinetiam instrumentum illud a Catalanis inventum: quod ab aliis ghiterra: ab aliis ghiterna vocatur: ex lyra prodiisse manifestissimum est. hec enim ut leutum (licet eo longe minor sit) et formam testudineam: et chordarum dispositionem atque contactum suscipit," Weinmann, *Johannes Tinctoris*, 42. It should also be noted that the related term *guidema*—a guitar played by Sicilian Jews—may be dated back to 1309, when, in the *Ordinationes* of Frederick III of Sicily, its use during funeral rites was expressly forbidden: "guideme, vel timpana vel alia solita instrumenta." See Giuseppe Donato, "Contributo alla storia delle siciliane," in *Proceedings of the 3rd International Symposium (Siena-Certaldo, 19–22 July 1975): La musica al tempo del Boccaccio e i suoi rapporti con la letteratura*, ed. Agostino Ziino. L'Ars Nova italiana del Trecento 4 (Certaldo: Centro Studi sull'Ars Nova Italiana del Trecento, 1978), 194.

25. The etymology of the term *viola* is addressed in Giulio Paulis, "I nomi delle 'launeddas' sarde e della 'viola' alla luce della tradizione musicale greco-romana," in *Sardinia antiqua: Studi in onore di Pietro Meloni* (Cagliari: Edizioni della Torre, 1992), 505–528.

26. See Meucci's preface to Woodfield, *La viola da gamba*, vii–xi.

27. See William F. Prizer, "Isabella d'Este and Lorenzo da Pavia, 'Master Instrument-Maker,'" *Early Music History* 2 (1982): 87–127.

28. See Meucci, "Alle origini della liuteria classica italiana," 1:15–17 and 34–39.

29. The notion that the term *alla spagnola* referred to a plucked string instrument was suggested by Prizer, "Isabella d'Este and Lorenzo da Pavia," 109–111. At the end of the sixteenth century, in fact, the terms *giterna* and *giterra*, which had previously, for about a century, been called simply "guitar," would be more frequently referred to as "Italian" to differentiate them from the nascent Spanish guitar. See Renato Meucci, "Da chitarra italiana a chitarrone: una nuova interpretazione," in *Enrico Radesca di Foggia e il suo tempo*, ed. Francesca Seller (Lucca: Libreria Musicale Italiana, 2001), 37–57.

30. See Meucci, "Alle origini della liuteria classica italiana," 1:78–81.

31. Silvestro Ganassi, *Lettione seconda pur della prattica di sonare il violone d'arco da tasti* (Venice, 1543), Cap. XX; translated as Silvestro Ganassi, *Regola Rubertina. First and Second Part: A Manual of Playing the Viola da Gamba and of Playing the Lute, Venice 1542 and 1543*, trans. and ed. Hildemarie Peter (Berlin–Lichterfelde: R. Lienau, 1972–1977), 91. For more on Giovanni Battista Sansone, "Il Siciliano," see Anthony M. Cummings, "Three *gigli*: Medici Musical Patronage in the Early Cinquecento," *Recercare* 15 (2003): 39–72, and Anthony M. Cummings, *The Politicized Muse: Music for Medici Festivals, 1512–1537* (Princeton, NJ: Princeton University Press, 1993), 227–228n9, which contains an extensive list of prior references. On the activities of other members of the same family, including Antonio I, Giovanni Battista, and Antonio II, see Laurence C. Witten, "Apollo, Orpheus, and David: A Study of the Crucial Century in the Development of Bowed Strings in North Italy 1480–1580 as Seen in Graphic Evidence and Some Surviving Instruments," *Journal of the American Musical Instrument Society* 1 (1975): 5–55. See also Stefano Toffolo, *Antichi strumenti veneziani, 1500–1800: quattro secoli di liuteria e cembalaria* (Venice: Arsenale, 1987), 137–141; and Willibald Leo von Lütgendorff, *Die Geigen und Lautenmacher vom Mittelalter bis zur Gegenwart*, originally 2 vols. (Frankfurt am Main and Berlin: Hesse, 1922; repr. Tutzing: Schneider, 1968 and 1975; vol. 3 containing supplements and updates by Thomas Drescher, Tutzing: Schneider, 1990), 3:97–98.

32. On the names of the Jews of Palermo, see Mariuccia Krasner, "L'onomastica degli ebrei di Palermo nei secoli XIV e XV: nuove prospettive di ricerca," *Materia Giudaica* 11, nos. 1–2 (2006): 97–112; on Jewish culture in Palermo, see also Mauro Zonta, "La filosofia ebraica medievale in Sicilia," in *Ebrei e Sicilia*, ed. Nicolò Bucaria, Michele Luzzati, and Angela Tarantino (Palermo: Flaccovio, 2002), 163–168.

33. ASNA, Notai del '500, lawyer Giovanni Giacomo Cavaliere, 1544–1545, c. 40; quoted in Filangieri, *Documenti*, 5:152.

34. On Giangiacomo de Rosa, see ASNA, Notai del '500, lawyer Giovanni Giacomo Cavaliere, 1544–1545, c. 403. On Marco de Callo, see ASNA, 1545–1546, c. 222.

35. See Filangieri, *Documenti*, 5:6–7; see also Francesco Nocerino, "La bottega dei violari Albanese e Matino," in *Liuteria, Musica, Cultura, 1999–2000*, ed. Renato Meucci (Lucca: Libreria Musicale Italiana, 2001), 3–9.

36. The origin of the surname Matino is documented in many sources from the Apulian area (particularly from Manduria near Taranto); see Gérard Delille, "Il Libro Magno di Manduria," *Storia e dossier* 2, no. 5 (March 1987).

37. Scipione Cerreto, *Della prattica musica vocale, et strumentale* (Naples: G. G. Carlino, 1601), 3:157.

38. The term *viola tastata* is used with increasing frequency to refer to the viola d'arco (with bow), starting from 1530 onward. We find, in fact, classifications of this type in

Giovanni Maria Lanfranco (*Scintille di musica*, 1533) and Ganassi (*Regola Rubertina*, 1542). See Woodfield, *La viola da gamba*, 111–112.

39. Woodfield, *The Early History of the Viol*, 96; Woodfield, *La viola da gamba*, 111.

40. "Tutto mi par che oggi si scorga nell'Illustrissimo Signor Don Carlo Gesualdo Principe di Venosa.... A questo Principe di più non basta, che si diletti della Musica, ma anche per gusto e intertenimento tiene in sua Corte, à sue spese, molti Compositori, Sonatori e Cantori eccellenti," Cerreto, *Della prattica musica vocale, et strumentale*, 3:155.

41. The description of this instrument is contained in the inventory of the properties of the castle of Gesualdo, preserved in Vatican City, Vatican Secret Archive, Boncompagni-Ludovisi Archive, "Inventario di tutte le robe si ritrovano nel castello di Gesualdo," prot. 274, serie V, n. 2, c. 711r. This instrument, along with others that belonged to Gesualdo, was reconstructed as part of my project; see Luigi Sisto, ed., *Carlo Gesualdo: Gli strumenti musicali* (Gesualdo: Gesualdo, 2017), 40–51.

42. "45. die 2 maij Joamnes bap.<tis>ta filius Mutij effrem et victoriae de donatellis bap.<tiza>tus / fuit a me sup.<radic>to archip.<resbite>ro levante Joamne bap.<tis>ta de paula," Gesualdo, Parish of San Nicola di Bari, Liber baptizatorum, vol. I, years 1599–1650, c. 9r. Published in Luigi Sisto, "Mutio Effrem e la corte del Principe di Venosa a Gesualdo," in *La musica del Principe: Studi e prospettive per Carlo Gesualdo*, Proceedings of the International Symposium (Venosa–Potenza, September 2003), ed. Luisa Curinga (Lucca: Libreria Musicale Italiana, 2008), 19–33.

43. The surnames Montella, De Paula (di Paola), and Stella are attested in many Jewish communities in southern Italy at that time. *Montella* suggests the name of a place, while *De Paula* had strong symbolic and theological value. See Michele Sisto, "Presenze multietniche in Irpinia," 159–169. See also Cesare Colafemmina, "Gli ebrei in Irpinia," in *Storia illustrata di Avellino e dell'Irpinia*, vol. 6, *Il novecento*, ed. Francesco Barra (Castel di Serra: Sellino & Barra Editore, 1996), 93–108.

44. Ruderman, *Early Modern Jewry*, 55.

45. Kirkendale suggests that Effrem was hired as a replacement for Frescobaldi, who left Mantua in early 1615, and also observes that Effrem was "possibly Jewish." See Warren Kirkendale, *The Court Musicians in Florence during the Principate of the Medici* (Florence: Leo S. Olschki, 1993), 360–361.

46. The music was published in *Musiche de alcuni eccellentissimi musici composte per la Maddalena, Sacra Rappresentazione di Gio. Battista Andreini Fiorentino* (Venice: Bartolomeo Magni, 1617). For more on the Mantuan production of *La Maddalena*, see Susan Parisi, "Ducal Patronage of Music in Mantua, 1587–1627: An Archival Study" (PhD diss., University of Illinois at Urbana-Champaign, 1989), 307–308 and 343n105.

47. On the d'Aponte dynasty, see Luigi Sisto, "I d'Aponte, costruttori di viole a Napoli al tempo dei Gesualdo," in *Carlo Gesualdo e il suo tempo*, Proceedings of the International Symposium (Gesualdo–Salerno 2013), ed. Alberto Granese and Luigi Sisto (Avellino: Il Terebinto, 2019), 157–182. Regarding the name of the organ builder Geronimo d'Amato, it is worth noting that Geronimo was one of the most commonly used names among "cristiani novelli." One example among many was Jehoshua ben Josef Lorki, instigator of the infamous Disputation of Tortosa in the fifteenth century, who took the name Geronimo (Hyeronimus) of Santa Fé. Sisto, *I liutai tedeschi a Napoli*, 115–118.

48. See Carlo Chiesa, "Qualche notizia storica su Andrea Amati / Some Historical Notes on Andrea Amati," in Meucci, *Un corpo alla ricerca dell'anima*, 1:106–107.

49. See Meucci, "Alle origini della liuteria classica italiana," 1:78–79. For more on the Bassano family's Jewish origins, see Roger Prior, "Jewish Musicians at the Tudor Court,"

Musical Quarterly 69, no. 2 (Spring 1983): 253–265. See also Dongmyung Ahn's chapter in the present volume.

50. See Meucci, "Alle origini della liuteria classica italiana," 1:52–53.

51. Meucci, 1:71

52. An analysis of parish registers consulted in southern Italy (which also have significant statistical value) reveals that the names most used to denote conversions were Bartolomeo and Bernardino. In many cases, the churches built in the place of ancient synagogues were dedicated to these two saints. See Sisto, "Presenze multietniche in Irpinia," 159–160.

> LUIGI SISTO is Curator of Musical Instruments at the Conservatorio di musica San Pietro a Majella in Naples. He is author of *I liutai tedeschi a Napoli. Storia di una migrazione in senso contrario.*

8

Salamone Rossi's *Songs of Solomon*
The Pleasures and Pains of Marginality

STEFANO PATUZZI

> *I am arriu'd for fruitfull* Lumbardie,
> *The pleasant garden of great* Italy.
>
> —William Shakespeare, *The Taming of the Shrew*, act 1, scene 1

An apparent contradiction lies at the heart of Salamone Rossi's *Ha-shirim 'asher li-Shlomo* (*The Songs of Solomon*), his volume of polyphonic compositions set to Hebrew texts published in Venice in 1622–1623. The rabbinical "copyright" attached to the music states in fact that Salamone became "'adam ha-rishon le-hadpis musiqah 'ivrit" ("the first man to print Hebrew music" or "Jewish music"; the term carries both meanings).[1] Given this claim of primacy, modern readers might expect Rossi's musical settings to display recognizably Jewish traits beyond their Hebrew texts. However, distinctive markers of Rossi's Jewish heritage are confined to those texts and to the introductory apparatus of the volume. Stylistically, the music itself bears all the hallmarks of Italian polyphonic motets and conservative secular madrigals of the late Renaissance.

It would be easy to explain away Rossi's compositions as a Judaization of some of the most important features of Italian musical culture of his day or, indeed, as a loss of cultural identity on the part of Rossi and his collaborators, including Rabbi Leon Modena, who was instrumental in seeing the volume through to publication. In fact, while Rossi's biographer Don Harrán agreed that Rossi's *Shirim* did not represent "a classic case of Jewish assimilation," he nevertheless argued that these works fall "into the category of cultural fusions, whereby disparate styles come together on common ground, losing some of their particularity in the course of their mutual accommodation."[2] And yet the rabbinical authorities' recognition of Rossi's status as the first man to print Hebrew music hints that they did not see his publication as effecting a loss of identity at all. Clearly, something more is at play.

In this essay, I reconsider the significance of Rossi's *Shirim*, adopting both emic and etic perspectives; ultimately, I show that there was no such loss of cultural "particularity." As I will argue, Rossi served as what Robert Bonfil has called a "marginal mediator," importing aspects of Italian musical culture into Jewish society and using them, in fact, to reaffirm Jewish identity and Jewish cultural practices. It was precisely within the apparent contradiction between Rossi's innovative publication and his adoption of a thoroughly conventional musical style that the significance of his complex cultural gesture lies.[3]

Salamone Rossi (Mantua, ca. 1570–ca. 1630?) lived in one of the most culturally important towns in the Italian peninsula at a time when that region hosted the largest Jewish population in Europe. The Jewish community of Mantua, located in Italy's Lombardy region, is today only a fraction of its size during Rossi's lifetime. When Rossi's *Shirim* were composed, rehearsed, and finally printed, Mantua's Jewish community was in the midst of a dramatic expansion. As Renata Segre explains, "At the beginning of the 16th century [the Jewish community of Mantua] numbered about 200 people; in 1587 it was almost five times as large, numbering 960 people; and by 1610 it had increased again, rapidly, to 2,325: these figures are near, or even beyond those in Venice," meaning that Mantua was "one of the four or five biggest Jewish communities of Western Europe."[4]

As is well known, Rossi's *Shirim* are the first examples of printed Hebrew compositions, although, as Leon Modena's introduction to the volume indicates, the synagogue in the city of Ferrara had included the performance of polyphonic vocal music with Hebrew texts around 1605.[5] In the Jewish year 5383, corresponding to 1622–1623, Rossi's *Ha-shirim 'asher li-Shlomo* were printed in Venice. Noteworthy among these is the setting of Psalm 8 ("O Lord, our Lord, how majestic is Thy name in all the earth"), Psalm 121 ("I lift my eyes to the mountains"), the particularly intense (and musically suggestive) Psalm 137 ("By the rivers of Babylon"), passages from Isaiah 35

("The wilderness and the parched land shall be glad"), and, notably, the *Qaddish shalem*. The volume's title page (see fig. 8.1) translates as follows:

> The Songs / of Solomon / Psalms, songs, and hymns / composed according to the science of song / and of [art] music / for three, four, five, six, seven and eight voices / by his honored eminence, master Shelomoh me-ha'Adumim [i.e. Salamone Rossi] (may his Rock / preserve him and grant him life!) / a resident of the holy community of Mantua / for thanking God and singing to His exalted name on all sacred occasions. / A new thing on earth. / Here in Venice, [5]383 [i.e. 1622–1623], / as a pious act of the lords / Pietro e Lorenzo Bragadini / in the house of Giovanni Calleoni, / *for the [publishing firm of the] illustrious lords / Pietro and Lorenzo Brag[adini]*.[6]

The printing of these thirty-three polyphonic vocal settings of Hebrew texts, together with extensive introductory texts by Leon Modena and other religious leaders, implies the expectation that the publication would achieve acceptance, at least to some degree, within the Mantuan Jewish community, as well as commercial success—and hence that it would be disseminated among other Jewish communities of the Italian peninsula. This prospect should be understood within the broader context of what David B. Ruderman has described as a "knowledge explosion" among these communities, facilitated especially by the advent of the printed book.[7] To be sure, the relatively low cost of printed books as compared with manuscript production, as well as their easier dissemination across a broad geographic range, undermined consolidated local traditions, which had for centuries been based on the patronage and production of manuscripts.[8] What is perhaps especially noteworthy about the *Shirim* is that they were published in the early 1620s, just a few years before the Italian music publishing industry (and the Venetian firms in particular) dramatically decreased its output; a short time later, production of this publication might not have been possible.[9]

If the spread of Hebrew books formed one important cultural pillar on which Rossi's *Ha-shirim 'asher li-Shlomo* stood, another was the creation of the Mantuan ghetto. Indeed, the *Shirim* may have been the most important cultural products following—perhaps even caused by—the establishment of the ghetto in 1612. The ghetto was built at the command of Duke Vincenzo Gonzaga (1587–1612) after a process of planning and implementation that lasted approximately a decade.[10] Some key principles that help to explain Vincenzo's motivations emerge quite clearly from the archives: first was his wish

FIGURE 8.1.

Salamone Rossi, title page of sesto partbook, from
Ha-shirim 'asher li-Shlomo (Venice: Bragadini, 1622–1623).
Image courtesy of the Bibliothèque nationale de France.

to emulate the policy of the popes and other Christian rulers concerning the management of the presence of the Jews within each given urban space, and second was his desire for an ordered management and shaping of the urban space itself under his control. As in other Italian states of that period, in fact, Vincenzo's plan for the management of the Jewish presence in the territory of his duchy involved the creation of a ghetto for Jews only in the urban space; ghettos were not created for Jews living in villages in the rural areas of the Duchy of Mantua, and those Jews were not forced to move to the capital city.[11]

Life within Mantua's ghetto allowed its inhabitants complete freedom of action, albeit within the very precise and restricted hours from the closing of the gates after sunset to their reopening the next morning. Not surprisingly, this was the time in which many specifically Jewish activities took place: theatrical and musical performances, acts of social proximity, and so forth. Most important, the closing of the gates brought with it a qualitative transformation of the internal space of the ghetto that, in a sense, was thus paradoxically liberating, as Stefanie B. Siegmund explains: "The Jews could use the streets of the ghetto and the open spaces to socialise and celebrate without being identified, spied upon, molested or monitored by both the crowd of Christians and by the authorities.... The night-time was the right moment to either rehearse and perform theatrical performances, or to organise choirs and musical concerts."[12]

For these and other reasons, far from being perceived exclusively as a punitive measure against the urban Jewish population, the institution of the ghetto may be understood as normalizing the Jewish presence within the social and urban grid. To quote Robert Bonfil, "The reception of Jews into Christian society was transformed by means of the ghetto from being exceptional and unnatural into being unexceptional and natural."[13] In Rossi's time, the "enclosure of the Jews" (*il recinto degli ebrei*, as it was sometimes called in Italian), which had earlier been, technically, voluntary, was transformed into a Jewish ghetto—that is, after 1612, it became a distinctively Jewish space. Far from being a generic expression, this is to be understood as the designation of "spatial environments in which Jewish things happen, where Jewish activities are performed, and which in turn are shaped and defined by those Jewish activities."[14]

Returning to Rossi's *Ha-shirim 'asher li-Shlomo*, both to the music and to its important prefatory material, one can infer some key factors. An emic (that is, insider or bottom-up) reading of the documents attached to the *Shirim* shows that the primary intent of Rabbi Leon Modena (the mastermind of the whole operation), of Rossi himself, and of the Venetian rabbis who signed the copyright was to demonstrate that music was not only permissible according to Jewish law but also intrinsic to Judaism and to Jewish worship in particular.[15] In other words, the authors of these documents claimed that music was originally a Jewish creation that was stolen by other peoples and lost by the Jewish people through their long exile. As a result, music constituted only a fragment of Jewish culture dispersed among the nations by Rossi's time, centuries later.[16] This vision, albeit historically problematic, was evidently necessary for the conception and printing of the *Shirim*: if one admits a Jewish origin of music as a whole, thus also of the highbrow Italian as well as the European music of that time, the foundations are laid for rehabilitating music within a Jewish and rabbinical collective imagination that perceived non-Jewish music to be essentially alien.[17] Thus, from an emic perspective, evidence of the musical tradition of the Jews and the lawfulness of music within Judaism constituted a means of both cultural and social elevation—a goal that the Jews of Mantua also pursued in other elements of their culture, including, for instance, their attire.[18]

This perspective sheds new light on the self-conscious statements of innovation that appear on the title page of the *Shirim*, in which these vocal compositions are labeled as *ḥadashah ba-'aretz*—that is, "a new thing on earth" (a reference to Jeremiah 31:21). And it is reiterated in Modena's prefatory material; Modena describes the *Shirim* as "something . . . that did not exist as such in Israel," observing that "there was no beginning like this any time before."[19] This observation adds weight to the rabbinical copyright that accompanies the *Shirim*, as stated previously, and helps us better comprehend the reason why, as Harrán notes, the very first occurrence of the expression "Hebrew music" appears here.

The etic perspective—the top-down view from our current historiographic position—brings another set of considerations to the forefront. First is the context of this music within the synagogue, to cite the most significant Jewish venue in which a number of these compositions were possibly performed. From a compositional as well as stylistic point of view, Rossi's *Shirim*, as explained previously, hint at both contemporary secular music (for example, the madrigal, albeit not in its most avant-garde incarnations, or instrumental dances) and sacred music of that period (the motet, to name just one example). Iconic instances include, on the one hand, the *Qaddish*, whose traits closely recall those of certain secular music of the early seventeenth century: it contains, for instance, some typical progressions and cadences found in instrumental *gagliarde* (of Rossi but also in general); the cadences also include hemiolas, also found very often in *gagliarde* and other dance movements in triple meter. More to the point, the mere choice of having composed the *Qaddish* in triple meter suggests a connection with dance movements. On the other hand, *'Elohim hashiveinu* alludes to sacred repertoire with an incipit that, as Joshua Jacobson has shown, includes some melodic and contrapuntal qualities that closely resemble those of *Cum essem parvulus*, a motet by Orlande de Lassus, who had died in 1594.[20]

It is therefore fair to assume that, to Rossi's Jewish contemporaries, the *Shirim* could have referenced the sound world of Catholic sacred music (for those among them who might have heard motets), as well as secular courtly music. Indeed, sacred and secular styles were already blurred in non-Jewish musical practice, and according to Bonfil, such a blurring began to manifest itself in Jewish culture during this very period.[21] For the Jewish community, then, *Ha-shirim 'asher li-Shlomo* contributed to this trend.

Such an etic reading of the *Shirim* leads to an interpretive outcome quite different from the preceding one. As already noted, the *Shirim* appear as Jewish artifacts in that, firstly, the texts are in Hebrew and, secondly, they were destined to be sung in Jewish social contexts and venues—some in the synagogue as part of the liturgy and some outside the liturgy and perhaps in other settings. These two layers are both distinct from each other and interconnected in the *Shirim*. The first layer—the Hebraization—comes from the use of Hebrew texts for the first time in the history of printed polyphonic music. However, it is worth pointing out that this layer, while important, constitutes only a single and insufficient element of Rossi's operation as a whole. Indeed, the second layer—the Judaization of the *Shirim*—was made possible not only by their composer's Jewish background but also by their use in the Jewish religious and social occasions during which those compositions were intended to be performed. To put it differently, if the *Shirim* could hypothetically be considered as anonymous compositions, they could even be viewed as the product of a non-Jewish composer interested in Jewish culture. In other words, it was their actual (in Mantua) and (postpublication) potential use and consumption within Jewish circles elsewhere that makes it possible to label them as Jewish artifacts. From a compositional point of view, even though the *Shirim* do constitute the first appearance of the expression "Jewish music" or "Hebrew music," what is actually happening is that Rossi is importing compositional practices from the non-Jewish world in an explicit manner.

Thus Rossi's *musiqah 'ivrit* represents a synthesis of only a limited number of Jewish elements—that is, the texts and usage—while other elements, including melody, rhythm, counterpoint, and compositional process, were drawn from non-Jewish musical practices. It is curious, therefore, that they are collectively defined as "Jewish" or "Hebrew," since this designation seems to overlook the many elements of the compositions that emerge from the non-Jewish musical world, foregrounding text and usage above all.

With regard to the places where these compositions were sung and heard, the prefatory material to the *Shirim* suggests that Rossi had numerous opportunities over the years to rehearse and perform some of the compositions that he later had published. It is crucial to observe that this must have meant considerable involvement with the Mantuan Jewish community. Far from being an outlier within the ghetto, Rossi relied on some of his coreligionists to practice the music with him—to read the notation, to work out the text underlay, to sing the polyphony, perhaps even to make suggestions or adjustments as they went—and on others to listen and provide feedback. All of this took place in advance of publication, as Modena explains in parts 18 and 19 of his lengthy introduction: "18. Day by day he would enter into his notebook a certain psalm of David or a formula for prayer or praise, reverence and divine song until he succeeded in gathering some of them into a collection, making several available. 19. When people sang them, they were delighted with their many good qualities; the listeners too were radiant, each of them finding it pleasant to hear them and wishing to hear the remainder."[22] This implies the cultivation of a considerable musical culture within the ghetto's Jewish community, notwithstanding the paucity of surviving notated compositions.

In light of the dynamic of cultural importation described previously, one might consider the influence, or perhaps the emulation, of courtly culture—specifically, and most obviously, from the Gonzaga court of Mantua. However, the general framework makes it plausible that there is some other factor of higher importance, since the vector previously suggested originated from within the court—even from the ducal chapel of Santa Barbara itself—and pointed toward the ghetto or even the synagogue, the very heart of the Jewish communal and sacred spheres. Another perspective on this dynamic is clearly illustrated by Bonfil: "Throughout the pre-modern era, the culture of the Jews is characterized clearly by the ambivalent mark of both the need and of the aspiration to participate in the space of the 'other,' and of the difficulties in doing this—and thus the penchant to force cultural discourse within the Jewish space. This state of things is a natural consequence of the strong amount of religiosity inherent in the perception of [Jewish] culture, hence of the rigidity of the (largely religious) definition of the plane on which the union between culture and society must take place."[23]

From the same angle, but focusing on the figure of Rossi, it is surely possible to interpret him as a "marginal mediator": "So, the 'chosen' few who, whether for vocation or contingent need, ventured in the external space, assumed the role of mediators for the importation of themes, contents, and forms of culture, not infrequently in the form of pure and simple translation into Hebrew."[24]

Rossi brought the music of both court and chapel into the Jewish world, apparently because of the desire to embrace a crucial distinctive feature of the culture of the "other." The principle here is one of synecdoche, in which a part (polyphonic music) is invoked for the whole (the larger, peculiar cultural traits of the portion of non-Jewish society that used this music as a point of reference). Such a dynamic of importation must be read within a broader framework than merely the narrow outlines of the events narrated here—a framework in which the gap between the Jewish minority and the Catholic majority was all too evident. The process of conception, composition, performance, and printing of the *Shirim* exemplifies the Jews' tendency toward mimesis rather than assimilation. In this case, the Jewish community imitated the surrounding Catholic society by adopting the polyphonic music of the Italian tradition as an unequivocal mark of the high culture of that era.[25]

The *Shirim*, if considered tout court as Jewish music, were thus the result of a double invention. They were both the first printed music set to Hebrew texts and the first attempt by Jews to emulate the compositional features of Italian courts and chapels in distinctively Jewish musical publications. This second invention suggests that Rossi, Modena, and the other rabbis who cooperated in the process of publishing the *Shirim* achieved a strong desire of the Jewish minority to borrow salient musical and compositional traits from the Catholic majority, legitimizing these traits within a Jewish framework. What is at work, then, is a simultaneous desire for cultural similarity and social differentiation. The hypothesis that the *Shirim* represented a dynamic of assimilation, hence of progressive loss of identity on the part of the Jewish minority, is thus illegitimate. The importation of the music of the majority into a Jewish space declares the Jews' desire to be like their non-Jewish models—but only to a certain extent—while affirming their Jewish identity.

By operating as a marginal mediator, Salamone Rossi (with the crucial contribution by Leon Modena) thus implemented a bridge, a cultural strategy, thanks to which the most refined products of the surrounding non-Jewish culture were not only admitted into the synagogue and possibly in other Jewish places but transformed into—and thus perceived as—Jewish artifacts. *Musiqah 'ivrit* was born.

NOTES

I am indebted to Susanna Vezzadini, University of Bologna, for her comments on an earlier draft of this article; to David Fligg, Royal Northern College of Music (Manchester), for his help in revising the English version of this article; and to Elam Rotem for his remarks on Rossi's *Qaddish*. I also thank the editors of this volume, whose observations have helped me to clarify a number of points in the present study. An earlier version of this essay appeared as "I Canti di Salomone Rossi e l'"invenzione' della musica ebraica," in *Lombardia judaica*, ed. Giulio Busi and Ermanno Finzi (Florence: Giuntina, 2017), 39–48. Translations are mine unless otherwise indicated.

1. Salamone Rossi, *Ha-shirim 'asher li-Shlomo* (Venice: Pietro and Lorenzo Bragadini, in the house of Giovanni Calleoni, [5]383 [=1622–1623]). Modern edition in Salamone Rossi, *Sacred Vocal Works in Hebrew: Hashirim 'asher lishlomo / "The Songs of Solomon,"* ed. with introduction and notes by Don Harrán, Complete Works, part 3, vols. 13a and 13b (S.l.: American Institute of Musicology and Neuhausen: Hänssler, 2003), 13a:220.

2. Don Harrán, "Tradition and Innovation in Jewish Music of the Later Renaissance," *Journal of Musicology* 7, no. 1 (1989): 119.

3. See Robert Bonfil, "A Cultural Profile," in *The Jews of Early Modern Venice*, ed. Robert C. Davis and Benjamin Ravid (Baltimore: Johns Hopkins University Press, 2001), 169–190; reprinted in *Cultural Change among the Jews of Early Modern Italy* (Farnham: Ashgate, 2010), chap. 12.

4. Renata Segre, "La Controriforma: espulsioni, conversioni, isolamento," in *Gli ebrei in Italia*, vol. 1, *Dall'alto Medioevo all'età dei ghetti*, Storia d'Italia, Annali 11, ed. Corrado Vivanti (Turin: Einaudi, 1996), 746.

5. See Don Harrán, *Salamone Rossi: Jewish Musician in Late Renaissance Mantua* (Oxford: Oxford University Press, 1999), 203.

6. Text on the sesto partbook title page; translation adapted from Don Harrán, Rossi, *Sacred Vocal Works*, 13a:161–162. The original title page reads as follows:

"השירים / אשר לשלמה / מזמרים ושירות ותשבחות אשר / הביא בחכמת הנגון והמוסיקה לשלשה ד' ה' ו' ז' ח' קולות / כ"מר שלמה מהאדומים י"צו / מדרי ק"ק מאנטובה / להודי' לה' ולזמר לשמו עליון בכל / דבר שבקדושה. חדשה / בארץ :פה וויניציאה שפ"ג / כמצות השרים / פייטרו ולורינצו בראגאדיני /.בבית ייואני קאליאוני Appresso gli Illust. / Sig. Pietro e Lorenzo Brag."

7. "The third and perhaps most significant element in defining an early modern Jewish culture I would call simply the 'knowledge explosion,' and by this I primarily mean the impact of the printed book." See David B. Ruderman, "Jewish Cultural History in Early Modern Europe: An Agenda for Future Study," in *Rethinking European Jewish History*, ed. Jeremy Cohen and Moshe Rosman (Portland, OR: Littman Library of Jewish Civilization, 2009), 105.

8. Adam Shear describes this as "a transitional moment in the passage from a culture dominated by manuscripts to a culture dominated by print." See Adam Shear, "Judah Moscato's Sources and Hebrew Printing in the Sixteenth Century: A Preliminary Survey," in *Rabbi Judah Moscato and the Jewish Intellectual World of Mantua in the 16th–17th Centuries*, ed. Giuseppe Veltri and Gianfranco Miletto (Leiden and Boston: Brill, 2012), 138.

9. See Lorenzo Bianconi, *Music in the Seventeenth Century* (Cambridge: Cambridge University Press, 1987), 76.

10. On the Mantuan ghetto, see Shlomo Simonsohn, *History of the Jews in the Duchy of Mantua* (Jerusalem: Kiryath Sefer, 1977); Luigi Carnevali, *Il ghetto di Mantova* (Mantua: Sartori, 1973); and Stefano Patuzzi, "Music from a Confined Space: Salomone Rossi's *Hashirim asher lishlomoh* (1622/23) and the Mantuan Ghetto," in "Sacred Space," special issue, *Journal of Synagogue Music* 37 (Fall 2012): 49–69.

11. The extremely well-documented volumes by Ermanno Finzi are especially important with regard to the Jewish communities in the Mantuan countryside, notably *La culla dei Finzi: Storia degli ebrei di Rivarolo Mantovano tratta dagli Archivi Notarili* (Mantua: Di Pellegrini, 2013); *Il giusto, come palma, fiorirà: Demografia ebraica sabbionetana* (Mantua: Di Pellegrini, 2014); and *Così uguali, così diversi: Le comunità ebraiche di Viadana e Pomponesco* (Mantua: Istituto Mantovano di Storia Contemporanea, 2015).

12. Stefanie B. Siegmund, "La vita nei ghetti," in Vivanti, *Dall'alto Medioevo all'età dei ghetti*, 863.

13. Robert Bonfil, "Change in the Cultural Patterns of a Jewish Society in Crisis: Italian Jewry at the Close of the Sixteenth Century," *Jewish History* 3, no. 2 (Fall 1988): 11–30; reprinted in Bonfil, *Cultural Change among the Jews of Early Modern Italy*, 18.

14. Anna Lipphardt, Julia Brauch, and Alexandra Nocke, "Exploring Jewish Space: An Approach," in *Jewish Topographies*, ed. Anna Lipphardt, Julia Brauch, and Alexandra Nocke (Farnham: Ashgate, 2008), 4.

15. I refer here to the juxtaposition of *emic* and *etic*: the original bibliographic milestone is Thomas N. Headland, Kenneth L. Pike, and Marvin Harris, eds., *Emics and Etics: The Insider/Outsider Debate* (Newbury Park, CA: Sage, 1990).

16. This constituted a *vulgata* very widespread in the Jewish circles: see, for all, Don Harrán, "An Early Modern Hebrew Poem on Music in Its Beginnings and at the End of Time," *Journal of the American Musicological Society* 64, no. 1 (Spring 2011): 30. This is analogous, for instance, to the stance of Leone de' Sommi's *Quattro dialoghi in materia di rappresentazioni sceniche*; as Bonfil explains, "Tragedy as a literary genre was considered an invention of classical Hebrew civilization, and the first tragedy was certainly the book of Job, which the

Talmudic tradition attributes to Moses." See Roberto Bonfil, "Lo spazio culturale degli ebrei d'Italia fra Rinascimento ed Età barocca," in Vivanti, *Dall'alto Medioevo all'età dei ghetti*, 468.

17. For more on this issue, see the chapter in the present volume by Rebecca Cypess and Lynette Bowring; as explained there, the idea of music as a science that originated among Jews but was then lost may be traced at least as far back as Don Isaac Abarbanel, and it recurs in a variety of sources from early modern Italy.

18. See, for example, Ariel Toaff, "La vita materiale," in Vivanti, *Dall'alto Medioevo all'età dei ghetti*, 257–261.

19. Rossi, *Sacred Vocal Works*, respectively pages 13a:180 and 182.

"אשר . . . לא נהיתה כזאת בישראל"; "לא נעשה כפתח הזה מאז מקדם"

20. Joshua Jacobson, in "Defending Salamone Rossi: The Transformation and Justification of Jewish Music in Renaissance Italy," *Yale University Institute of Sacred Music Colloquium: Music, Worship, Arts* 5 (Autumn 2008; issued April 2010): 85–92, states very clearly that "Rossi even borrowed from the styles of Christian sacred music" and sees precise analogies with the incipit of the cited motet by Orlande de Lassus. I thank here Daniele Torelli for the exchange of opinions on some stylistic aspects of Rossi's compositions at hand.

21. See Bonfil, *Lo spazio culturale*, 469.

22. Rossi, *Sacred Vocal Works*, 13a:179–180.

"18.ויום יום לעומת מחברתו היה מביא איזה מזמור לדוד או ממכשירי תפלה או שבחות הלל וזמרת יה עד כי משכיל לאסף קבץ כמה מהם והיו לאחדים בידו. 19. וכאשר שוררו אנשי' אותם והתענגו על רוב טובם והמקשיבי' הזהירו כל אחד ערבה אזנו משמוע וישמע יתרו'."

23. Bonfil, *Lo spazio culturale*, 420.

24. Bonfil, 422.

25. Some assonance can be seen with the work by Alberto Castaldini, *L'ipotesi mimetica. Contributo a una antropologia dell'ebraismo* (Florence: Leo S. Olschki, 2001). The roots of this study go deep into the theory of René Girard's "mimetic desire," a vision first formulated in his *Mensonge romantique et Vérité romanesque* (Paris: Grasset, 1961), trans. Yvonne Freccero as *Deceit, Desire and the Novel: Self and Other in Literary Structure* (Baltimore: Johns Hopkins University Press, 1966), and progressively developed over the decades.

STEFANO PATUZZI, who holds a PhD in musicology and a *diploma* in organ and organ composition, is Director of Research at Teatro San Cassiano (London and Venice) and member of the Jewish Music Study Group at the Fondazione Levi in Venice. He studied under Claudio Gallico, Tim Carter, and Lorenzo Bianconi; has published in Italy, England, and the United States on Claudio Monteverdi, Girolamo Frescobaldi, and Salamone Rossi; and is currently working on Venetian baroque theaters and Salomon Sulzer.

9

Orality and Literacy in the Worlds of Salamone Rossi

REBECCA CYPESS AND LYNETTE BOWRING

The innovative nature of Salamone Rossi's *Ha-shirim 'asher li-Shlomo* (*The Songs of Solomon*) has long been recognized.[1] The volume consists of thirty-three polyphonic compositions on liturgical Hebrew texts—apparently the only such notated polyphonic Hebrew works printed before the nineteenth century. The publication involved a collaboration of numerous individuals, including the composer; his foremost supporter in the Jewish community, the rabbi and cantor Leon Modena; Rossi's dedicatee, Moses Sulam, who had encouraged the composer in this project; the writers who penned poetry in praise of the composer; and a Christian printing house that catered to the needs of the literate Jewish communities of early modern Italy.[2]

The issue of typography in the *Shirim* has been discussed in the past.[3] The music runs from left to right, as would be expected by any reader of Italian or Latin. The text, however, is printed in Hebrew characters, which read from right to left, meaning that reconciliation was required of the directionality of the musical notation and the written text. Rossi's solution was to print each Hebrew word as a single unit (apparently underneath the last note to which the word applies) from right to left but the order of words from left to right.

Beneath this curious feature of the printed volume, however, runs a deeper and more complex undercurrent: the tension between orality and literacy. While Hebrew and Italian literacy was more common among Jews than among their non-Jewish neighbors, it is unclear whether and to what extent this literacy encompassed the reading of staff notation used in the non-Jewish musical tradition, though the presence of Jewish musicians and dancing masters discussed throughout the present volume suggests that it was not unheard of.[4] The written system of cantillation markings for the reading of the Hebrew Bible did not record specific pitches, and it did not capture polyphonic elements. The musical modes used for prayers were unnotated, as was any polyphonic rendering. While these systems of liturgical music had served Jewish communities for centuries (and continue to do so today), a number of Jewish writers in the early modern era remarked on the problems that arose from the oral nature of the Jewish musical tradition. Observing the flourishing of church music among their Christian neighbors, prominent rabbinic writers expressed frustration with what they perceived as a lack of understanding of musical theory and refinement in musical performance. Leon Modena summarized these difficulties and used them as a polemical tool in support of Rossi's publication. In this context, the printed volume of *Ha-shirim* may be understood as an effort to open spaces of convergence between traditional oral cultures and the medium of printed staff notation.

It was not only in his contributions to Jewish music that Rossi brought orality and literacy into dialogue: his secular compositions—and specifically his instrumental works—sought to reconcile oral traditions within printed music. In addition to his literacy in both Hebrew language and music, Rossi seemed to be trained in the most professionally useful aspects of secular music: viol and violin playing; singing of polyphonic music; and composition in the most common secular genres, both vocal and instrumental. Rossi's published volumes of instrumental music, Italian madrigals, and strophic *canzonette* catered to the demand for secular entertainments in the Mantuan court of the Gonzaga family.[5] Most of Rossi's documented professional performance activities consisted of playing with a small group of string players (his *concerto*) at the Gonzaga court, providing dances and other short pieces for courtly entertainment; such a group may have operated at least partially within a lingering oral tradition of group improvisation—a tradition that we will discuss in the following pages.[6] He was sometimes paid for his musical activities within the court but was presumably removed from the rich musical culture at Santa Barbara and the other Mantuan churches by his Jewish faith; this may have prevented him from holding a higher-level court appointment too, despite his evidently valued services as a violinist, ensemble leader, and composer.

The publication of Rossi's collections of instrumental music spanned a period that saw widespread developments in the lives and work of ensemble instrumentalists—developments that probed the lines between their oral traditions and growing literacy skills.[7] Previous generations of Italian ensemble instrumentalists seldom notated or published full compositions; instead, they largely operated within what Walter Ong would classify as a "primary oral culture," where the performers were generally removed from written exemplars of the music they played.[8] Most earlier instrumental ensemble repertoires are only fragmentarily preserved in text: the basse danse repertoire, for example, consists of a small surviving body of notated repertoire supplemented by sources showing only a tenor cantus firmus in breves, over which improvisors created polyphony.[9] Such notations may have been largely unnecessary for musicians in this tradition who could rely on memorized formulas and familiar cantus firmi. In such a tradition, written composition was frequently unnecessary and unhelpful; instrumentalists who were illiterate or partially or fully literate all participated in these practices.[10] By the end of the sixteenth century, however, many instrumentalists were fully literate in both language and music: they were participating in the written and printed cultures of the time, and considerable numbers of notated, original compositions for instrumental ensembles have been preserved through print and manuscript.

Rossi was among the composers who participated in the nascent literate cultures of instrumentalists, and his compositions for instrumental ensembles show both the interplay and the fault lines between oral and literate musical traditions. His four main instrumental publications, printed in Venice between 1607 and 1622, demonstrate a clear effort to organize carefully crafted compositions within unified printed volumes, suggesting that he was aware of the novelty of published instrumental music and sought to establish himself as a leader in its new genres and styles. However, many of his musical materials were dependent on formulas and improvisatory practices from the oral tradition, and his notations and publications represent a decisive meeting of oral and literate traditions.

Rossi's participation in the gradual shift from an oral to a literate culture of instrumental music may be fruitfully considered in relation to his attempts to introduce a new kind of musical literacy in the form of staff notation alongside traditional cantillation markings and the oral systems of synagogue worship. As we will demonstrate in subsequent passages, Rossi's Hebrew vocal works seem to evade some of the markers of orally transmitted practices that left noticeable traces on his instrumental works. Most obviously, in strophic hymns that invite a formulaic treatment—treatment that, as Leon Modena explained, was already common in oral traditions in some Jewish communities—Rossi instead subverts the stanzaic structure of the text, creating through-composed works that require musical literacy for performance. Because of the interplay between orality and literacy in instrumental practice, we argue that viewing Rossi's instrumental works alongside these Hebrew vocal works is particularly productive. (A more complete consideration of these phenomena in relation to Rossi's Italian vocal works must await further study.)

Rossi's intentions in adopting these compositional methods, which diverge from those in his instrumental works, will never be fully known. However, the contrast between the two approaches seems significant. While the formula-based nature of his instrumental music builds on the models of an oral culture, Rossi's approach to the Hebrew motets seems to move away from that oral culture in a more dramatic way, instead calling attention to the act of composition and a print-based practice that would supplement the dominant oral tradition of synagogue music. The influence of the *Shirim* was limited, fostering no immediate successors, yet Rossi's attempted inclusion of the literate medium of the book alongside traditional forms of cantillation and worship may shed light on the convergence of cultures that he experienced.

ORALITY AND LITERACY IN ROSSI'S INSTRUMENTAL MUSIC

Walter Ong, in his groundbreaking 1982 study *Orality and Literacy*, addressed the transitions between oral and literate cultures, proposing that literacy acquisition can power large-scale cultural and intellectual changes. By conceiving of writing as a technology, an artificial construction that causes "interior transformations of consciousness,"[11] Ong suggested that literacy restructures thought processes, changing how individuals understand the world around them and react to its stimuli.[12] While other studies have considered musical instruments as technologies that can shape creative acts, Ong considered writing to be "an even more deeply interiorized technology than instrumental musical performance."[13]

Spoken languages, in Ong's formulation, are intrinsically related to the sense of hearing, and—despite their fundamentally evanescent nature—verbal, oral utterances are dynamic, immediate, and extraordinarily powerful.[14] A "primary oral culture," in which the technology of writing has not taken root, is inclined to thinking that is formulaic, additive, and deeply embedded in the memory.[15] For Ong, this culture was represented by the singers and reciters of epic poetry who were studied by Milman Parry and Albert Lord, whose research showed that orally trained storytellers memorize a repertoire of themes and formulas, which they order and bring together with copious ornament in the moment of performance.[16] Through assessing societies in varying stages of literacy, Ong concluded that the technology of writing is "separative"—that is, it holds the potential to break down language into constituent parts that may be analyzed, critiqued, and contemplated objectively.[17] The fixed themes and formulas of the oral tradition can be readily separated into smaller units—individual words—that can be infinitely reordered and manipulated. By enabling a slowing of the creative process, writing also allows the mind to cultivate different modes of thought and expression, and it brings the ability to contemplate and edit writing atemporally.[18] At the oral-literate interface, when these two systems coexist and perhaps conflict, some aspects of oral traditions may be seen represented in writing and gradually taking on some characteristics of literate thinking.[19]

Ong's study was primarily concerned with literacy in human languages; he did not consider other semiotic systems such as the notation of musical sounds, but his arguments contain strong implications for an understanding of the effects of musical literacy. Given that music is an evanescent sonic phenomenon that can be represented (albeit incompletely) by a written semiotic system, the theories of Ong and other scholars in this field may illuminate aspects of the oral-literate interface in the history of music. For an individual such as Salamone Rossi, such theories help to situate his works within the oral-literate interface of his time.[20]

Rossi's collections of instrumental music show his close reliance on the forms and styles of music—many of them oral in nature—that he used as a primarily secular instrumentalist. His first two volumes are dominated by large numbers of dances and short sinfonie, which are likely representative of the repertoire that he performed with his Mantuan string ensemble. Such ensembles had traditionally relied on oral tradition by improvising on formulas, so the works in these genres may represent a certain transfer of oral instrumental traditions into the written realm.[21] Although the dances and sinfonie show some effective writing for a small instrumental ensemble, most show no particular development of extended or ambitious counterpoint or of a distinctive personal style. Frequently, either a simple imitative or homophonic opening devolves into loose polyphony where there are rarely any breaks in any of the parts. Such writing is reminiscent of improvised polyphony, where a continuous interplay of parts, relatively undogmatic approach, and the generation of effective but not particularly striking musical material must have been commonplace.[22]

Rossi shows some more polyphonic rigor in the genres conventionally associated with contrapuntal practices than in the dances and sinfonie. Rossi's single *canzona* in the *Primo libro* and the three *canzoni per sonar* in the *Secondo libro* are noticeably more focused on the presentation of a *soggetto* and its imitation around the ensemble in the manner of a ricercare, showing Rossi working out his counterpoint with more rigor while engaging with the many notated contrapuntal compositions for instruments within these genres. The improvisation of sophisticated imitative polyphonic textures was a required skill for many church organists, but it is highly unlikely that ordinary instrumental ensembles could improvise such detailed imitative counterpoint at length.[23] At times, he uses gestures that are familiar from the ricercare and canzona repertoire, such as the soggetto heard in m. 22 of the first *Canzon per sonar* (see ex. 9.1), which features the three repeated notes common to many such contrapuntal pieces. While the notated dances and sinfonie may represent the manner of pieces that Rossi and his colleagues could have improvised with some awareness of a long oral heritage, these canzonas show Rossi engaging with a tradition that, while potentially oral for some of his colleagues, could likely only be recreated for an instrumental ensemble using writing.

These canzonas relying on counterpoint made up only a minority of Rossi's published instrumental works. Most of the rest were variation sonatas, in which some kind of schema—a bass line, chord progression, or

EXAMPLE 9.1.

Salamone Rossi, "Canzon [prima] per sonar," from *Il secondo libro delle sinfonie è gagliarde à tre voci* (Venice: Amadino, 1608), mm. 1–6 and mm. 22–26.

melody—provided the impetus for a set of variations. Although such *stile moderno* sonatas were cultivated by a number of his contemporary composers, Rossi's contributions to this distinctive genre are substantial: his *Terzo libro* featured six variation sonatas, and his *Quarto libro* included eight variation sonatas.[24]

The types of schemas on which these sonatas were based are testament to the oral heritage of improvising on tunes that were widely known. Some are based on popular songs, such as "Questo è quel luoco," "L'è tanto tempo hormai," and "Porto celato il mio nobil pensiero."[25] Also used are dance themes from the common *passamezzo* through to the rarely encountered *tordiglione*, both of which appeared in the encyclopedic dance manual of Fabritio Caroso; such dances were presumably heard frequently in the secular society within and around the Gonzaga court.²⁶ Other sonatas are based on standard formulas, or *arie*, that were commonly employed in performing epics—such *arie per cantar stanze* as the *Romanesca* and *Ruggiero* were used by *cantastorie*, semi-improvising performers who based their singing or recitation of works such as *Orlando furioso* on these musical formulas.²⁷ Many of these practices can be strongly connected to the traditions of oral storytelling described in Albert Lord's *Singer of Tales*, since they consist of a standard repertoire of formulas and themes, together with musical ideas that encourage metrical structures in sung or spoken stanzas.²⁸

The early example of Diego Ortiz shows that the *Romanesca* had a heritage of being used for instrumental elaboration, since it featured alongside passamezzi and other similar schemes in his manual demonstrating the ornamental procedures known as "diminution."²⁹ By the beginning of the seventeenth century, formulas such as arie and basic dance progressions were also being set down in the notational shorthand of *alfabeto* for the guitar, broadening their distribution.³⁰ It may be an indication of Rossi's essentially secular outlook as an instrumentalist that he cultivated themes that were popular in secular society and that would have been recognized by listeners. Such sonatas were likely written for use in secular entertainment, combining secular tunes that everyone knew with more impressive instrumental techniques.

The variation sonatas of Rossi's *Terzo libro* rely substantially on their oral roots and demonstrate a number of oral practices being carried over and transformed into written structures. The material on which each sonata is based—the *Romanesca*, *Ruggiero*, and other popular themes—is invariably clearly audible at the beginning of each piece and continues to guide the listener throughout the variations. While the theme itself is derived from the realm of oral performance, Rossi benefited from the ability to use the medium of writing to refine and plan carefully the style and effect of each variation. This aspect of the written text seems to have hastened a distinction between different stylistic traits and enabled composers to create stylistically contrasting variations. The inclusion of stylistic contrast would have been more difficult in an improvised ensemble setting, where the level of communication among players would have rendered impractical the consistent execution of stylistic transformations across the ensemble.

Some of Rossi's sonatas contain a variation in a different meter, such as a dance idiom featuring a characteristic rhythm, and there are instances of controlled syncopations or suspensions, sometimes approaching the complex harmonies of the organists' *durezze e ligature* (dissonances and suspensions) idiom. It was probable that organists, as highly trained individuals, could improvise such sudden changes, intricate textures, and dissonant harmonies; for an ensemble of instrumentalists, however, a written composition was a more reliable way to introduce these kinds of details into a framework. On a larger scale, this written working out of variations made it easy for broader concerns of development, structure, and pacing to be worked into the composition.

The first of Rossi's published variation sonatas, the "Sonata sopra l'aria della Romanesca" from *Il terzo libro de varie sonate, sinfonie, gagliarde, brandi, e corrente*, established many hallmarks of this notated variation style. After his initial presentation of the *Romanesca* theme with the characteristic harmonic scheme and a melody in the canto parts (presumably intended for violins), Rossi added seven variations; see example 9.2 for the incipits of the variations. The *Romanesca* harmonies remain clearly audible throughout, since Rossi does not attempt any substantial reharmonizations or alterations that may impede awareness and appreciation of this recognizable scheme. However, Rossi does make a clear attempt to order his diminutions so as to vary the surface motion. The first two variations use only a moderate level of motion, in mainly eighth notes, and the third variation provides a calmer interlude in a *ligature* texture. The subsequent four variations alternate between variations featuring some quicker sixteenth notes and variations that combine a busy texture of eighth notes in the upper parts with constant motion from the bass. The increase of activity that this scheme generates is emphasized by Rossi's direction to repeat the final variation at a quicker tempo (*Si replica l'ultima parte ma più presto*). The use of perpetual motion in all three parts and a quicker repeat recurs in several of Rossi's sonatas, demonstrating his interest in leading the sonatas to exciting endings.

In terms of surface ornamentation, many of the variations in Rossi's sonatas are reliant on the technique of diminution. This technique of breaking down the notes of a melody line into smaller, ornamental note values lends itself naturally to variation forms. While the early example of Ortiz included the use of a *Romanesca* formula as a basis for diminutions, the later instrumentalists who published diminution manuals in the 1580s–1590s tended to draw melodic lines from the sophisticated polyphonic genres of chansons

Romanesca theme

Variation 1: eighth notes, ascending then descending, hocketing

Variation 2: eighth notes, mainly descending, hocketing

EXAMPLE 9.2.

Salamone Rossi, "Sonata sopra l'aria della Romanesca," from *Il terzo libro de varie sonate, sinfonie, gagliarde, brandi, e corrente* (Venice: Vincenti, [1613?]), incipits.

and madrigals.[31] These instrumentalists used the leading genres of written composition as ideal vehicles to carry the diminution tradition from its presumably oral origins toward a notated, literate practice. Much as a musical formula could encourage an epic singer to obey set metrical and poetic structures,[32] the use of a formula as the basis for diminutions also had the potential to organize this previously varied ornamental detail. It was in writing that this potential could be fully realized, since notation encouraged the delineation and repetition of clearly characterized variants.

Variation 3: half notes, suspensions

Variation 4: sixteenth notes, descending, hocketing

Variation 5: eighth notes, both descending and irregular, hocketing

EXAMPLE 9.2. (*Continued*)

Salamone Rossi, "Sonata sopra l'aria della Romanesca," from *Il terzo libro de varie sonate, sinfonie, gagliarde, brandi, e corrente* (Venice: Vincenti, [1613?]), incipits.

Variation 6: quick eighth/sixteenth-note motif in sequences, hocketing

Variation 7: both violins playing constant eighth notes; variation repeated faster

EXAMPLE 9.2. (*Continued*)

Salamone Rossi, "Sonata sopra l'aria della Romanesca," from *Il terzo libro de varie sonate, sinfonie, gagliarde, brandi, e corrente* (Venice: Vincenti, [1613?]), incipits.

The written medium also allowed for a coherent ensemble approach to variation. Rather than a single instrumentalist controlling the ornamental surface, as in Ortiz's diminutions, or each part having to ornament in turn, as in Girolamo Dalla Casa's decorated ensemble madrigals, the single creative mind could direct multiple parts in writing and generate interesting new options for interaction and interplay between the parts.[33] One feature that frequently occurs in these sonatas is a focus on one particular type of diminution, either a single note value or a distinctive rhythmic or melodic unit that functions as a motif. This recalls Dalla Casa's pedagogical idea of providing examples of diminutions that focused on a single note value, or Riccardo Rognoni's tendency to repeat units of diminution in sequences until they give the impression of motifs;[34] it also returns to Ong's conception of writing as a separative activity. In these variation sonatas of the early seventeenth century, focus on a particular category of diminution established some standard types of variations that recur in a number of compositions, and it became a way to evoke different characters in successive variations.

A basic method of variation was to confine the rhythmic surface to mainly eighth notes; this was used for the first variation in several of Rossi's sonatas. There were two main options for executing this: either to have a short motif in eighth notes passed between the parts (as in variations 1, 2, and 5 of the "Sonata sopra l'aria della Romanesca") or to use a lengthier stream of eighth-note diminutions running in one or both upper parts (as in the last variation of this sonata). When eighth-note motifs are passed between the parts, the written medium allows for great control over the consistency and dovetailing of gestures, and in places the instruments can create a compound melody through the interaction of their parts. The fifth variation of this sonata shows Rossi crafting an intricate effect through writing, with the two violin parts carefully interlocking their motifs over a moto perpetuo version of the *Romanesca* bass line.

Similar procedures are available for variations that focus on sixteenth notes: distinct motifs can be passed between the parts, the instruments can alternate to form a single melody line, or they can coordinate in a show of harmony that would be practically impossible in an extemporization. Variation 4 uses sixteenth notes in a distinctive descending gesture, passed between the parts—this variation forms a natural culmination to the first half of the sonata, particularly since Rossi uses sixteenth notes in both parts at the midpoint and end of the phrase. Variation 6 increases the surface rhythm considerably with sequential repetitions of a distinctive motif; after alternating for much of the variation, the two violins join together in the final measure for a written-out *groppo* ornament.

Rossi's "Sonata sopra l'aria della Romanesca" shows the composer balancing his oral heritage and skills in written composition, and it shows many of the characteristics that scholars such as Ong and Goody observed at the oral-literate interface. The borrowed *Romanesca* tune remains clearly perceivable by listeners throughout and was recognizable aurally, not hidden deep in a written texture. These kinds of themes probably represented the type of repertoire that Rossi was familiar with as a violinist in a small ensemble; although we have no record of his precise ensemble activities, improvisation on such common themes was likely. Much of his writing on the theme is similarly informed by the oral heritage of instrumentalists, with the use of diminutions reflecting back on sixteenth-century improvisatory skills that seemed quite widespread. He was, however, clearly prepared to benefit from the organization and close detail that written composition can facilitate, since his variations demonstrate both intricacies of part writing and a larger structural coherence that is enabled by notation.

ORALITY, LITERACY, AND THE CONTEXTS OF ROSSI'S *HA-SHIRIM 'ASHER LI-SHLOMO*

Rossi's compositional practice in his instrumental works resided at the intersection of oral and literate musical traditions. Similarly, *Ha-shirim 'asher li-Shlomo* shows his engagement with a range of possibilities in Jewish practice, as he introduced polyphony, written in pitch-specific staff notation, as a supplement to the oral practices already prevalent in Jewish communities. Indeed, for centuries, musical practice among the Jews had remained an oral tradition; this was a purposeful decision based on Jewish history and legal considerations, as explained in the following pages. In his publication of a collection of Hebrew-language vocal works, Rossi introduced a new ontological possibility in Jewish musical practice. Even if *Ha-shirim 'asher li-Shlomo* did not have any immediate successors in the form of similar Hebrew publications, it represented a foray into music notation that was in dialogue with Jewish discourse on music.

In 1605, the Jewish community of Ferrara experienced a musical crisis.[35] While congregational singing, led by a cantor, was common, the community's rabbi, the young Leon Modena, attempted to introduce improvised polyphony into his synagogue's practice, encouraging some congregants to complement the melody of the cantor. One man in attendance, Rabbi Moses Coimbram, objected loudly. He cited the body of *halakhic* (Jewish legal) literature debating the propriety of singing—often taken as a marker of joy—following the destruction of the Temple in Jerusalem in the year 70 CE. In sources reaching as far back as the Mishnah (before 200 CE) and the Babylonian Talmud (compiled ca. 200–700 CE), Jewish legal authorities had debated the permissibility of music making, with some arguing that a total ban on music was required as a sign of mourning and exile. Other writers had taken a more lenient position, arguing that the prohibition on music applied only to instruments, or only to instruments in synagogues, or only to the singing of secular songs while the singer is experiencing the intoxicating effects of wine.[36]

Modena answered a formal *she'elah* (legal question) about whether the singing of (probably unnotated) polyphony in synagogue was acceptable or prohibited. As the author of the she'elah explained, "We have with us, from among the members of our congregation (may its Rock preserve it and give it life!) six or eight intelligent persons who, knowing something about the science of song, viz., music, lift their voices and sing in joy in the synagogue. ... Yet a man arose to expel them with the speech of his lips, answering [others] by saying that it is improper to do so, for rejoicing is prohibited."[37] In his responsum, Modena surveyed the halakhic literature on the subject and drew his own conclusion: "The cantor is required to make his voice sound as pleasant as possible in prayer. And if he were able to make his one voice sound like ten singers together, would it not be good? Or if, at his side, he had assistants whom the Lord favored with a sweet voice and they sang along with him not in [compositional] order but rather a[d] aria, as is customary all day long in the Ashkenazi congregations, and it should happen that they relate to and coordinate with him, would it be considered a sin on their part?"[38]

Here Modena argues in favor of allowing the cantor to have assistants by his side who would create polyphony *all'improvviso*. Noting that this was a frequent occurrence in Ashkenazic communities (rather than the Sephardic communities who had come to Italy following expulsion from

Spain in 1492), Modena suggests using arie—the harmonic-melodic formulas that, as we have seen, were in common use in both vocal and instrumental music in early modern Italy—as the basis of improvised synagogue polyphony. Avery Gosfield has shown that Italian Jews frequently used arie designed for terza rima or ottava rima poetry, adapting them for poetry on Jewish subjects, whether in Italian, Hebrew, or Yiddish.[39] Formulas such as the *Romanesca* and the *Ruggiero*, as well as other folk songs, appear to have been used for such purposes. Modena's responsum seems to suggest merely expanding this practice to include it in Sephardic synagogue worship.

When Rossi and Modena assembled the materials for *Ha-shirim 'asher li-Shlomo*, they included Modena's *teshuva* (Jewish legal responsum) in the volume's prefatory material, clearly anticipating objections of a nature similar to those that had been raised in Ferrara some eighteen years earlier. As Modena writes in his foreword to the *Shirim*:

> It could be that among the exiled [i.e., the Jewish community] there is one of those sanctimonious persons who eliminate anything new or any example of learning in which they have no part and that he may wish to prohibit this work because of what he learned, though inexactly. In order to remove any resentment from a stubborn heart, I decided to reproduce here in print what I wrote in an answer to a question eighteen years ago—I was then a teacher of Tora in the holy community of Ferrara (may God protect it!)—with the intent of sealing the mouth of someone speaking nonsense about this matter, and all the learned men of Venice at that time signed it.[40]

Modena's foreword glosses over the distinctions between the 1605 Ferrara case and that of Rossi's *Shirim*. Most notable among these distinctions is the fact that Rossi's polyphony is composed and notated rather than improvised. In this context, it seems significant that Rossi's Hebrew works do not include any of the arie to which Modena had referred in his teshuva and that Rossi used so extensively in his instrumental works. Indeed, Rossi seems to have gone out of his way to avoid any semblance of formula-based composition. The question from the Ferrara community makes special mention of hymns such as *Yigdal 'Elohim ḥai* (May the living Lord be magnified), *'Ein kelohenu* (There is none like our Lord), and *'Adon 'olam* (Master of the world)—three texts for which Rossi composed musical settings.[41] All three are stanzaic, and they use poetic meters that clearly invite strophic musical treatment, perhaps with elaboration and ornamentation along the lines found in Rossi's

EXAMPLE 9.3A.

Salamone Rossi, "'Ein kelohenu," from *Ha-shirim 'asher li-Shlomo* (Venice: Bragadini, 1622–1623), mm. 46–53, Chorus I (Chorus II omitted).

variation sonatas, as discussed previously. Rossi's settings of these texts respect their stanzaic poetry, especially through the alternation of choirs with the start of each stanza. However, there is virtually no musical repetition from one stanza to the next, such that improvised congregational participation is practically impossible. Unlike in the variation sonatas, there is no underlying strophic theme that allows the listener to follow aurally from one stanza to the next. The last stanza of Rossi's "'Ein kelohenu" demonstrates these points clearly. After four stanzas in which each syllable of each line is stated only once (see ex. 9.3a), the last stanza is subjected to text repetition and motivic fragmentation in the manner of a through-composed madrigal (ex. 9.3b).

The *Shirim* were certainly not intended to replace the oral tradition of synagogue music. The presence in his publications of double bar lines to signal moments for congregational responses at liturgically mandated points confirms this. The singers of polyphony would pause the progress of their music as they awaited those responses, which might have been spoken or sung, with the singers' performance reflecting varying degrees of musical training. Moreover, the *Shirim* cover only a fraction of the music that would have been sung in a synagogue service, the rest of which would have been rendered in the traditional manner; they might also have been

EXAMPLE 9.3B.

Salamone Rossi, "'Ein kelohenu," from *Ha-shirim 'asher li-Shlomo* (Venice: Bragadini, 1622–1623), mm. 59–100.

used in contexts outside synagogue worship. Additionally, Rossi would not have expected these pieces to be used on an everyday basis. As indicated in Modena's foreword, Rossi published the *Shirim* so that his people would "rejoice on festivals and on the return of sacred observances."[42] Nevertheless, Rossi's divergence from the oral tradition of improvised singing, including the use of strophic arie, is noteworthy. Whereas his instrumental variation sonatas built on the oral tradition of instrumental practice to create a more complex work, the *Shirim* seem to avoid reference to techniques that highlight the continuity of orality and literacy. Vestiges of the oral tradition are

EXAMPLE 9.3B. (*Continued*)

Salamone Rossi, "'Ein kelohenu," from *Ha-shirim 'asher li-Shlomo* (Venice: Bragadini, 1622–1623), mm. 59–100.

obscured within the text itself, even while they remained evident elsewhere in the service.

For Modena, Rossi's *Shirim* constituted part of an ongoing effort to foster musicianship and musical literacy in the Jewish communities of northern Italy. Modena encouraged learned musical activities among Jews through a variety of activities and documents, including writing halakhic responsa on the subject; fostering music in synagogues; and leading his Venetian academy, the Accademia degli Impediti, of which he assumed direction in 1628. Harrán and others have speculated that Modena composed as well.[43]

EXAMPLE 9.3B. (Continued)

Salamone Rossi, "'Ein kelohenu," from *Ha-shirim 'asher li-Shlomo* (Venice: Bragadini, 1622–1623), mm. 59–100.

Modena's musical literacy seems highly likely given his statement, in the preface to *Ha-Shirim*, that he proofread Rossi's work.[44] His engagement with staff notation is further demonstrated by the recent discovery that he was the author of a poetic contrafactum of an Italian vocal work by Orazio Vecchi— a piece that would likely have required him to read from a score; the other singers who participated in this polyphonic performance would have had to either read along with him or learn the piece by rote.[45] Rossi was one of many professional performers in Mantua who worked in music and musical theater, and the Gonzagas cultivated these activities among the Jewish community and brought them to the court for performances.[46] Celebrations

EXAMPLE 9.3B. (*Continued*)

Salamone Rossi, "'Ein kelohenu," from *Ha-shirim 'asher li-Shlomo* (Venice: Bragadini, 1622–1623), mm. 59–100.

of festivals such as Simḥat Torah sometimes involved elaborate musical performances, including polyphony with instruments.[47] While it is difficult to know whether all these activities relied on musical literacy, it is clear that such literacy was not uncommon in the Jewish community. Inventories taken of Jewish-owned libraries indicate that "many Jews owned books on music theory by Christian authors such as Gaffurio."[48] Moreover, the issue of literacy in music notation was a matter of some import for Jewish writers in Italy, raising a host of issues concerning the status of the Jewish community in the Diaspora and its relationship with its non-Jewish neighbors.

EXAMPLE 9.3B. (*Continued*)

Salamone Rossi, "'Ein kelohenu," from *Ha-shirim 'asher li-Shlomo* (Venice: Bragadini, 1622–1623), mm. 59–100.

Jewish communities had long been linguistically literate. Despite the emphasis in the Jewish tradition on the "oral law" (a term that refers to the laws said to have been transmitted through divine communication at the same time as the "written law," or Torah), the major corpus of legal works stemming from the oral tradition had been committed to writing (albeit terse and elliptical) as the Mishnah, Midrash, and Talmud between roughly 200 BCE and 700 CE in response to the existential threat posed by life in exile.[49]

Just as Jewish communities had engaged in a literate tradition early on, the Jews of early modern Italy adopted printed texts in great numbers almost immediately following the introduction of print technology. As Adam

EXAMPLE 9.3B. (*Continued*)

Salamone Rossi, "'Ein kelohenu," from *Ha-shirim 'asher li-Shlomo* (Venice: Bragadini, 1622–1623), mm. 59–100.

Shear and Joseph R. Hacker explain, "Despite the continuing production of manuscripts, the evidence tells us a story of print displacing manuscript production, even in the late fifteenth century."[50] Jewish authors published Hebrew-language books through partnerships with Christian printing houses, and Jewish readers collected such volumes in great numbers. (A similar partnership was required for the publication of the *Shirim*.) Although, as Robert Bonfil has noted, printed books were still "luxury items,"[51] there is evidence that Jews were proportionally more literate than their Christian neighbors.[52] David B. Ruderman has suggested that the increase in the production of Hebrew books in the early modern era may have been a reaction to the heightened mobility that characterized early modern Jewry as a whole: "In a society in constant movement, the publishing of books also constituted a means of arresting motion, of preserving and storing the memory of the past and its traditions as an attempt—albeit elusive—of fixing and stabilizing the present."[53]

As noted previously, Jews had, early on, also adopted a set of cantillation markings resembling neumes, which governed the music for liturgical recitation of the Torah and other books of the Hebrew Bible. While Christian detractors had long claimed that these cantillation markings were an invention at the end of the first millennium by the group of scholars known as the "Masoretes" (the Hebrew word *mesorah* meaning "tradition"), Jewish sources hold that they date to the period of the ancient Israelites and that the Masoretes merely codified the tradition.[54] Whatever the case, these cantillation markings represent a form of musical literacy for the liturgical reading of biblical passages. No similar system was applied to liturgical prayers not taken from the Bible.

The indication of specific pitches for Jewish liturgical music in Western musical notation had, with only a few exceptions, not been attempted.[55] The rare instances, prior to the seventeenth century, in which Western musical notation had been applied to either the cantillation markings or the composition of melodies for prayers stemmed from cases of cross-confessional interaction, as Francesco Spagnolo notes in his chapter in the present volume. One such instance is that of the twelfth-century Norman convert Johannes, or Obadiah "Ha-Ger" (the Norman Proselyte), whose manuscripts showing Hebrew texts of Psalms with Western chant notation were uncovered in the Cairo Genizah.[56] Another, the *Opus de prosodia Hebraeorum* of 1545 by the Christian writer Johannes Vallensis, transcribed the cantillation markings for the liturgical chanting of the Torah but found them nonsensical.[57]

The early seventeenth-century Hebrew writer Abraham Portaleone, whose *Shiltei Ha-Gibborim* (Shields of the heroes, Mantua, 1612) sought to explain the art of music among other practices of the Temple of the ancient Israelites, exposed the pitfalls of such interreligious mixing. For Portaleone, Vallensis's evaluation of Hebrew cantillation represented a betrayal. Portaleone claimed that Vallensis had studied with one Rabbi Eliyahu but had "deceived him" with false pretenses, approaching his task of explicating the Jewish cantillation markings with the prior intention of "discovering" their faults. Portaleone provided his own explanation of the value and import of the cantillation marks in both exegetical and musical terms.[58] He concluded this section of the *Shiltei Ha-Gibborim* with a confident statement that "when our Messiah comes, He will restore the pristine splendor; and our priests, Levites and prophets will teach us, by God's command, the proper intervals of music ... which we have forgotten in our exile."[59]

Throughout the *Shiltei Ha-Gibborim*, Portaleone expresses discomfort with the knowledge that Christians had a more fully developed tradition of music, including musical literacy, while Jews did not. He defined the musical instruments and modes listed in the Hebrew Bible in terms of modern Italian instruments, likening, for example, the biblical nevel to the lute.[60] In this system, musical literacy was equally important. As Portaleone explained, "Since there was a great number of all the players and musical instruments and singers, we may assume that the Levites had many books which taught them all sorts of instrumental melodies and all kinds of tunes for the Psalms of David, son of Jesse; and with this book we sing today. These books, therefore, along with all the other musical instruments, were placed in chambers which opened onto the Women's Court [of the Temple], so that the books might be ready for use [literally, "to speak of them," a quotation from Deuteronomy 6:7] when needed."[61] Borrowing language of the Italian Renaissance, he explains further that some ancient Israelite instruments were "perfect" (that is, they could play both melody and harmony together, as keyboard instruments) and had their own *intavolatura*, while players of "imperfect" (that is, melody) instruments learned their parts from partbooks.[62] Portaleone's claim, whether meant literally or not, is that the notation of Italian music in the seventeenth century was preceded by similar forms of notation used in the ancient Temple.[63] This notation, together with the science of music in general, would be restored during messianic times.

In his longing for the restoration of a literate musical tradition, Portaleone was not alone. Don Isaac Abravanel, the leader of the Jewish community of Spain who settled in Italy following the expulsion of the Jews in 1492, wrote in an introductory essay to Exodus 15, which contains the Song at the Sea, that music was an integral part of ancient Israelite practice. Enumerating various types of Hebrew poetry, some of which included music by definition, Abravanel explained that song served an essential purpose in the transmission of traditions and texts: "For most people forget plain texts [i.e., those that are not sung], even if they study them day and night. But when [the texts] are set to melodies to which they can be sung and played, they will be remembered forever by means of their melodies."[64] For Abravanel, music impresses the meanings of the words in the memory of those who sing and hear them—an observation that was, for him, borne out by the survival of the cantillation system and the texts that it was meant to deliver.

Abravanel was clear that the oral tradition that had existed prior to the exile was a rich one, perhaps involving rhythmic modes like the ones he knew from his Muslim neighbors in Spain. However, prefiguring Portaleone, Abravanel cited the unstable nature of oral transmission as a reason for the loss of this knowledge: "There is no doubt that they once had known melodies, but those were forgotten because of the passage of time and the length of the exile."[65] And it was not only the melodies and rhythmic modes that were lost; so, too, was the tradition of musical instruments: "In their practice everything was done according to the various instruments and their types: their strings, their threads, and their holes: kinor [harp] and 'ugav [viola da gamba] and tof [drum] and ḥalil [flute] and minim [clavichord] and metzaltim [cymbals] and neginot [meaning unclear, lit. "melodies"] and gitit [harp] and the sheminit [eight-stringed harp] and the 'asor [ten-stringed harp, interpreted by Portaleone as a theorbo], and the nevel [lute] and the maḥol [bell] and their like ... for this science [of music] holds great powers—wondrous matters pertaining to divinity."[66]

Modena picked up on these themes in the prefatory material that he contributed to Rossi's *Ha-shirim 'asher li-Shlomo*. Quoting the medieval Italian poet Immanuel HaRomi, Modena asked, "What will the science of music [*niggun*] say to others? 'I was surely stolen from the land of the Hebrews.'"[67] And Modena placed Rossi within the lineage of the ancient musicians, including King David and the Levites who sang and played instruments in the Temple, writing that Rossi may be "compared to many famous persons, in yesteryear, among the families of the earth."[68] Describing Rossi's compositional process, Modena writes, "Day by day he would enter into his notebook a certain psalm of David or a formula for prayer or praise, reverence and divine song [*zimra*] until he succeeded in gathering some of them into a collection, making several available ... He ordered me to prevent any mishap from coming to the composition, to prepare it [for setting], embellish it, proofread it and keep my eyes open for typographical errors and defects."[69]

Through these statements, Modena calls attention to the physical artifact of the book, which would allow the composer to "leave behind a name better than sons, for he is beginning something that will not be outdone and that did not exist as such in Israel; and in order to let his fellows be their beneficiaries." Lacing his statements with scriptural citations, Modena emphasizes the novelty and lasting import of the printed artifact: "Blessed are you now, congregation of believers, for we have succeeded in a peaceful beginning: an inkwell may be seen, in our days, alongside that wise man who writes and prints these praises in song."[70] To judge from this statement, he expected that Rossi's introduction of a literate musical tradition into synagogue liturgical practice would inspire others to follow in his footsteps. Modena expects that congregants would hear the contrast between Rossi's compositions and the sounds of other forms of synagogue prayer, and he suggests that Rossi's works would inspire other composers to create notated polyphonic compositions: "Will we, who were masters of music in our prayers and our praises, now become a laughingstock to the nations, for them to say that no longer is [this] science in our midst? Will we shout to the God of our fathers as a dog and as a crow? ... No sensible person or sage would think of prohibiting the praise of the Lord (may He be blessed) with the most pleasant voice possible and with this science that awakens souls to his glory."[71]

It is noteworthy that Modena adopts the language of the "music libel against the Jews," identified by Ruth HaCohen as a persistent and insidious feature of European discourse for centuries.[72] In this mode of discourse, Jews are incapable of making music and instead create nothing but noise. Modena's likening of synagogue music to the shouting of barnyard animals is not far from the opinion of the English traveler Thomas Coryat, who claimed that chanting in synagogue was nothing more than an "exceeding loud yaling, undecent roaring, and as it were a beastly bellowing of it forth."[73]

Modena's foreword to Rossi's *Shirim* sheds light on one additional element of the publication, already remarked on: its counterintuitive typography. While the music is written according to the European custom, from left to right, each Hebrew word appears under the musical notation such that it must be read from left to right. The reader's eye must constantly skip to the right to locate the next Hebrew word, which is again read from right to left. As Modena notes, "He who sees will see that, in the eyes of the composer, it seemed better to have the readers pronounce the letters backwards, yet read in reverse order the words of the song with which they are all familiar than to invert the musical order from what is customary.... For that reason, too, he felt no misgivings about there being no vowels for the words, for, in singing, the majority of those versed in the system of notation are also skilled in reading."[74]

The incongruous layout of the Hebrew text and the musical notation is yet one more element of Rossi's publication that depends on the readers' possession and study of the book itself. Modena's explanation of this typography also represents an admission that musical literacy was still limited among the Jewish communities that formed the primary audience for his publication. Rossi did not anticipate problems omitting the diacritical markings that indicate vowels—at least no more problem than was posed by the system of music notation.

Indeed, while there were clearly some Jews who were musically literate, and Modena seems to have intended to expand his advocacy for musical literacy, his statement here suggests that musical literacy was not yet widespread. Rossi clearly intended his *Shirim* for performance by skilled musicians. The throughcomposed treatment of stanzaic poetry points to a nonparticipatory medium that relied on the use of the printed volume. Rossi seems consciously to have eschewed the techniques of formula-based composition that he embraced in his instrumental works and his strophic canzonette.

CONCLUSION

The level of success of Rossi's experiment with notated Hebrew polyphony is unclear. The volume was apparently never reprinted, and as noted previously, it inspired no immediate followers or imitators. The plague that swept across Italy in 1630 hit the Jewish communities with great force, and it appears that the already small number of Jews who were musically literate was reduced significantly. If this is true, then the singular nature of the *Shirim* as a polyphonic Hebrew work of the early modern era may have been nothing more than the result of historical happenstance.

And yet, although Rossi's *Shirim* was a unique publication, it should be understood within the context of the musical polemics that appeared in other Hebrew sources of this period. Abravanel and Portaleone seem to have had a great deal invested in the claim that composed art music had been an important component of religious practice in the ancient Temple. Admitting to what they saw as the decline of the Jewish musical tradition since ancient times, they argued that this decline was a result of the Jews' exile and dispersion. Systems of notation were one of the components that they claimed had been lost in the many centuries of this exile. Reviving the art of notated music was essential for the rebuilding of a musical tradition.

Salamone Rossi was uniquely positioned to mediate between oral and written musical traditions and to introduce—albeit only briefly—notated polyphonic compositions into Jewish practice. A highly regarded, published composer of secular Italian vocal works as well as instrumental music, Rossi witnessed—and contributed to—a transition toward literacy in instrumental music. He composed numerous variation sonatas that, as shown previously, draw on the oral tradition of instrumental performance but build on them to create large, well-crafted, notated musical edifices.

Whether Rossi was conscious of the influences of oral musical culture on his instrumental compositions, he seems to have avoided such influences in his Hebrew motets. Despite evidence that musical formulas like the ones he used in his instrumental sonatas were likewise used in improvised synagogue polyphony, the *Shirim* do not take up those formulas—even in settings of poetry that could easily accommodate them. His compositions draw attention to their rootedness in musical literacy. This effect is consciously amplified in the volume's typography and the prefatory material by Leon Modena, which emphasizes the novelty of the "inkwell"—that is, of Rossi's musical literacy. Although a historical curiosity with no clear or immediate successors, his Hebrew compositions shed light on the meeting of orality and literacy in Rossi's worlds.

NOTES

1. Salamone Rossi, *Ha-shirim 'asher li-Shlomo* (Venice: Pietro and Lorenzo Bragadini, in the house of Giovanni Calleoni, [5]383 [=1622–1623]). Throughout, we refer to the prefatory material as printed in Salamone Rossi, *Sacred Vocal Works in Hebrew: Hashirim 'asher lishlomo / "The Songs of Solomon,"* ed. with introduction and notes by Don Harrán, Complete Works, part 3, vols. 13a and 13b (S.l.: American Institute of Musicology and Neuhausen: Hänssler, 2003).

2. Leon Modena's autobiography provides a great deal of information about his life; see Leon Modena, *The Autobiography of a Seventeenth-Century Venetian Rabbi: Leon Modena's Life of Judah*, trans. and ed. Mark R. Cohen (Princeton, NJ: Princeton University Press,

1988). See also Don Harrán, "'Dum recordaremur Sion': Music in the Life and Thought of the Venetian Rabbi Leon Modena (1571–1648)," *AJS Review* 23, no. 1 (1998): 17–61. Moses Sulam was the father-in-law of Sarra Copia Sulam, a prominent Jewish poet whose work may have crossed over into music. See Don Harrán, "Doubly Tainted, Doubly Talented: The Jewish Poet Sara Copio (d. 1641) as a Heroic Singer," in *Musica Franca: Essays in Honor of Frank A. D'Accone*, ed. Irene Alm, Alyson McLamore, and Colleen Reardon (Stuyvesant, NY: Pendragon, 1996), 367–422. Harrán transcribed and translated Sarra Copia Sulam's writings in Sarra Copia Sulam et al., *Jewish Poet and Intellectual in Seventeenth-Century Venice: The Works of Sarra Copia Sulam in Verse and Prose, along with Writings of Her Contemporaries in Her Praise, Condemnation, or Defense*, ed. and trans. with introduction by Don Harrán (Chicago: University of Chicago Press, 2009). For more on Sulam, see Lynn Lara Westwater, *Sarra Copia Sulam: A Jewish Salonnière and the Press in Counter-Reformation Rome* (Toronto: University of Toronto Press, 2020), and Umberto Fortis, *La "bella ebrea": Sara Copio Sullam, poetessa nel ghetto di Venezia del '600* (Turin: Silvio Zamorani editore, 2003). On partnerships between Jews and Christians in the printing of Hebrew books, see Bruce Nielsen, "Daniel van Bombergen, a Bookman of Two Worlds," in *The Hebrew Book in Early Modern Italy*, ed. Joseph R. Hacker and Adam Shear (Philadelphia: University of Pennsylvania Press, 2011), 56–75, and David Werner Amram, *The Makers of Hebrew Books in Italy, Being Chapters in the History of the Hebrew Printing Press* (Philadelphia: Julius H. Greenstone, 1909).

3. Don Harrán, *Salamone Rossi: Jewish Musician in Late Renaissance Mantua* (Oxford: Oxford University Press, 1999), 210. This volume contains the most complete overview of Rossi's life and works.

4. On Jewish literacy as a whole, see Robert Bonfil, *Jewish Life in Renaissance Italy*, trans. Anthony Oldcorn (Berkeley: University of California Press, 1994), 146–151.

5. The volumes of compositions by Rossi considered in this study are *Il secondo libro delle sinfonie è gagliarde à tre voci* (Venice: Amadino, 1608) and *Il terzo libro de varie sonate, sinfonie, gagliarde, brandi, e corrente* (Venice: Vincenti, [1613?]). All of Rossi's extant instrumental works appear in Salamone Rossi, *Instrumental Works: Sonatas, Sinfonie, etc., Book 3*, ed. with introduction and notes by Don Harrán, Complete Works, part 2, vol. 11 (S.l.: American Institute of Musicology and Neuhausen: Hänssler, 1995). That the Gonzaga family kept copies of Rossi's instrumental publications as well as his vocal works is shown in Susan Parisi, "Ducal Patronage of Music in Mantua, 1587–1627: An Archival Study" (PhD diss., University of Illinois at Urbana-Champaign, 1989), 713–714.

6. For further details on his salary and courtly duties, see Harrán, *Salamone Rossi*, 18–24.

7. The situations for keyboardists, lutenists, and amateur instrumentalists are quite different and will not be considered in detail here.

8. Walter J. Ong, *Orality and Literacy: The Technologizing of the Word*, 30th anniversary ed. with additional chapters by John Hartley (Abingdon: Routledge, 2012), 11–13.

9. For more on the basse danse repertoire and the role of improvisation over a cantus firmus, see Jon Banks, *The Instrumental Consort Repertory of the Late Fifteenth Century* (Aldershot: Ashgate, 2006), 60–64, and Ross W. Duffin, "Ensemble Improvisation in 15th-Century Mensural Dance," in *Instruments, Ensembles, and Repertory, 1300–1600: Essays in Honour of Keith Polk*, ed. Timothy J. McGee and Stewart Carter (Turnhout: Brepols, 2013), 201–206.

10. This attitude is akin to traditional jazz practices, in which standard versions of tunes are preserved on lead sheets yet practicing jazz musicians rely primarily on their memorized versions of the tune when they improvise on it in performance.

11. Ong, *Orality and Literacy*, 81.

12. Ong, 75.

13. Ong, 82. An earlier study that considered musical instruments as technologies is Rebecca Cypess, *Curious and Modern Inventions: Instrumental Music as Discovery in Galileo's Italy* (Chicago: University of Chicago Press, 2016).

14. Ong, *Orality and Literacy*, 32. Ong builds on the far-reaching ideas of Marshall McLuhan (1962), who proposed that "the interiorization of the technology of the phonetic alphabet translates man from the magical world of the ear to the neutral visual world." See Marshall McLuhan, *The Gutenberg Galaxy: The Making of Typographic Man*, new ed. with essays by W. Terrence Gordon, Elena Lamberti, and Dominique Scheffel-Dunand (Toronto: University of Toronto Press, 2011), 21–26. These ideas are also developed further in Jack Goody, *The Interface between the Written and the Oral* (Cambridge: Cambridge University Press, 1987), 186–187.

15. Ong, *Orality and Literacy*, 33–57. Goody, in *The Interface between the Written and the Oral*, followed Ong's work by discussing the distinction between purely oral cultures and those in which orality continues to persist even while written or printed culture is ascendant; his research draws on ethnographic studies of a range of cultures where orality has persisted further into the modern age.

16. For the most thorough development of Parry-Lord Theory, see Albert B. Lord, *The Singer of Tales* (Cambridge, MA: Harvard University Press, 1960). A prominent later response to these ideas was John M. Foley, *The Singer of Tales in Performance* (Bloomington: Indiana University Press, 1995).

17. Ong, *Orality and Literacy*, 45. This was developed further in Goody, *The Interface between the Written and the Oral*, 186–188.

18. Ong referred to writing as a "time-obviating technology"; see Ong, *Orality and Literacy*, 40.

19. See Ong, 38 and 41, for some examples of this.

20. The implications of Ong's and Goody's theories to instrumental composers of Rossi's generation are addressed in Lynette Bowring, "Orality, Literacy, and the Learning of Instruments: Professional Instrumentalists and Their Music in Early Modern Italy" (PhD diss., Rutgers University, 2017). Other studies that have applied theories of orality and literacy to musical topics are, for example, Anna Maria Busse Berger, "Mnemotechnics and Notre Dame Polyphony," *Journal of Musicology* 14, no. 3 (1996): 263–298, and Anna Maria Busse Berger, *Medieval Music and the Art of Memory* (Berkeley: University of California Press, 2005).

21. For a discussion of Rossi's dances and their relationships with the works of Buonamente, see Don Harrán, "From Mantua to Vienna: A New Look at the Early Seventeenth-Century Dance Suite," *Journal of the Royal Musical Association* 129 (2004): 181–219. On earlier contexts for dancing and the oral and improvisatory heritage of dance musicians, see Victor Coelho and Keith Polk, *Instrumentalists and Renaissance Culture, 1420–1600: Players of Function and Fantasy* (Cambridge: Cambridge University Press, 2016), 177–180.

22. Improvised polyphony, variously referred with terms such as *contrapunto alla mente*, *contraponto all'improvviso*, and *cantare super librum*, appeared to be widespread throughout much of this period, although direct evidence is sparse and is only just being assessed by musicologists. An early study and extensive preliminary assessment of sources was Ernest T. Ferand, "Improvised Vocal Counterpoint in the Late Renaissance and Early Baroque," *Annales Musicologiques* 4 (1956): 129–174; for some more recent research, see Philippe Canguilhem, "Singing upon the Book according to Vicente Lusitano," *Early Music History* 30 (2011): 55–103; Rob C. Wegman, "What Is Counterpoint?" in *Improvising Early Music: The*

History of Musical Improvisation from the Late Middle Ages to the Early Baroque, Collected Writings of the Orpheus Institute 11, ed. Dirk Moelants (Leuven: Leuven University Press, 2014), 9–68; and Philippe Canguilhem, *L'Improvisation polyphonique à la Renaissance* (Paris: Classiques Garnier, 2015).

23. That improvisational skills were required of church organists is attested, for example, in a *regolamento* setting out audition procedures for organists at San Marco, Venice, that requires the organist to improvise at length in multiple imitative and contrapuntal parts on portions of chant and other compositions. For the Italian and a translation, see Edward J. Soehnlen, "Diruta on the Art of Keyboard-Playing: An Annotated Translation and Transcription of *Il Transilvano*, Parts I (1593) and II (1609)" (PhD diss., University of Michigan, 1975), 10–11.

24. For an overview of other significant composers who contributed to the variation sonata, see Peter Allsop, *The Italian "Trio" Sonata: From Its Origins until Corelli* (Oxford: Oxford University Press, 1992), 85–125. The other prominent composer of variation sonatas in Mantua was Giovanni Battista Buonamente (rumored to have been Rossi's student); see Peter Allsop, *Cavalier Giovanni Battista Buonamente: Franciscan Violinist* (Aldershot: Ashgate, 2005), 93–109; for a discussion of Buonamente's variation sonatas in relation to the issues addressed here, see Bowring, "Orality, Literacy, and the Learning of Instruments," 211–228.

25. Some studies of popular songs that influenced compositions of this era include John Wendland, "'Madre non mi far Monaca': The Biography of a Renaissance Folksong," *Acta Musicologica* 48, fasc. 2 (1976): 185–204, and Warren Kirkendale, "Franceschina, Girometta, and Their Companions in a Madrigal 'a diversi linguaggi' by Luca Marenzio and Orazio Vecchi," *Acta Musicologica* 44 (1972): 181–235.

26. For an English translation of Caroso's treatise, see Fabritio Caroso, *Courtly Dance of the Renaissance: A New Translation and Edition of the "Nobiltà di Dame" (1600)*, trans. Julia Sutton and F. Marian Walker, rev. ed. (New York: Dover, 1995). The *passo e mezzo* appears on 38–39 and 177–181; the *tordiglione*, which is related to the *gagliarda*, appears on 41–43 and 287.

27. For further detail about the *Ruggiero* as an aria for oral recitation, see Alfred Einstein, "Die Aria di Ruggiero," *Sammelbände der Internationalen Musikgesellschaft* 13 (1912): 444–454, and James Haar, "Arie per cantar stanze ariostesche," in *L'Ariosto, la musica, i musicisti: Quattro studi e sette madrigali ariosteschi*, ed. Maria Antonella Balsano, Quaderni della Rivista Italiana di Musicologia 5 (Florence: Leo S. Olschki, 1981), 31–46. For a more general discussion of these kinds of progressions in instrumental music, see Richard Hudson, *Passacaglio and Ciaccona: From Guitar Music to Italian Keyboard Variations in the 17th Century*, Studies in Musicology 37 (Ann Arbor, MI: University Microfilms International, 1981).

28. The more general concept of how "music may act as a constraint to fix a verbatim oral narrative" was also factored into Ong's theory; see Ong, *Orality and Literacy*, 62–63.

29. For diminutions on the *Romanesca*, see Diego Ortiz, "Recercada settima," *Trattado de glosas sobre clausulas* (Rome: Dorico, 1553), 2:58–59. For more on diminution-style ornamentation in the sixteenth and early seventeenth centuries, see Bruce Dickey, "Ornamentation in Early Seventeenth-Century Italian Music," in *A Performer's Guide to Seventeenth-Century Music*, ed. Stewart Carter, rev. by Jeffery T. Kite-Powell (Bloomington: Indiana University Press, 2012), 293–316; Howard Mayer Brown, *Embellishing Sixteenth-Century Music* (London: Oxford University Press, 1976); and Liza Nicole Malamut, "Sounding History: A Diminution Method for Modern Trombonists" (DMA diss., Boston University, 2018), 14–47.

30. On the growing popularity of chord progressions in alfabeto notation, see Cory M. Gavito, "The *Alfabeto* Song in Print, 1610–ca. 1665: Neapolitan Roots, Roman Codification, and '*Il gusto popolare*'" (PhD diss., University of Texas at Austin, 2006).

31. On Ortiz's use of the *Romanesca*, see note 29. Some leading instrumentalists to publish diminution manuals in the late sixteenth century were Girolamo Dalla Casa, *Il vero modo di diminuire*, 2 vols. (Venice: Gardano, 1584); Giovanni Bassano, *Ricercate, passaggi et cadentie, per potersi essercitar nel diminuir terminatamente con ogni sorte d'istrumento* (Venice: Vincenti and Amadino, 1585, 2/1598); and Riccardo Rognoni (Richardo Rogniono), *Passaggi per potersi essercitare nel diminuire terminatamente con ogni sorte d'instromenti*, 2 vols. (Venice: Vincenti, 1592).

32. Lord, *The Singer of Tales*, 37–38; see also Ong, *Orality and Literacy*, 62–63.

33. Dalla Casa demonstrates ensemble diminution with four-part diminutions on Cipriano de Rore's "Alla dolc'ombra" in *Il vero modo di diminuire*, 2:38–49. This composition shows a conversational conception of diminutions, in which each part is ornamented in turn; written for voices and presented in choirbook format, these diminutions may acknowledge the greater desire of amateurs to sing such pieces and share both the responsibility for ornamentation and the chance to momentarily shine.

34. See Dalla Casa, *Il vero modo di diminuire*, 1:7–11, for model diminutions that focus on just one note value, and Rognoni, *Passaggi*, 1:5–9, for an example of each unit of diminution being transposed along ascending and descending scales, thus forming sequences.

35. The sources are discussed in Rossi, *Sacred Vocal Works*, and in Harrán, "'Dum recordaremur Sion,'" 21–23.

36. A survey of these sources is in Boaz Cohen, *Law and Tradition in Judaism* (New York: Ktav, 1959), 167–181. Harrán's conjecture that Coimbram objected to Modena's innovations because of "the proximity of the Sabbath [in question] to the doleful Ninth of Av" is clearly incorrect; see Harrán, "'Dum recordaremur Sion,'" 23.

37. Rossi, *Sacred Vocal Works*, 13a:193–194. The full text of Modena's responsum is also transcribed in Shlomo Simonsohn, ed., *She'elot u-teshuvot: Ziqne Yehuda* (Jerusalem: Rabbi Kuk Foundation, 1956), 15–20.

"יש אתנו יודע עד מה בחכמת השיר ר"ל המוסיקא ששה אושמנה בני דעת מבני קהלנו יצ"ו אשר בחגים ובמועדים ישאו קולם וירונו בבית הכנסת . . . ויקם אדם לגרשם בשיח שפתותיו עונה ואומר כי לא נכון לעשות כן כי אם לשוש אסור."

38. Rossi, *Sacred Vocal Works*, 13a:206–207.

"והמצוה על הש"ץ להנעי' קולו בתפלתו ביותר. ואם יוכל להשמיע קולו יחידי כאילו עשרה משוררים יחד האם לא יהיה טוב? או אם יעמדו אצלו מסייעים אשר חננם ה' קול ערב ובלי סדר רק אַה אַרְיֵאה כנהוג כל היום בין קהלות האשכנים יזמרו עמו ויקרה שיתיחסו ויערכו לו האם יחשב להם לחטא?"

39. Avery Gosfield, "I Sing It to an Italian Tune . . . Thoughts on Performing Sixteenth-Century Italian-Jewish Sung Poetry Today," *European Journal of Jewish Studies* 8, no. 1 (June 2014): 9–52. See also Gosfield's contribution to this volume, which documents other formulaic melodies that were commonly used within the Jewish community for the recitation of both sacred and secular poetry.

40. Rossi, *Sacred Vocal Works*, 13a:184.

"אולי ימצא בבני הגולה איזה אחד מן המתחסדי' המרחיקי' כל חדש וכל בינה אשר אין להם חלק בה יחפץ לאסור אסר דבר זה מדגריס ולא דייק ראיתי להעלות פה על ספר אשר כתבתי בתשובת שאלה זה י"ח שני' בהיותי מרביץ תורה בק"ק פֵירָארָא יע"א לסתום פה דובר בלבלה בנדון זה וחתמו עליו כל גאוני ויניציאה אשר בימים ההם."

41. Rossi, 13a:193. We italicize titles of general prayers but place quotation marks around Rossi's settings of those prayers contained in his *Ha-shirim*.

42. Rossi, 13a:180.

"ירונו במועדים ובחדשים של מצוה."

43. Harrán, "'Dum recordaremur Sion,'" 56–59.

44. Rossi, *Sacred Vocal Works*, 13a:181.

45. Kedem Golden, "An Italian Tune in the Synagogue: An Unexplored Contrafactum by Leon Modena," *Revue des études juives* 177, nos. 3–4 (July–December 2018): 391–420. As Seroussi has discussed, a manuscript sermon by Modena includes the names of singers who sang polyphony with him between 1624 and 1628; see Edwin Seroussi, "Ghetto Soundscapes: Venice and Beyond," in *Shirat Dvora: Essays in Honor of Professor Dvora Bregman*, ed. Haviva Ishay (Beer-Sheva: Ben Gurion University in the Negev Press, 2019), 166.

46. See the references in "'Dum recordaremur Sion,'" 23–24, and Cecil Roth, *The Jews in the Renaissance* (Philadelphia: Jewish Publication Society of America, 1959), 271–304. On the Gonzaga patronage of Jewish performers, see Emily Wilbourne, "*Lo Schiavetto* (1612): Travestied Sound, Ethnic Performance, and the Eloquence of the Body," *Journal of the American Musicological Society* 63, no. 1 (Spring 2010): 9–11.

47. Seroussi, "Ghetto Soundscapes," 6 and 8.

48. Daniel Jütte, "The Place of Music in Early Modern Italian Jewish Culture," in *Musical Exodus: Al-Andalus and Its Jewish Diasporas*, ed. Ruth F. Davis (Lanham, MD: Rowman and Littlefield, 2015), 47. See Shlomo Simonsohn, "Sefarim ve-Sifriyot shel Yehudei Mantova 1595," *Kiryat Sefer* 37 (1961–1962): 103–122.

49. Definitions of these terms, as well as a methodological overview of the texts, can be found in Adin Steinsaltz, *The Talmud: The Steinsaltz Edition: A Reference Guide*, trans. Israel V. Berman (S.l.: The Israel Institute for Talmudic Publications and Milta Books, 1989).

50. Adam Shear and Joseph R. Hacker, "Introduction," in Hacker and Shear, *The Hebrew Book in Early Modern Italy*, 3.

51. A recent study of the collaboration and mediation required for the production of printed books is in Michela Andreatta, "The Poet in the Printing Shop: Leon Modena and the Para-textual Production of Authority in Early Modern Venice," in *Shirat Dvora: Essays in Honor of Professor Dvora Bregman*, ed. Haviva Ishay (Beer-Sheva: Ben Gurion University in the Negev Press, 2019), 9–29.

52. Bonfil, *Jewish Life in Renaissance Italy*, 146–151.

53. David B. Ruderman, *Early Modern Jewry: A New Cultural History* (Princeton, NJ: Princeton University Press, 2010), 55.

54. An overview of the Masoretic tradition is in Geoffrey Khan, *A Short Introduction to the Tiberian Masoretic Bible and Its Reading Tradition*, 2nd ed. (Piscataway, NJ: Gorgias, 2014).

55. On this topic, see Francesco Spagnolo's contribution to the present volume.

56. See the website devoted to Ovadiah's life and work, curated by Gary A. Rendsburg and Peter M. Smith, at http://johannes-obadiah.org/ (accessed August 2018). The music manuscripts are housed in New York, Jewish Theological Seminary, J.T.S. ENA 4096b. See Norman Golb, "המוסיקולוגית ועבודתו רגה הידוע ויינעב" [The musicologist and his work: Obadiah the Proselyte], *Tarbiz* 35 (1965–1966): 81–83, and Norman Golb, "The Music of Obadiah the Proselyte and His Conversion," *Journal of Jewish Studies* 18 (1967): 43–63.

57. Johannes Vallensis, *Opus de prosodia Hebraeorum in quatuor libros divisum* (Paris: Jacobum Bogardum, 1545). The transcription of the Jewish cantillation markings appears in book 2 of this publication, as an insert after page 42.

58. Abraham Portaleone, *Shiltei Ha-Gibborim* [The shields of the heroes] (Mantua: Avraham mi-Sha'ar 'Aryeh [the Author], 5372 [=1612]); translated in Daniel Sandler, "The Music Chapters of the *Shiltei Ha-Gibborim*" (PhD diss., University of Tel Aviv, 1987), 157–159. Other sections of Portaleone's publication are translated in Don Harrán, *Three Early Modern Hebrew Scholars on the Mysteries of Song* (Leiden and Boston: Brill, 2015).

59. Sandler, "The Music Chapters," 158–159. Original in Portaleone, *Shiltei Ha-Gibborim*, ch. 197.

"שבביאת משיחנו תשוב העטרה ליושנה וילמדו אותנו כהנינו לויינו ובניאנו במצות ה' הקולות הנאותים אל הזמרה . . . אשר שכחנו בגלותנו."

60. Sandler, "The Music Chapters," 121.

61. Translation adapted from Sandler, "The Music Chapters," 76–77. Original in Portaleone, *Shiltei Ha-Gibborim*, 32.

"ועל כי רבו המנגנים וכלי הנגון והמשוררים גם יחד ראוי הוא להאמין שיהיו ללוים ספרים רבים המלמדים כל מיני הנגונים בכלים וגם כל מיני השיר על תהלות דוד בן ישי ועם הספר ישירו כיום הזה. ועל כן הספרים האלה עם כלי הנגון כלם היו מונחים בלשכות שהן פתוחות לעזרת הנשים וזה כדי שיהיו להם הספרי' מן המוכן לדבר בם בעת המצטרך."

62. See Portaleone, *Shiltei Ha-Gibborim*, 40–41, and Sandler, "The Music Chapters," 136–137.

63. The claim that Jews had preceded non-Jews in this aspect of knowledge forms an example of a pattern that Abraham Melamed has identified in numerous areas of Jewish thought in the Renaissance. See Abraham Melamed, "The Myth of the Jewish Origins of Philosophy in the Renaissance: From Aristotle to Plato," *Jewish History* 26, nos. 1–2 (May 2012): 41–59, and Abraham Melamed, *Raqah̠ot ve-tabah̠ot: Ha-mitos 'al meqor ha-h̠okhmot* [The myth of the Jewish origins of philosophy and science: A history] (Haifa: Haifa University Press; Jerusalem: Magnes Press, 2010). For a more extensive interpretation of Portaleone's work, see Rebecca Cypess and Yoel Greenberg, "Hearing the Ancient Temple in Early Modern Mantua: Abraham Portaleone and the Cultivation of Music within the Mantuan Jewish Community," in *The Oxford Handbook of Jewish Music*, ed. Tina Frühauf (Oxford: Oxford University Press, forthcoming).

64. Don Isaac Abravanel, *Perush Abravanel 'al ha-Torah* [Abravanel's commentary on the Torah] (Jerusalem: H̠oreb, 5757 [=1996–1997]), 2:212. Translations from this source are by Rebecca Cypess.

"לפי שהספורים הפשוטים רוב בני אדם שוכחים אותם ואפילו שיהגו בהם יומם ולילה. אך כשהם על מערכת הנגונים לשורר ולנגן אותם יהיו נזכרים תמיד באמצעות נגוניהם."

65. Abravanel, *Perush Abravanel 'al ha-Torah*, 2:212.

"ואין ספק שהיו להם נגונים ידועים ונשתכחו מרוב הזמנים אשר חלפו למו ובאורך הגליות."

The eighteenth-century philosopher Moses Mendelssohn followed Abravanel in including a lengthy essay on the art of biblical music as an introduction to his commentary on Exodus 15 in his own extensive commentary on the Torah known as the *Bi'ur* (Explanation). Mendelssohn's approach is discussed in Elias Sacks, "Poetry, Music, and the Limits of Harmony: Mendelssohn's Aesthetic Critique of Christianity," in *Sara Levy's World: Gender, Judaism, and the Bach Tradition in Enlightenment Berlin*, ed. Rebecca Cypess and Nancy Sinkoff (Rochester, NY: University of Rochester Press, 2018), 122–146, and in Rebecca Cypess, "Music Historicism: Sara Levy and the Jewish Enlightenment," in *Bach Perspectives*, ed. Robin A. Leaver (Urbana: University of Illinois Press, 2018), 12:129–152.

66. Abravanel, *Perush Abravanel 'al ha-Torah*, 2:212. Abravanel uses the biblical terms for these instruments, but later sources, including Portaleone, equate them with instruments of their own day. The bracketed terms in this translation follow Portaleone's understanding of the biblical instruments, though these date to over a century after Abravanel.

"והכל היה אצלם כפי תנועות הכלים המתחלפים ומנין חוטיהם נימיהם ונקביהם כנור ועוגב ותוף וחליל ומינים ומצלתים ונגינות וגתית ושמינית ועשור ונבל ומחול ודומיהם . . . כי הנה יוכללו בחכמה הזאת ענינים נפלאים בהשגות האלהות."

67. Translation adapted from Rossi, *Sacred Vocal Works*, 13a:175.
"מה תאמר חכמת הנגון אל האחרים גנב גנבתי מארץ העברים."
68. Rossi, 13a:178.
"וישוה ערוך מאתמול לרבים אנשי שם ממשפחות האדמה."
69. Rossi, 13a:179 and 181.
"ויום יום לעומת מחברתו היה מביא איזה מזמור לדוד או ממכשירי תפלה או שבחה הלל וזמרת יה עד כי משכיל לאסף קבץ כמה מהם והיו לאחדים בידו . . . ואותי צוה לעמוד על כל צרה שלא תבא על החבור לסדרו להגיה אורו ולפקוח עינים על עבירות וחטאות הדפוס."
70. Rossi, 13a:183.
"ועתה ברוכים אתם קהל אמוני אחרי אשר זכינו להתחיל לשלום ונראתה הקסת בימינו מהנבון הלז כותב וחוקק תהלות אלו בשיה."
71. Rossi, 13a:208.
"ואנו אשר היינו ובעלי המוסיקא בתפילותינו והודאותינו עתה נהיה לבוז אל העמי׳ אשר יאמרו כי אין אתנו עוד חכמה ונצעק אל אלהי אבותינו ככלב וכעורב . . . ולא עלה על דעת שום ב״ד או חכם לאסור מלשבח לה׳ ית׳ בקול היותר נעים שאפשר ובחכמה הזאת המעוררת הנפשות לכבודו."
72. Ruth HaCohen, *The Music Libel against the Jews* (New Haven, CT: Yale University Press, 2011).
73. Thomas Coryat, *Coryat's Crudities* (London: Stansby, 1611), 231–233.
74. Rossi, *Sacred Vocal Works*, 13a, 183.
"וירא הרואה כי נראה לעין המחבר טוב שהקוראי׳ יגידו האותיו׳ לאחור ויקראו למפרע מלו׳ הזמרה שגורי׳ בפי כל מלהפך סדר הצורות מהמורגל . . . ולסבה זו ג״כ לא חש על כל אשר איננו נקוד מהתבו׳ כי בשיר רוב מצויין אצל השטה מומחין הן בקריאה."

REBECCA CYPESS is Associate Dean for Academic Affairs at the Mason Gross School of the Arts, Rutgers University, where she is also Associate Professor of Music. She is author of *Women and Musical Salons in the Enlightenment* and *Curious and Modern Inventions: Instrumental Music as Discovery in Galileo's Italy* and editor (with Nancy Sinkoff) of *Sara Levy's World: Gender, Judaism, and the Bach Tradition in Enlightenment Berlin*.

LYNETTE BOWRING is Assistant Professor Adjunct of Music History at the Yale School of Music. She received her PhD in musicology from Rutgers University and has published on the intersections of orality and literacy in early modern Italian musical culture.

10

L'Accademia degli Impediti
A Reevaluation

LIZA MALAMUT

In 1628, the Venetian ghetto absorbed a significant number of Jewish refugees from Mantua, most of whom had fled the city during the War of Succession (1628–1631) prior to the expulsion of the Jewish population in 1630.[1] Among these refugees was an unknown number of professional musicians who had frequently been employed as performers for events at the Gonzaga court. These musicians—composers, instrumentalists, and singers—participated in elaborate theatrical spectacles put on by the Gonzaga family, who showed particular preference for high-quality productions mounted by Jewish theater troupes.[2]

The favor shown to participants in these events had allowed for the cultivation of high-caliber artistry, with some musicians—Salamone Rossi, Isaachino Massarano, and Abramino Halevi dall'Arpa, to name a few—rising to a level of fame that was acknowledged by Jews and Christians throughout Italy.[3] This prolificacy was nevertheless halted when the Austrians gained control of Mantua, and the fate of many Jewish Mantuan court musicians was never known. Some of those who surfaced among the refugees in Venice joined Leon Modena in forming L'Accademia degli Impediti (the Academy of the Impeded Ones), a musical society that gained significant fame in its relatively short existence.

The Accademia degli Impediti was one of hundreds of self-designated Italian academies (*accademie*), intellectual societies that embraced poetry, literature, art, science, rhetoric, music, theater, and other humanistic disciplines. Members of these academies—usually upper-class scholars, scientists, artists, musicians, and literati—prided themselves on the advancement of knowledge, and many academies gained renown by producing works that influenced popular culture.[4] The Impediti followed the model of non-Jewish practice-based music academies: it focused on performance and composition, boasted a talented membership of professional-level musicians, and held regularly scheduled meetings that included performances of its members' works. Like other Italian academies, the Impediti had an *impresa*, or linguistic-pictorial device, consisting of a title with a double meaning, a motto, and an engraving.[5] As Evelien Chayes observes, evidence of the academy's impresa survives in a letter written by Modena in 1639: "The impresa was three willows upon which hung many scores of music and sounding instruments, with the motto *Cum recordaremur Sion*, the concept from Psalm 136 *Super flumina Babilonici*, and the name was of the Impeded Ones, all of which alludes to the unhappy state of our captivity that impedes any virtuous act from completion."[6]

According to Modena's description, the title Impeded Ones refers to the condition of the Jewish people after the Roman destruction of the second Temple in Jerusalem in 70 CE. The Diaspora, or the Jewish population's subsequent departure and dispersal across Europe, Asia, and Africa following that event, effectively prevented Jews from carrying out certain traditions—"virtuous acts"—that would customarily have been performed within the Temple's walls. For example, many Jewish communities mourned the destruction of the Temple by refraining from playing musical instruments during certain religious services, a practice that directly affected the Impediti.[7] The academy's motto, "Cum recordaremur Sion"—"when we remembered Zion"—underscores this hampered state by referencing Psalm 136:1, "By the rivers of Babylon we wept when we remembered Zion." The academy's engraving—musical scores and instruments hanging from the branches of three willows—carries the same allusion.[8]

The impresa of the Impediti may also reference the "impeded" or "captive" state of Venetian Jews during Modena's lifetime. Because of persecution, many ghetto residents had migrated from Spain, Portugal, Turkey, Germany, and other regions throughout Europe; others were descendants of those who had done so. As a result, the Venetian ghetto was home to a vibrant, diverse population of Jews who, while displaced, enjoyed relative intellectual and artistic freedom.[9] In spite of this, Don Harrán notes that Modena lamented the "foreign dwellings and restless runnings" of the Jewish people, a sentiment that no doubt influenced the academy's impresa.[10]

The Accademia degli Impediti has been acknowledged by many scholars of Jewish music but rarely discussed at length.[11] No extant primary-source publications or records bear its name or impresa, and its self-ascribed designation as a musical "academy" makes it unique among Jewish societies. However, its existence has been confirmed in accounts by seventeenth-century eyewitnesses, including the convert Giulio Morosini, Leon Modena's former student:

> I remember well what happened during my time in Venice around 1628. It was around then, if I am not mistaken, when the Jews fled Mantua because of the war and came to Venice. Since the city of Mantua flourished in all sorts of studies, the Jews also applied themselves to music and to musical instruments. Those who arrived in Venice founded an academy of music in the ghetto, where they sang twice per week in the evening, and only the most important and wealthy congregants of the ghetto attended and sustained it, of which I myself was one. My master Rabbi Leon da Modena was maestro di cappella.[12]

Accounts such as this one have been explored by scholars including Harrán, Israel Adler, Alfred Sendrey, Eduard Birnbaum, and, of course, Cecil Roth, whose essay on Jewish musicians in Mantua and Venice has been the basis for much of the subsequent scholarship on the subject.[13] In spite of this, the academy has only recently reemerged in studies by Giuseppe Veltri and Evelien Chayes, who have begun the important work of contextualizing it within the Italian academic tradition more generally.[14] Although other authors have given ample attention to the significance of humanistic Jewish activities in Venice, including medicine, polemics, literature, and music in general, the importance of the academy has been, for the most part, under-researched. Indeed, Abraham Zvi Idelsohn once asserted that after the sack of the Mantuan ghetto, "all desire for the *ars nova* was killed in the Jew. He abandoned his ambition to become a co-worker in the Renaissance and the few attempts made toward the introduction of European achievements in music were deserted."[15] This nihilistic sentiment seems overly pessimistic in light of the academy's strong presence in Venice, as well as its parallels to other humanistic societies, both Jewish and Christian. The academy had a significant impact on Jewish musical identity in Venice—especially the practice of composing and performing Italian art music. In fact, as I will argue, it embodies the paradox between early modern Jewish identity and its surrounding culture—an example of what historian Robert Bonfil has, in another context, called "agents of modernity."

"Paradox," Bonfil wrote, "is essentially a mediating element between opposites." The case that Bonfil was addressing was the study of Qabbalah, which was, for Jews, "one of the most effective mediators between the medieval and the modern worlds, and as such, functioned as an agent of modernity."[16] Indeed, Bonfil and other scholars address many mediums that fit this description: on Jewish literature, Bonfil writes that "the affinity between Jewish and non-Jewish literary production manifested itself at the center, not at the edges, of the Jewish cultural space."[17] A paradox of language has also been addressed in depth by Howard Adelman, who wrote at length about Modena's desire to demonstrate linguistic kinships between Hebrew and Italian, which formed an "effort to establish and to embellish the legends and symbols of shared experience and common culture with their host country in the hope that this would make a small contribution to the elevation of Jewish dignity."[18] Paradoxes also proliferated in the tensions revealed in Jewish political thought. For example, the *Discorso circa il stato degli Hebrei* (1638) of Simone Luzzato, chief rabbi of the Ashkenazic Jewish community in the Venetian ghetto, used the Renaissance preoccupation with classicism to form masterful polemics in the style of Machiavelli and Tacitus, wherein he argued for the importance of the Jewish community to the economic, political, and civic operations of the Venetian state—an impressive literary feat, given the anti-Jewish leanings of those two historians.[19] Agents of modernity also appeared in the sciences: Mantuan physician Abraham Portaleone attempted to reconcile fundamental Judaism with modern medicine. (He also devoted a large portion of one of his treatises to a discussion of music in the ancient Temple, which he claimed was equivalent to Italian polyphonic music.[20])

The role of the Accademia degli Impediti warrants reappraisal in light of these examples. Considering its extensive activity in the Venetian ghetto, especially its performances of non-Jewish art music by high-profile Jewish musicians, the impact of the academy deserves reevaluation and recognition as an important seventeenth-century agent of modernity.

THE MUSICIANS OF THE ACADEMY AND THEIR MUSICAL ACTIVITIES

An in-depth study of the Accademia degli Impediti is difficult because of the lack of surviving records confirming its membership and regular activities.

Further reading from Morosini's account of the Spanish Synagogue's lavish Simḥat Torah celebrations, for which the academy played a part, provides some insight into its capabilities:

> In that year, two rich and splendid persons—one of whom was a member of the same Academy—had already been designated as *sposi* for this festival, held at the Spanish Synagogue (richly decorated and adorned with silver and great jewels). As per our custom, the musicians organized themselves into two choirs, and on the two evenings beginning on the eighth day of Shemini 'Atzeret and Simḥat Torah, they sang figured music, in the Hebrew language, parts of the 'arvit and several Psalms; as well as the Minchà—that is, the Vespers of the last day—with solemn music, which lasted several hours into the night. Many noblemen and ladies gathered, offering great applause, so that it was necessary to guard the door with many captains and policemen so that things might pass calmly. Among the instruments, the organ was also brought to the synagogue, though it was not permitted by the Rabbis, as it is an instrument that is normally played in our churches. But what of it? All of this was a flash in the pan ["straw on fire"], the Academy lasted only a short time, and music returned to its former practices.[21]

From this description and the one cited previously, we can determine several points with relative certainty. We know that Modena served as the academy's maestro di cappella and that the members were accomplished professional musicians and (likely) high-level amateurs, many of them Mantuan refugees. We know they met two times a week at the Spanish Synagogue, and we know that they performed in liturgical and paraliturgical settings. We know that the academy was established in 1628 and that it performed at an elaborate Simḥat Torah celebration in 1629.

Morosini's account describes a large group that both sang and played instruments at an astoundingly high level. These observations—though not sufficient evidence on their own—support his earlier assertions that many of the participants were former Mantuan musicians who had appeared at court. The date of the performance, however, adds significant weight to this theory. Morosini writes that it was around 1628 when the Mantuan Jews fled their city and came to Venice. Modena's 1639 letter reveals the diminished state of the academy after the plague of 1630, which claimed the lives of the society's best musicians and left the group without a "fertile plant of composers."[22] Written in response to an unidentified Jewish colleague who apparently expressed interest in collaborating with Modena and the Impediti, this letter confirms the high quality of the academy's musicianship prior to the onset of the plague, as well as its decline in the nine years following. Taken in tandem with Morosini's account, the letter reveals that the academy was at its most prolific after the War of Succession and before the plague. This information has led Adler to pin down the exact year for the academy's lavish performance as 1629, supporting Morosini's theory that Mantuan Jewish musicians performed with the academy for the celebration.[23]

The idea that many members of the academy were Mantuan refugees is further supported by Claudia Burattelli's observation that those involved in the production of Mantuan *balli* and *commedie* were also involved in organizational aspects of the events and that they were very efficient in this regard.[24] The holiday festivities that Morosini describes lasted multiple days and could only have been successfully planned by those experienced in the mounting of large productions. Though Venice was not without Jewish theatrical activity, there is no record of any musical event of equivalent scale to the Shemini 'Atzeret celebrations of 1629.[25]

There is unfortunately a dearth of other information about the activities of the academy. Aside from Modena, we do not know the specific names of the participating musicians. Likewise, knowledge of their training is largely speculative; the scant evidence consists of brief references to musical tutelage in Jewish schools for boys and secular liberal arts universities, which presumably complemented the usual master-apprentice tradition evident through familial musical relationships in the court of Mantua.[26] We also lack evidence of the participants' ages, though an observation of vocal ranges in extant polyphonic works opens the possibility for the inclusion of grown men and boys.[27]

There are also no surviving payment records for academy musicians. Morosini describes wealthy residents of the ghetto who "attended and sustained" the meetings, perhaps implying that funds were allocated for the academy's biweekly performances. The distribution of these funds is more mysterious. Were the musicians themselves paid for their work? If so, the lack of extant payment records is curious, since detailed accounts for most professional artistic services provided by Jews still survive, even those that were self-funded by Jewish organizations. For example, the Venetian Università announced payment for the *suonatore del sabato*, the trumpeter who called the hour of the Sabbath in the ghetto, beginning in 1604.[28] The

Mantuan Università also kept detailed bookkeeping records for participants in Gonzaga court productions, including performing artists, backstage workers, costume makers, and light carriers.[29] If the members of the academy were paid, we have lost the evidence that would have provided an important window to the society's individual membership.

The mystery of the academy's membership could be attributed to multiple causes, but the likeliest are the losses of musicians due to war, plague, and conversion to Christianity. Prior to 1628, the Gonzaga court kept records of important Jewish musicians who regularly performed in Mantuan court spectacles. Burattelli's exhaustive search of the Gonzaga archives reveals a thick register of those involved in Jewish theatrical productions in Mantua, but only the most prominent members are named.[30] Interestingly, this register provides another hint of what Jewish musical training might have looked like: Burattelli observes that entire families often worked at court together with a homogenous function. One of these families was the Rossi family, which included Salamone's sister Madama Europa, her sons Bonaiuto and Angelo, and Angelo's sons Giuseppe and Bonaiuto.[31] Another family of musicians also played the harp at the Gonzaga court: Abraham Halevi dall'Arpa and his grandson Abramino. The latter converted to Catholicism under duress, and the family name henceforth disappeared into obscurity.[32] The remaining names are absent from the records after 1628.[33] It is surely no coincidence that the disappearance of well-known Mantuan Jewish musicians coincides with the sack of the city by imperial troops.

Who, then, were the Mantuan refugees active in the academy? Certainly, none of the aforementioned names found in the Gonzaga archives make an appearance in Venice after 1628; while this could be due to poor record keeping, surely the appearance of a musician such as Rossi, who had such a close relationship with Modena, would have been mentioned in the latter's detailed accounts.[34] Modena's letter, as described previously, reveals no individual names.

As for the repertoire that the academy played and sang, here, too, we can only speculate. Morosini's account states that "the musicians organized themselves into two choirs" and that "among the instruments, the organ was also brought to the synagogue." At a minimum, this information describes a musical society large enough to provide singers and instrumentalists for double-choir pieces. If the academy regularly performed polychoral works in a liturgical setting, it would need to have in its ranks at least eight capable singers. If it did not, that number could be even fewer.[35] On the other hand, nonliturgical settings—such as the Simḥat Torah festivities that Morosini describes—allowed for the addition of instruments.[36] But what instruments? And what parts did they play? Functionally, the instruments Morosini describes—including, curiously, the organ—could have served to fill in missing vocal lines, play concertato parts, or bolster the existing voices. These forces, however, are mysterious. Hints come to us from Mantua: performance accounts refer to Jewish lutenists and harpists, and Rossi is known to have played the violin.[37] The appearance of the organ suggests that some Jewish musicians played keyboard instruments. There are no extant records of Jewish reed players or trombonists in either Mantua or Venice, though this does not preclude their existence. Rossi's instrumental music may provide further clues; it is scored for "two violins or two cornetti, and chittarrone or other istromento da corpo" (literally, "instruments of the body," or instruments capable of playing figured continuo lines, such as the theorbo, lute, organ, and harp), among "other similar instruments."[38] His sonata for four violins could imply that other Mantuan Jewish violinists shared his expertise in bowed instruments. Even here, though, we must tread with care: while it is easy to imagine Rossi's company of musicians performing his instrumental music, the publications give no indication that they were intended specifically for his Jewish colleagues. In short, the available sources only give us a hint of what might have been possible among the members of the academy.

THE ACADEMY AND LEON MODENA

Leon Modena is the only figure whose musical activities are known with any clarity. He is reported to have had a beautiful tenor voice and was continually reelected to the role of ḥazzan, or cantor, of the Italian Synagogue in Venice, a position he would keep for most of his life.[39] Indeed, Modena's enthusiasm for music prompted legal responsa on the subject of the propriety of polyphony in synagogues. Modena, a master of rhetoric, famously argued in defense of art music after a performance of vocal polyphony for a Jewish festival celebrating the fifteenth day of the Hebrew month of Av (a joyous annual event) in Ferrara in 1605. As I will show in the following pages, that event is significant for several reasons: first, the introduction of polyphony into liturgical Jewish services can likely be traced to this occurrence; second, the event garnered a vehement outcry from pietist rabbis against the mixture of art music with Jewish liturgy; and third, Modena's successful defense, inspired by his teacher Samuel Archivolti and famed Jewish thinker Simone Luzzato, influenced the acceptance and success of future endeavors in Italian art music by Jewish musicians in Venice.[40]

Modena's impact on the Accademia degli Impediti cannot be understated, and his role as its leader has tremendous significance for the society's function within Jewish and Italian culture. Indeed, the figure of Modena personifies the characteristics of Bonfil's "agent of modernity," and it was his leadership that lent the academy as a whole that same status. Modena's complex relationships with both Jews and Christians, his fascination with humanistic subjects, and his attraction to the secular arts demonstrate his cultural hybridity. More specifically, his ardent defense of art music in the synagogue reveals his role as a mediator between customs ancient and new, Jewish and non-Jewish. In light of his wide-ranging intellect and artistry, it is not surprising that Modena assumed leadership of this new musical society.

Modena's musical and intellectual interests manifested throughout his life. Growing up, he was educated in the liberal arts as well as Jewish studies, and as with other Jewish boys, music and languages were part of his curriculum.[41] His teacher Samuel Archivolti, who had a tremendous influence on Modena, wrote poetry for religious and secular events, including for books published by Christians.[42] This affinity for poetry was reflected in Archivolti's young student: at the age of twelve, Modena demonstrated his talent for languages by translating large portions of Ariosto's *Orlando furioso* into Hebrew, expertly preserving the poetic form; he also began to compose original poetry in both Italian and Hebrew. As Adelman relates, Modena was motivated by "his desire to show Jews and Italians the linguistic affinity between their languages."[43]

In adulthood, Modena became known for his linguistic brilliance even beyond the boundaries of the ghetto, and as a result, he gained prestige in non-Jewish circles as well as Jewish ones. Indeed, there is ample evidence of collaboration between Modena and his Christian colleagues. Modena apparently composed a poem to be sung in honor of the doge's visit to a local monastery, and he was also known to attend meetings of an unnamed humanistic Christian society—perhaps one of the *ridotti*, or even a fraternity that met at the Scuola Grande or one of the monasteries in the vicinity.[44] Even more interestingly, Modena was known to make appearances at church services, where he was almost certainly influenced by the integration of art music with Christian liturgy.[45] He taught his Christian friends Hebrew and Qabbalah (the latter of which he later regretted, renouncing kabbalistic practices in favor of traditional rabbinic Judaism in his seminal critique, *Ari Nohem*).[46] A master of rhetoric, Modena participated in religious debates and often acted as an arbiter in conflicts between Christians and Jews.[47]

Modena's enthusiasm for linguistic activities was not motivated by personal interest alone. He lamented what he saw as a severe deficit in the education of young Jews, many of whom were refugees or descendants of refugees from the Inquisition in Spain and Portugal. By this time, the Venetian ghetto had become a multicultural center that boasted German, Spanish, Italian, and Turkish synagogues and was home to Jews from all over Europe and the Middle East. The influx of multilingual immigrants into a relatively liberal Italy in the late fifteenth and early sixteenth centuries did not always support what Modena viewed as a traditional Jewish education, which would have emphasized fluency in Hebrew reading and writing. Indeed, Modena feared that the constant relocation of the Jewish people had depleted their knowledge of their own language and heritage. He sought not only to bridge a gap between Jewish writers and their Christian compatriots but to reacquaint his fellow Jews with what he saw as a core aspect of their own history.[48]

This is particularly apparent in Modena's involvement with Rossi's publication of his volume of Hebrew motets, *Ha-shirim 'asher li-Shlomo*. Modena's mentorship of Rossi, and the obvious associations between Rossi's sacred music and Modena's love for art music, has been discussed at length by others.[49] However, there were other levels to Modena's involvement with the *Shirim*. The publication itself reflects the linguistic bridge building that was so important to Modena. Rossi's choice to use Hebrew texts, meticulously set in conjunction with polyphonic music, certainly served Modena's goal of reintegrating the Hebrew language with contemporary Jewish knowledge and practice.

Indeed, the melding of Italian art forms with traditional Jewish texts in their original language parallels Modena's own endeavors in this area, including his Hebrew translations of Italian poetic forms and, of course, his own music, most of which has been lost.[50] Of particular interest is the contrafactum *Yoshev marom ḥazaq*, an unnotated poem found in Modena's

Divan and introduced with the text "To the Tune of *Trà verdi campi a la stagion novella*, for Singing and Chanting."[51] The tune in question originates in the first book of four-voice *canzonette* by Orazio Vecchi, and Kedem Golden has observed that Modena's Hebrew poem precisely copies the Italian canzonetta form. According to Edwin Seroussi, it is even possible that Modena sang this Hebrew canzonetta himself: in an unpublished sermon delivered between 1624 and 1628, he recounts the names of three singers with whom he enjoyed performing music in four parts.[52]

The Accademia degli Impediti became a vehicle for bringing these and other similar works to life, ushering them into the heart of the Jewish community: the synagogue.[53] With Modena as its leader, then, the academy assumed its role as an agent of modernity, melding art music, the ancient Hebrew language, and contemporary Jewish life.

THE ACADEMY AS REPLACEMENT FOR MUSICAL LIFE AT THE GONZAGA COURT

The overarching hybridity of the Accademia degli Impediti, as embodied by Modena, is also relevant in a more general way. While Modena's leadership no doubt drove the Venetian academy's activities, the society also served as an outlet for the displaced Mantuan musicians as described previously. Venetian Jewish musicians, including Jewish refugees, lacked the performance opportunities that were provided (for better or for worse) by the Gonzaga family. More than a century earlier, on March 29, 1516, the Venetian Senate had ordered the segregation of Jews in Venice. Restrictions on Jewish activities had gradually intensified after that event, including those prohibiting Jews from serving as music teachers to Christians. While that law was not new, it began to be enforced with more rigor during the Catholic Reformation.[54] Without the opportunities provided by the Gonzaga court, and with the increased restrictions of Venice, Jewish refugees naturally sought to create their own opportunities. The formation of a music academy would have provided a practical means to accomplish these efforts.

Harrán has suggested that the musicians themselves founded the academy and persuaded Modena to lead it, rather than the other way around.[55] This would be curious indeed, since there is no evidence of a similar artist-founded Jewish music society in Mantua that regularly performed sacred art music, whether liturgical or nonliturgical.[56] The lack of a Mantuan music academy could be due to any number of factors, including the contested acceptance of polyphonic music in synagogues that instigated Modena's responsum of 1605.[57] It could also reflect a musical scene that already provided ample professional opportunities for Jewish musicians, unlike that in Venice. In any case, if Harrán is correct, the impetus to form a music academy by Mantuan musicians in Venice—when they did not do so in Mantua—emphasizes the need of a displaced population to reestablish its identity as a highly regarded society of skilled and employable musicians.

The choice of Modena as leader of the Accademia degli Impediti could also have been an attempt to find a replacement for the figure of Leone de' Sommi, the polymath who led the Mantuan Jewish theatrical company and its overarching guild of merchants and artisans, the Università degli Ebrei.[58] De' Sommi, while not a composer himself, collaborated with celebrated composers of art music in the Gonzaga court, including Giaches de Wert and Giovanni Giacomo Gastoldi. Often put in charge of entire productions, de' Sommi collaborated with Rossi's company of musicians as well as non-Jewish musicians at the ducal court to provide intermedii that would have been performed as part of Italian theatrical spectacles.[59]

It is important to note that performances by members of the Mantuan Università were self-funded; while the ducal court desired the participation of Jewish theatrical performers, all financial obligations fell to the Jews themselves.[60] This does not in itself eliminate the theater as a source of livelihood, but the source of that livelihood never came directly from Gonzaga coffers. The main benefit to Jewish performers in the ducal court appeared to be prestige, which was accompanied by extremely desirable benefits. Esteemed performers such as de' Sommi and Rossi were exempt from wearing the Jewish badge mandated for most Jews by Italian leadership,[61] and the high-profile venue elevated the performers in the eyes of their compatriots and allowed Jewish actors and musicians to develop their talents to the fullest potential. Moreover, friendly interactions with Italian gentry must have had positive effects on the Jewish community as a whole. The Venetian Accademia degli Impediti, then, did not serve as a career replacement in a financial sense (though one can conjecture that this was a long-term goal of its founding members), but it may have filled personal and pragmatic gaps that were created in absence of the Università's activities.

Incidentally, the Venetian ghetto was not devoid of theatrical activity by its Jewish inhabitants prior to the formation of the academy. An irate responsum by Rabbi Samuel Aboab, published posthumously in 1705, confirms the existence of a Jewish theater company that performed secular plays. Participants included women and children, which no doubt contributed to the ire of more traditional rabbis.[62] There were musicians as well: as early as 1609, references to a certain "Rachel," a talented Jewish singer, can be found in accounts of Venetian theatrical performances, especially in a play written by Modena himself, *Rachele e Giacobbe* (1603).[63] The first extant Jewish play, *L'Ester*, was written for Purim around 1558 by Solomon Usque, and Modena rewrote it in 1619.[64] Considering Modena's fascination with Italian drama, it seems likely that a performance would have integrated standard elements of theatrical performances at the time, including musical intermedii.[65] The influx of Mantuan musicians in 1628, which would have included many Jewish musicians who had been active in Gonzaga productions, would then have been a welcome addition to the enthusiasts of Venice.

THE ACADEMY AS AN AGENT OF MODERNITY

The Venetian Accademia degli Impediti was not an isolated society. Its roots lay in other humanistic societies both in the ghetto and beyond, and academies with an exclusively musical focus were not uncommon.[66] Some, like the Venetian Accademia della Fama, focused on music theory, and others, like the Accademia Filarmonica in Verona, focused on music performance, composition, and criticism.[67] While most music academies were short lived, with varying levels of formality, a few still survive today. The extant Accademia Filarmonica of Bologna, founded in 1666, had a schedule similar to that of the Impediti: it met two times a week to perform music written by its members.[68] Modena himself had previously directed another society that aimed to cultivate "the science of music." Founded around 1604, this amateur Jewish musical organization performed on feast days and festivals in Ferrara.[69]

It is worth noting, however, that the Impediti's use of the designation "accademia" was apparently unique among Jewish music societies. Given that members of Italian academies inherently viewed their organizations as closed circles limited to a privileged elite, the title could have served to elevate the Impediti while simultaneously carrying an implication of modesty.[70] As described by Veltri and Chayes, Italian academies "aroused the curiosity of the Jewish intellectuals who, although excluded, tried at least to establish a discourse with them, with greater or lesser success."[71] In Mantua, for example, de' Sommi balanced a close, if fraught, connection with the theatrically focused L'Accademia degli Invaghiti. Being Jewish, de' Sommi was denied official membership in the society; he was instead tasked with writing works for the Invaghiti and freed from the requirement to wear the standard Jewish badge. As noted by both David Kaufman and Veltri, this position gave him all the responsibilities of membership without the honor of belonging.[72]

In the Venetian ghetto, this curiosity manifested in another society that embraced humanistic activities. Sarra Copia Sulam, a close contact of Modena, hosted salons at her home that included Jewish and Christian intellectuals. These salons welcomed a close circle of highly educated individuals who discussed literature, art, music, and philosophical subjects. Copia Sulam, like Modena, was a master of poetry and rhetoric; Harrán has suggested that she was also a musician.[73] Her patronage of several Christian colleagues may have played a pivotal role in the formation of another academy, the famous Accademia degli Incogniti.[74] The origins and philosophies of the Accademia degli Incogniti have been dealt with at length by other scholars, but it is significant that its members were connected so closely with Jewish intellectuals and musicians such as Modena and Copia Sulam.[75] The Incogniti embraced tenets of Renaissance humanistic practice that are reminiscent of Jewish thinkers such as Luzzato, Portaleone, and others.[76] Indeed, topics of debate among Christian and Jewish intellectuals frequently overlapped: immortality of the soul, Jewish and Christian historiography, science and religion, and art and music. This is evidenced by Luzzato's historiographies of the Jewish people, which are written in the style of the classicists, as well as Copia Sulam's discussions of immortality with her teacher and admirer (and eventual betrayer) Ansaldo Cebà, a Genoese monk and member of the Incogniti. Modena also produced polemics on that same subject.[77]

The Accademia degli Impediti seems to have been a society for practitioners rather than theorists. If it was also home to rhetorical or intellectual explorations, we will never know. However, it is significant that its leader had such a strong connection to Copia Sulam's intellectual circle, and Modena's own sphere of Jewish and non-Jewish thinkers suggests that the establishment of the academy may have had some grounding in the preexistence of other societies for humanistic thought. This is further supported by evidence, as described earlier, that Modena's intellectual interests overlapped with his practical pursuits. A Jewish musical society that specialized in the "science of music" would have been an ideal setting with which to continue these pursuits, and its classification as an "academy," recalling the names of the Incogniti and other non-Jewish societies, may have lent it—at least to its members' ears and perhaps also to non-Jewish onlookers—an air of prestige.

Even so, the Accademia degli Impediti and other Jewish societies differed distinctly from those of their Christian peers by nature of their paradoxical position, their role as a "mediating element between opposites"—as an "agent of modernity." The relative freedom that Jews experienced within the walls of the Venetian ghetto provided a space to explore intellectual, scientific, and cultural ideas—but those ideas still needed to align with Jewish philosophy and law. Modena's initial fascination with Qabbalah, and his eventual abandonment of it, provides a convenient illustration of such a paradox. Qabbalah, according to Bonfil, acted as a vehicle that propelled Jews to modernity, transforming the way they prayed, worshipped, and viewed the world around them. Bonfil keenly observes that Qabbalah connects directly to musical practice, creating a more "open" view of music and theater that was still couched in restriction and ambivalence.[78]

This paradox is further illustrated by Luzzato's historiographies. While writing in the style of Machiavelli and Tacitus, Luzzato nevertheless had to reconcile his admiration for the classicists with their inherent anti-Jewish positions. This was achieved by a feat of sheer rhetorical genius, in which Luzzato stresses his admiration for Greek and Roman culture while arguing for the intellectual superiority of the Jewish people that resulted from their captivity by those same societies.[79]

These apologetics are also employed in relation to music. The Mantuan rabbi Judah Moscato attributed the discovery of music to the Levantine Jews of the ancient Temple, as did Abraham Portaleone, essentially rebutting the assertions by Christian critics that Jewish music was simple and primitive.[80] Veltri eloquently observes that Portaleone simultaneously wanted to "glorify the Jewish past while recognizing the greatness of contemporary culture, which was non-Jewish in origin. He beholds two privileged eras, that of the Judaism of the First and Second Temple and the contemporary age, out of which he fashions an imperfect synthesis bespeaking a tension that is difficult to resolve."[81] I have noted in the previous pages that Modena argued for the inclusion of art music in the synagogue, framing it as a necessity for praising God through song as commanded by the Torah. Modena's polemics magnify his lamentations for the perceived loss of the cultural and intellectual superiority of his coreligionists.

The formation of the Accademia degli Impediti, then, was in some ways a natural outgrowth of these philosophies, and its existence, however short lived, embodied the paradox inherent in Jewish agents of modernity. While never replacing the prestige of the Gonzaga court, the academy provided a means for Mantuan refugees to simultaneously hold on to their identities as composers and musicians and maintain a connection with the artistic developments of contemporary society. The high performance standards of the academy attest to its role as a vehicle for the elevation of Jewish cultural achievement. It was also an answer, like Luzzato's *Discorso*, to Christian notions of Jewish society. If Morosini's account is to be believed, the academy's activities served to combat perceptions of primitivism in Jewish music by Christian intellectuals. While it is easy for modern historians to determine the anti-Jewish roots of these perceptions, they were nonetheless pervasive, and Modena clearly took them seriously.[82] The academy's pursuit of art music may have helped to dampen these perceptions while simultaneously enhancing and rebuilding the Jewish identity of its members and surrounding community.

The academy's role as an agent of modernity is underlined, finally, by the academy's motto, "Cum recordaremur Sion." How remarkable that these words—a remembrance of a better time, a lament for things lost—were chosen for a group of Jewish musicians who performed the music of their non-Jewish contemporaries, seeking not only to master it but to magnify and perfect it. It is here that the scope of the academy's impact is revealed. The Accademia degli Impediti was, among all else, an answer to exile: the recent exile of the Mantuan refugee musicians and the ongoing exile of the Jewish people from their ancient homeland. It was a means, however brief, to return glory and dignity to Jewish music and cultural tradition, within both the Venetian Jewish community and the society in which it operated.

NOTES

1. Israel Adler, *La pratique musicale savante dans quelques communautés juives en Europe aux XVIIe et XVIIIe siècles*, 2 vols. (Paris and Den Haag: Mouton, 1966), 531; Don Harrán, "'Dum recordaremur Sion': Music in the Life and Thought of the Venetian Rabbi Leon Modena (1571–1648)," *AJS Review* 23 no. 1 (1998): 53–54; and Israel Adler, "The Rise of Art Music in the Italian Ghetto," in *Jewish Medieval and Renaissance Studies*, ed. Alexander Altmann (Cambridge, MA: Harvard University Press, 1967), 343.

2. A detailed description of these activities, especially accounts of professionals such as Isaachino Massarano and Simone Basilea, can be found in Claudia Burattelli, *Spettacoli di corte a Mantova tra Cinque e Seicento* (Florence: Casa editrice Le Lettere, 1999), 158.

3. Burattelli, 155.

4. The definition of the word *academy* has evolved over time. See David S. Chambers, "The Earlier 'Academies' in Italy," in *Italian Academies of the Sixteenth Century*, ed. David S. Chambers and François Quiviger (London: Warburg Institute, University of London, 1995), 1–14; Frances A. Yates, "The Italian Academies," in *Selected Works of Frances A. Yates*, vol. 9, *Renaissance and Reform: The Italian Contribution* (London, New York: Routledge, 1983), 6–10; Iain Fenlon, "Gioseffo Zarlino and the Accademia Venetiana della Fama," in *Music and Culture in Late Renaissance Italy* (Oxford: Oxford University Press, 2002), 119; and "The Italian Academies—Definitions and Interests," Database of Italian Academies, British Library, accessed December 2020, https://www.bl.uk/catalogues/ItalianAcademies/Definitions AndInterests.aspx.

5. For discussions on imprese, see Yates, "The Italian Academies," 10–14, 16–17; Ian F. McNeely, "The Renaissance Academies between Science and the Humanities," *Configurations* 13, no. 3 (2009): 237–238; Dorigen Caldwell, "The *Paragone* between Word and Image in Impresa Literature," *Journal of the Warburg and Courtauld Institutes* 63 (2000): 277–286, esp. 277–278; Evelien Chayes, "Crossing Cultures in the Venetian Ghetto: Leone Modena, the Accademia degli Incogniti and Imprese Literature," *Bollettino di italianistica* 2 (2017), 78–81, 87–88; and Jennifer Montagu, *An Index of Emblems of the Italian Academies Based on Michele Maylender's* Storie delle accademie d'Italia (London: Warburg Institute, University of London, 1988). The Impediti's impresa does not appear in Montagu's index (see note 11).

6. "Era impresa tre salici con molti libretti di musicanti, istrumenti da suono appesi, col motto *Cum recordaremur Sion*, il concetto preso dal Salmo 136 *Super flumina Babilonici*, et il nome era de gli impediti, tutto per alluder all'infelice stato della captività nostra che si impedisce d'ogni atto virtuoso la compitezza," British Library, MS Or. 5395, f. 23; transcribed in Evelien Chayes, "L'Accademia degli Incogniti: tra Talmud e Kabbalah," in *Oltre le mura del Ghetto: Accademie, scetticismo e tolleranza nella Venezia barocca*, by Giuseppe Veltri and Evelien Chayes (Palermo: New Digital Frontiers, 2016), 102–105; and Cecil Roth, "L'accademia musicale del ghetto veneziano," *La Rassegna mensile di Israel* 3, no. 4 (Tebheth 5688 [=1927–1928]): 157–162. See also Chayes, "Crossing Cultures," 78–81, 87–88.

7. Tim Dowley and Nick Rowland, "The Jewish Diaspora," in *Atlas of World Religions* (Minneapolis: 1517 Media, 2018), 66–67, and Rebecca Cypess, "The Anxiety of Specificity," in "Colloquy: Jewish Studies and Music," convened by Klára Móricz and Ronit Seter, *Journal of the American Musicological Society* 65, no. 2 (Summer 2012): 580.

8. Based on a reevaluation of the manuscript, discovered by Cecil Roth, Chayes convincingly argues for a corrected version of this motto, used here. It was originally transcribed by Roth as "Dum recordaremur Sion," or "while we remembered Zion." The phrase appears in Psalm 136:1 in the Latin Vulgate and later versions of Psalm 137:1: "Super flumina Babylonis

illic sedimus et flevimus cum recordaremur Sion." The engraving of the willows matches the psalm's continuation, 137:2–3: "There on the willows we hung our harps / for there our captors requested a song; our tormentors demanded songs of joy: 'Sing us a song of Zion.' / How can we sing a song of the Lord in a foreign land?" Chayes, "L'Accademia degli Incogniti," 102–105; Chayes, "Crossing Cultures," 78n53, 79; Cecil Roth, "L'accademia musicale," 161–162; and Philip V. Bohlman, "On Non-Jewish Music," *International Review of the Aesthetics and Sociology of Music* 50, no. 1/2 (2019): 106.

9. David B. Ruderman, *Early Modern Jewry: A New Cultural History* (Princeton, NJ: Princeton University Press, 2010), 37–40.

10. Harrán, "'Dum recordaremur Sion,'" 59–60.

11. The Accademia degli Impediti left no publications bearing its impresa and has largely been left out of seminal sources for Italian academy study, including Michele Maylender, *Storia delle accademie d'Italia* (Bologna: Cappelli, 1926); Montagu, *An Index of Emblems*; Fenlon, *Music and Culture*; Jane E. Everson, Denis V. Reidy, and Lisa Sampson, eds., *The Italian Acadamies, 1525–1700: Networks of Cultures, Innovation and Dissent* (London: Routledge, 2016); and the Database of Italian Academies.

12. Io mi ricordo bene di quello, che à tempi miei successe in Venetia del 1628. In circa, se non erro, quando da Mantova per causa della guerra fuggiti gli Ebrei, se ne vènero in Venetia. E coll'occasione che fioriva la Città di Mantova in molte sorti di studii, anche gli Ebrei havevano applicato alla musica, & agl'istromenti. Arrivati questi in Venetia si formò nel Ghetto, che ivistà, un'Accademia di Musica, nella quale per ordinario si cantava due volte per settimana di sera e vi si congregavano solamente alcuni principali, e ricchi di quel Ghetto che la sostentavano, tra i quali io pure mi travavano: e'l mio maestro Rabbì Leon da Modena era maestro di Capella.

Giulio Morosini, *Via della fede mostrata a'gli ebrei* (Rome: Stamperia della Cong. de prop. fide, 1683), 793. Translations are mine unless otherwise indicated.

13. Israel Adler, "The Rise of Art Music," 346; Harrán, "'Dum recordaremur Sion,'" 53–54, 57, 59–60; Alfred Sendrey, *The Music of the Jews in the Diaspora (up to 1800): A Contribution to the Social and Cultural History of the Jews* (New York: Yoseloff, 1970), 330–333; and Cecil Roth, "L'accademia musicale," 157–162. Accounts of Mantuan Jewish musicians prior to the War of Succession have been explored by Eduard Birnbaum, *Jewish Musicians at the Court of the Mantuan Dukes (1542–1628)*, ed. Hanoch Avenary, trans. Judith Cohen (Tel Aviv: Publications of the Department of Musicology and the Chaim Rosenberg School of Jewish Studies, Tel-Aviv University, 1987).

14. Giuseppe Veltri, *Alienated Wisdom: Enquiry into Jewish Philosophy and Scepticism* (Berlin and Boston: De Gruyter, 2018), 193; Giuseppe Veltri, "Le accademie ebraiche a Venezia," in Veltri and Chayes, *Oltre le mura*, 43–45; Chayes, "L'Accademia degli Incogniti," 102–105; and Chayes, "Crossing Cultures," 65–66, 78–80.

15. Abraham Z. Idelsohn, *Jewish Music: Its Historical Development*, introduction by Arbie Orenstein (New York: Henry Holt, 1929; New York: Dover, 1992/R), 201.

16. Robert Bonfil, "Change in the Cultural Patterns of a Jewish Society in Crisis: Italian Jewry at the Close of the Sixteenth Century," *Jewish History* 3, no. 2 (Fall 1988): 14; reprinted in *Cultural Change among the Jews of Early Modern Italy* (Farnham: Ashgate, 2010), 14.

17. Robert Bonfil, *Jewish Life in Renaissance Italy*, trans. Anthony Oldcorn (Berkeley: University of California Press, 1994), 151.

18. Howard Ernest Adelman, "Success and Failure in the Seventeenth-Century Ghetto of Venice: The Life and Thought of Leon Modena, 1571–1648" (PhD diss, Brandeis University, 1985), 234.

19. Luzzato is only one example among many Jewish thinkers who used rhetoric to bridge Jewish and classical philosophies. Discussion can be found in Abraham Melamed, "The Perception of Jewish History in Italian Jewish Thought of the Sixteenth and Seventeenth Centuries: A Re-examination," in *Italia Judaica* 2 (1986): 157–158.

20. Alessandro Guetta, "Can Fundamentalism Be Modern? The Case of Avraham Portaleone, the Repentant Scientist," in *Italian Jewry in the Early Modern Era: Essays in Intellectual History*, ed. Giuseppe Veltri (Boston: Academic Studies Press, 2014), 51, 53, and Don Harrán, "In Search of the 'Song of Zion': Abraham Portaleone on Music in the Ancient Temple," *European Journal of Jewish Studies* 4, no. 2 (2010): 215–239. See also Rebecca Cypess and Lynette Bowring's contribution to the present volume.

21. Simḥat Torah is the second day of Shemini 'Atzeret, a festival that follows and concludes the seven days of Sukkot (a festival that celebrates the agricultural harvest and commemorates the Exodus); this second day is observed only in the Diaspora. On Simḥat Torah, the last portion of the Torah is read, and the Torah scrolls are unwound, rerolled, and chanted from the beginning. The term *sposi* refers to the two congregation members who are honored with reading the final and opening verses of the Torah.

> In quell'anno essendo stati per sposi già descritti in questa festa due persone ricche e splendidi, delli quali uno era della medesima Accademia, fecero nella Scuola Spagnuola (ricchissimamente apparata, e adornata di gran argenterie e gioie) fare due cori ad usanza nostra per li musici, e le due sere cioè nell'ottava della festa Scemini Nghatzeret e Allegrezza della Legga, si cantò in musica figurata in lingua ebraica parte della Ngharbith, e diversi Salmi; e la Minchà, cioè il Vespero dell'ultimo giorno con musica solenne, che durò alcune hore della notte, dove vi concorse molta nobilità di Signori, e di Dame con grand'applauso, si che vi convenne tenere alle porte molti Capitani e Birri, acciò si passasse con quiete. Tra gl'istromenti fù portato in Sinagoga anche l'Organo, il qual però non fù permesso da i Rabbini, che si sonasse per essere instromento che per ordinario si suona nelle nostre chiese. Ma' che? Tutto questo fu un fuoco di paglia, durò poco l'Accademia, e la Musica, si ritornò al pristino.

Morosini, *Via della fede*, 793. Many thanks to Massino Ossi for his assistance with the last sentence of this translation.

22. "Non havendo pianta fertile di Compositori," Roth, "L'accademia musicale," 160–161; British Library, MS Or. 5395, f. 23.

23. Adler argues convincingly that the Simḥat Torah celebrations took place during this year. See Adler, *La pratique musicale*, 530–531. While Morosini's accounts of Jewish activities have rightly been treated with skepticism by some scholars because of his status as a converted Christian and the polemical nature of *Via della fede*, his observations of the Simḥat Torah celebrations are largely considered accurate because of the corresponding information in Modena's letter and as described in this chapter. For an extensive discussion of Morosini and a summary of the *Via della fede*, see Benjamin Ravid, "Contra Judaeos in Seventeenth Century Italy: Two Responses to the Discorso of Simone Luzzato by Melchiore Palontrotti and Giulio Morosini," *AJS Review* 7 (1982): 328–348.

24. Burattelli's search of the Jewish Community Archives reveals records of Jews active in Mantuan theatrical productions, such as Abramo Sarfati, Jacob Melli, and Abramo da

Udine, who "avevano responsabilità di carattere organizzativo, occupandosi delle questioni amministrative, del reperimento di costumi e oggetti di scena, della convocazione dei recitanti, e facendo da intermediari tra la corte e la comunità [had organizational responsibilities, dealing with administrative matters, finding costumes and props, calling the reciters, and acting as intermediaries between the court and the community]." Burattelli, *Spettacoli*, 155–156.

25. A possible exception can be found in records from the Libro Grande describing plans for "something tasteful, such as ballets or similar things" ("cosa di gusto, come per esempio balletti et cose simili") to be performed by members of the Venetian Jewish community in honor of the doge's visit in 1610. However, if this performance actually happened, no descriptions have survived. Daniel Jütte, "The Place of Music in Early Modern Italian Jewish Culture," in *Musical Exodus: Al-Andalus and Its Jewish Diasporas*, ed. Ruth F. Davis (Lanham, MD: Rowman & Littlefield, 2015), 54; Benjamin Ravid, "How 'Other' Really Was the Jewish Other? The Evidence from Venice," in *Acculturation and Its Discontents: The Italian Jewish Experience between Exclusion and Inclusion*, ed. David N. Myers, Massimo Ciavolella, et al. (Toronto: University of Toronto Press, 2008), 34; David Joshua Malkiel, *A Separate Republic: The Mechanics and Dynamics of Venetian Jewish Self-Government, 1607–1624* (Jerusalem: Magnes Press, 1991), 160, 231; and Archivio di Stato di Venezia, MS 242/1: Libro grande dell'università degli ebrei, traduzione ufficiale di Sebastiano Venier, 1632, 77r–77v.

26. For discussions about musical tutelage for Jewish boys, see Bonfil, *Jewish Life in Renaissance Italy*, 134–135; Shlomo Simonsohn, *History of the Jews in the Duchy of Mantua* (Jerusalem: Kiryath Sefer, 1977), 582; Adelman, "Success and Failure," 212; and Adler, "The Rise of Art Music," 325. See also Burattelli's commentary on Jewish musical families in Mantua, 156–157.

27. Salamone Rossi's *Ha-shirim 'asher li-Shlomo* include cantus lines with the clefs G_1, C_1, and C_2. While it is feasible that some of the pieces for smaller ensembles could have been transposed down a fourth or fifth, this option becomes considerably less viable for the seven- and eight-part pieces. If the academy sang this music, the higher cantus lines could have been sung by men or boys. Salamone Rossi, *Ha-shirim 'asher li-Shlomo* (Venice: Pietro and Lorenzo Bragadini, in the house of Giovanni Calleoni, [5]383 [=1622–1623]).

28. A record of this payment can be found in a document contained in the Libro Grande dell'Università degli Ebrei, preserved in the Archivio di Stato di Venezia, *Ufficiali al Cattaver*, busta 242, carta 153. The document is transcribed fully by Carla Boccato, "Ordinanze contro il lusso e sul 'suonatore del sabato' nel Ghetto di Venezia nel secolo XVII," *La Rassegna mensile di Israel*, series 3, 45, no. 6/7 (June/July 1979): 254.

29. Erith Jaffe-Berg, "Performance as Exchange: Taxation and Jewish Theatre in Early Modern Italy," *Theatre Survey: The Journal of the American Society for Theatre Research* 54, no. 3 (2013): 402.

30. Burattelli, *Spettacoli*, 155–156.

31. The life and career of Madama Europa is discussed at length in Don Harrán, "Madama Europa, Jewish Singer in Late Renaissance Mantua," in *Festa Musicologica: Essays in Honor of George J. Buelow*, ed. Thomas J. Mathiesen and Benito V. Rivera (New York: Pendragon, 1995), 197–231. For Europa's activities at the Mantuan court, see 200–201. For accounts of her sons' musical (and other) activities, see 214–219. Angelo and his sons eventually ended up in the employ of the duke of Savoy, though they apparently retained a presence in Mantua. See Harrán, "The Man," in *Salamone Rossi: Jewish Musician in Late Renaissance Mantua* (Oxford: Oxford University Press, 1999), 38.

32. For an account of the Levi musician dynasty, especially the saga of Abramino's conversion, see Don Harrán, "The Levi Dynasty: Three Generations of Jewish Musicians in Sixteenth-Century Mantua," in *Rabbi Judah Moscato and the Jewish Intellectual World of Mantua in the Sixteenth-Seventeenth Centuries*, ed. Giuseppe Veltri and Gianfranco Miletto (Leiden and Boston: Brill, 2012), 174–186.

33. Burattelli, 156–157.

34. Harrán reminds us that Rossi indeed made an appearance in Venice in 1628 to oversee the publication of his *Madrigaletti*. His name, however, does not appear in conjunction with any mentions of the academy that same year, and he does not appear to have interacted with Modena following that appearance. Harrán, "'Dum recordaremur Sion,'" 54.

35. The use of instruments to replace voices, a common practice in Christian venues, would not have been widely accepted because of rabbinical prohibition of musical instruments in liturgical synagogue services. To successfully perform a double-choir piece in a liturgical setting, then, an ensemble would need a minimum of eight singers.

36. Modena argued that instruments were permissible in some settings, including "over wine," and for weddings and similar festive occasions, as stated by the Rambam in Mishnah Torah, Hilchot Taaniot, chap. 5, Halakhah 14. These arguments, found in Modena's 1605 responsum and his *Historia de'riti hebraici* [IV.iii.4–5, 91–92], are summarized by Harrán in "'Dum recordaremur Sion,'" 38–40. A translation of the responsum can also be found in Salamone Rossi, *Sacred Vocal Works in Hebrew: Hashirim 'asher lishlomo / "The Songs of Solomon,"* ed. with introduction and notes by Don Harrán, Complete Works, part 3, vols. 13a and 13b (S.l.: American Institute of Musicology and Neuhausen: Hänssler, 2003), 193–211. Many thanks to Rebecca Cypess for her assistance with the Mishnah resource and translation.

37. The few extant names of Jewish instrumentalists in the Gonzaga court have been well documented. See Adler, "The Rise of Art Music," 322; Eduard Birnbaum, *Jewish Musicians*, 16–17; Roth, "L'accademia musicale," 155; Harrán, "'Dum recordaremur Sion,'" 58–59; Idelsohn, *Jewish Music*, 196–197; and Burattelli, *Spettacoli*, 158.

38. "Due Viole, overo doi Cornetti, & un Chittarrone o altro istromento da corpo," Salamone Rossi, *Il primo libro delle sinfonie et gagliarde a tre, quatro, & cinque voci* (Venice: Amadino, 1607); "altro stromento simile," Salamone Rossi, *Il terzo libro de varie sonate, sinfonie, gagliarde, brandi, e corrente* (Venice: Vincenti, [1613?]). Agostino Agazzari defines the term *istromento da corpo* as a continuo instrument capable of playing all the voices in a given ensemble. See Agostino Agazzari, *Del sonare sopra'l basso con tutti li stromenti e dell'uso loro nel conserto* (Siena: Domenico Falconi, 1607), esp. 3, 6.

39. Idelsohn, "Success and Failure," 422–423.

40. Rossi, *Sacred Vocal Works*, especially Modena's responsum, 13a:193–211. See also Adler, *La pratique musicale*, 530–531, and Adelman, "Success and Failure," 378–382. Modena's responsum regarding the musical performance in Ferrara is number 6 in Shlomo Simonsohn, ed., *She'elot u-teshuvot: Ziqne Yehuda* (Jerusalem: Rabbi Kuk Foundation, 1956), 15–20.

41. Harrán, "'Dum recordaremur Sion,'" 20.

42. Adelman, "Success and Failure," 215.

43. Ellis Rivkin, "Leon da Modena and the *Kol Sakhal* [Continued, part III]," *Jewish Quarterly Review* 38, no. 4 (April 1948): 370; Adelman, "Success and Failure," 222; and Leon Modena, *The Divan of Leo de Modena: Collection of His Hebrew Poetical Works, Edited from a Unique MS in the Bodleian Library*, ed. Simon Bernstein (Philadelphia: Jewish Publication Society of America, 1932), 33–45, 234.

44. The original poem is number 53 in *Divan*. The ridotti were private societies that welcomed an elite membership. They bore some resemblances to academies and in some cases even overlapped with them, since many were comprised of specialist groups that included scientists, writers, and intellectuals. However, the word *ridotti* was most often associated with gambling parlors. See Jonathan Walker, "Gambling and Venetian Noblemen, c. 1500–1700," *Past & Present* 162 (February 1999): 32–37. Theories as to the society frequented by Modena are discussed in Adelman, "Success and Failure," 305–307.

45. Modena was evidently present at a service at San Geremia, as related in his autobiography *Hayye Yehudah*, ed. Abraham Kahana (Kiev: s.n., 1911), 34; translated in Leon Modena, *The Autobiography of a Seventeenth-Century Venetian Rabbi: Leon Modena's Life of Judah*, trans. and ed. Mark Cohen (Princeton, NJ: Princeton University Press, 1988), 95, 102. Adelman states that Modena's presence at church services was "not an uncommon occurrence," though I have had difficulty confirming this assertion. See Adelman, "Success and Failure," 486, and Marc Saperstein, "Italian Jewish Preaching: An Overview," in *Preachers of the Italian Ghetto*, ed. David B. Ruderman (Berkeley and Los Angeles: University of California Press, 1992), 85–104.

46. Adelman, "Success and Failure," 836–838; Howard Tzvi Adelman, "Rabbi Leon Modena and the Christian Kabbalists," in *Renaissance Rereadings: Intertext and Context*, ed. Maryanne Cline Horowitz, Anne J. Cruz, and Wendy A. Furman (Urbana: University of Illinois Press, 1988), 271–286; and Moshe Idel, "Differing Conceptions of Kabbalah in the Early Seventeenth Century," in *Jewish Thought in the Seventeenth Century*, ed. Isadore Twersky and Bernard Septimus (Cambridge, MA: Harvard University Press, 1987), 137–200. See also Yaacob Dweck, *The Scandal of Kabbalah: Leon Modena, Jewish Mysticism, Early Modern Venice* (Princeton, NJ: Princeton University Press, 2011), 1–2, 10–13.

47. Chayes, "L'Accademia degli Incogniti," 47; Adelman, "Success and Failure," 836–838.

48. Adelman, "Success and Failure," 427; this fear is also expressed by Luzzato in *Preparatio Evengelica*. See Melamed, "Perception," 157. Ruderman notes that Jewish mobility directly affected languages and linguistic outputs in Venice, especially the publication of Jewish books in Hebrew and vernacular languages. Ruderman, *Early Modern Jewry*, 55, 107–108.

49. Significant studies on Rossi's *Shirim* include Don Harrán, "The Songs of Solomon," in *Salamone Rossi*, 201–220; Idelsohn, *Jewish Music*; Don Harrán, "Tradition and Innovation in Jewish Music of the Later Renaissance," *Journal of Musicology* 7, no. 1 (1989): 116; Rossi, *Sacred Vocal Works*, esp. 13a:40–49; Harrán, "'Dum recordaremur Sion,'" 18, 45–52; and Stefano Patuzzi, "Music from a Confined Space: Salomone Rossi's *Ha-shirim asher lishlomoh* (1622/23) and the Mantuan Ghetto," in "Sacred Space," special issue, *Synagogue Music* 37 (Fall 2012): 61–62. See also Jütte, "Place of Music," 47, 50–51, 56–57.

50. Many of Modena's poems were set to music, likely his own. His son, Zebulun, may have sung some of these on the second day of the Jewish month of Shevat; Modena's grandson also reported that Modena presented poems that he "composed and sang." See Harrán, "'Dum recordaremur Sion,'" 31–33. Attempts have also been made to attribute MS Mus. 101 to Modena, though these claims have not been verified (see note 53).

51. Modena, *Divan*, 200–201; Oxford, Bodleian Library, MS Mich. 528, fol. 43r, no. 232.

52. Kedem Golden, "An Italian Tune in the Synagogue: An Unexplored Contrafactum by Leon Modena," *Revue des études juives* 177 nos. 3–4 (July–December 2018): 399; Edwin Seroussi, "Ghetto Soundscapes: Venice and Beyond," in *Shirat Dvora: Essays in Honor of Professor Dvora Bregman*, ed. Haviva Ishay (Beer-Sheva: Ben Gurion University in the Negev Press, 2019), 166–167. The four-voice canzonetta is in Orazio Vecchi, *Canzonette di Oratio*

Vecchi da Modona, *Libro primo a quattro voci* (Venice: Angelo Gardano, 1580), four partbooks, all on p. 22.

53. Evidence of the existence of polyphonic Jewish liturgical works for synagogue services can be found in the Eduard Birnbaum collection, Library of Hebrew Union College, Cincinnati. Specifically, MS Mus. 101 contains the *canto secondo* line of twenty-one double-choir settings of Hebrew texts. Descriptions of MS Mus. 101 can be found in Harrán, "'Dum recordaremur Sion,'" 56–57; Werner, "Manuscripts of Jewish Music"; and Israel Adler, *Hebrew Notated Manuscript Sources up to circa 1840: A Descriptive and Thematic Catalogue with a Checklist of Printed Sources*, with the assistance of Lea Shalem, 2 vols., RISM B/IX/1 (Munich: G. Henle, 1989), 1:394–401.

54. There is evidence that some Jewish musicians taught music to Christian students during the sixteenth century, including Abraham Halevi dall'Arpa of the Gonzaga court, who apparently tutored the children of Ferdinand I in Austria. See Simonsohn, *History*, 670–671. Jütte explores a number of similar cases in which Jewish musicians taught Christian students in Italy, though these activities became more severely restricted as the religious pressures of the Catholic Reformation increased. Venice was particularly affected by these restrictions. See Jütte, "The Place of Music," especially 51–55.

55. Harrán infers this from Morosini's account in *Via della fede*, quoted earlier (see note 21). See "'Dum recordaremur Sion,'" 53–54.

56. For more commentary on this, see Adler, "The Rise of Art Music," 340, 344.

57. Rossi, *Sacred Vocal Works*, 13a:193–211.

58. Jaffe-Berg, "Performance as Exchange," 394–395.

59. Burattelli, *Spettacoli*, 155; Veltri, "Le accademie italiane e gli ebrei," in Veltri and Chayes, *Oltre le mura*, 34–36; Roth, "L'Accademia musicale," 153–154; and Adler, "The Rise of Art Music," 341.

60. Burattelli, *Spettacoli*, 145.

61. Veltri notes that de' Sommi's exemption was granted on request. See Veltri, "Le accademie italiane e gli ebrei," 36; Roth discusses Rossi's exemption from the "infamous red cap" in "L'accademia musicale," 154.

62. Adler, "The Rise of Art Music," 345; Roth, "L'accademia musicale," 155; and Adler, *La pratique musicale*, 234, commenting on a responsum by Rabbi Samuel Aboab, *Devar Shemuel* (Venice, 1705), fol. 2a. The responsum was published after Aboab's death in 1694. Alex Kerner notes that a version published in 1702 appears in the H. Lindo, *Catalogue of the Library of the College of Portuguese and Spanish Jews in London*. See Alex Kermer, *Lost in Translation, Found in Transliteration: Books, Censorship, and the Evolution of the Spanish and Portuguese Jews' Congregation of London as a Linguistic Community, 1663–1810*, Studies in Jewish History and Culture 53 (Leiden: Koninklijke Brill NV, 2018), 83n.

63. Modena, *Hayye Yehudah*, 45; Adler, "Success and Failure," 199, 433–434; Adler, "The Rise of Art Music," 332; Roth, "L'accademia musicale," 155; Harrán, "'Dum recordaremur Sion,'" 58; and Modena, *Autobiography*, 5, 127, 210, 239.

64. Usque's *L'Ester* was performed for members of the Venetian Jewish community and some of the Venetian nobility by Jewish actors and musicians in 1559. Adelman draws a parallel between Modena's revival of *L'Ester* and Monteverdi's music dramas, but this is not explored in depth, perhaps because there is little record of *L'Ester*'s musical elements. Modena's version of *L'Ester* was dedicated to Sarra Copia Sulam, a Jewish intellectual and patron of both Jewish and non-Jewish artists. See Adelman, "Success and Failure," 433–434, and Leon Modena, *L'Ester, tragedia tratta dalla sacra scrittura* (Venice: Giacomo Sarzina, 1619). A

translation of Modena's dedication can be found in "Dedication to Sarra Copia from Leon Modena's Play *Ester*," in Sarra Copia Sulam et al., *Jewish Poet and Intellectual in Seventeenth-Century Venice: The Works of Sarra Copia Sulam in Verse and Prose, along with Writings of Her Contemporaries in Her Praise, Condemnation, or Defense*, ed. and trans., with introduction by Don Harrán (Chicago: University of Chicago Press, 2009), 511–514.

65. Emily Wilbourne discusses this practice at length in *Seventeenth-Century Opera and the Sound of Commedia dell'Arte* (Chicago: University of Chicago Press, 2016), especially 20, 26, 36–38.

66. Yates, "Italian Academies," 22.

67. Fenlon notes that the Filarmonici in Verona focused primarily on the practice of music, as opposed to the "traditional study of its theoretical and philosophical aspects." Fenlon, "Gioseffo Zarlino," 120.

68. Maylender, "Accademia dei Filarmonici—Bologna," *Storia delle accademie d'Italia*, vol. 2, 377–381; Howard Mayer Brown and Iain Fenlon, "Academy," Grove Music Online (2001), accessed December 2020, https://doi.org/10.1093/gmo/9781561592630.article.00084. For information on all of these academies, see the Database of Italian Academies, accessed December 2020, https://www.bl.uk/catalogues/ItalianAcademies/Default.aspx.

69. Harrán, "'Dum recordaremur Sion,'" 21–22; Modena includes this information in a letter to Judah Saltaro da Fano in 1605, found in Yacob Boksenboin, ed., *Letters of Rabbi Leon Modena* (Tel-Aviv: Tel-Aviv University Press, 1984), 110–111.

70. Adler, "La pratique musicale," 532.

71. Giuseppe Veltri and Evelien Chayes, introduction to *Oltre le mura del Ghetto: Accademie, scetticismo e tolleranza nella Venezia barocca* (Palermo: New Digital Frontiers, 2016), 12.

72. Veltri, "Le accademie italiane e gli ebrei," 35; Adler, "The Rise of Art Music," 341; Roth, "L'accademia musicale," 154; and David Kaufman, "Leone de Sommi Portaleone (1527–92), Dramatist and Founder of a Synagogue at Mantua," *Jewish Quarterly Review* 10 no. 3 (April 1898): 451.

73. Don Harrán, "Doubly Tainted, Doubly Talented: The Jewish Poet Sara Copio (d. 1641) as a Heroic Singer," in *Musica Franca: Essays in Honor of Frank D'Accone*, ed. Irene Alm, Alyson McLamore, and Colleen Reardon (New York: Pendragon, 1996) 367–422. See also Lynn Lara Westwater, *Sarra Copia Sulam: A Jewish Salonnière and the Press in Counter-Reformation Rome* (Toronto: University of Toronto Press, 2020), 47.

74. See the tables provided by Chayes that demonstrate the connections among members of the Accademia degli Incogniti and members of Copia Sulam's circle. Chayes, "L'Accademia degli Incogniti," 106–107. Chayes further explores these connections in "Crossing Cultures," esp. 85–86.

75. Studies on the Accademia degli Incogniti include Monica Miato, *Accademia degli Incogniti di Giovan Francesco Loredan: Venezia, 1630–1661* (Florence: Leo S. Olschki, 1998); Edward Muir, "The Libertines: The Celestial Divorce," in *The Culture Wars of the Late Renaissance: Skeptics, Libertines, and Opera* (Cambridge, MA: Harvard University Press, 2007), 70–75; and Wendy Heller, "Tacitus Incognito: Opera as History in *L'incoronazione di Poppea*," *Journal of the American Musicological Society* 52, no. 1 (1999): 39–96. See also Girolamo Brusoni, Giovanni Francesco Loredano, et al, *Le glorie de gli incogniti: o vero gli hvomini illvstri dell'Accademia de'signori Incogniti di Venetia* (Venice: Francesco Valuasense, 1647).

76. For more commentary regarding the significance of Sarra Copia Sulam and the Incogniti, see Veltri, "Le accademie ebraiche a Venezia," 38–45; Chayes, "L'Accademia degli Incogniti," 74–75; and Veltri and Chayes, introduction to *Oltre le mura*, 12–13. See also

Howard Tzvi Adelman, "Sarra Copia Sullam," in *Jewish Women: A Comprehensive Historical Encyclopedia*, Jewish Women's Archive, March 2009, accessed December 2018, https://jwa.org/encyclopedia/article/sullam-sara-coppia.

77. On the relationship between Copia Sulam and Ansaldo Cebà, see their letters in part 1, "Sarra Copia and Ansaldo Cebà," in *Jewish Poet and Intellectual*, 115–267, and Westwater, *Sarra Copia Sulam*, esp. 48–52. For discussions on the immortality of the soul, especially the dire results of this debate for Copia Sulam, see Westwater, *Sarra Copia Sulam*, "A Rupture in the Salon," 53–74; part 2, "A Controversy on the Immortality of the Soul," in *Jewish Poet and Intellectual*, 269–348; and Ravid's summary in "How 'Other' Really Was the Jewish Other?" 28–29.

78. Bonfil, "Change in the Cultural Patterns," 19.

79. Simone Luzzato, *Discorso circa il stato de gl'hebrei, et in particolar dimoranti nell'inclita Città di Venetia* (Venice: Gioanne Calleoni, 1638); see also Melamed, "Perception," 156–158, and Veltri, "Un accademico scettico: Simone Luzzatto," in Veltri and Chayes, *Oltre le mura*, 147–173, especially 152–157.

80. Translations and commentary on Moscato's sermon can be found in Don Harrán, "Sounds for Contemplation on a Lyre," in *Three Early Modern Hebrew Scholars on the Mysteries of Song* (Leiden and Boston: Brill, 2015), 47–128; For commentary on Portaleone, see Guetta, "Fundamentalism," 53, and Melamed, "Perception," 160. The original text can be found in Abraham Portaleone, *Shiltei ha-Gibborim* [The shields of the heroes] (Mantua: Avraham mi-Shaʿar ʾAryeh, 5372 [=1612]). Among other unflattering descriptions of Jewish music, see Thomas Coryat, *Coryat's Crudities* (London: Stansby, 1611), 232, discussed in Cypess's introduction to this volume.

81. Guetta, "Fundamentalism," 53.

82. The association of synagogue music with "noise" in sixteenth- and seventeenth-century Italy is addressed by Ruth HaCohen in *The Music Libel against the Jews* (New Haven, CT: Yale University Press, 2011), esp. 64–66.

LIZA MALAMUT is an independent scholar, educator, and historical trombonist; she is Co-Artistic Director of the ensemble Incantare and has been appointed Artistic Director of the Newberry Consort.

BIBLIOGRAPHY

MANUSCRIPT SOURCES

Bologna, Archivio di Stato di Bologna. Rogiti del notaio Melchiorre Zanetti. Busta III. 1499–1508.
Budapest, Akademie der Wissenschaften. Kauffman Collection, No. 397, Gumprecht von Szczebrszyn. Venice, ca. 1553–1554.
Cambridge, Trinity College Library. MS F.12.45.
Cincinnati, Library of Hebrew Union College. Eduard Birnbaum collection, MS Mus. 101.
Ferrara, Archivio di Stato di Ferrara. Antichi Notai. Matr. 283. Ser Bartolomeo Codegori. Pacco 21. 1502–1503.
Florence, Archivio di Stato di Firenze. Notarile Antecosimiano. No. 17996, olim R 189. 1440–1442/1443.
Florence, Archivio di Stato di Firenze. Notarile Antecosimiano. No. 10198, olim G 619. 1456–1496.
Florence, Archivio di Stato di Firenze. Notarile Antecosiminiano. No. 16838, olim P 356. 1499–1502.
Florence, Archivio di Stato di Firenze. Otto di Guardia e Balìa della Repubblica. No. 92.
Gesualdo, Parish of San Nicola di Bari. Liber baptizatorum. Vol. I. 1599–1650.
London, British Library. MS Or. 5395.
Modena, Biblioteca Estense. MS C311. 1574. Cosimo Bottegari. "Arie e Canzoni in musica di Cosimo Bottegari."
Munich, Universitätsbibliothek der Ludwig-Maximilians-Universität München. 4° Cod. MS 757. Accessed April 10, 2019. Digitized at https://epub.ub.uni-muenchen.de/22791/.
Naples, State Archive of Naples. Notai del '400. Lawyer Giovanni de Carpanis. 1486–1487.
Naples, State Archive of Naples. Notai del '500. Lawyer Giovanni Giacomo Cavaliere. 1544–1546.
New York, Jewish Theological Seminary. J.T.S. ENA 4096b.
Oxford, Bodleian Library. MS Canonici Or. 6. Ludovico Ariosto. "Orlando furioso." Accessed April 10, 2019. Digitized at https://digital.bodleian.ox.ac.uk/inquire/p/bcf48b43-f81c-4dce-9aa5-f33d3ad079b9.
Oxford, Bodleian Library. MS Canonici Or. 12. Accessed July 19, 2021. Digitized at https://digital.bodleian.ox.ac.uk/objects/2303b438-073b-4e0e-81b6-4955acffb6b0/.
Oxford, Bodleian Library. MS Michael 528.
Palermo, State Archive of Palermo. Tribunale del Santo Uffizio. Ricevitoria, register 8 bis.

Rome, Roma Biblioteca Casanatense. MS 805. 1513. Raffaello Lippo Brandolini. *De musica et poetica opusclum*.
Siena, Archivio di Stato di Siena. Notarile Antecosimiano. No. 361. 1436–1439.
Urbino, Sezione di Archivio di Stato di Urbino. Quadra di Pusteria. N. 1 (1407–1408); n. 2 (1408–1409).
Vatican City, Biblioteca Apostolica Vaticana. MS Urb.lat.1204. Digitized at DigiVatLib. Accessed January 30, 2019. https://digi.vatlib.it/view/MSS_Urb.lat.1204.
Vatican City, Biblioteca Apostolica Vaticana. MS Vat.gr.725. Digitized at DigiVatLib. Accessed June 3, 2019. https://digi.vatlib.it/view/MSS_Vat.gr.725.
Vatican City, Biblioteca Apostolica Vaticana. MS Urb.lat.899. Ordine delle nozze dello illustrissimo messer Costanzo Sforza e Camilla d'Aragona. Digitized at DigiVatLib. Accessed January 30, 2019. https://digi.vatlib.it/view/MSS_Urb.lat.899.
Vatican City, Biblioteca Apostolica Vaticana. "Psalterium David secundum traductionem Septuaginta interpetrum [*sic*] a beato Hieronymo ex Greco in Latinum traductum." MS Urb.lat.9. Digitized at DigiVatLib. Accessed January 30, 2019. https://digi.vatlib.it/view/MSS_Urb.lat.9.
Vatican City, Vatican Secret Archive. Boncompagni-Ludovisi Archive. "Inventario di tutte le robe si ritrovano nel castello di Gesualdo." Prot. 274, serie V, n. 2.
Venice, Archivio di Stato di Venezia. MS 242/1: Libro grande dell'università degli ebrei, traduzione ufficiale di Sebastiano Venier, 1632.
Venice, Archivio di Stato di Venezia. *Ufficiali al Cattaver*. Busta 242, carta 153.

PRINTED SOURCES

Aaron, Pietro. *Compendiolo di molti dubbi, segreti et sentenze intorno al canto fermo, et figurato, da molti eccellenti & consumati Musici dichiarate, Raccolte dallo Eccellente & scienzato Autore frate Pietro Aron del ordine de Crosachieri & della Inclita Città di Firenze*. Milan: Giovanni Antonio Castiglione, [1550?]. Reprinted, Bologna: Editrice Forni, 1971.

———. *Libri tres de institutione harmonica editi a Petro Aaron florentino interprete Io. Antonio Flam. Forocornelite*. Bologna: Benedetto di Ettore, 1516. Facsimile, New York: Broude Brothers, 1976.

———. *Lucidario in musica di alcune oppenioni antiche, et moderne con le loro Oppositioni, & Resolutioni . . . dall'eccellente, & consumato Musico Pietro Aron del Ordine de Crosachieri, & della città di Firenze*. Venice: Girolamo Scotto, 1545. Facsimile, Bologna: Editrice Forni, 1969.

———. *Thoscanello de la musica di Messer Pietro Aaron fiorentino canonico da Rimini*. Venice, 1523. Second edition, *Toscanello in musica di Messer Piero Aron fiorentino del ordine Hierosolimitano et canonico in Rimini*. Venice: Bernardino & Matheo de Vitali, 1529. Reprinted with preface by Willem Elders, Bologna: Forni, 1969.

———. *Trattato della natura et cognitione di tutti gli tuoni di canto figurato*. Venice: Bernardino de Vitali, 1525. Reprinted with a preface by Willem Elders, Utrecht: Joachimsthal, 1966.

Aboab, Samuel. *Devar Shemuel*. Venice, 1705.
Abramov-van Rijk, Elena. *Parlar cantando: The Practice of Reciting Verses in Italy from 1300 to 1600*. New York: Peter Lang, 2009.
Abravanel, Don Isaac. *Perush Abravanel 'al ha-Torah* [Abravanel's commentary on the Torah]. Jerusalem: Ḥoreb, 5757 [=1996–1997].

Abulafia, David. "The Diffusion of the Italian Renaissance: Southern Italy and Beyond." In *Palgrave Advances in Renaissance Historiography*, edited by Jonathan Woolfson, 27–51. Houndmills, Basingstoke: Palgrave Macmillan, 2005.

Achinstein, Sharon. "John Foxe and the Jews." *Renaissance Quarterly* 54, no. 1 (Spring 2001): 86–120.

Acts of the Privy Council of England. Vol. 1, 1542–1547. London: H. M. Stationery Office, 1890.

Adelman, Howard Ernest. "Success and Failure in the Seventeenth-Century Ghetto of Venice: The Life and Thought of Leon Modena, 1571–1648." PhD diss., Brandeis University, 1985.

Adelman, Howard Tzvi. "Rabbi Leon Modena and the Christian Kabbalists." In *Renaissance Rereadings: Intertext and Context*, edited by Maryanne Cline Horowitz, Anne J. Cruz, and Wendy A. Furman, 271–286. Urbana: University of Illinois Press, 1988.

———. "Sarra Copia Sullam." In *Jewish Women: A Comprehensive Historical Encyclopedia*, Jewish Women's Archive. March 2009. Accessed December 2018. https://jwa.org/encyclopedia/article/sullam-sara-coppia.

Adler, Israel. "The Earliest Notation of a Sabbath Table Song (ca. 1508–1518)." *Journal of Synagogue Music* 16, no. 2 (1986): 17–37.

———. *Hebrew Notated Manuscript Sources up to circa 1840: A Descriptive and Thematic Catalogue with a Checklist of Printed Sources*, with the assistance of Lea Shalem, 2 vols. RISM B/IX/1. Munich: G. Henle, 1989.

———, ed. *Hebrew Writings concerning Music in Manuscripts and Printed Books from Geonic Times up to 1800*. Munich: G. Henle, 1975.

———. "La pénétration de la musique savante dans les synagogues italiennes au XVIIe siècle: le cas particulier de Venise." In *Gli ebrei a Venezia: secoli XIV–XVIII, Atti del Convegno Internazionale organizzato dall'Istituto di storia della società e dello stato veneziano della fondazione Giorgio Cini (Venezia 1983)*, edited by Gaetano Cozzi, 527–535. Milan: Edizioni di Comunità, 1987.

———. *La pratique musicale savante dans quelques communautés juives en Europe aux XVIIe et XVIIIe siècles*, 2 vols. Paris and Den Haag: Mouton, 1966.

———. "The Rise of Art Music in the Italian Ghetto." In *Jewish Medieval and Renaissance Studies*, edited by Alexander Altmann, 321–364. Cambridge, MA: Harvard University Press, 1967.

———. "Sheloshah teqasim musiqaliim lehosha'na rabah baqehilat qasale monferato (1732, 1733, 1735)." In *Yuval: Studies of the Jewish Music Research Center*, vol. 5, *The Abraham Zvi Idelsohn Memorial Volume*, edited by Israel Adler, Bathja Bayer, Eliyahu Schleifer, 51–137 (Hebrew section). Jerusalem: Magnes Press, the Hebrew University, 1986.

Agamennone, Maurizio, dir. *APORIE (Archivio e Portale informatico sulla Poesia in Ottava Rima Estemporanea)*. Accessed December 28, 2019. http://www.aporie.it/.

———, ed. *Cantar ottave: Per una storia culturale dell'intonazione cantata in ottava rima*. Lucca: Libreria Musicale Italiana, 2017.

Agazzari, Agostino. *Del sonare sopra'l basso con tutti li stromenti e dell'uso loro nel conserto*. Siena: Domenico Falconi, 1607.

Agostini, Grazia, and Claudia Pedrini, eds. *Innocenzo da Imola: Il tironcinio di un artista*. Imola: Trafis, 1993. Exhibition catalog.

Alexander-Skipnes, Ingrid. "'Bound with Wond'rous Beauty': Eastern Codices in the Library of Federico da Montefeltro." *Mediterranean Studies* 19 (2010): 67–85.

Allsop, Peter. *Cavalier Giovanni Battista Buonamente: Franciscan Violinist*. Aldershot: Ashgate, 2005.

———. *The Italian "Trio" Sonata: From Its Origins until Corelli*. Oxford: Oxford University Press, 1992.
Ambrose. *Hexameron, Paradise, and Cain and Abel*. Translated by John J. Savage. Washington, DC: Catholic University of America Press, 1961.
———. *Sancti Ambrosii Opera*. Vol. 32. Edited by Karl Schenkl. Vienna: F. Tempsky, 1897.
Amram, David Werner. *The Makers of Hebrew Books in Italy, Being Chapters in the History of the Hebrew Printing Press*. Philadelphia: Julius H. Greenstone, 1909.
Andreatta, Michela. "The Poet in the Printing Shop: Leon Modena and the Para-textual Production of Authority in Early Modern Venice." In *Shirat Dvora: Essays in Honor of Professor Dvora Bregman*, edited by Haviva Ishay, 9–29. Beer-Sheva: Ben Gurion University in the Negev Press, 2019.
Ariosto, Ludovico. *Orlando Furioso . . . traduzido en Romance Castellano por Don Ieronimo di Vrrea*. Antwerp: Martin Nuncio, 1549.
———. *Orlando Fvrioso di M. Ludovico Ariosto*. Translated by Jeronimo De Urrea. Venice: Gabriel Iolito di Ferrari, 1542.
Ashbee, Andrew. *Records of English Court Music*. Vol. 7, 1485–1558. Aldershot: Scolar, 1993.
Atlas, Allan William. *Music at the Aragonese Court of Naples*. Cambridge: Cambridge University Press, 1985.
Avenary, Hanoch. "The Earliest Notation of Ashkenazi Bible Chant." *Journal of Jewish Studies* 26 (1975): 132–150.
Babylonian Talmud, Tractate *Gittin* and Tractate *Ḥagigah*.
Backhouse, Janet. "Illuminated Manuscripts and the Development of the Portrait Miniature." In *Henry VIII: A European Court in England*, edited by David Starkey, 88–93. London: Collins and Brown, 1991.
Baines, Anthony. "Fifteenth-Century Instruments in Tinctoris's *De Inventione et Usu Musicae*." *Galpin Society Journal* 3 (March 1950): 19–26.
Balsano, Maria Antonella, and James Haar. "L'Ariosto in musica." In *L'Ariosto: la musica, i musicisti: Quattro studi e sette madrigali ariosteschi*, edited by Maria Antonella Balsano, 47–88. Quaderni della Rivista Italiana di Musicologia 5. Florence: Leo S. Olschki, 1981.
Banks, Jon. *The Instrumental Consort Repertory of the Late Fifteenth Century*. Aldershot: Ashgate, 2006.
Barber, Peter. "England I: Pageantry, Defense, and Government: Maps at Court to 1550." In *Monarchs, Ministers, and Maps: The Emergence of Cartography as a Tool of Government in Early Modern Europe*, edited by David Buisseret, 26–56. Chicago: University of Chicago Press, 1992.
Barile, Nicola Lorenzo. "Renaissance Monti di Pietà in Modern Scholarship: Themes, Studies, and Historiographic Trends." *Renaissance and Reformation / Renaissance et Réforme* 35, no. 3 (2012): 85–114.
Barkan, Elazar, and Karen Barkey. *Choreographies of Shared Sacred Sites: Religion, Politics, and Conflict Resolution*. New York: Columbia University Press, 2016.
Barolini, Teodolinda. "The Wheel of the 'Decameron.'" *Romance Philology* 36, no. 4 (1983): 521–539.
Barrington, Robert. "Two Houses Both Alike in Dignity: Reginald Pole and Edmund Harvell." *Historical Journal* 39, no. 4 (December 1996): 895–913.
Bartolocci, Giulio. *Qiryat sefer. Bibliotheca magna Rabbinica de scriptoribus, et scriptis Hebraicis, ordine alphabetico Hebraicè, et Latinè digestis. . . . 4 partes*. Edited by Carlo Imbonati. Rome: Typographia Sacrae Congregationis de Propaganda Fide, 1675–1693.

Beck, Eleonora M. [Aaron.] *Giotto's Harmony: Music and Art in Padua at the Crossroads of the Renaissance*. Florence: European Press Academic Publishing, 2005.

———. "Mirrors and Music in the *Decameron*." *Heliotropia* 7, nos. 1–2 (2010): 81–103.

———. *Singing in the Garden: Music and Culture in the Tuscan Trecento*. Florence: Libreria Musicale Italiana, 1998.

Beinfeld, Solon, and Harry Bochner. *Comprehensive Yiddish–English Dictionary*. Bloomington: Indiana University Press, 2013.

Ben-Naeh, Yaron. "Research on Ottoman Jewish History and Culture: The State of the Art." *Revue Européenne des Études Hébraïques* 18 (2016): 53–89.

Bent, Margaret. "Accidentals, Counterpoint, and Notation in Aaron's *Aggiunta* to the *Toscanello*." *Journal of Musicology* 12 (1994): 306–344.

Bergquist, Peter. "The Theoretical Writings of Pietro Aaron." PhD diss., Columbia University, 1964.

Bernardy, Amy A. "Les juifs dans la république de San Marin du XIV au XVII siècle." *Revue des études juives* 48 (1904): 241–264.

Bianconi, Lorenzo. *Music in the Seventeenth Century*. Cambridge: Cambridge University Press, 1987.

Biggi, Francis. "La *Fabula di Orpheo* d'Ange Politien ou comment rendre une oeuvre à l'espace de l'interprétation?" In *La Musique ancienne entre historiens et musiciens*, edited by Xavier Bisaro and Rémy Campos, 491–512. Musique & Recherche 3. Geneva: Droz, Haute Ecole de musique de Genève, 2014.

———. Liner notes for Ensemble Lucidarium, *Una musa plebea: Everyday Music from Renaissance Italy*. Audio recording. Raumklang, RK2410, 2011.

Birnbaum, Eduard. *Jewish Musicians at the Court of the Mantuan Dukes (1542–1628)*. Edited by Hanoch Avenary. Translated by Judith Cohen. Tel-Aviv: Publications of the Department of Musicology and the Chaim Rosenberg School of Jewish Studies, Tel-Aviv University, 1987.

Blackburn, Bonnie J. "Cipriano de Rore's Early Italian Years: The Brescian Connection." In *Cipriano de Rore: New Perspectives on His Life and Music*, edited by Jessie Ann Owens and Katelijne Schiltz, 29–74. Turnhout: Brepols, 2016.

———. "Fortunato Martinengo and His Musical Tour around Lake Garda: The Place of Music and Poetry in Silvan Cattaneo's *Dodici giornate*." In *Fortunato Martinengo: Un gentiluomo del Rinascimento fra arti, lettere e musica*, edited by Elisabetta Selmi and Marco Bizzarini, 181–211. Annali di Storia Bresciana. Brescia: Morcelliana, 2018.

———. "Publishing Music Theory in Early Cinquecento Venice and Bologna: Friends and Foes." In *Music in Print and Beyond: Hildegard von Bingen to the Beatles*, edited by Craig A. Monson and Roberta Montemorra Marvin, 36–61. Eastman Studies in Music. Rochester, NY: Rochester University Press, 2013.

———, Edward E. Lowinsky, and Clement A. Miller, eds. *A Correspondence of Renaissance Musicians*. Oxford: Clarendon, 1991.

Boccaccio, Giovanni. *Boccaccio on Poetry: Being the Preface and the Fourteenth and Fifteenth Books of Boccaccio's* Genealogia deorum gentilium *in an English Version with Introductory Essay and Commentary*. Translated by Charles G. Osgood. New York: Liberal Arts, 1956.

———. *Decameron*. Edited by Vittore Branca. Turin: Einaudi, 1987.

———. *The Decameron*. Translated by George Henry McWilliam. 2nd edition. London: Penguin Books, 1995.

———. *The Decameron*. Translated and edited by Wayne A. Rebhorn. New York: W. W. Norton, 2015.

———. *In Defence of Poetry = Genealogiae deorum gentilium liber XIV*. Edited by Jeremiah Reedy. Toronto: Pontifical Institute of Mediaeval Studies, 1978.
———. *Genealogie deorum gentilium*. Accessed July 18, 2021. http://www.bibliotecaitaliana.it/testo/bibit000673.
———. *Un autografo del Decameron (Codice Hamiltoniano 90)*. Edited by Vittore Branca and Pier Giorgio Ricci. Padua: Casa editrice Dott. Antonio Milani, 1962.
Boccato, Carla. "Ordinanze contro il lusso e sul 'suonatore del sabato' nel Ghetto di Venezia nel secolo XVII." *La Rassegna mensile di Israel*, series 3, 45, no. 6/7 (June/July 1979): 239–254.
Boesch Cajano, Sofia. "Il Comune di Siena e il prestito ebraico nei secoli XIV e XV: Fonti e problem." In *Aspetti e problemi della presenza ebraica nell'Italia centro-settentrionale (secoli XIV e XV)*, 175–225. Quaderni 2. Rome: Istituto di Scienze Storiche dell'Università di Roma, 1983.
Bohlman, Philip V. *Jewish Music and Modernity*. Oxford: Oxford University Press, 2008.
———. "On Non-Jewish Music." *International Review of the Aesthetics and Sociology of Music* 50, no. 1/2 (2019): 105–122.
Bokher, Elye. *Bovo d'Antona by Elye Bokher: A Yiddish Romance: A Critical Edition with Commentary*. Edited by Claudia Rosenzweig. Leiden and Boston: Brill, 2016.
———. *Due canti yiddish: rime di un poeta ashkenazita nella Venezia del Cinquecento*. Translated and edited by Claudia Rosenzweig; translated by Anna Linda Callow. Quaderni di traduzione 4. Arezzo: Bibliotheca Arentina, 2010.
Boksenboin, Yacob, ed. *Letters of Rabbi Leon Modena*. Tel-Aviv: Tel-Aviv University Press, 1984.
Bombardini, Sanzio. *Il diavolo nel tamburo: Lotte e tragedie nella storia di una città romagnola e nel diario di un guelfo imolese (1500–1525)*. Bologna: University Press, 1982.
Bonaventura, Arnaldo. *Il Boccaccio e la musica: Studio e trascrizioni musicali*. Turin: Fratelli Bocca, 1914.
Bonfil, Robert. "Change in the Cultural Patterns of a Jewish Society in Crisis: Italian Jewry at the Close of the Sixteenth Century." *Jewish History* 3, no. 2 (Fall 1988): 11–30. Reprinted in *Cultural Change among the Jews of Early Modern Italy*, chapter 6. Farnham: Ashgate, 2010.
———. "A Cultural Profile." In *The Jews of Early Modern Venice*, edited by Robert C. Davis and Benjamin Ravid, 169–190. Baltimore: Johns Hopkins University Press, 2001. Reprinted in *Cultural Change among the Jews of Early Modern Italy*, chapter 12. Farnham: Ashgate, 2010.
———. *Jewish Life in Renaissance Italy*. Translated by Anthony Oldcorn. Berkeley: University of California Press, 1994.
Bonfil, Roberto. "Lo spazio culturale degli ebrei d'Italia fra Rinascimento ed Età barocca." In *Gli ebrei in Italia*, vol. 1, *Dall'alto Medioevo all'età dei ghetti*, Storia d'Italia, Annali 11, edited by Corrado Vivanti, 411–473. Turin: Einaudi, 1996.
Borgó, András. "Miriam's Musical Instruments in Medieval Hebrew Representations." *Music in Art* 1–2 (2006): 175–193.
Botticini, Maristella. "A Tale of 'Benevolent' Governments: Private Credit Markets, Public Finance, and the Role of Jewish Lenders in Medieval and Renaissance Italy." *Journal of Economic History* 60, no. 1 (2000): 164–189.
Bowring, Lynette. "Orality, Literacy, and the Learning of Instruments: Professional Instrumentalists and Their Music in Early Modern Italy." PhD diss., Rutgers University, 2017.
Branca, Daniela Delcorno, ed. *Buovo d'Antona: cantari in ottava rima (1480)*. Biblioteca medievale 118. Rome: Carocci, 2008.
———. "Fortuna e trasformazioni del *Buovo d'Antona*." In *Testi, cotesti e contesti del franco-italiano*, edited by Gunter Holtus, Henning Krauss, and Peter Wunderli, 285–306. Tubingen: Max Niemeyer, 1989.

British Library. "Database of Italian Academies." Accessed December 2020. https://www.bl.uk/catalogues/ItalianAcademies/.
Brooks, Andrée Aelion. *The Woman Who Defied Kings: The Life and Times of Doña Gracia Nasi*. Saint Paul, MN: Paragon House, 2002.
Brown, Howard Mayer. *Embellishing Sixteenth-Century Music*. London: Oxford University Press, 1976.
———. "Fantasia on a Theme by Boccaccio." *Early Music* 5 (1977): 324–339.
———. "St. Augustine, Lady Music, and the Gittern in Fourteenth-Century Italy." *Musica Disciplina* 38 (1984): 25–65.
Brusoni, Girolamo, Giovanni Francesco Loredano, et al. *Le glorie de gli incogniti: o vero gli hvomini illvstri dell'Accademia de'signori Incogniti di Venetia*. Venice: Francesco Valuasense, 1647.
Buovo di Antona di Guidone Palladino, Rezunto e Revisto. Bologna: Caligola de' Bazalieri, 1497.
Burattelli, Claudia. *Spettacoli di corte a Mantova tra Cinque e Seicento*. Florence: Casa editrice Le Lettere, 1999.
Busse Berger, Anna Maria. *Medieval Music and the Art of Memory*. Berkeley: University of California Press, 2005.
———. "Mnemotechnics and Notre Dame Polyphony." *Journal of Musicology* 14, no. 3 (1996): 263–298.
Caldwell, Dorigen. "The *Paragone* between Word and Image in *Impresa* Literature." *Journal of the Warburg and Courtauld Institutes* 63 (2000): 277–286.
Calimani, Riccardo. *Storia degli ebrei italiani*. Milan: Mondadori, 2013.
Canguilhem, Philippe. *L'Improvisation polyphonique à la Renaissance*. Paris: Classiques Garnier, 2015.
———. "Singing upon the Book according to Vicente Lusitano." *Early Music History* 30 (2011): 55–103.
Capitula regni utriusque Siciliae. Edited by Antonio Cervoni. Constitutionum Regni Siciliarum Libri III 2. Naples, 1773.
Carmi, T. (pseudonym of Carmi Chamay), ed. *The Penguin Book of Hebrew Verse*. London: Penguin Books, 2006.
Carnevali, Luigi. *Il ghetto di Mantova*. Mantua: Sartori, 1973.
Caroso, Fabritio. *Courtly Dance of the Renaissance: A New Translation and Edition of the "Nobiltà di Dame" (1600)*. Translated by Julia Sutton and F. Marian Walker. Rev. ed. New York: Dover, 1995.
Carter, Tim. Review of Don Harrán, *Salamone Rossi: Jewish Musician in [sic] Renaissance Mantua*. *Journal of the Royal Musical Association* 125, no. 2 (2000): 299–306.
Cassuto, Umberto. *Gli ebrei a Firenze nell'età del Rinascimento*. Florence: Galletti e Cocci, 1918.
Castaldini, Alberto. *L'ipotesi mimetica. Contributo a una antropologia dell'ebraismo*. Florence: Olschki, 2001.
Castex, Jean. *Architecture of Italy*. Westport, CT: Greenwood, 2008.
Castiglione, Baldassare. *Il libro del Cortegiano*. Venice: Gabriel Giolito di Ferrarii, 1544.
Cerreto, Scipione. *Della prattica musica vocale, et strumentale*. Naples: G. G. Carlino, 1601.
Chambers, David S. "The Earlier 'Academies' in Italy." In *Italian Academies of the Sixteenth Century*, edited by David S. Chambers and François Quiviger, 1–14. London: Warburg Institute, University of London, 1995.
Chayes, Evelien. "Crossing Cultures in the Venetian Ghetto: Leone Modena, the Accademia degli Incogniti and Imprese Literature." *Bollettino di italianistica* 2 (2017): 62–88.
———. "L'Accademia degli Incogniti: tra Talmud e Kabbalah." In *Oltre le mura del Ghetto: Accademie, scetticismo e tolleranza nella Venezia barocca*, by Giuseppe Veltri and Evelien Chayes, 47–119. Palermo: New Digital Frontiers, 2016.

Cheles, Luciano. "The Inlaid Decorations of Federico da Montefeltro's Urbino Studiolo: An Iconographic Study." *Mitteilungen des Kunsthistorischen Institutes in Florenz* 26, no. 1 (1982): 1–46.
Chiesa, Carlo. "Qualche notizia storica su Andrea Amati / Some Historical Notes on Andrea Amati." In *Un corpo alla ricerca dell'anima: Andrea Amati e la nascita del violino 1505–2005*, edited by Renato Meucci, 1:92–107. Cremona: Ente Triennale Internazionale degli Strumenti ad Arco, 2005.
Clough, Cecil H. "Federigo da Montefeltro's Artistic Patronage." *Journal of the Royal Society for the Encouragement of Arts, Manufactures and Commerce* 126 (1978): 718–734.
Coelho, Victor, and Keith Polk. *Instrumentalists and Renaissance Culture, 1420–1600: Players of Function and Fantasy*. Cambridge: Cambridge University Press, 2016.
Cohen, Boaz. *Law and Tradition in Judaism*. New York: Ktav, 1959.
Cohen, Jeremy, and Richard I. Cohen, eds. *The Jewish Contribution to Civilization: Reassessing an Idea*. Oxford: Littman Library of Jewish Civilization, 2008.
Cohen, Judith. "'This Drum I Play': Women and Square Frame Drums in Portugal and Spain." *Ethnomusicology Forum* 17, no. 1 (2008): 95–124.
Colafemmina, Cesare. "Gli ebrei in Irpinia." In *Storia illustrata di Avellino e dell'Irpinia*, vol. 6, *Il novecento*, edited by Francesco Barra, 93–108. Castel di Serra: Sellino & Barra, 1996.
Copia Sulam, Sarra, et al. *Jewish Poet and Intellectual in Seventeenth-Century Venice: The Works of Sarra Copia Sulam in Verse and Prose, along with Writings of Her Contemporaries in Her Praise, Condemnation, or Defense*. Edited and translated by Don Harrán. Chicago: University of Chicago Press, 2009.
Coryat, Thomas. *Coryat's Crudities*. London: Stansby, 1611.
Coulter, Cornelia C. "The Library of the Angevin Kings of Naples." *Transactions and Proceedings of the American Philological Association* 75 (1944): 141–155.
Cummings, Anthony M. *The Politicized Muse: Music for Medici Festivals, 1512–1537*. Princeton, NJ: Princeton University Press, 1993.
———. "Three *gigli*: Medici Musical Patronage in the Early Cinquecento." *Recercare* 15 (2003): 39–72.
Cypess, Rebecca. "The Anxiety of Specificity." In "Colloquy: Jewish Studies and Music," convened by Klára Móricz and Ronit Seter. *Journal of the American Musicological Society* 65, no. 2 (Summer 2012): 576–582.
———. *Curious and Modern Inventions: Instrumental Music as Discovery in Galileo's Italy*. Chicago: University of Chicago Press, 2016.
———. "Music Historicism: Sara Levy and the Jewish Enlightenment." In *Bach and the Counterpoint of Religion*, edited by Robin A. Leaver, 129–152. Vol. 12 of *Bach Perspectives*. Urbana: University of Illinois Press, 2018.
Cypess, Rebecca, and Yoel Greenberg. "Hearing the Ancient Temple in Early Modern Mantua: Abraham Portaleone and the Cultivation of Music within the Mantuan Jewish Community." In *The Oxford Handbook of Jewish Music*, edited by Tina Frühauf. Oxford: Oxford University Press, forthcoming.
d'Arco, Niccolò. *Hieronymi Fracastorii Veronensis, Adami Fumani canonici Veronensis, et Nicolai Archii comitis Carminum editio II*. 2 vols. Padua: Giuseppe Comino, 1739.
Dato, Mordechai. "Megillat Ester in Ottava rima." In *La Istoria de Purim io ve racconto . . . Il Libro di Ester secondo un rabbino emiliano del Cinquecento*, edited by Giulio Busi. Venice: Luis, 1987.
Delille, Gérard. "Il Libro Magno di Manduria." *Storia e dossier* 2, no. 5 (March 1987).

Del Lago, Giovanni. *Breve introduttione di musica misurata, composta per il venerabile Pre Giovanni del Lago Venetiano: scritta al Magnifico Lorenzo Moresino patricio Venetiano patron suo honorendissimo*. Venice: Brandino and Ottaviano Scotto, 1540. Facsimile, Bologna: Forni, 1969.

Dickey, Bruce. "Ornamentation in Early Seventeenth-Century Italian Music." In *A Performer's Guide to Seventeenth-Century Music*, edited by Stewart Carter, revised and expanded by Jeffery T. Kite-Powell, 293–316. Bloomington: Indiana University Press, 2012.

Di Flavio, Vincenzo, and Alessandro Papò. *Res publica hebreorum de Reate*. Rieti: Comune di Rieti, 2000.

Donato, Giuseppe. "Contributo alla storia delle siciliane." In *Proceedings of the 3rd International Symposium (Siena-Certaldo, 19–22 July 1975): La musica al tempo del Boccaccio e i suoi rapporti con la letteratura*, edited by Agostino Ziino, 183–209. L'Ars Nova italiana del Trecento 4. Certaldo: Centro Studi sull'Ars Nova Italiana del Trecento, 1978.

Dowley, Tim, and Nick Rowland. *Atlas of World Religions*. Minneapolis: 1517 Media, 2018.

Duffin, Ross W. "Ensemble Improvisation in 15th-Century Mensural Dance." In *Instruments, Ensembles, and Repertory, 1300–1600: Essays in Honour of Keith Polk*, edited by Timothy J. McGee and Stewart Carter, 195–219. Turnhout: Brepols, 2013.

———. *A Performer's Guide to Medieval Music*. Bloomington: Indiana University Press, 2000.

Dumitrescu, Theodor. *The Early Tudor Court and International Musical Relations*. Burlington, VT: Ashgate, 2007.

Dweck, Yaacob. *The Scandal of Kabbalah: Leon Modena, Jewish Mysticism, Early Modern Venice*. Princeton, NJ: Princeton University Press, 2011.

Ebreo da Pesaro, Guglielmo. *De pratica seu arte tripudii: On the Practice or Art of Dancing*. Edited, translated, and introduced by Barbara Sparti. Oxford: Clarendon, 1993.

Einstein, Alfred. "Die Aria di Ruggiero." *Sammelbände der Internationalen Musikgesellschaft* 13 (1912): 444–454.

Epstein, Marc. *The Medieval Haggadah: Art, Narrative, and Religious Imagination*. New Haven, CT: Yale University Press, 2011.

Erik, Maks. *Di geshikte von der yidisher literature fun di eltste tsaytn biz der Haskole-tkufe*. Warsaw: Furlag Kultur-lige 1928; repr. Publications of the Congress for Jewish Culture, New York: Shulsinger Bros., 1979.

Everson, Jane E., Denis V. Reidy, and Lisa Sampson, eds. *The Italian Academies, 1525–1700: Networks of Culture, Innovation and Dissent*. London: Routledge, 2016.

Fabiański, Marcin. "Federigo da Montefeltro's 'Studiolo' in Gubbio Reconsidered. Its Decoration and Its Iconographic Program: An Interpretation." *Artibus et Historiae* 11, no. 21 (1990): 199–214.

Fassler, Margot. *The Virgin of Chartres: Making History through the Arts*. New Haven, CT: Yale University Press, 2010.

Federico da Montefeltro. *Lettere di stato e d'arte (1470–1480)*. Edited by Paolo Alatri. Rome: Edizioni di Storia e Letteratura, 1949.

Fenlon, Iain. "Gioseffo Zarlino and the Accademia Venetiana della Fama." In *Music and Culture in Late Renaissance Italy*, 118–138. Oxford: Oxford University Press, 2002.

Ferand, Ernest T. "Improvised Vocal Counterpoint in the Late Renaissance and Early Baroque." *Annales Musicologiques* 4 (1956): 129–174.

Filangieri, Gaetano, ed. *Documenti per la storia delle arti e le industrie delle province napoletane raccolti e pubblicati*. 6 vols. Naples: Tipografia dell'Accademia Reale delle Scienze, 1883–1891.

Finlay, Robert. "Foundation of the Ghetto: Venice, the Jews, and the War of the League of Cambrai." *Proceedings of the American Philosophical Society* 126, no. 2 (April 1982): 140–154.

Finzi, Ermanno. *Così uguali, così diversi: Le comunità ebraiche di Viadana e Pomponesco*. Mantua: Istituto Mantovano di Storia Contemporanea, 2015.

———. *Il giusto, come palma, fiorirà: Demografia ebraica sabbionetana*. Mantua: Di Pellegrini, 2014.

———. *La culla dei Finzi: Storia degli ebrei di Rivarolo Mantovano tratta dagli Archivi Notarili*. Mantua: Di Pellegrini, 2013.

Flender, Reinhard. *Hebrew Psalmody: A Structural Investigation*. Jerusalem: Magnes Press, the Hebrew University, 1992.

Foley, John M. *The Singer of Tales in Performance*. Bloomington: Indiana University Press, 1995.

Fortis, Umberto. *La "bella ebrea": Sara Copio Sullam, poetessa nel ghetto di Venezia del '600*. Turin: Silvio Zamorani, 2003.

Foster, Susan. "Holbein as Court Painter." In *Henry VIII: A European Court in England*, edited by David Starkey, 58–63. London: Collins and Brown, 1991.

Foxe, John, and George Townsend. *The Acts and Monuments of John Foxe: With a Life and Defence of the Martyrologist, by the Late Rev. George Townsend*. 8 vols. London: G. Seeley, 1870.

Frakes, Jerold C., ed. *Early Yiddish Texts, 1100–1750*. Oxford: Oxford University Press, 2008.

Fresta, Mariano, ed. "Glossario del teatro popolare tradizionale." In *Guida al Museo Te.Po.Tra.Tos.—Scene del teatro popolare tradizionale Toscano*. Siena: Protagon, 2010.

———. *La Val d'Orcia di Iris. Storia, vita e cultura dei mezzadri*. Montepulciano: Le Balze, 2003.

Galvin, Carol, and Phillip Lindley. "Pietro Torrigiano's Portrait Bust of King Henry VII." *Burlington Magazine* 130, no. 1029 (December 1988): 892–902.

Ganassi, Silvestro. *Lettione seconda pur della prattica di sonare il violone d'arco da tasti*. Venice, 1543.

———. *Regola Rubertina. First and Second Part: A Manual of Playing the Viola da Gamba and of Playing the Lute, Venice 1542 and 1543*. Translated and edited by Hildemarie Peter. Berlin-Lichterfelde: R. Lienau, 1972–1977.

Garruto, Maria Emilia. "Ebrei in Valdelsa nel Quattrocento: Una storia di famiglia (I Poggibonsi)." Doctoral thesis, Università degli Studi di Pisa, Dottorato in Storia, ciclo XVI, 2001–2003.

Gavito, Cory M. "The *Alfabeto* Song in Print, 1610–ca. 1665: Neapolitan Roots, Roman Codification, and 'Il gusto popolare.'" PhD diss., University of Texas at Austin, 2006.

Gillingham, Susan E. *The Poems and the Psalms of the Hebrew Bible*. Oxford: Oxford University Press, 1994.

Ginio, Alisa Meyuhas, ed. *Jews, Christians, and Muslims in the Mediterranean World after 1492*. New York: Routledge, 2013/R.

Girard, René. *Mensonge romantique et Vérité Romanesque*. Paris: Grasset, 1961. Translated by Yvonne Freccero as *Deceit, Desire and the Novel: Self and Other in Literary Structure*. Baltimore: Johns Hopkins University Press, 1966.

Giusti, Maria Elena. "Etnografia sul teatro dei Maggi. Un bilancio degli ultimi 30 anni." In *Progetto Incontro. Materiali di ricerca e analisi*, edited by Ignazio Macchiarella and Duilio Caocci, 440–461. Isre: Nuoro, 2011.

———. "Scrittura e oralità nell'ottava Toscana." In *L'albicocco e la rigaglia. Un ritratto del poeta di Realdo Tonti*, edited by Pietro Clemente and Antonio Fanelli, 277–306. Siena: Edizioni Gorée, 2009.

Glixon, Jonathan. "Music at the Venetian Scuole Grande, 1440–1540." PhD diss., Princeton University, 1979.

Gnoli, Domenico. *La Roma di Leon X*. Milan: Hoepli, 1938.

Golb, Norman. "The Music of Obadiah the Proselyte and His Conversion." *Journal of Jewish Studies* 18 (1967): 43–63.

———. "המוסיקולוגית ועבודתו הגר עובדיה בעניין" [The musicologist and his work: Obadiah the Proselyte]. *Tarbiz* 35 (1965–1966): 81–83.

Golden, Kedem. "An Italian Tune in the Synagogue: An Unexplored Contrafactum by Leon Modena." *Revue des études juives* 177, nos. 3–4 (July–December 2018): 391–420.

Goody, Jack. *The Interface between the Written and the Oral*. Cambridge: Cambridge University Press, 1987.

Gosfield, Avery. "Gratias post mensam in diebus festiuis cum cantico העבריים: A New Look at an Early Sixteenth-Century *Tzur Mishelo*." In *Revealing the Secrets of the Jews: Johannes Pfefferkorn and Christian Writings about Jewish Life and Literature in Early Modern Europe*, edited by Jonathan Adams and Cordelia Heß, 275–296. Berlin: De Gruyter, 2017.

———. "I Sing It to an Italian Tune ... Thoughts on Performing Sixteenth-Century Italian-Jewish Sung Poetry Today." *European Journal of Jewish Studies* 8, no. 1 (June 2014): 9–52.

Gregory of Tours. *Glory of the Martyrs*. Translated by Raymond Van Dam. Liverpool: Liverpool University Press, 1988.

Grossvogel, Steven M. "A Fable of the World's Creation and Phaeton (*Allegorica mitologica*)." In *Boccaccio: A Critical Guide to the Complete Works*, edited by Victoria Kirkham, Michael Sherberg, and Janet Smarr, 63–68. Chicago: University of Chicago Press, 2013.

Guetta, Alessandro. "Can Fundamentalism Be Modern? The Case of Avraham Portaleone, the Repentant Scientist." In *Italian Jewry in the Early Modern Era: Essays in Intellectual History*, edited by Giuseppe Veltri, 30–61. Boston: Academic Studies Press, 2014.

———. "Le opere italiane e latine di Lazzaro da Viterbo, ebreo umanista del XVI secolo." In *Giacobbe e l'angelo. Figure ebraiche alle radici della modernità europea*, edited by Emilia D'Anruono et al., 31–69. Rome: Lithos libri, 2012.

Guidobaldi, Nicoletta. *La Musica di Federico: Immagini e suoni alla corte di Urbino*. Florence: Leo S. Olschki, 1995.

Haar, James. "Arie per cantar stanze ariostesche." In *L'Ariosto: la musica, i musicisti: Quattro studi e sette madrigali ariosteschi*, edited by Maria Antonella Balsano, 31–46. Quaderni della Rivista Italiana di Musicologia 5. Florence: Leo S. Olschki, 1981.

———. "*Improvvisatori* and Their Relationship to Sixteenth-Century Music." In *Essays on Italian Poetry and Music in the Renaissance, 1350–1600*, 76–99. Berkeley: University of California Press, 1986.

HaCohen, Ruth. *The Music Libel against the Jews*. New Haven, CT: Yale University Press, 2011.

Harrán, Don. "Between Exclusion and Inclusion: Jews as Portrayed in Italian Music from the Late Fifteenth to the Early Seventeenth Centuries." In *Acculturation and Its Discontents: The Italian Jewish Experience between Exclusion and Inclusion*, edited by David N. Myers, Massimo Ciavolella, Peter H. Reill, and Geoffrey Symcox, 72–98. Toronto: University of Toronto Press, 2008.

———. "Doubly Tainted, Doubly Talented: The Jewish Poet Sara Copio (d. 1641) as a Heroic Singer." In *Musica Franca: Essays in Honor of Frank D'Accone*, edited by Irene Alm, Alyson McLamore, and Colleen Reardon, 367–422. New York: Pendragon, 1996.

———. "'Dum recordaremur Sion': Music in the Life and Thought of the Venetian Rabbi Leon Modena (1571–1648)." *AJS Review* 23 no. 1 (1998): 17–61.

———. "An Early Modern Hebrew Poem on Music in Its Beginnings and at the End of Time." *Journal of the American Musicological Society* 64, no. 1 (Spring 2011): 3–50.

———. "From Mantua to Vienna: A New Look at the Early Seventeenth-Century Dance Suite." *Journal of the Royal Musical Association* 129 (2004): 181–219.
———. *In Search of Harmony: Hebrew and Humanist Elements in Sixteenth-Century Musical Thought*. Amsterdam: American Institute of Musicology, 1988.
———. "In Search of the 'Song of Zion': Abraham Portaleone on Music in the Ancient Temple." *European Journal of Jewish Studies* 4, no. 2 (2010): 215–239.
———. "The Levi Dynasty: Three Generations of Jewish Musicians in Sixteenth-Century Mantua." In *Rabbi Judah Moscato and the Jewish Intellectual World of Mantua in the Sixteenth-Seventeenth Centuries*, edited by Giuseppe Veltri and Gianfranco Miletto, 161–198. Leiden and Boston: Brill, 2012.
———. "Madama Europa, Jewish Singer in Late Renaissance Mantua." In *Festa Musicologica: Essays in Honor of George J. Buelow*, edited by Thomas J. Mathiesen and Benito V. Rivera, 197–231. New York: Pendragon, 1995.
———. *Salamone Rossi: Jewish Musician in Late Renaissance Mantua*. Oxford: Oxford University Press, 1999.
———. "Sounds for Contemplation on a Lyre." In *Three Early Modern Hebrew Scholars on the Mysteries of Song*, 47–128. Leiden and Boston: Brill, 2015.
———. *Three Early Modern Hebrew Scholars on the Mysteries of Song*. Leiden and Boston: Brill, 2015.
———. "Tradition and Innovation in Jewish Music of the Later Renaissance." *Journal of Musicology* 7, no. 1 (1989): 107–130.
Headland, Thomas N., Kenneth L. Pike, and Marvin Harris, eds. *Emics and Etics: The Insider/Outsider Debate*. Newbury Park, CA: Sage, 1990.
Heller, Wendy. "Tacitus Incognito: Opera as History in *L'incoronazione di Poppea*." *Journal of the American Musicological Society* 52, no. 1 (1999): 39–96.
Hoffman, Joseph. "Piero della Francesca's 'Flagellation': A Reading from Jewish History." *Zeitschrift für Kunstgeschichte* 44, no. 4 (1981): 340–357.
Holman, Peter. *Four and Twenty Fiddlers: The Violin at the English Court, 1540–1690*. Oxford: Clarendon, 1993.
The Holy Bible Faithfully Translated into English out of the Authentical Latin, Diligently Conferred with the Hebrew, Greek, & Other Editions in Diverse Languages. Translated by the English College of Doway. Rheims: John Cousturier, 1635.
Hudson, Richard. *Passacaglio and Ciaccona: From Guitar Music to Italian Keyboard Variations in the 17th Century*. Studies in Musicology 37. Ann Arbor, MI: University Microfilms International, 1981.
Idel, Moshe. "Differing Conceptions of Kabbalah in the Early Seventeenth Century." In *Jewish Thought in the Seventeenth Century*, edited by Isadore Twersky and Bernard Septimus, 137–200. Cambridge, MA: Harvard University Press, 1987.
Idelsohn, Abraham Zvi. *Jewish Music in Its Historical Development*. New York: Henry Holt, 1929; New York: Tudor, 1948/R; New York: Dover, 1992/R.
Jacobson, Joshua. "Art Music and Jewish Culture before the Jewish Enlightenment: Negotiating Identities in Late Renaissance Italy." In *The Cambridge Companion to Jewish Music*, edited by Joshua S. Walden, 143–155. Cambridge: Cambridge University Press, 2015.
———. "Defending Salamone Rossi: The Transformation and Justification of Jewish Music in Renaissance Italy." *Yale University Institute of Sacred Music Colloquium: Music, Worship, Arts* 5 (Autumn 2008; issued April 2010): 85–92.
———. "A Possible Influence of Traditional Chant on a Synagogue Motet of Salamone Rossi." *Musica Judaica* 10 (1987–1988): 52–58.

Jacoby, David. "New Evidence on Jewish Bankers in Venice and the Venetian Terraferma (ca. 1450–1550)." In *The Mediterranean and the Jews*, edited by Ariel Toaff, 151–178. Ramat-Gan: Bar-Ilan University Press, 1989.

Jaffe-Berg, Erith. "Performance as Exchange: Taxation and Jewish Theatre in Early Modern Italy." *Theatre Survey: The Journal of the American Society for Theatre Research* 54, no. 3 (2013): 389–417.

Judd, Cristle Collins. *Reading Renaissance Music Theory: Hearing with the Eyes*. Cambridge Studies in Music Theory and Analysis. Cambridge: Cambridge University Press, 2000.

Jütte, Daniel. "The Place of Music in Early Modern Italian Jewish Culture." In *Musical Exodus: Al-Andalus and Its Jewish Diasporas*, edited by Ruth F. Davis, 45–61. Lanham, MD: Rowman and Littlefield, 2015.

Katz, Dana E. *The Jew in the Art of the Italian Renaissance*. Philadelphia: University of Pennsylvania Press, 2008.

———. *The Jewish Ghetto and the Visual Imagination of Early Modern Venice*. Cambridge: Cambridge University Press, 2017.

Katz, David S. *The Jews in the History of England, 1485–1850*. Oxford: Clarendon, 1994.

Kaufman, David. "Leone de Sommi Portaleone (1527–92), Dramatist and Founder of a Synagogue at Mantua." *Jewish Quarterly Review* 10, no. 3 (April 1898): 445–461.

———. "Nathanael Trabot über die Behandlung der Gebete in der Composition." *Monatsschrift für die Geschichte und Wissenschaft des Judenthums* 39, n.s., 3, vol. 8 (1895): 350–357.

Kermer, Alex. *Lost in Translation, Found in Transliteration: Books, Censorship, and the Evolution of the Spanish and Portuguese Jews' Congregation of London as a Linguistic Community, 1663–1810*. Studies in Jewish History and Culture 53. Leiden: Koninklijke Brill NV, 2018.

Kezich, Giovanni, and Maurizio Agamennone. *I poeti contadini: introduzione all'ottava rima popolare: immaginario poetico e paesaggio sociale*. Rome: Bulzoni, 1986.

Khan, Geoffrey. *A Short Introduction to the Tiberian Masoretic Bible and Its Reading Tradition*. 2nd ed. Piscataway, NJ: Gorgias, 2014.

Kinkeldey, Otto. "A Jewish Dancing Master of the Renaissance (Guglielmo Ebreo)." In *Studies in Jewish Bibliography and Related Subjects, in Memory of Abraham Solomon Freidus (1867–1923)*, 329–372. New York: Alexander Kohut Memorial Foundation, 1929.

Kirkendale, Warren. *The Court Musicians in Florence during the Principate of the Medici*. Florence: Leo S. Olschki, 1993.

———. "Franceschina, Girometta, and Their Companions in a Madrigal 'a diversi linguaggi' by Luca Marenzio and Orazio Vecchi." *Acta Musicologica* 44 (1972): 181–235.

Kligman, Mark. "Jewish Liturgical Music." In *The Cambridge Companion to Jewish Music*, edited by Joshua S. Walden, 84–103. Cambridge: Cambridge University Press, 2015.

Kogman-Appel, Katrin. "Portrayals of Women with Books: Female (Il)literacy in Medieval Jewish Culture." In *Reassessing the Roles of Women as "Makers" of Medieval Art and Architecture*, edited by Therese Martin, 2 vols., 2:525–563. Leiden: Brill, 2012.

Kokin, David Stein. "Isaac ha-Kohen's Letter to Marco Lippomano: Jewish-Christian Exchange and Arabic Learning in Renaissance Italy." *Jewish Quarterly Review* 104, no. 2 (Spring 2014): 192–233.

Krasner, Mariuccia. "L'onomastica degli ebrei di Palermo nei secoli XIV e XV: nuove prospettive di ricercar." *Materia Giudaica* 11, nos. 1–2 (2006): 97–112.

Kurtzman, Jeffrey. "Instruments, Instrument Makers, and Instrumentalists in the Second Half of the Sixteenth Century." In *A Companion to Music in Sixteenth-Century Venice*, edited by Katelijne Schiltz, 292–320. Leiden: Brill, 2018.

Lasocki, David, with Roger Prior. *The Bassanos: Venetian Musicians and Instrument Makers in England, 1531–1665*. Aldershot: Scolar and Brookfield, VT: Ashgate, 1995.

Lavin, Marilyn Aronberg. "The Altar of Corpus Domini in Urbino: Joos Van Ghent, Piero della Francesca." *Art Bulletin* 49, no. 1 (1967): 1–24.

Letters and Papers, Foreign and Domestic, of the Reign of Henry VIII: Preserved in the Public Record Office, the British Museum, and Elsewhere in England, arranged and catalogued by J. S. Brewer. 21 vols. London: Longman, Green, Longman, and Roberts, 1862–1932.

Levi, Leo. "Le due più antiche trascrizioni musicali di melodie ebraico-italiane." In *Scritti sull'ebraismo in memoria di Guido Bedarida*, 105–136. Florence: Tipografia Giuntina, 1966.

Levita, Elia [a.k.a. Elye Bokher]. *Paris un Wiene: Ein jiddischer Stanzenroman des 16. Jahrhunderts*. Translated and edited by Erika Timm and Gustav Adolf Beckmann. Tübingen: M. Niemeyer, 1996.

Lieto, Bartolomeo. *Dialogo quarto di musica*. Naples, 1559. Reprint edited by Patrizio Barbieri, Lucca: Libreria Musicale Italiana, 1993.

Lipphardt, Anna, Julia Brauch, and Alexandra Nocke. "Exploring Jewish Space: An Approach." In *Jewish Topographies*, edited by Anna Lipphardt, Julia Brauch, and Alexandra Nocke, 1–23. Farnham: Ashgate, 2008.

Liptzin, Sol. *A History of Yiddish Literature*. Middle Village, NY: Jonathan David, 1972.

Lockwood, Lewis. "Adrian Willaert and Cardinal Ippolito I d'Este: New Light on Willaert's Early Career in Italy, 1515–21." *Early Music History* 5 (1985): 85–112.

———. "Aspects of the 'L'homme armé' Tradition." *Proceedings of the Royal Musical Association* 100, no. 1 (1973): 97–122.

Lord, Albert B. *The Singer of Tales*. Cambridge, MA: Harvard University Press, 1960.

Lütgendorff, Willibald Leo von. *Die Geigen und Lautenmacher vom Mittelalter bis zur Gegenwart*. 2 vols. Frankfurt am Main and Berlin: Hesse, 1922. Reprint, Tutzing: Schneider, 1968 and 1975; vol. 3 containing supplements and updates by Thomas Drescher, Tutzing: Schneider, 1990.

Luzzati, Michele. *La casa dell'ebreo: Saggi sugli ebrei a Pisa e in Toscana nel Medioevo e nel Rinascimento*. Pisa: Nistri Lischi, 1985.

———. "Una 'condotta' con divieto di prestito e con scadenza *sine die*: Gli Alpilinc e altri sefarditi nello Stato fiorentino agli inizi del Cinquecento." In *Studi sul mondo sefardita in memoria de Aron Leoni*, edited by Pier Cesare Joly Zorattini, Michele Luzzati, and Michele Sarfatti, 13–21. Florence: Leo S. Olschki, 2012.

Luzzato, Simone. *Discorso circa il stato de gl'hebrei, et in particolar dimoranti nell'inclita Città di Venetia*. Venice: Gioanne Calleoni, 1638.

Luzzatto, Gina. *I banchieri ebrei in Urbino nell'età ducale*. Padua: Arnoldi Forni, 1902.

Malamut, Liza Nicole. "Sounding History: A Diminution Method for Modern Trombonists." DMA diss., Boston University, 2018.

Malkiel, David Joshua. *A Separate Republic: The Mechanics and Dynamics of Venetian Jewish Self-Government, 1607–1624*. Jerusalem: Magnes Press, 1991.

Mann, Vivian B., ed. *Gardens and Ghettos: The Art of Jewish Life in Italy*. Art catalogue by the Jewish Museum, New York. Berkeley: University of California Press, 1989.

———. "The Recovery of a Known Work." *Jewish Art* 12–13 (1986–1987): 269–278.

Marshall, Peter. "Forgery and Miracles in the Reign of Henry VIII." *Past and Present* 178 (February 2003): 39–73.

Matut, Diana. *Dichtung und Musik im frühneuzeitlichen Aschkenas*. Leiden: Brill, 2011.

Maylender, Michele. *Storia delle accademie d'Italia*. Bologna: Cappelli, 1926.

McGee, Timothy J. "Dancing Masters and the Medici Court in the 15th Century." *Studi Musicali* 17 (1988): 201–224.
McLuhan, Marshall. *The Gutenberg Galaxy: The Making of Typographic Man*. New ed. with essays by W. Terrence Gordon, Elena Lamberti, and Dominique Scheffel-Dunand. Toronto: University of Toronto Press, 2011.
McNeely, Ian F. "The Renaissance Academies between Science and the Humanities." *Configurations* 13, no. 3 (2009): 227–258.
Melamed, Abraham. "The Myth of the Jewish Origins of Philosophy in the Renaissance: From Aristotle to Plato." *Jewish History* 26, nos. 1–2 (May 2012): 41–59.
———. "The Perception of Jewish History in Italian Jewish Thought of the Sixteenth and Seventeenth Centuries: A Re-examination." *Italia Judaica* 2 (1986): 139–170.
———. *Raqaḥot ve-tabaḥot: Ha-mitos 'al meqor ha-ḥokhmot* [The myth of the Jewish origins of philosophy and science: A history]. Haifa: Haifa University Press; Jerusalem: Magnes Press, 2010.
Meucci, Renato. "Alle origini della liuteria classica italiana: come in una gara ad ostacoli . . . / The Origins of Italian Violin Making: Rather like an Obstacle Course." In *Un corpo alla ricerca dell'anima: Andrea Amati e la nascita del violino 1505–2005*, edited by Renato Meucci, 1:10–88. Cremona: Ente Triennale Internazionale degli Strumenti ad Arco, 2005.
———. "Da chitarra italiana a chitarrone: una nuova interpretazione." In *Enrico Radesca di Foggia e il suo tempo*, edited by Francesca Seller, 37–57. Lucca: Libreria Musicale Italiana, 2001.
———, ed. *Un corpo alla ricerca dell'anima: Andrea Amati e la nascita del violino 1505–2005*. 2 vols. Cremona: Ente Triennale Internazionale degli Strumenti ad Arco, 2005.
Miato, Monica. *Accademia degli Incogniti di Giovan Francesco Loredan: Venezia, 1630–1661*. Florence: Leo S. Olschki, 1998.
Minervini, Laura. "Una versione giudeospagnola dell'*Orlando Furioso*." *Annali di Ca' Foscari* 32, no. 3 (1993): 35–45.
Modena, Leon. *The Autobiography of a Seventeenth-Century Venetian Rabbi: Leon Modena's Life of Judah*. Translated and edited by Mark R. Cohen, with introduction and essays by Mark R. Cohen, Theodore K. Rabb, Howard E. Adelman, and Natalie Zemon Davis, with historical notes by Howard E. Adelman and Benjamin C. I. Ravid. Princeton, NJ: Princeton University Press, 1988.
———. *The Divan of Leo de Modena: Collection of His Hebrew Poetical Works, Edited from a Unique MS in the Bodleian Library*. Edited by Simon Bernstein. Philadelphia: Jewish Publication Society of America, 1932.
———. *Hayye Yehudah*. Edited by Abraham Kahana. Kiev: s.n., 1911.
———. *Historia de' riti hebraici*. Venice: Appresso il Miloco, 1673.
———. *L'Ester, tragedia tratta dalla sacra scrittura*. Venice: Giacomo Sarzina, 1619.
Modona, Leonello. "Una poesia inedita di Manuello, giudeo." In *Il vessillo israelitico: rivista mensile per la storia, la scienza e lo spirito del giudaismo*, edited by Flaminio Servi, 380–386. Casale: Pane, 1885.
Molina, Mauricio. "Frame Drums in the Medieval Iberian Peninsula." PhD diss., New York University, 2006.
Montagu, Jennifer. *An Index of Emblems of the Italian Academies Based on Michele Maylender's Storie delle accademie d'Italia*. London: Warburg Institute, University of London, 1988.
Montaigne, Michel. *Journal du voyage en Italie, par la Suisse & l'Allemagne en 1580 et 1581. Avec des notes-par M. de Querlon*. Paris: Le Jay, 1774.
Morgan, Leslie Zarker. "*Bovo d'Antona* in the *Geste Francor* (V 13): Unity of Composition and Clan Destiny." *Italian Culture* 16, no. 2 (1998): 15–38.

Morosini, Giulio. *Via della fede mostrata a'gli ebrei*. Rome: Stamperia della Cong. de prop. fide, 1683.

Moscati Benigni, Maria Luisa. *Marche itinerari ebraici: i luoghi, la storia, l'arte*. Venice: Marsilio, 1996.

———. "Urbino 1633: nasce il ghetto." In *La presenza ebraica nelle Marche: secoli XIII–XX*, edited by Sergio Anselmi and Viviana Bonazzoli, 121–138. Ancona: Proposte e ricerche, 1993.

Muir, Edward. *The Culture Wars of the Late Renaissance: Skeptics, Libertines, and Opera*. Cambridge, MA: Harvard University Press, 2007.

Myers, David N., Massimo Ciavolella, Peter H. Reill, and Geoffrey Symcox, eds. *Acculturation and Its Discontents: The Italian Jewish Experience between Exclusion and Inclusion*. Toronto: University of Toronto Press, 2008.

Narkiss, Bezalel. *The Golden Haggadah*. Rohnert Park, CA: Pomegranate Artbooks, 1997.

Neubauer, Adolf. *Catalogue of the Hebrew Manuscripts in the Bodleian Library and in the College Libraries of Oxford*. Oxford: Clarendon, 1886.

———. *Catalogue of the Hebrew Manuscripts in the Bodleian Library: Supplement of Addenda and Corrigenda to Vol. I (A. Neubauer's Catalogue)*. Edited by Malachi Beit-Arié and Ron A. May. Oxford: Clarendon, 1994.

Neuberg, Simon, ed. *Das schwedesch lid: ein westjiddischer Bericht über Ereignisse in Prag im Jahre 1684*. Hamburg: H. Buske, 2000.

Nielsen, Bruce. "Daniel van Bombergen, a Bookman of Two Worlds." In *The Hebrew Book in Early Modern Italy*, edited by Joseph R. Hacker and Adam Shear, 56–75. Philadelphia: University of Pennsylvania Press, 2011.

Nissim, Paolo. "Le tappe del soggiorno in Italia di Elia Levita." *La Rassegna mensile di Israel* 32, no. 8 (1966): 359–364.

Nocerino, Francesco. "La bottega dei violari Albanese e Matino." In *Liuteria, Musica, Cultura, 1999–2000*, edited by Renato Meucci, 3–9. Lucca: Libreria Musicale Italiana, 2001.

Ong, Walter J. *Orality and Literacy: The Technologizing of the Word*. 30th anniversary ed. with additional chapters by John Hartley. Abingdon, UK: Routledge, 2012.

Osborne, June. *Urbino: The Story of a Renaissance City*. Chicago: University of Chicago Press, 2003.

Ottolenghi, Emanuele. *Autodafé: l'Europa, gli Ebrei e l'antisemitismo*. Turin: Lindau, 2007.

Parish, Helen. *Monks, Miracles, and Magic: Reformation Representations of the Medieval Church*. London: Routledge, 2005.

Parisi, Susan. "Ducal Patronage of Music in Mantua, 1587–1627: An Archival Study." PhD diss., University of Illinois at Urbana-Champaign, 1989.

Patuzzi, Stefano. "*I Canti* di Salomone Rossi e l'"invenzione' della musica ebraica." In *Lombardia judaica*, edited by Giulio Busi and Ermanno Finzi, 39–48. Florence: Giuntina, 2017.

———. "Music from a Confined Space: Salomone Rossi's *Ha-shirim asher lishlomoh* (1622/23) and the Mantuan Ghetto." In "Sacred Space." Special issue, *Journal of Synagogue Music* 37 (Fall 2012): 49–69.

Paulis, Giulio. "I nomi delle 'launeddas' sarde e della 'viola' alla luce della tradizione musicale greco-romana." In *Sardinia antiqua: Studi in onore di Pietro Meloni*, 505–528. Cagliari: Edizioni della Torre, 1992.

Pearsall, Eileen Sharpe. "Tudor Court Musicians, 1485–1547: Their Number, Status and Function." PhD diss., New York University, 1986.

Perosino, Aldo. "La comunità ebraica di Alessandria dal 1842 a oggi: indagine statistica." *Rassegna mensile di Israel* 68, no. 2 (May–August 2002): 43–82.

Peruzzi, Marcella. *Cultura, potere immagine: La biblioteca di Federico di Montefeltro*. Collana di Studi e Testi 20. Urbino: Accademia Raffaello, 2004.

———, Lorenza Mochi Onori, and Claudia Caldari, eds. *Ornatissimo codice: La biblioteca di Federico di Montefeltro*. Milan: Skira, 2008.

Philo. *Philo*. Vol. 6, *On Abraham. On Joseph. On Moses*. Translated by Francis H. Colson. Cambridge, MA: Harvard University Press, 1966.

Picone, Michelangelo. "Il *Decamerone* come macrotesto: il problema della cornice." In *Introduzione al Decameron*, edited by Michelangelo Picone and Margherita Mesirca, 9–34. Florence: Cesati, 2004.

Pirrotta, Nino. *Li due Orfei*. Turin: Einaudi, 1975.

———, ed. *The Music of Fourteenth-Century Italy*. Amsterdam: American Institute of Musicology, 1960.

———. "Rhapsodic Elements of North-Italian Polyphony of the 14th Century." *Musica Disciplina* 37 (1983): 83–99.

———. "Tradizione orale e tradizione scritta nella musica." In *L'Ars Nova italiana del Trecento* 3, edited by F. Albert Gallo, 431–441. Certaldo: Centro di studi sull' Ars Nova italiana del Trecento, 1970.

Portaleone, Abraham. *Shiltei ha-Gibborim* [The shields of the heroes]. Mantua: Avraham mi-Sha'ar 'Aryeh [the Author], 5372 [=1612].

Potter, Joy. *Five Frames for the Decameron: Communication and Social Systems in the Cornice*. Princeton, NJ: Princeton University Press, 1982.

Prior, Roger. "Jewish Musicians at the Tudor Court." *Musical Quarterly* 69, no. 2 (Spring 1983): 253–265.

———. "A Second Jewish Community in Tudor England." *Jewish Historical Studies: Transactions of the Jewish Historical Society of England* 31 (1988–1990): 137–152.

Prizer, William F. "Isabella d'Este and Lorenzo da Pavia, 'Master Instrument-Maker.'" *Early Music History* 2 (1982): 87–127.

Proverbio, Delio. "Notes on the Diaspora of the Hebrew Manuscripts: From Volterra to Urbino." In *Federico da Montefeltro and His Library*, edited by Marcello Simonetta, 51–62. Milan: Y-Press, 2007.

Pullan, Brian. "Jewish Banks and Monti di Pietà." In *The Jews of Early Modern Venice*, edited by Robert C. Davis and Benjamin Ravid, 53–72. Baltimore: Johns Hopkins University Press, 2001.

———. *Rich and Poor in Renaissance Venice: The Social Institutions of a Catholic State, to 1620*. Cambridge, MA: Harvard University Press, 1971.

Ravid, Benjamin. "*Contra Judaeos* in Seventeenth Century Italy: Two Responses to the *Discorso* of Simone Luzzato by Melchiore Palontrotti and Giulio Morosini." *AJS Review* 7/8 (1982): 301–351.

———. "How 'Other' Really Was the Jewish Other? Evidence from Venice." In *Acculturation and Its Discontents: The Italian Jewish Experience between Exclusion and Inclusion*, edited by David N. Myers, Massimo Ciavolella, et al., 19–55. Toronto: University of Toronto Press, 2008.

———. "The Legal Status of the Jews in Venice to 1509." *Proceedings of the American Academy for Jewish Research* 54 (1987): 169–202.

———. *Studies on the Jews of Venice, 1382–1797*. Aldershot, UK: Ashgate, 2003.

Renda, Francesco. *L'Inquisizione in Sicilia*. Palermo: Sellerio, 1997.

Rendsburg, Gary A., and Peter M. Smith, cur. Johannes of Oppido = Obadiah the Proselyte = הגר עבדיה. Accessed August 2018. http://johannes-obadiah.org/.

Reusner, Nikolaus. *Icones sive imagines vivae*. Basel: Conr. Valdkirch, 1589.
Richardson, Brian. "The Social Connotations of Singing Verse in Cinquecento Italy." *Italianist* 34, no. 3 (2014): 362–378.
Rivière, Jean-Marc. "Les Juifs florentins dans l'espace politique republicain (1494–1496)." In *Ebrei migranti: Le voci della diaspora*, edited by Raniero Speelman, Monica Jansen, and Silvia Gaiga, 14–30. Italistica Ultraiectina 7. Utrecht: Igitur, 2012.
Rivkin, Ellis. "Leon da Modena and the *Kol Sakhal* [continued; part III]." *Jewish Quarterly Review* 38, no. 4 (April 1948): 369–408.
Rosellini, Aldo, ed. *La "Geste Francor" di Venezia. Edizione integrale del Codice XIII del Fondo francese della Marciana*. Centro di Linguistica dell'Universita Cattolica, Saggi e monografie 6. Brescia: La Scuola, 1986.
Rosenzweig, Claudia. "From the Square and the Court to the Private Room: Some Remarks on the Yiddish Version of the Chivalric Poem *Bovo d'Antona*." *Zutot: Perspectives on Jewish Culture* 5, no. 1 (2008): 51–60.
———. "Rhymes to Sing and Rhymes to Hang Up." In *The Italia Judaica Jubilee Conference*, edited by Shlomo Simonsohn and Joseph Shatzmiller, 149–153. Brill's Series in Jewish Studies 48. Leiden and Boston: Brill, 2012.
Rosman, Moshe. *How Jewish Is Jewish History?* Oxford: Littman Library of Jewish Civilization, 2007.
Roth, Cecil. *A History of the Jews in England*. Oxford: Clarendon, 1941.
———. *The History of the Jews of Italy*. Philadelphia: Jewish Publication Society of America, 1946. Reprinted Farnborough: Gregg International, 1969.
———. *The Jewish Contribution to Civilization*. London: MacMillan, 1938.
———. *The Jews in the Renaissance*. Philadelphia: Jewish Publication Society of America, 1959.
———. "L'accademia musicale del ghetto veneziano." *La Rassegna mensile di Israel* 3, no. 4 (Tebheth 5688 [=1927–1928]): 152–162.
———. *Personalities and Events in Jewish History*. Philadelphia: Jewish Publication Society of America, 1953.
Ruderman, David B. *Early Modern Jewry: A New Cultural History*. Princeton, NJ: Princeton University Press, 2010.
———, ed. *Essential Papers on Jewish Culture in Renaissance and Baroque Italy*. New York: New York University Press, 1992.
———. "Jewish Cultural History in Early Modern Europe: An Agenda for Future Study." In *Rethinking European Jewish History*, edited by Jeremy Cohen and Moshe Rosman, 95–111. Portland, OR: Littman Library of Jewish Civilization, 2009.
——— and Giuseppe Veltri, eds. *Cultural Intermediaries: Jewish Intellectuals in Early Modern Italy*. Philadelphia: University of Pennsylvania Press, 2004.
Ruffatti, Alessio. "Italian Musicians at the Tudor Court." *Jewish Historical Studies* 35 (1996–1998): 1–14.
The Rylands Haggadah: A Medieval Sephardi Masterpiece in Facsimile. With introduction, notes on illuminations, transcription, and English translation by Raphael Loewe. London: Thames and Hudson, 1988.
Sacerdoti, Annie. *Guida all'Italia ebraica*. Genova: Casa Editrice Marietti S.p.A, 1986.
Sacks, Elias. "Poetry, Music, and the Limits of Harmony: Mendelssohn's Aesthetic Critique of Christianity." In *Sara Levy's World: Gender, Judaism, and the Bach Tradition in Enlightenment Berlin*, edited by Rebecca Cypess and Nancy Sinkoff, 122–146. Rochester, NY: University of Rochester Press, 2018.

Saggio, Francesco. "Improvvisazione e scrittura nel tardo-quattrocento cortese: lo strambotto al tempo di Leonardo Giustinian e Serafino Aquilano." In *Cantar ottave: Per una storia culturale dell'intonazione cantata in ottava rima*, ed. Maurizio Agamennone, 25–47. Lucca: Libreria Musicale Italiana, 2017.

Salvadori, Roberto. *Gli ebrei di Firenze: dalle origini ai giorni nostri*. Florence: Giuntina, 2000.

Salzberg, Rosa. "In the Mouths of Charlatans: Street Performers and the Dissemination of Pamphlets in Renaissance Italy." *Renaissance Studies* 24 (2010): 638–653.

——— and Massimo Rospocher. "Street Singers in Italian Renaissance Culture and Communication." *Cultural and Social History* 9 (2012): 9–26.

Sandler, Daniel. "The Music Chapters of the *Shiltei Ha-Gibborim*." PhD diss., University of Tel Aviv, 1987.

Sanuto, Marino. *I diarii di Marino Sanuto*. Edited by Rinaldo Fulin et al., vol. 34. Venice: F. Visentini, 1892.

Saperstein, Marc. "Italian Jewish Preaching: An Overview." In *Preachers of the Italian Ghetto*, edited by David B. Ruderman, 85–104. Berkeley and Los Angeles: University of California Press, 1992.

Schaerf, Samuele. *I cognomi degli ebrei d'Italia*. Florence: Casa Editrice "Israel," 1925.

Seebass, Tilman. "Iconography and Dance Research." *Yearbook for Traditional Music* 23 (1991): 33–51.

Segre, Renata. "La Controriforma: espulsioni, conversioni, isolamento." In *Gli ebrei in Italia*, vol. 1, *Dall'alto Medioevo all'età dei ghetti*, Storia d'Italia, Annali 11, edited by Corrado Vivanti, 707–778. Turin: Einaudi, 1996.

Sendrey, Alfred. *Music in Ancient Israel*. London: Vision, 1969.

———. *The Music of the Jews in the Diaspora (up to 1800): A Contribution to the Social and Cultural History of the Jews*. New York: Yoseloff, 1970.

Seroussi, Edwin. "Ghetto Soundscapes: Venice and Beyond." In *Shirat Dvora: Essays in Honor of Professor Dvora Bregman*, edited by Haviva Ishay, 157–171. Beer-Sheva: Ben Gurion University in the Negev Press, 2019.

———. "In Search of Jewish Musical Antiquity in the 18th-Century Venetian Ghetto: Reconsidering the Hebrew Melodies in Benedetto Marcello's *Estro poetico-armonico*." *Jewish Quarterly Review* 93, nos. 1–2 (July–October 2002): 149–199.

———. "In the Footsteps of the Great Jewish Composer." Review of Harrán, *Salamone Rossi*, *Min Ad: Israel Studies in Musicology* 3 (2004): 14–20.

———. "Music: The 'Jew' of Jewish Studies." *Jewish Studies* 46 (2009): 3–84.

———. "The Turkish *Makam* in the Musical Culture of the Ottoman Jews: Sources and Examples." *Israeli Studies in Musicology* 5 (1989): 43–68.

Shear, Adam. "Judah Moscato's Sources and Hebrew Printing in the Sixteenth Century: A Preliminary Survey." In *Rabbi Judah Moscato and the Jewish Intellectual World of Mantua in the 16th–17th Centuries*, edited by Giuseppe Veltri and Gianfranco Miletto, 121–142. Leiden and Boston: Brill, 2012.

——— and Joseph R. Hacker. "Introduction." In *The Hebrew Book in Early Modern Italy*, edited by Joseph R. Hacker and Adam Shear, 1–16. Philadelphia: University of Pennsylvania Press, 2011.

Shtif, Nokhum. "Naye materialn tsu Elye Halevi's *Hamavdil-lid*." *Shriftn* 1 (1928): 148–179.

Shulvass, Moses A. "The Jewish Population in Renaissance Italy." *Jewish Social Studies* 13, no. 1 (1951): 3–24.

Siegmund, Stefanie B. "La vita nei ghetti." In *Gli ebrei in Italia*, vol. 1, *Dall'alto Medioevo all'età dei ghetti*, Storia d'Italia, Annali 11, edited by Corrado Vivanti, 845–892. Turin: Einaudi, 1996.

———. *The Medici State and the Ghetto of Florence: The Construction of an Early Modern Jewish Community*. Stanford, CA: Stanford University Press, 2006.

Simonsohn, Shlomo. *History of the Jews in the Duchy of Mantua*. Jerusalem: Kiryath Sefer, 1977.

———. "Sefarim ve-Sifriyot shel Yehudei Mantova 1595." *Kiryat Sefer* 37 (1961–1962): 103–122.

———, ed. *She'elot u-teshuvot: Ziqne Yehuda*. Jerusalem: Rabbi Kuk Foundation, 1956.

Sisto, Luigi, ed. *Carlo Gesualdo: Gli strumenti musicali*. Gesualdo: Gesualdo, 2017.

———. "I d'Aponte, costruttori di viole a Napoli al tempo dei Gesualdo." In *Carlo Gesualdo e il suo tempo*, Proceedings of the International Symposium (Gesualdo–Salerno 2013), edited by Alberto Granese and Luigi Sisto, 157–182. Avellino: Il Terebinto, 2019.

———. *I liutai tedeschi a Napoli tra Cinque e Seicento. Storia di una migrazione in senso contrario*. Rome: Istituto Italiano per la Storia della Musica, 2010.

———. "La confisca dei beni di Matteo Sansone, musico sefardita (Palermo 1513). Considerazioni sull'introduzione della violecta spagnola in Italia." In *Musica tra storia e filologia*, edited by Federica Nardacci, 1–12. Rome: Istituto Italiano per la Storia della Musica, 2010.

———. "Mutio Effrem e la corte del Principe di Venosa a Gesualdo." In *La musica del Principe: Studi e prospettive per Carlo Gesualdo*, Proceedings of the International Symposium (Venosa–Potenza, September 2003), edited by Luisa Curinga, 19–33. Lucca: Libreria Musicale Italiana, 2008.

Sisto, Michele. "Presenze multietniche in Irpinia: Cristiani novelli ed altre minoranze etniche nell'età Moderna." *Grammata* 2 (2000): 141–185.

Slim, H. Colin. "Some Fifteenth- and Sixteenth-Century Namesakes." *Musical Quarterly* 57 (1971): 562–574.

Slonik, Benjamin Aaron ben Abraham. *Precetti d'esser imparati dalle donne hebree*. Translated by Giacob Alpron. Venice: Gioanni de' Paoli, 1710.

Smith, John Arthur. "Musical Aspects of Old Testament Canticles in Their Biblical Setting." *Early Music History* 17 (1998): 232–233.

Smith, William A. "Jewish Dancing in Wedding Pageantry at Pesaro, Italy in 1475." *Israel Dance Annual* (1987–1988): 11–24.

Soehnlen, Edward J. "Diruta on the Art of Keyboard-Playing: An Annotated Translation and Transcription of *Il Transilvano*, Parts I (1593) and II (1609)." PhD diss., University of Michigan, 1975.

Spagnolo, Francesco. "The Bimah and the Stage: Synagogue Music and Cultural Production in the Italian Ghettos." In *Venice, the Jews, and Europe*, edited by Donatella Calabi, 264–269. Venice: Marsilio, 2016.

———. "La stampa periodica ebraica come fonte per la ricostruzione della vita sinagogale nell'Italia dell'emancipazione." *Materia Giudaica* 9, nos. 1–2 (2004): 265–273.

———. "Music and Synagogue Life" [in Hebrew]. In *Jewish Communities in the East in the Nineteenth and Twentieth Centuries: Italy*, edited by Roni Weinstein, 143–150. Jerusalem: Ben Zvi Institute, 2012.

———. "Scritto in italiano, ascoltato in ebraico: A proposito delle fonti scritte della musica ebraica in Italia." In *Ebraismo in musica: Da Mantova all'Europa e ritorno*, edited by Stefano Patuzzi, 87–101. Mantua: Di Pellegrini, 2011.

Sparti, Barbara. "Dancing in Fifteenth-Century Italian Society." In *Guglielmo Ebreo da Pesaro, De pratica seu arte tripudii: On the Practice or Art of Dancing*, edited and translated by Barbara Sparti, 47–61. Oxford: Clarendon, 1993.

———. "Guglielmo's Life." In Guglielmo Ebreo da Pesaro, *De pratica seu arte tripudii: On the Practice or Art of Dancing*, edited and translated by Barbara Sparti, 23–45. Oxford: Clarendon, 1993.

———. "Jewish Dancing-Masters and 'Jewish Dance' in Renaissance Italy: Guglielmo Ebreo and Beyond." In *Seeing Israeli and Jewish Dance*, edited by Judith Brin Ingber, 235–250. Detroit: Wayne State University Press, 2011.

———. "The Moresca and Mattaccino in Italy—circa 1450–1630." In *Proceedings of the Symposium "Moreska: Past and Present,"* edited by Elsie Ivancich Dunin, 129–142. Zabreb: Institute of Ethnology and Folklore Research, 2002.

———. "Questions concerning the Life and Works of Guglielmo Ebreo." In *Guglielmo Ebreo da Pesaro e la danza nelle corti italiane del XV secolo: Atti del Convegno Internazionale di Studi, Pesaro 16/18 luglio 1987*, edited by Maurizio Padovan, 35–50. Pisa: Pacini, 1990.

———. "Status and Description of *De pratica*." In Guglielmo Ebreo da Pesaro, *De pratica seu arte tripudii: On the Practice or Art of Dancing*, edited and translated by Barbara Sparti, 3–22. Oxford: Clarendon, 1993.

Starkey, David, ed. *Henry VIII: A European Court in England*. London: Collins and Brown, 1991.

Steinsaltz, Adin. *The Talmud: The Steinsaltz Edition: A Reference Guide*. Translated by Israel V. Berman. S.l.: The Israel Institute for Talmudic Publications and Milta Books, 1989.

Stern, Moritz, ed. *Die Lieder des venezianischen Lehrers Gumprecht von Szczebrszyn*. Berlin: Hausfreund, 1922.

Straeten, Edmond Van der. *La musique aux Pays-Bas avant le XIXe siècle*. 8 vols. Brussels, 1867–1888.

Timm, Erika. "Wie Elia Levita sein Bovobuch für den Druck überarbeitete: ein Kapitel aus der italo-jiddischen Literatur der Renaissancezeit." *Germanisch-romanische Monatsschrift* 41, no. 1 (1991): 61–81.

Tinctoris, Johannes. *De inventione et usu musicae*. Naples, ca. 1497.

———. *Johannes Tinctoris (1445–1511) und sein unbekannter Traktat, "De inventione et usu musicae."* Edited by Karl Weinmann. Regensburg: F. Pustet, 1917. Reprint, Tutzing: Wilhelm Fischer, Schneider, 1961.

Toaff, Ariel. "La vita materiale." In *Gli ebrei in Italia*, vol. 1, *Dall'alto Medioevo all'età dei ghetti*, Storia d'Italia, Annali 11, edited by Corrado Vivanti, 237–263. Turin: Einaudi, 1996.

———. *Pasque di sangue: ebrei d'Europa e omicidi rituali*. Bologna: Il mulino, 2008.

Toffolo, Stefano. *Antichi strumenti veneziani, 1500–1800: quattro secoli di liuteria e cembalaria*. Venice: Arsenale, 1987.

Torrefranca, Massimo Acanfora. "Sulle musiche degli ebrei in Italia." In *Gli ebrei in Italia*, vol. 1, *Dall'alto Medioevo all'età dei ghetti*, Storia d'Italia, Annali 11, edited by Corrado Vivanti, 478–493. Turin: Einaudi, 1996.

Traube, Alexandre. "Traces de déclamation dans les recueils de frottole à la fin du XVe siècle: Quelques pistes pour une recherche." In *La Musique ancienne entre historiens et musiciens*, edited by Xavier Bisaro and Rémy Campos, 513–520. Musique & Recherche 3. Geneva: Droz, Haute Ecole de musique de Genève, 2014.

Turniansky, Chava, and Erika Timm, eds., with the collaboration of Claudia Rosenzweig. *Yiddish in Italia: Yiddish Manuscripts and Printed Books from the 15th to the 17th Century*. Milan: Associazione Italiana Amici dell'Università di Gerusalemme, 2003.

Tyndale, William. *An Answer to Sir Thomas More's Dialogue, the Supper of the Lord after the True Meaning of John VI and 1 Cor. XI*. Cambridge: Cambridge University Press, 1850.

———. *Doctrinal Treatises and Introductions to Different Portions of the Holy Scriptures*. Edited by Henry Walter. Cambridge: Parker Society, 1848.

———. *The Works of English Reformers: William Tyndale and John Frith*. Edited by Thomas Russell. Vol. 2. London: Ebenezer Palmer, 1831.

Vallensis, Johannes. *Opus de prosodia Hebraeorum in quatuor libros divisum*. Paris: Jacobum Bogardum, 1545.

Veltri, Giuseppe. *Alienated Wisdom: Enquiry into Jewish Philosophy and Scepticism*. Berlin and Boston: De Gruyter, 2018.

———. "Le accademie ebraiche a Venezia." In *Oltre le mura del Ghetto: Accademie, scetticismo e tolleranza nella Venezia barocca*, by Giuseppe Veltri and Evelien Chayes, 37–45. Palermo: New Digital Frontiers, 2016.

———. "Le accademie italiane e gli ebrei." In *Oltre le mura del Ghetto: Accademie, scetticismo e tolleranza nella Venezia barocca*, by Giuseppe Veltri and Evelien Chayes, 15–36 Palermo: New Digital Frontiers, 2016.

———. "Un accademico scettico: Simone Luzzatto." In *Oltre le mura del Ghetto: Accademie, scetticismo e tolleranza nella Venezia barocca*, by Giuseppe Veltri and Evelien Chayes, 147–173. Palermo: New Digital Frontiers, 2016.

——— and Evelien Chayes. Introduction to *Oltre le mura del Ghetto: Accademie, scetticismo e tolleranza nella Venezia barocca*, 9–14. Palermo: New Digital Frontiers, 2016.

Veronese, Alessandra. "Gli ebrei nel ducato di Urbino tra cinque e seicento: insediamenti, economia e societa." *Materia giudaica: Rivista dell'associazione italiana per lo studio del giudaismo* 10, no. 1 (2005): 111–122.

———. "La presenza ebraica nel ducato di Urbino nel Quattrocento." In *Italia Judaica: Gli ebrei nello Stato pontificio fino al Ghetto (1555): Atti del VI Convegno internazionale, Tel Aviv, 18–22 giugno 1995*, 251–283. Rome: Ministero per i beni culturali e ambientali ufficio centrale per i beni archivistici, 1998.

———. *Una famiglia di banchieri ebrei tra XIV e XVI secolo: I da Volterra. Reti di credito nell'Italia del Rinascimento*. Pisa: Edizioni ETS, 1998.

———. "Una societas ebraico-christiana *in docendo tripudiare ac cantare* nella Firenze del Quattrocento." In *Guglielmo Ebreo da Pesaro e la danza nelle corti italiane del XV secolo: Atti del Convegno Internazionale di Studi, Pesaro 16/18 luglio 1987*, edited by Maurizio Padovan, 51–57. Pisa: Pacini, 1990.

Vespasiano da Bisticci. *Vite di uomini illustri del secolo XV*. Edited by Paolo d'Ancona and Erhard Aeschlimann. Milan: Ulrico Hoepli, 1951.

Virdung, Sebastian. *Musica getutscht*. Basel: M. Furter, 1511.

Viterbo, Lazzaro da. *Il Tempio di M. Moise di Riete, trasportato in vulgare Italiano*. Venice: Giovanni De Gara, ca. 1585. Facsimile: Hebrew Books. Accessed April 10, 2019. http://www.hebrewbooks.org/pdfpager.aspx?req=42193.

Vivarelli, Carla. "'Di una pretesa scuola napoletana': Sowing the Seeds of the *Ars nova* at the Court of Robert of Anjou." *Journal of Musicology* 24, no. 2 (2007): 272–296.

Volterra, Mešullam da. *Viaggio in Terra d'Israele*. Translated by Alessandra Veronese. Rimini: Luisè, 1989.

Walker, Jonathan. "Gambling and Venetian Noblemen, c. 1500–1700." *Past & Present* 162 (February 1999): 28–69.

Wegman, Rob C. "What Is Counterpoint?" In *Improvising Early Music: The History of Musical Improvisation from the Late Middle Ages to the Early Baroque*, Collected Writings of the Orpheus Institute 11, edited by Dirk Moelants, 9–68. Leuven: Leuven University Press, 2014.

Weil, Gérard. *Élie Lévita: humaniste et massorète*. Studia Post Biblica 7. Leiden: E. J. Brill, 1963.
Weir, Alison. *Henry VIII: King and Court*. London: Jonathan Cape, 2001.
Wendland, John. "'Madre non mi far Monaca': The Biography of a Renaissance Folksong." *Acta Musicologica* 48, fasc. 2 (1976): 185–204.
Westwater, Lynn Lara. *Sarra Copia Sulam: A Jewish Salonnière and the Press in Counter-Reformation Rome*. Toronto: University of Toronto Press, 2020.
Wilbourne, Emily. "*Lo Schiavetto* (1612): Travestied Sound, Ethnic Performance, and the Eloquence of the Body." *Journal of the American Musicological Society* 63, no. 1 (Spring 2010): 1–43.
———. *Seventeenth-Century Opera and the Sound of Commedia dell'Arte*. Chicago: University of Chicago Press, 2016.
Wilson, Blake. "The *Cantastoria/Canterino/Cantimbanco* as Musician." *Italian Studies* 71, no. 2 (2016): 154–170.
———. "*Canterino* and *improvvisatore*: Oral Poetry and Performance." In *The Cambridge History of Fifteenth-Century Music*, edited by Anna Maria Busse Berger and Jesse Rodin, 292–310. Cambridge: Cambridge University Press, 2015.
———. "Dominion of the Ear: Singing the Vernacular in Piazza San Martino." *Tatti Studies in the Italian Renaissance* 16, no. 1/2 (2013): 273–287.
Witten, Lawrence C. "Apollo, Orpheus, and David: A Study of the Crucial Century in the Development of Bowed Strings in North Italy 1480–1580 as Seen in Graphic Evidence and Some Surviving Instruments." *Journal of the American Musical Instrument Society* 1 (1975): 5–55.
Wolf, Lucien. "Jews in Tudor England." In *Essays in Jewish History*, edited by Cecil Roth, 73–90. London: Jewish Historical Society of England, 1934.
Woodfield, Ian. *The Early History of the Viol*. Cambridge: Cambridge University Press, 1984. Translated by Cristiano Contadin and Alberto Ponchio and edited by Renato Meucci as *La viola da gamba dalle origini al Rinascimento*. Torino: EDT, 1999.
Wriothesley, Charles. *A Chronicle of England during the Reigns of the Tudors, from A.D. 1485 to 1559*. Edited by William Douglas Hamilton. Vol. 1. London: Camden Society, 1875–1877.
Yates, Frances A. "The Italian Academies." In *Selected Works of Frances A. Yates*, vol. 9, *Renaissance and Reform: The Italian Contribution*, 6–28. London, New York: Routledge, 1983.
Zambotti, Bernardo. *Diario ferrarese dall'anno 1476 sino al 1504*. Edited by Giuseppe Pardi. Rerum italicarum scriptores XXIV, parte VII. Bologna: Nicola Zanichelli, 1934.
Zeldes, Nadia. "The Converted Jews of Sicily before and after the Expulsion (1460–1550)." PhD diss., Tel Aviv University, 1997.
———. "Dress, Dancing and Music: Aspects of Renaissance Culture among Sicilian Jews and Converts." In *Le usate leggiadrie. I cortei, le cerimonie, le feste e il costume nel Mediterraneo tra XV e XVI secolo*, edited by Gemma T. Colesanti, 222–236. Montella: Edizioni Dragonetti, 2009.
———. *"The Former Jews of This Kingdom": Sicilian Converts after the Expulsion, 1492–1516*. Leiden and Boston: Brill, 2003.
Zonta, Mauro. "La filosofia ebraica medievale in Sicilia." In *Ebrei e Sicilia*, edited by Nicolò Bucaria, Michele Luzzati, and Angela Tarantino, 163–168. Palermo: Flaccovio, 2002.

PRINTED SCORES

Bassano, Giovanni. *Ricercate, passaggi et cadentie, per potersi essercitar nel diminuir terminatamente con ogni sorte d'istrumento*. Venice: Vincenti and Amadino, 1585, 2/1598.

Dalla Casa, Girolamo. *Il vero modo di diminuire*. 2 vols. Venice: Gardano, 1584.
Marcello, Benedetto. *Estro poetico-armonico: Parafrasi sopra li salmi*. Venice: Domenico Lovisa, 1724–1726.
Milano, Francesco da. *Intavolatura per viola overo lauto*. Naples, 1536. Reprint, Geneva: Minkoff, 1988.
Musiche de alcuni eccellentissimi musici composte per la Maddalena, Sacra Rappresentazione di Gio. Battista Andreini Fiorentino. Venice: Bartolomeo Magni, 1617.
Nanino, Giovanni Maria. *Il primo libro delle canzonette a tre voci*. Venice: Angelo Gardano, 1593.
Ortiz, Diego. *Trattado de glosas sobre clausulas*. 2 vols. Rome: Dorico, 1553.
Rognoni, Riccardo (Richard Rogniono). *Passaggi per potersi essercitare nel diminuire terminatamente con ogni sorte d'instromenti*. 2 vols. Venice: Vincenti, 1592.
Rossi, Salamone. *Complete Works*. 13 vols. S.l.: American Institute of Musicology and Neuhausen: Hänssler, 1995–.
———. *Ha-shirim 'asher li-Shlomo*. Venice: Pietro and Lorenzo Bragadini, in the house of Giovanni Calleoni, [5]383 [=1622–1623].
———. *Il primo libro delle sinfonie et gagliarde a tre, quatro, & cinque voci*. Venice: Amadino, 1607.
———. *Il secondo libro delle sinfonie è gagliarde à tre voci*. Venice: Amadino, 1608.
———. *Il terzo libro de varie sonate, sinfonie, gagliarde, brandi, e corrente*. Venice: Vincenti, [1613?].
———. *Instrumental Works: Sonatas, Sinfonie, etc., Book 3*. Edited with introduction and notes by Don Harrán. Complete Works, part 2, vol. 11. S.l.: American Institute of Musicology and Neuhausen: Hänssler, 1995.
———. *Sacred Vocal Works in Hebrew: Hashirim 'asher lishlomo / "The Songs of Solomon."* Edited with introduction and notes by Don Harrán. Complete Works, part 3, vols. 13a and 13b. S.l.: American Institute of Musicology and Neuhausen: Hänssler, 2003.
Strambotti, ode, sonetti et modo de cantar versi latini e capituli, Libro quarto. Petrucci: Venice, [1505].
Vecchi, Oratio. *Canzonette di Oratio Vecchi da Modona, Libro primo a quattro voci*. Venice: Angelo Gardano, 1580.

DISCOGRAPHY

APORIE (Archivio e Portale informatico sulla Poesia in Ottava Rima Estemporanea): Filmographia. Accessed December 28, 2019. http://www.aporie.it/filmografia.html.
Banca della Memoria del Casentino. Accessed December 28, 2019. https://www.youtube.com/channel/UCPlyRdTc9JdrU3i3hz-mZOA.
Borbona—Festival di canto a braccio 2009—Ottave di saluto. June 23, 2010. Accessed December 28, 2019. https://www.youtube.com/watch?v=iwGCCx9Po5A.
Buzzetta, Flavia. *Ottava di Morgana, dall'Orlando Innamorato per Flavia Buzzetta*. January 4, 2013. Accessed December 28, 2019. https://www.youtube.com/watch?v=elFosR9pw4M.
Centro Tradizioni Popolare della Provincia di Lucca. Accessed December 28, 2019. http://www.centrotradizionipopolari.it/index.php?id=1&lang=it.
D'Amico, Leonardo. *Cantar l'ottava: Progetto pilota per un documentario sui poeti in ottava rima realizzato da Leonardo D'Amico*. July 27, 2016. Accessed December 28, 2019. https://www.youtube.com/watch?v=bMXdDJzfomw and https://www.youtube.com/watch?v=iwGCCx9Po5A.

Ensemble Lucidarium. *La Istoria de Purim: Musique et poésie des Juifs en Italie à la Renaissance.* Audio recording. Sarrebourg: K617, 2005.

———. *Sounds from Shylock's Venice.* Audio recording. Abbaye de Bonmont: Ramée / Outhere, in production.

———. *Una musa plebea: Everyday Music from Renaissance Italy.* Audio recording. Raumklang, RK 2410, 2011. Accessed December 28, 2019. https://soundcloud.com/ensemble-lucidarium /ottave-from-orlando-furioso.

——— with Enrico Fink, Gloria Moretti, and Marie-Pierre Duceau. "Tzur mi-shelo," live performance at the Musica Cortese Early Music Festival, Gorizia, 2011. https://www.youtube .com/watch?v=uim-XWuj8MQ&list=FLe6CoIDQQfEZsxvCN9oqtpw&index=7&t=0s.

Poliziano, Angelo. *La fabula di Orpheo.* Audio recording. La Compagnia dell'Orpheo, directed by Francis Biggi. Sarrebourg: K617, 2007.

Spadi, Gelasio. *L'Orlando innamorato di Gelasio Spadi.* Banca della Memoria del Casentino. October 25, 2016. Accessed December 28, 2019. https://www.youtube.com/watch?v=4B5hTcluyEQ.

INDEX

Page numbers in italics refer to figures, tables, and musical examples.

Aaron, Pietro: as cantor, 97; *Compendio di molti dubbi, segreti et sentenze intorno al canto fermo* (attributed), 106n4; as convert, 8, 9, 16, 92–105; education of, 93–96, 105; family members of, 100–103; as friar of the Order of the Crociferi, 99; "Io non posso più durare" (frottola), 94; *Libri tres de institutione harmonica*, 93, 96–97, 100, 106n3, 108n23; *Lucidario in musica*, 99–100, 105, 106n4, 108n22; name of, 103; as priest, 97; salary of, 98; *Toscanello de la musica*, 92–93, 94, 95, 98, 100, 106n1, 106n2, 107n5, 108n23; *Trattato della natura et cognition di tutti gli tuoni di canto figurato*, 100, 106n4, 108n22
Abel (biblical), 48
Aboab, Samuel, 245
Abravanel, Don Isaac, 221–222, 224, 231n66
academies, 233–234, 245–246, 247, 249n4, 250n11, 254n44; Accademia degli Impediti, 3, 18, 215, 233–248; Accademia degli Incogniti, 246–247, 256n74, 256n75, 256n76; Accademia della Fama, 245; Accademia Filarmonica (Bologna), 245; Accademia Filarmonica (Verona), 245, 256n67; L'Accademia degli Invaghiti, 246
Achinstein, Sharon, 150, 155
Adam (biblical), 46
Adelkind, Conrad, 139n31
Adelman, Howard, 236, 241, 254n45, 255n64
Adler, Israel, 4, 25, 27, 35, 35n1, 124, 235, 238, 251n23
Agricola, Alexander, 93
Albanese, Orazio, 174

Alberti, Gasparo, 99
Alessandria, 33
Alessandro VI (pope), 167
Alexander-Skipnes, Ingrid, 73
alfabeto notation, 204, 228n30
Alfonso of Aragon (king of Aragon, king of Naples), 104, 167
Alpron, Giacob, 118
Amadis of Gaul (poem), 118
Amati family, 178
d'Amato, Geronimo, 178, 183n47
Ambrose (Saint), 15, 37, 38, 42–45; *Hexameron*, 15, 37–38, 42–45
Anatoli, Jacob, 45
Andreini, Giovan Battista, 178
Angevin family, 46, 60n39
anti-Judaism, antisemitism, 1–2, 6, 11–12, 67, 72–73, 78, 103, 147, 149–152, 154, 156, 236, 247, 248. *See also* Jews
Antonio, Vito, 176
Antwerp, 151, 152, 158
d'Aponte dynasty, 178
Apuleius, *Metamorphoses, Golden Ass*, 37
Apulia, 174, 177, 182n36
Aquinas, Thomas, 46
Arabic grammar, texts, 45, 46, 87n31, 156
Arabic poetry, Arabic-Andalusian poetry, 37, 124, 142n56
d'Aragona, Camilla, 74
Aragonese court, 75, 167–168, 180n10. *See also* Ferdinando I
Arbëreshë, 174
Archivolti, Samuel (Shemuel), 28, 241
d'Arco, Niccolò, 105, 110n57

285

arie, arie per cantar stanze (recitation formulas), 16, 111–114, 119, 123–136, 140n39, 204, 212, 214; *Romanesca*, 204–210, 212, 228n29, 229n31; *Ruggiero*, 204, 212, 228n27
Ariosto, Ludovico, 113, 118, *121*, 138n14, 140n38, 141–142n54, 124, 204, 241
Aronne da Este, Buonaventura (Ventura) di (also Giovanni Battista), 100–103
dall'Arpa, Abraham Halevi, 239, 255n54
dall'Arpa, Abramino Halevi, 20n12, 233, 239, 253n32
dell'Arpa, Giovan Leonardo, *176*
'asor. *See* musical instruments
Avenary, Hanoch, 25

bagpipe (*cornamusa*). *See* musical instruments
ballerini. *See* dance: dancing masters
balli, 238
Barbad (musician at the court of Khosrow II), 83
Bardi family, 46
Bartolocci, Giulio, 24, 30, 32, 35n1
Basel, 154, 158
Bassano family, 144–159, 179; banishment from Bassano del Grappa, 146; Bassano, Alvise, 145, 148–149; Bassano, Anthony I, 146; Bassano, Antony "the Sagbut," 153; Bassano, Jacomo, 146; Bassano, Jasper, 153; Bassano, Jeronimo, 148; Bassano, John, 153; Bassano, Loyses, 153; move to England, 144–159; responses to economic circumstances, 148; surname of, 145, 160n5
basse danse, 80, 199, 226n9
Beit-Arié, Malachi, 141–142n54
Bellafiore, daughter of Dolce di Daniele di Vitale da Pisa, 102–103, 109n39
"Bella gerit," 80. *See also* Montefeltro (dynasty)
Benigni, Maria Luisa Moscati, 73
Bergamo, 108n24; Confraternity of Santa Maria Maggiore, 99
Bernardino "dalli violini," 179
Bible, 58n5, 72, 74, 151, 154, 220; Hebrew Bible, 54, 37–45, 47–49, 83, 103, 119, 122, 139n22, 152, 198, 220–221; Hosea, 19n7; influence on *Decameron*, 37–50, 57; New Testament, 48; poetry and prose in, 39, 48–49, 58n4, 58n8; Psalms, 4, 28, 39, 44–45, 48–49, 55, 62n77, 116, 139n31, 140n32, 186–187, 192, 220–222, 234, 237, 249–250n8; Song at the

Sea (Miriam's Song), 15, 37, 39, 42, 43, 44, 51, 57, 221
Birnbaum, Eduard, 235, 250n13, 255n53
birdsong, 44–45, 53
Bisticci, Vespasiano da, 72
blood libel, 22n38, 146–147, 150
Boccaccio, Giovanni, 12, 15, 37–38, 43, 45–57, 113; connection to Jewish/Hebrew musical thought, 37–38, 48, 52, 57; connection to Jewish writings, 45–46, 48, 49; *Decameron*, 15, 37–57; exposure to Jewish culture, 45–47; *Genealogy of the Pagan Gods (De Genealogia Deorum Gentilium)*, 38, 46–49, 58n4; laude, 47, 49, 52, 54, 61n54
Bokher, Elye (also Eliyahu ben Asher HaLevi Ashkenazi, Elia Bachur Levita, Elijah Levita), 12, 16, 111–136; *Bovo d'Antona* (also *Bovo Bukh*), 111–116, 118, 120–122, 124, 135, 140n32; *Dás lid ouf di śěrěfę yun Wěnědig* (also *Śěrěfę lid*), 111, 112, 114, 116, *117*, 120, *121, 122, 123*–130, 131–132, 142n61; *HaMav̆dil lid*, 111–112, 114, 116, *118*, 120–122, 130–135, *134, 135*, 142n61; *Paris un Wiene* (attributed), 115–116
Bolino, Luca, *176*
Bologna, 93, 96, 102, 107n9, 110n57; Concerto Palatino, 149; Convent of Corpus Domini, 172. *See also* academies: Accademia Filarmonica (Bologna)
Bologna, Jacopo da, 49
Bolognese, Annibale, *176*
Bonaventura, Arnaldo, 50, 52
Bonfil, Robert, 9–12, 18, 146–148, 186, 189, 191, 193, 195n16, 219, 235–236, 241, 247
Bonini, Pier Maria, 93
Borgia dynasty, 166–167; Borgia, Alonso, 166 (*see also* Callistus III); Borgia, Rodrigo, 167. *See also* Alessandro VI
Borzi, Camillo, 89n56
Bragadini (printers), 27, 30, 187. *See also* Rossi, Salamone: *Ha-shirim 'asher li-Shlomo*
Branca, Vittoria, 37, 61n65
Brancaleone, Gentile, 75
Brescia, 100, 105, 147, 178
Brescia, Giovan Maria of, 179
brigata. *See* Boccaccio, Giovanni: *Decameron*
Brown, Howard Meyer, 49
Bubbe mayses (Yiddish phrase), 111
Buonaventura da Este, Aronne di, 100–102
Burattelli, Claudia, 238–239, 251n24, 252n26

Cain (biblical), 48
Cairo Genizah, 220
Callistus III (pope), 166–167
Callo, Marco de, 174
Caltelano, Fabio, 176
cantastorie, 113, 119, 138n11, 204.
    See also *arie, arie per cantar stanze* (recitation formulas)
cantata, cantatas, 34
cantillation, 48, 200, 220, 222
cantillation marks (for liturgical recitation of Hebrew texts), *te'amim*, 32, 198, 200, 220–221, 230n57
cantor, 1, 2, 11, 24, 28, 32, 197, 211, 240.
    See also Aaron, Pietro: as cantor; Modena, Leon: as cantor
cantus firmus, 199, 226n9
canzona, 202
canzonetta, canzonette, 53, 140n39, 198, 224, 243, 254n52
canzon per sonar, 202, 203
Capistrano, Giovanni da, 67
Cardone, F., 176
Caroso, Fabritio, 203, 228n26
Casale, John, 151–152
Casale Monferrato, 24, 25, 28, 29, 33–34
Caso, Luise, 176
Casteldurante, 65
Castiglione, Baldassare, 63–64, 85n2
Catalano, Antonio, 174
Catalans, 166–167, 171
Catherine of Aragon, 144, 151
Catholicism, 33, 92, 93, 97, 146, 151, 153, 155–159, 179, 191, 193–194; Catholic musicians, 33–34; Catholic Reformation, 153–154, 243, 255n54; conversion to, 77, 151, 239
Cebà, Ansaldo, 246, 257n77
Cerreto, Scipione, 175, 176
Certaldo, 46
chanson, 80, 137n6, 205
Charlemagne, 137n6
Charles I (Charles of Anjou), 45
Charles V (Holy Roman Emperor), 152
Charles VIII (king of France), 102
Chayes, Evelien, 234–236, 249n8, 256n74
chitarrone. See musical instruments
choir, choirs, 31, 33, 39, 52, 61n65, 99, 189, 213, 237, 239–240, 253n35, 255n53

Christianity, 1, 3–5, 7–12, 14–17, 30, 38–40, 42, 43, 45–50, 64, 66–69, 72, 74, 75, 77, 84, 93, 100, 102–105, 112, 114–115, 166, 168, 177, 178, 179, 189, 198, 217, 219–221, 235, 239, 241–243, 246–248; Catholics in England, 146, 151, 153–158; Christian Hebraism, 10, 142n57, 156; Christian musical cultures, 24–28, 30, 32–34, 37, 242; Protestants in England; 144–158. See also Catholicism; church; conversion; Jewish/Hebrew music: compared to Christian music; Jews: interactions with non-Jews
church, 2, 3, 12, 43, 44, 67, 86n13, 93, 98, 99, 103–105, 109n48, 145, 148, 149, 154–158, 162n67, 170, 184n52, 198, 202, 228n23, 237, 242, 254n45
Cicilia, Moysè de (Musetto or Moses of Sicily), 75
classicism, 78, 236–247, 251n19
Clement VII (pope), 151
Clough, Cecil, 63
Coelho, Victor, 152–153
Cohen, Judith, 40, 59n20
Coimbram, Rabbi Moses, 3, 19–20n7, 211, 229n36
Collegium Neophytorum (Venice), 30
commedie, 238
Consiglio da Toscanella, Jacob di, 101
Constantinople, fall of, 71
"contribution discourse," 4, 6, 64, 160n4, 165–166
conversion, 2, 4, 8, 9, 14, 16, 20n12, 26, 28, 46–47, 67, 69–71, 77–78, 84, 89n55, 92–105, 150, 152, 156, 160n5, 165–166, 170, 172, 175, 177–179, 180n8, 181n16, 184n52, 220, 235, 239, 251n23, 253n32
Cornaro, Giacomo, 99
cornetto. See musical instruments
Cortese, Martio, 176
Cortese, Ottavio, 175, 176
Coryat, Thomas (*Coryat's Crudities*), 1–2, 223, 257n80
Coulter, Cornelia C., 46
counterpoint, 96, 99, 192, 202
Cromwell, Thomas, 149
Crusades, 80
Cuccurullo, Jacopo Antonio, 174
Cuneo, Zatri di, 121
cymbal. See musical instruments

Dalla Casa, Girolamo, 209, 229n33
dance, 3, 5, 37–40, 42, 49–57, 58n9, 73–80, 82–83, 90n67, 104, 146, 191, 198, 202–204; as a cultural intermediary between Jews and Christians, 74, 83, 146; dancing masters, 78, 82, 89n59, 110n52 (*see also* Jews: as teachers of dance; Ebreo da Pesaro, Guglielmo [later Giovanni Ambrosio]); in Exodus (Miriam's Song at the Sea), 38, 39, 49, 57; *gagliarda*, 191, 228n26; as a humanistic art, 78–79, 83–84; images of, 39, 40–42, 58n12, 58n13, 82; instrumental dance music, 191, 198, 202–204, 227n21; at the marriage of Costanzo Sforza and Camilla d'Aragona in Pesaro, 74–75, 76; *moresca, moresche*, 74, 76, 88n40; in the *Music* panel, 80–82; *passamezzo*, 203–204; as praise, 39, 50; role in Jewish life and culture, 3, 5, 40, 50, 58n9, 73–74, 83–84; *tordiglione*, 203. *See also* Boccaccio, Giovanni: *Decameron*
Daniele, Isaia di maestro, 65
Dante Alighieri (*Divine Comedy*), 52, *121*
Dato, Mordechai, 119, *121*, 122, 124
David (biblical king of Israel), 27, 28, 43, 48–49, 192, 221–222
Dentice, Fabrizio, *176*
Dentice, Scipione, 177
desecration of the Host, 67, 145
Des Prez, Josquin, 93
Diaspora, 217, 234, 251n21
diminution, 204–206, 209–210, 228n29, 229n33, 229n34; manual of, 205, 229n31, 229n33, 229n34
Drei, Francesco, 34
drum. *See* musical instruments
durezze e ligature (dissonances and suspensions), 205

early modern as a term and concept, 7–10
Ebreo da Pesaro, Giuseppe, 75, 77, 89n44, 89n55, 104
Ebreo da Pesaro, Guglielmo (later Giovanni Ambrosio), 7, 14, 16, 75–84, 89n47, 90n66, 104; conversion to Christianity, 77–78, 84; at the court of Urbino, 76, 78–84; *De pratica seu arte tripudii*, 75, 77, 79, 82, 104; as Knight of the Golden Spur, 75, 77, 78, 104; as musician, 14, 16, 78–79, 80, 82, 84; Pietro Paolo (Pierpaolo) (son of Guglielmo Ebreo da Pesaro), 76; presence in Urbino imagery, 79–84; as theorist, 79, 84. *See also* Ghent, Joos van: *Music*
education, musical, 47, 93–94. *See also* Jews: musical education of
Edward IV (king of England), 158
Effrem, Mutio, 177–178, 183n45
Egypt, Egyptian, 38, 43, 47, 61n50
Emancipation, 23, 27, 33
Emanuele da Volterra, Buonaventura di, 101, 102, 109n36
emic vs. etic, 186, 189–191, 195n15
England, 17, 144–146, 148, 152–153, 158; Act of the Six Articles, 154; status of Jews in, 145, 148–152, 159, 178; tensions between Protestants and Catholics, 153–155. *See also* Bassano family: move to England; Jews: expulsion from England
Epstein, Marc, 40
Esslingen, 125
Este dynasty: d'Este, Eleonora, 103; d'Este, Ercole, 103; d'Este, Ippolito I (cardinal), 110n53; d'Este, Isabella, 78, 171, 179; d'Este, Leonello, 104
Este (town of), 100
Esther (biblical book), 119, 120, 124, 141n49
estrangement, 28
Ettore, Benedetto di, 96
Eucharist, 71, 155, 157, 159, 162n67
Europa, Madama, 6, 239
Exodus (biblical book), 15, 37, 38–40, 42–44, 48–52, 57, 58n12, 221, 231n65, 251n21

Fagius, Paul, 114–115
Faraj of Girgenti, 45
Farissol, Abraham, 28
Fassler, Margot, 163n76
Felis, Stefano, 177
Feltre, Bernardino da, 67, 103
Ferdinand I (Holy Roman Emperor), 255n54
Ferdinand II of Aragon (king of Spain), 151
Ferdinando I (Ferrante d'Aragona, king of Naples), 167, 168
Ferrara, 93, 103–104, 110n53, 132, 177; musical society in, 245; Sala del tesoro, Palazzo Costabili, 172; synagogue practice in, 2–3, 186, 211–212, 240, 253n40
Ferrer, Antonio, 168
Filelfo, Giovanni Mario, 79
Finlay, Robert, 147
Finzi, Ya'aqov Halewi, 28

Flaminio, Giovanni Antonio, 96–97, 105; *Sylvarum libri II*, 96
Flaminio, Marc'Antonio, 105
Flanders, 158
Florence, 12, 46, 57, 75, 92–93, 96, 97, 101–104, 158; Otto di guardia, 101, 103; SS. Annunziata, 93
flute. *See* musical instruments
folk music and practices, 111, 113, 132, 212
Fossombrone, 65
Foxe, John (*Acts and Monuments*—also called *Book of Martyrs*), 17, 144–145, 149–151, 153–159, 159n2
Frakes, Jerold C., 123
Francesco Maria II (duke of Urbino), 85, 87n31
Francese, Enrico (Herrico), 175, 176
Franciscan order, 66, 77, 147
Frederick II (king of Sicily and Holy Roman Emperor), 45, 47
Frederick III (Holy Roman Emperor), 75, 104
Frederick III (king of Sicily), 181n24
Friuli, Cividale del, 132
Fulbert of Chartres, 163n76

Gaffurio, Franchino, 107n7, 217
Gallichi, Volunio (Zevulun), 34
Gallo, Domenico, 176
Ganassi, Silvestro, 174
Gastoldi, Giovanni Giacomo, 244
Genesis, 42–44, 52, 59n22
Germany, 4, 13, 24, 74, 114–115, 234, 242; German-Jewish song and poetry, 32, 112, 115, 124–125, 142n61; German Jews, 9, 74, 111, 113, 114, 116, 121, 132, 136
Geste Francor, 113. *See also* Matter of France
Gesualdo, Carlo (prince of Venosa), 175, 177, 183n41
Ghent, Joos van, 69–83; *Communion of the Apostles*, 69–72; *Dialectic*, 82, 90n70; *Music*, 80–83, *81*
ghettos, 2, 3, 9, 11–12, 23, 27, 30, 34, 147, 189; Mantua, 4, 17, 18, 186–189, 192, 193, 235; Urbino, 16, 64, 85, 88n32; Venice, 11, 12, 114, 145, 147, 233–236, 238, 241–242, 245–248 (*see also* Venice)
Ghivizzani, Alessandro, 178
Giles of Viterbo, 114
gitit. *See* musical instruments
Golb, Norman, 25

Golden, Kedem, 243
Gonzaga, Ferdinando (duke of Mantua), 178
Gonzaga, Vincenzo (duke of Mantua), 187, 189
Gonzaga court, 17–18, 178, 192–193, 198, 204, 216, 233, 239, 243–245, 248, 253n37, 255n54; ducal chapel of Santa Barbara, 193, 198; musicians at, 17–18, 178, 198, 216, 230n46, 233, 239, 243–245, 248, 253n37, 255n54; productions at, 198, 216, 233, 239, 243–245. *See also* Gonzaga, Ferdinando (duke of Mantua); Gonzaga, Vincenzo (duke of Mantua); Mantua
Gonzaga family, 175, 198, 216, 226n5, 230n46, 233, 243
Goody, Jack, 210, 226n15, 227n15, 227n20
Graziano, Shelomoh ben Mordekhai, 28
Greek arts and thought, 50, 64, 73, 87n31, 97, 247; concepts of justice and harmony, 40; "Greek song" (Talmudic discussion), 19n7; music of the spheres, 43; narratives, 37; poetry, 48 (*see also* poetry); texts, 46
Gregory of Tours, 157, 163n76; *Glory of the Martyrs*, 157
Grimani, Marco, 109n48
Grindal (chaplain of Bishop Nicholas Ridley), 154
Grossi, Carlo, 34
Gubbio, 65, 73, 82
Gugnasco, Lorenzo, 171, 179
Guidobaldi, Nicoletta, 79–80, 82–83
guitar (*giterra, chitarra a sette corde*). *See* musical instruments

Hacker, Joseph R., 219
HaCohen, Ruth, 1, 223, 227n82
Haggadahs, 14, 15, 40, 41, 42, 58n14, 140n35; Golden Haggadah, 40–42, *42*; Sarajevo Haggadah, 40, 42; Sephardic and Ashkenazic, 40
Ha-Kohen, Rabbi Isaac, 156
halakha (Jewish law), 3–5, 10, 47, 139n22, 152, 190, 210–212, 240, 247; pertaining to music, 210–212
Halfan, Elijah Menahem, 152
ḥalil. *See* musical instruments
Ha-mavdil bein qodesh le-ḥol (*piyyut*), 131–132, 142n61, 142–143n64
HaRomi, Immanuel (also Immanuel Romano), 47, 54, 222

harp. *See* musical instruments
harpsichord, chromatic (*cimbalo cromatico*). *See* musical instruments
Harrán, Don, 6–7, 19n7, 20–21n19, 27, 37–38, 185–186, 190, 215, 229n36, 234, 235, 243–244, 246, 253n34, 255n55
Harvell, Edmund, 149, 152, 158
Hasan, Uzun (king of Persia), 69, 87n26
Hebreo, Giovan Maria (also Johannes Maria de Medicis) (count of Verucchio), 104, 110n53
Hebrew (language), 4, 6, 13, 15, 18, 20n9, 24–25, 28, 32–33, 37, 45–46, 58n5, 64, 72–74, 83, 84, 87n31, 109n36, 112, 114–117, 120, 121, 124, 125, 142n61, 152, 156, 163n72, 210, 212, 220, 237, 242, 243; book printing, 4, 9, 17–18, 25, 30, 114, 139n31, 185–187, 190–191, 193, 195n7, 197–198, 219–220, 223–224, 226n2, 230n51; diacritic vowel markings, 224; linguistic kinship with Italian, 236, 241–243; in traditional education, 242
Henry VII (king of England), 158
Henry VIII (king of England), 17, 144–145, 151–155, 158–159, 163–164n85, 174, 178; correspondence with Venetian rabbis concerning his divorce from Catherine of Aragon, 144, 151–152
Holbein the younger, Hans, 158
Horenbout family, 158–159
host desecration, 67, 68, 72
humanism, 3, 5, 6, 14, 32, 38, 63–64, 78–79, 96–97, 110n57, 115, 233, 235, 241, 245–247
hunting horn (*cornecto di caccia*). *See* musical instruments
hymns, 44, 52, 187, 200, 212

Ibn Ghayyat, Isaac Judah, 142–143n64
Idelsohn, Abraham, 4, 235
Imola, 96–98, 107n9, 107n12, 110n57; San Cassiano, 97–98
improvisation, 4, 18, 118, 138n14, 198–199, 202–205, 209–214, 226n9, 228n23; formulas for, 113, 199–204, 206. *See also arie, arie per cantar stanze* (recitation formulas); *cantastorie*; poetry: epic (heroic verse); polyphony: improvised
Inquisition, 151–152, 159, 170, 174, 242
intermedio, 244–245
Isaac, Heinrich, 93
Isaac (Persian ambassador), 69–72, 84, 87n21, 87n26

Isabella I of Castille (queen of Spain), 151
Isacco da Pisa, Vitale di, 101, 102
Israelites, 38–39, 43, 48, 220
istromento da corpo. *See* musical instruments
Italian (language), 121, 197, 236, 241–242

Jesus (biblical), 48, 69, 71, 155, 158
Jewish/Hebrew music: ancient tradition, 38, 40, 44, 50, 141n45, 190, 220–221, 225; chant, 48, 132; Christian perceptions of, 1–2, 33, 223, 247–248; Christian performers of, 25, 27, 33; compared to Christian music, 2–3, 15, 112, 185–186, 191–194, 198; fieldwork concerning, 32–33, 125; historiography of, 4–7, 23–25; imitation by non-Jewish composers, 3; "Jewish music" or "Hebrew music" as terms, 7–8, 185–186, 190, 192; librettos, 25, 33; liturgical, 1–2, 4, 25, 26, 33–34, 11, 190–194, 197–198, 200, 239–241, 243–244; and *makam*, rhythmic modes, 11, 222; manuscript production of, 23, 25, 28, 33, 130–131, 141n46, 187; musical theater, 3, 4, 189; mutual collaboration with and influence from Christian music, 3, 8, 9, 15, 25, 30, 112–113, 178, 191–194; notation and typography of, 4, 15, 24–26, 28, 29, 30, 32, 119–120, 126, 125, 197–198, 210–212, 220–223 (*see also* cantillation marks [for liturgical recitation of Hebrew texts], *te'amim*); oral tradition of, 24, 26, 66, 112, 113–114, 119, 198, 200, 210, 214–215, 222; participatory nature of, 1–2, 211, 224; performance of, 1–2, 112–114, 118, 120–122, 125, 135–136, 192, 213–214, 243; as praise, 39, 45, 47, 51, 192, 223; printing of, 4, 23, 25, 30, 32, 33, 186–187, 197, 200; prohibition by Venetian authorities, 146, 243; responsorial song, 38–39, 44, 52; in synagogues, 24–25, 33–34, 132, 239–240, 243, 248; Talmudic/halakhic prohibition on music, 2, 3, 20n7, 211–212, 223, 234, 241, 253n35; texts of, 24, 25, 116–132, 141n44, 191–192, 197; transcription of, 32, 125, 127–128, 128–129, 130, 133–135, *135*; troping, 48; written sources of, 26, 27
Jewish musicians, 3, 104, 144, 145, 148–149, 151, 168, 233, 235, 236–240, 243–245, 246; and improvisation, 4; and instrumental performance, 4, 148, 152–153, 217, 235, 236–237, 239–240 (*see also* musical instruments); Levites (ancient), 43, 221–222; and musical literacy, 216–217, 221;

possible status as converts or Jews, 103–104, 145–146, 166, 172, 174–175, 177–179. *See also entries for individual musicians*
Jewish mysticism, 34
Jewish studies, 24. *See also* Wissenschaft des Judentums
Jewish theater, 233, 238, 245. *See also* theater
Jews: as advisers at court, 64, 45, 151–152; Albanian, 174; Ashkenazic Jews, Ashkenazic traditions, 10–11, 26, 28, 40, 100, 112, 115, 116, 124, 211, 236 (*see also* Germany: German Jews); and book trade, 9; compared to animals, 1, 223; conceptions of music among, 5, 190; as "contributors" to European music and culture (*see* "contribution discourse"); as doctors and scientists, 65, 69, 236; education of, 73, 94, 105, 139n22, 241–242; enclosure in ghettos, 23, 27, 160n21, 189 (*see also* ghettos); as entertainers, 28, 244–245; expulsion from the Duchy of Milan, 11; expulsion from England, 17, 144, 150, 153, 179; expulsion from the Iberian Peninsula, 10, 151, 152, 165–167, 211–212; expulsion from the Kingdom of Naples, 11, 12, 174; expulsion from Mantua, 233; expulsion from the Papal States, 11; expulsion of non-native Florentines, 103; and fabric trade, 85; as instrument builders, designers, and traders, 3, 8, 165–170, 171, 174, 178–179 (*see also* musical instruments); intellectual life of, 9, 26, 28, 187, 246–248; interactions with non-Jews, 7, 10, 11, 14, 23–34, 45–46, 64–66, 69–72, 103, 112, 114–115, 144, 154–159, 163n85, 166, 216–217, 220, 241–242 (*see also* Jewish/Hebrew music: Christian performers of); international connections of, 8, 11, 166, 169, 172, 174; in Italian courts, 5, 178, 192; literacy among, 9, 28, 197–198, 218–220, 242; living as Christians, Marranos, 145, 151, 152, 159 (*see also* conversion); as mediators or "marginal mediators," 74, 112, 166, 178, 186, 193–194, 241; migration of, 8–9, 12, 74, 151, 165–167, 174, 178–179, 234; mobility of, 166; and moneylending, 11–12, 65–67, 71, 72, 84, 103, 114, 146–147, 150; musical education of, 2, 146, 238, 239; and musical theater, 216; as music theorists, 3, 5, 6, 13; naming of, 103, 146; Ottoman/Levantine, 11, 174, 141–142n54, 247; participation in trade networks, 11, 166, 169, 174; as patrons of theater, 246; perception of Christian music, 190; as performers/practitioners of music, 3, 5, 198, 216–217 (*see also* Jewish musicians); and precious metals trade, 65; and rabbinic authority, 9; restrictions on dress, 84, 139n21, 146, 244, 246; in secular culture, 5, 66, 189; self-identification of, 4, 9, 10; as sellers of leather and paper, 65; sense of community, 9, 189; Sephardic, 11, 15, 26, 30, 40, 124, 146, 165–168, 171, 174, 179, 211–212; socioeconomic status, 10, 12, 26, 145–152; Spanish, 30; as tailors, 65, 85; as teachers of dance, 5, 16, 73–79, 83–84, 89n44, 89n56, 104, 110n52, 146, 198 (*see also* Ebreo da Pesaro, Guglielmo [later Giovanni Ambrosio]); as teachers of music, 3, 5, 74, 243; as translators, 45; violence against, 103, 147, 150; women, women's issues, 115, 117–118, 122

Johannes of Oppido, 25
Jubal, 83
Judas (biblical), 69, 71
Jütte, Daniel, 7, 12, 74, 255n54

Katz, Dana E., 11, 12, 71, 87n19
Kaufman, David, 246
keyboard instruments. *See* musical instruments
Khosrow II (Sassanian king of Persia), 83
kinor. *See* musical instruments
Kircher, Athanasius, 10
Kokin, Daniel Stein, 156, 163n73
Koran, 83
Kufic script, 83

Lago, Giovanni del, 99–100, 108n22
Lambardi, Camillo, 176
Lasocki, David, 145–146, 151, 153, 162n48
Lassus, Orlande de, 191, 196n20
Latin, 15, 37, 38, 46, 58n5, 59n21, 59n23, 60n46, 64, 73, 87n31, 93, 96–97, 104, 121, 141n52, 142n61, 152, 154, 197, 249n8
Lavin, Marilyn, 69–71, 87n21
Leonessa, Fra Domenico de, 67
Leo X (pope), 92–93, 104, 106n1
L'homme armé, 80
Lieto, Bartolomeo, 168
Linarol, Ventura, 179
Lippomano, Marco, 156, 163n72
lira da braccio. *See* musical instruments
lira da gamba. *See* musical instruments

literacy, 18, 197–202, 204, 206, 209–210, 214–215. *See also* Jews: literacy among
Loewe, Raphael, 40
Lord, Albert B., 201, 204
Lorenzetti, Ambrogio, 40, 58n12, 61n63
Lowinsky, Edward, 100
Lupo, Ambrose, 145
lute. *See* musical instruments
Luzzati, Michele, 100–102, 108n28, 109n39, 109n41
Luzzato, Simone (*Discorso circa il stato degli Hebrei*), 236, 241, 246–248, 251n19, 254n48

Machiavelli, 236, 247
Macque, Jean de, 177
madrigal, 94, 99, 107n20, 177, 185, 190, 198, 206, 209, 213
Maggio drammatico, 113–114, 138–139n16
Maglione, Garzia, *176*
Maglione, Luise, *176*
Magnus, Albertus, 46
maḥol. *See* musical instruments
Mai, Miguel, 152
makam, rhythmic modes, 11, 222
Malatesta, Roberto, 76
Malatesta family, 75
Mann, Vivian, 73
Mantua, 2, 4, 12, 18, 33, 105, 140n32, 178, 183n45, 183n46, 186–187, 189–192, 195n11, 198, 202, 216, 220, 228n24, 233–240, 243–248, 250n13, 251n24. *See also* ghettos: Mantua; Gonzaga court
Mantua, Duchy of, 189
Marcello, Benedetto, 24, 27, 30, 32, 112, 132, *133, 134, 135*
Maria (daughter of King Alfonso of Aragon), 104
Marillac, Charles de, 158
Marranos. *See* Jews: living as Christians, Marranos
Martinengo, Fortunato, 99, 105, 108n24
Martino, Sebastiano de, 168, 180–181n13
Mary (biblical), 157, 159
Masoretes, 220, 230n54
Massa, Giovanni, 177
Massa, Raffaele, 168, 180–181n13
Massarano, Isaachino, 233, 249n2
Matino, Giovanni Tommaso, 174
Matter of France, 113, 137n6, 138n11
Maximillian I (Holy Roman Emperor), 147

Mayone (Maione), Ascanio, *176*, 177
McLuhan, Marshall, 227n14
Medici dynasty, 93; Medici, Caterina de', 178; Medici, Cosimo de', 101; Medici, Giovanni de' (cardinal) (*see* Leo X [pope]); Medici, Giovanni de' (son of Cosimo), 101; Medici, Ippolito de' (cardinal), 174; Medici, Lorenzo de, 50, 75–77, 93, 103, 104
Melamed, Abraham, 231n63
Mendelssohn, Moses, 231n65
Mendes, Diego, 152
Mendes, Francisco, 151
Mendes, Gracia, 151
Meshullam, Asher (also Anselmo Meshullam, Anselmo del Banco), 114, 123, 160n21
messianism, 9
Messina, 170
Mestre, 114, 116
metzaltim. *See* musical instruments
Michiel, Sebastiano, 92–93, 98, 106n4, 110n48
Midrash, 121, 218
Milan, 54, 75–78, 89n54, 89n56, 93, 106–107n4, 147
Milan, Duchy of, 11
Milan Commission, 151
Milano, Francesco Canova da, 168, 180n9
Minervini, Laura, 141–142n54
minim. *See* musical instruments
minstrel (*spilman*), 123
Miriam (biblical), 15, 38–43, 48, 57, 58n5, 58n12, 58n13
Miriam's Song. *See* Song at the Sea
Miroballo, Ottavio, *176*
Miscia, Antonio, 175, *176*
Mishnah, 211, 218, 253n36
Miracle of the Profaned Host, 67–69, *68*. *See also* Uccello, Paolo
Modena, Leon, 2–3, 5, 7, 9, 13, 14, 18, 33, 121, 122, 123–124, 185–187, 190, 192, 194, 197–198, 200, 211, 215–216, 229n36, 239–242, 245–248, 253n34, 254n44; as cantor, 2, 240; collaboration with Christians, 241–242, 246–247; in defense of art music, 5, 18, 190, 211–212, 215, 240–241, 244, 248, 253n36; *Divan*, 243; friendship with Sarra Copia Sulam, 246; introduction to Rossi's *Ha-shirim 'asher li-Shlomo*, 18, 30, 185–187, 190, 192, 212, 214, 216, 222–225, 230n45, 340; as leader of L'Accademia degli Impediti, 3, 18, 233–235, 237–241, 243–244, 248;

L'Ester (reworked by Modena, originally by Solomon Usque), 245, 255–256n64; as linguist, 121, 236, 241–242, 243; as playwright, 245; as poet, 122, 123–124, 241–243, 246, 254n50; *Rachele e Giaccobbe*, 245; as singer, 122, 123, 230n45, 243, 254n50; views on Qabbalah, 247
monochord. *See* musical instruments
Monte degli Ebrei (Mount of the Jews), 74
Montefeltro court (Urbino), 63–64, 66, 72–73, 75–76, 78–80, 82–85, 85n2
Montefeltro (dynasty): Montefeltro, Count Antonio II, 65; Montefeltro, Count Guidantonio da, 66; Montefeltro, Federico da (duke of Urbino), 16, 63–67, 69, 72–73, 75–84, 85n2, 87n26, 89n48, 90n67; Montefeltro, Guidobaldo da (duke of Urbino, I), 69, 72, 84–85, 85n2; Montefeltro, Guidobaldo da (duke of Urbino, II), 84–85; Montefeltro, Sveva Colonna, 76; Montefeltro era, 65
Montella, Giovanni (or Giovan) Domenico, 177, 183n43
Monteverdi, Claudio, 178, 255n64
monte di pietà, 12, 67–69, 72, 86n12, 86n14, 87n19, 103, 146–147. *See also* Jews: and moneylending
Montmorency, Anne de, 158
More, Thomas, 155
Morosini, Giulio, 33, 235–240, 248, 251n23, 255n55
Moscato, Judah, 9, 247
Moses (biblical), 38–39, 43–44, 48, 57, 58n4, 60n46, 61n50, 61n56, 72, 103, 118
motet, 2, 94, 185, 191, 196n20, 200, 225, 242
musical instruments: 'asor, 222; bagpipe (*cornamusa*), 53, 55; biblical/ancient Israelite, 221–222; builders of, 165–170, 171, 174, 178–179 (*see also* Jews: as instrument builders, designers, and traders); chitarrone, 240; collection of, 170–171; cornetto, 148, 240; cymbal, 40; drum, 50; flute, 47, 148; gitit, 222; guitar (*giterra, chitarra a sette corde*), 47, 171, 176, 204 (see also *alfabeto* notation); ḥalil, 222; harmonium, 33; harp, 158, 176, 239, 240, 249–250n8; harpsichord, chromatic (*cimbalo cromatico*), 177; hunting horn (*corneto di caccia*), 170; iconography of, 168, 171–172; istromento da corpo, 240;

keyboard instruments, 170; kinor, 222; *lira da braccio*, 94, 171; *lira da gamba*, 176; lute, 40, 47, 50, 53, 94, 104, 168–169, 171–170, 176, 221, 240; maḥol, 222; metzaltim, 222; minim, 222; monochord, 94; neginot, 222; nevel, 221, 222; organ, 33, 82, 94, 177, 178, 202, 205, 228n23, 237, 239, 240; *pandero cuadrado*, 40; psaltery, 39; rebec (*ribeca*), 171; recorder, 94, 153; reed instruments, 240; sackbut (trombone), 148, 153, 240; shawm, 148; sheminit, 222; in synagogues, 33; theorbo, 240; timbrel, 39, 40, 42, 50, 53, 57; tof, 222; trumpet, 47, 148, 153, 238; 'ugav, 222; vielle, 53; viol, 145, 159, 198; viola d'arco (*vihuela de arco, viola cum arculo, viola tastata*), 168, 170–171, 175, 176, 182n38; viola da gamba, 168; viola da mano (*vihuela de mano, viola sine arculo*), 168–171; violecta, violecta spagnola, 170–171; *violetta* of Santa Caterina de' Vigri, 172; violin, 170, 171, 174, 175, 178, 179, 198, 199, 205, 209, 210, 240; wind instruments, 178; woodblock, 40
Muslim entertainers, 47
Muslims, music among. *See makam*, rhythmic modes; *muwashshah*
muwashshah, 124

Naples, 45, 46, 60n39, 76, 104, 158, 165, 167–169, 174–178; Boccaccio's connection to, 45, 46; Royal Chapel, 177. *See also* Aragonese court; Boccaccio, Giovanni; Naples, Kingdom of
Naples, Kingdom of, 11, 12, 17, 165, 167, 174–175
neginot. *See* musical instruments
Nenna, Pompiono, 177
Neustadt an der Aisch, 114
nevel. *See* musical instruments
Nicola, Giovan Battista di, 176
Noah (biblical), 46, 48
Nürnberg, 12

Obadiah the Proselyte (also Obadiah Ha-Ger, Johannes of Oppido, or Johannes the Proselyte), 25–26, 220
Obrecht, Jacob, 93
Ong, Walter, 199–201, 209–210, 227n14
orality, 18, 197–204, 206, 210, 213–215, 225; "primary oral culture," 199, 201. *See also* Jewish/Hebrew music: oral tradition of; Mishnah; Talmud

oratorios, 34
organ. *See* musical instruments
organists, improvisational practices of, 202, 228n23
ornamentation, 133, 201, 206, 209–210, 212. *See also* diminution
Ortiz, Diego, 204–205, 209, 229n31
Osborne, June, 80
ottava rima, 113–114, 119, 120, *121*, *122*, 124, 137n6, 137n7, 138n11, 138n12, 138n13, 143n67, 212
Ottoman Empire, 8, 11, 80, 90n67, 174. *See also* Jews: Ottoman/Levantine
Ovid, 170

Padua, 12, 99, 100, 107n19, 111, 114, 116, 132, 152
Palermo, 165, 167, 170, 174, 182n32
Panchatantra (The Five Heads), 37
pandero cuadrado. *See* musical instruments
Paola, Francesco di (also Francesco de Paula), 175, *176*, 183n43
Papal States, 11, 85, 167
paradox, 3, 18, 235–236, 247–248
Paris, 67
Parish, Helen, 162n67
parody (as musical adaptation), 111–112, 120, *121*, *122*
Parry, Milman, 201
pasquinata, *katoves*, 117, 120, 131, 141n45
Passover, 40, *41*, 140n35
Paul II (pope), 69
Pavia, 75, 79
pawnbrokers, 65, 67, 71. *See also* Jews: and moneylending
Pearsall, Eileen, 153
Perfino, Diego, 177
Persia, 69–72, 83, 87n26
Pesaro, 28, 74–76, 82, 85, 89n47
Peter (biblical), 71
Petrarch, 170
Petrucci, Ottaviano, 96, 107n6; *Frottole libro quinto*, 94
Pius II (pope), 69, 160n15
piyyut, 112, *121*, 124, 125, 131
plague, 3, 9, 57, 77, 129, 150, 224, 237–239
plainchant, 96, 97, 132
Planterio, Prospero, 176
poetry, 6, 13, 16, 38, 47–48, 50–57, 60n41, 79, 96, 105, 110n57, 111–124, 125, 128–129, 130–133, 135, 241–243; biblical origins of, 48–49, 58n4, 58n8; as a disseminator of Jewish culture, 16, 45, 111–112; epic (heroic verse), 16, 38, 112–113, 115, 201, 206; evidence for sung performance, 117–118, 123, 140n39; in the Haggadah, 40; in humanist societies, 233, 246; lauda, 47, 49; lauda-ballata, 49, 52, 54; piedi (rhythmic feet), 50; ripresa (refrain), 50, 51; volta (turn), 50. See also *arie, arie per cantar stanze* (recitation formulas); Boccaccio, Giovanni: *Decameron*; Bokher, Elye (also Eliyahu ben Asher HaLevi Ashkenazi, Elia Bachur Levita, Elijah Levita); ottava rima
Polk, Keith, 153
polyphony, 2, 4, 18, 186, 192–193, 197–199, 202, 205, 210–213, 216–217, 223–225, 227n22, 230n45, 237, 238, 242; in the ancient Temple, 236; in synagogues, 19n7, 212–213, 225, 240–241, 244, 255n53; improvised, 202, 211, 225, 227n22
Portaleone, Abraham (*Shiltei Ha-Gibborim*), 9, 220–222, 224–225, 231n63, 231n66, 236, 246–248
Porta Valbona, 85
Porto, Matteo, 170
Portogruaro, 132
Prior, Roger, 145–146, 162n48, 163n85
prostitutes, 12
Provenzal, Abraham ben David, 28
psaltery. *See* musical instruments
Pullan, Brian, 147
Purim, 115, 119, *121*, 123, 141n49, 245

Qabbalah, 5, 10, 18, 25, 34, 114, 236, 242, 247

Raphael, Marco, 152
Ravid, Benjamin, 14
rebec (*ribeca*). *See* musical instruments
Rebhorn, Wayne, 37
recitation formula. See *arie, arie per cantar stanze* (recitation formulas)
recorder. *See* musical instruments
reed instruments. *See* musical instruments
Reform movement, Jewish, 4
refugees, 5, 85, 114, 174, 233, 237–239, 242, 243, 248
Renhart, Johannes, 125
ricercare, 202
Ridley, Nicholas (bishop), 154
ridotti, 241, 254n44

Rieti, Moses da, *Il Tempio* (*Me'on ha-sho'alim*), 120, 121
Rimini, 76
Robert of Anjou (king of Naples), 45–46
Rodio, Rocco, 177
Rognoni, Riccardo (Richardo Rogniono), 209
Romanesca. See *arie*, *arie per cantar stanze* (recitation formulas)
Romano, Andrea, 176
Romano, Judah, 45
Rome, 12, 24, 85n2, 86n6, 87n31, 93, 104, 114, 116, 152, 167, 177; Sack of (1527), 114
Rosa, Giangiacomo de, 174
Rosenzweig, Claudia, 120–123, 140n32, 141n45, 141n46
Rosman, Moshe, 5–6, 20n16, 165–166
Rossi, Angelo (grandson of Madama Europa), 239
Rossi, Angelo (son of Madama Europa), 239
Rossi, Bonaiuto, 239
Rossi, Guiseppe, 239
Rossi, Luigi, 177
Rossi, Salamone, 4–7, 9, 13–14, 17–18, 24, 27–28, 178, 185–194, 197–225, 239, 253n34; *concerto* of, 198, 202, 210; in the court of Mantua, 178, 233, 216, 244; "'Ein kelohenu," 213, 213–219; *Ha-shirim 'asher li-Shlomo*, 2, 4, 5, 17–18, 27–28, 30, 31, 32, 185–194, 197–198, 200, 210–216, 213, 214–219, 219, 222–225, 242, 252n27; instrumental music of, 191, 198–210, 212–214, 224–225, 240; name, spelling of, 19n5; "Sonata sopra l'aria della Romanesca," 205–210, 206–208
Rossi Codex, 49–51
Roth, Cecil, 4–6, 73–74, 89n47, 141n54, 151, 235, 249n8
Roy, Bartolomeo, 176
Ruderman, David B., 8–10, 12, 14, 166, 178, 181n16, 187, 219–220, 254n48
Ruffatti, Alessio, 145, 148, 149, 160n5

Sabbath, 112, 131, 150, 238
sackbut (trombone). See musical instruments
salon, 246
San Gimignano (town), 101
San Marino, 75
San Pietro, Girolamo, 96
Sansone, Giovanni Battista (*Il Siciliano*), 173, 174, 179

Sansone, Matteo, 170–172
Sanuto, Marino, 33, 103, 110n48
Saracens, 47
Savonarola, Girolamo, 93
Scacco, Cristoforo, 168–169
Segre, Avraham, 24, 28
Sendrey, Alfred, 39, 235
Seroussi, Edwin, 6–8, 11, 24, 27, 30, 32, 230n45, 243
Seven Wise Masters, 37
Severino (family): Severino, Giovanni Antonio, 176; Severino, Giulio, 176; Severino, Pompeo, 176; Severino, Vicencello, 176
Sforza (family): Sforza, Alessandro, 75, 76, 77; Sforza, Battista, 67, 69, 72; Sforza, Bianca Maria, 77; Sforza, Camilla (d'Aragona), 75; Sforza, Costanzo, 74–75, 82; Sforza, Francesco, 75, 76; Sforza, Galeazzo Maria (duke of Milan), 78–79; Sforza court in Milan, 77; Sforza court in Pesaro, 76; Sforza family, 76
shawm. See musical instruments
Shear, Adam, 218–219
Sheba (biblical), 74, 88n41
sheminit. See musical instruments
Sicily, 45, 167, 169
Siegmund, Stefanie B., 14, 189
Siena, 33, 100, 101, 102; synagogue in, 25, 34
silk farming and trade, 146
Simḥat Torah, 217, 237, 240, 251n21, 251n23
sinfonia, 202
singing, 47, 51–57, 80, 111–113, 117–120, 122–123, 124, 125, 211–212, 221–222, 224, 243, 245; in the *Decameron* (*see* Boccaccio, Giovanni: *Decameron*); images of, 40; in Jewish practice, 3, 27, 30, 32, 48, 52; paired with dance, 37–39, 40, 50; polychoral, 239, 253n35; popular, 203; as praise, 38–39, 43, 44–45, 49, 55, 248. *See also* poetry: evidence for sung performance
Sixtus IV (pope), 69
Solomon (Jewish moneylender in Urbino), 72
Solomon (king, biblical), 74
Sommi, Leone de', 244, 246, 255n61
sonata, 202–209
Soncino, Gershon, 114
Song at the Sea, 15, 37, 38–39, 42–44, 51, 57, 58n13, 221
Song of Songs (Song of Solomon), 49, 52

Spain, 40, 69, 151, 165, 167, 172, 174, 179, 212, 221–222, 242. *See also* Jews: expulsion from the Iberian Peninsula
Sparti, Barbara, 78, 79, 84, 89n47
Spataro, Giovanni, 97, 98, 107n17, 108n22
Staivalo, Prospero, *176*
Stella, Scipione "Pietro Paulo," 175, 177, 183n43
Stellatello, G. C., *176*
stile moderno, 203
strambotto, 113, *121–122*
Sulam, Moses, 197
Sulam, Sarra Copia, 6, 7, 246, 255–256n64
suonatore del sabato, 238
Szczebrszyn, Gumprecht von, 119

Tacitus, 236, 247
Talmud, 74, 84, 211, 218; Tractate *Gittin*, 3; Tractate Ḥagigah, 20n7
Tanzhaus (dancing house), 74
Tarquinia (town), 101
Tasso, Torquato (*Gerusalemme liberata*), 113
Temple (ancient, in Jerusalem), 3, 27, 43, 211, 220, 234, 248; musical performance in, 221–222, 225, 234, 236, 247
terza rima, 120, *121–122*, 212
theater, 3, 4, 74, 178, 189, 216, 233, 244, 245, 247
theorbo. *See* musical instruments
The Thousand and One Nights, 37
timbrel. *See* musical instruments
Tinctoris, Johannes, 168, 171
Tisi, Benvenuto, 172
tof. *See* musical instruments
Torah, Pentateuch, 32, 117, 220, 248
Torrigiano, Pietro, 158
Townsend, George (*Life of the Martyrologist*), 154
Trabaci, Giovanni Maria, 177
transubstantiation, 71, 145, 154–159
trumpet. *See* musical instruments
Turks, 66, 69–72, 83
Tuscania (town), 101
Tyndale, William, 155
Tzarfati, Josef, *121*, 122
Tzur mi-shelo (late-medieval *piyyut*), 112, 120, 122, *124–131*, *126*, *127*, *128*, *132–133*

Uccello, Paolo, 67, *68*, 69. *See also Miracle of the Profaned Host*
Udine, 132

'ugav. *See* musical instruments
Umbria, 49
universities: Mantuan, 239; Università degli Ebrei, 244, 242n28; Venetian, 238
Urbino, 12, 15–16, 63–69, 72–73, 75–79, 82–85, 87n26, 87n31; artworks, 66, 67, *68*, 69, *71* (*see also* Ghent, Joos van; *Miracle of the Profaned Host*; Uccello, Paolo); Church of Corpus Domini, 67; Confraternity of Corpus Domini, 67, 69, 71, 72; Corpus Domini procession, 69; Jewish community in, 64–66, 85, 86n6, 90n79; Jewish musical activities in, 64, 85; Jewish property ownership in, 65, 84; Pusterla district, 65, 73, 84; restrictions against Jews in, 84; synagogue in, 65, 73, 84, 85, 88n32; Torah Ark, *73*. *See also* Montefeltro court (Urbino); Montefeltro (dynasty): Montefeltro, Federico da (duke of Urbino)
Urbino, Duchy of, 80, 85
Urrea, Jerónimo de, 124
Usque, Solomon, 245, 255–256n64

Vallensis, Johannes (*Opus de prosodia Hebraeorum*), 220–221
variation, 202–206, 209–210. *See also* sonata
Vecchi, Orazio, 216, 243
Veltri, Giuseppe, 14, 235, 246, 247–248
Venice, 1–3, 11–13, 17, 18, 25, 27, 33, 92, 98, 99, 103, 104, 112, 116, 121, 132, 141–142n54, 145–149, 151–152, 179, 235, 240, 241, 243–245, 253n34, 254n48; Doge's trombe e piffari, 148–149; fire on the Rialto (1514), 123, 129; German Synagogue, 132; Italian Synagogue (Scuola Italiana), 2, 240; Jewish refugees in, 233, 235, 237–240; Jewish theatrical activity in, 238, 245; Knights of Saint John of Jerusalem, 92, 98; plague of 1630, 237; printers in, 30, 114; restrictions against Jews in, 146, 243; San Marco, 103, 109n48, 145, 147, 148, 161n33; Scuola della Misericordia, 148; Scuola Grande di San Rocco, 179, 242; Spanish Synagogue, 237, 242; synagogue practice in, 25
Verona, 47, 50, 147, 152, 245. *See also* academies: Accademia Filarmonica (Verona)
Veronese court of Can Grande, 47
vielle. *See* musical instruments

viol. *See* musical instruments
viola da gamba. *See* musical instruments
viola da mano (*vihuela de mano, viola sine arculo*). *See* musical instruments
viola d'arco (*vihuela de arco, viola cum arculo, viola tastata*). *See* musical instruments
violecta, violecta spagnola. *See* musical instruments
violin. *See* musical instruments
Violone, Orazio del, *176*
Virdung, Sebastian, 171, *172*
Virgil, 170
Vitale da Pisa, Dolce di Daniele di, 101, 102
Viterbo, Lazzaro da, 120, *122*
Volpe, Preposito della, 97
Volpe, Vincenzo, 158
Volterra, Buonaventura di Emanuele da, 101, 102, 109n36

Volterra, Emanuele di Buonaventura da, 102
Volterra, Lazzaro di Emanuele da, 101, 102

Wallich manuscript, 120, 141n44
War of the League of Cambrai, 114, 146–147
War of Succession, 233, 238
Wert, Giaches de, 244
wind instrument players, status of, 149, 152–153. *See also* musical instruments: wind instruments
Wissenschaft des Judentums, 4–6
woodblock. *See* musical instruments

yeshiva, 114
Yiddish, 16, 111, 114–117, *121*, 123–124, 125–128, 135, 140n35, 212
Yoshev marom ḥazaq (poem set as a contrafactum by Leon Modena), 242–243

www.ingramcontent.com/pod-product-compliance
Lightning Source LLC
Chambersburg PA
CBHW021943240426
43668CB00037B/579